THE SOURCE
OF THE NILE

THE SOURCE OF THE NILE

JOHN HANNING SPEKE

AMBERLEY

First published 1863, this edition 2015

Amberley Publishing
The Hill, Stroud
Gloucestershire, GL5 4EP

www.amberley-books.com

British Library Cataloguing in Publication Data.
A catalogue record for this book is available from the British Library.

ISBN 978 1 4456 4423 3 (print)
ISBN 978 1 4456 4436 3 (ebook)

Typeset in 10pt on 13pt Minion.
Typesetting and Origination by Amberley Publishing.
Printed in the UK.

Editor's Note

This is an abridged version of John Hanning Speke's original text detailing his travels in Africa that began in 1859, during which he hoped to prove that the Victoria N'yanza was the source of the Nile. It details the main sites visited on his journey, and was originally published as *Journal of the Discovery of the Source of the Nile* in 1863. The original language has been retained as it appeared in this 1863 edition, and this displays Speke's personal style, but also a very different way of thinking from the modern day. At times, views expressed in the text may appear rather shocking, but it is important to remember that at the time of writing certain (no-longer held) views regarding various populations of countries of the world prevailed. Although sometimes surprising, this volume nevertheless offers the reader an important historical insight into a fascinating journey.

Contents

To those kind friends who thought of us, and raised an expedition to succour us when we were supposed to be in great danger in the centre of Africa, this work is gratefully dedicated.

J. H. Speke.
Jordans, December 1863.

CHAPTER I

London to Zanzibar, 1859

My third expedition in Africa, which was avowedly for the purpose of establishing the truth of my assertion that the Victoria N'yanza, which I discovered on the 30th July 1858, would eventually prove to be the source of the Nile, may be said to have commenced on the 9th May 1859, the first day after my return to England from my second expedition, when, at the invitation of Sir R. I. Murchison, I called at his house to show him my map for the information of the Royal Geographical Society. Sir Roderick, I need only say, at once accepted my views; and, knowing my ardent desire to prove to the world, by actual inspection of the exit, that the Victoria N'yanza was the source of the Nile, seized the enlightened view, that such a discovery should not be lost to the glory of England and the Society of which he was President; and said to me, 'Speke, we must send you there again.' I was then officially directed, much against my own inclination, to lecture at the Royal Geographical Society on the geography of Africa, which I had, as the sole surveyor of the second expedition, laid down on our maps. A council of the Geographical Society was now convened to ascertain what projects I had in view for making good my discovery by connecting the lake with the Nile, as also what assistance I should want for that purpose.

Some thought my best plan would be to go up the Nile, which seemed to them the natural course to pursue, especially as the Nile was said, though nobody believed it, to have been navigated by expeditions sent out by Mehemet Ali, Viceroy of Egypt, up to 3° 22' north latitude. To this I objected, as so many had tried it and failed, from reasons which had not transpired; and, at the same time, I said that if they would give me £5000 down at once, I would return to Zanzibar at the end of the year, march to Kazé again, and make the necessary investigations of the Victoria lake. Although, in addition to the journey to the source of the river, I also proposed spending three years in the country, looking up tributaries, inspecting watersheds, navigating the lake, and making collections on all branches of natural history, yet £5000 was thought by the Geographical Society too large a sum to expect from the Government; so I accepted the half, saying that, whatever the expedition might cost, I would make good the rest, as, under any circumstances, I would complete what I had begun, or die in the attempt.

This beautiful project, I am sorry to say, was doomed from the first; for I did not get the £2500 grant of money or appointment to the command until fully nine months had elapsed, when I wrote to Colonel Rigby, our Consul at Zanzibar, to send on the first instalment of property towards the interior.

As time then advanced, the Indian branch of the Government very graciously gave me fifty artillery carbines, with belts and sword-bayonets attached, and 20,000 rounds of ball ammunition. They lent me as many surveying instruments as I wanted; and, through Sir George Clerk, put at my disposal some rich presents, in gold watches, for the chief Arabs who had so generously assisted us in the last expedition. Captain Grant, hearing that I was bound on this journey, being an old friend and brother sportsman in India, asked me to take him with me, and his appointment was settled by Colonel Sykes, then chairman of a committee of the Royal Geographical Society, who said it would only be a 'matter of charity' to allow me a companion.

Much at the same time, Mr Petherick, an ivory merchant, who had spent many years on the Nile, arrived in England, and gratuitously offered, as it would not interfere with his trade, to place boats at Gondokoro, and send a party of men up the White River to collect ivory in the meanwhile, and eventually to assist me in coming down. Mr Petherick, I may add, showed great zeal for geographical exploits; so, as I could not get money enough to do all that I wished to accomplish myself, I drew out a project for him to ascend the stream now known as the Usŭa river (reported to be the larger branch of the Nile), and, if possible, ascertain what connection it had with my lake. This being agreed to, I did my best, through the medium of Earl de Grey (then President of the Royal Geographical Society), to advance him money to carry out this desirable object.

The last difficulty I had now before me was to obtain a passage to Zanzibar. The Indian Government had promised me a vessel of war to convey me from Aden, to Zanzibar, provided it did not interfere with the public interests. This doubtful proviso induced me to apply to Captain Playfair, Assistant-Political at Aden, to know what Government vessel would be available; and should there be none, to get for me a passage by some American trader. The China war, he assured me, had taken up all the Government vessels, and there appeared no hope left for me that season, as the last American trader was just then leaving for Zanzibar. In this dilemma it appeared that I must inevitably lose the travelling season, and come in for the droughts and famines. The tide, however, turned in my favour a little; for I obtained, by permission of the Admiralty, a passage in the British screw steam-frigate Forte, under orders to convey Admiral Sir H. Keppel to his command at the Cape; and Sir Charles Wood most obligingly made a request that I should be forwarded thence to Zanzibar in one of our slaver-hunting cruisers by the earliest opportunity.

On the 27th April, Captain Grant and I embarked on board the new steam-frigate Forte, commanded by Captain E. W. Tumour, at Portsmouth; and after a long voyage, touching at Madeira and Eio de Janeiro, we arrived at the Cape of Good Hope on the 4th July. Here Sir George Grey, the Governor of the colony, who took a warm and enlightened interest in the cause of the expedition, invited both Grant and myself to reside at his house. Sir George had been an old explorer himself – was once wounded by savages in Australia, much in the same manner as I had been in the Somali country – and, with a spirit of sympathy, he called me his son, and said he hoped I would succeed. Then, thinking how best he could serve me, he induced the Cape Parliament to advance to the expedition a sum of £300, for the purpose of buying baggage-mules; and induced Lieut-General Wynyard, the Commander-in-Chief, to detach ten volunteers from the Cape Mounted Rifle Corps to accompany me. When this addition was made to my force, of twelve mules and ten Hottentots, the Admiral of the station placed the screw steam-corvette Brisk at my disposal, and we all sailed for Zanzibar on the 16th July, under the command of Captain A. F. de Horsey – the Admiral himself accompanying us, on one of his annual inspections to visit the east coast of Africa and the Mauritius. In five days more we touched at East London, and, thence proceeding north, made a short stay at Delagoa Bay, where I first became acquainted with the Zŭlŭ Kafirs, a naked set of negroes, whose national costume principally consists in having their hair trussed up like a hoop on the top of the head, and an appendage like a thimble, to which they attach a mysterious importance. They wear additional ornaments, charms, etc, of birds' claws, hoofs and horns of wild animals tied on with strings, and sometimes an article like a kilt, made of loose strips of skin, or the entire skins of vermin strung close together. These things I have merely noticed in passing, because I shall hereafter have occasion to allude to a migratory people, the Watŭta, who, dressing much in the same manner, extend from Lake N'yassa to Uzinza, and may originally have been a part of this same Kafir race, who are themselves supposed to have migrated from the regions at present occupied by the Gallas. Next day (the 28th) we went on to Europa, a small island of coralline, covered with salsolacious shrubs, and tenanted only by sea-birds, owls, finches, rats, and turtles. Of the last we succeeded in turning three, the average weight of each being 360 lb, and we took large numbers of their eggs.

We then went to Mozambique, and visited the Portuguese Governor, John Travers de Almeida, who showed considerable interest in the prospects of the expedition, and regretted that, as it cost so much money to visit the interior from that place, his officers were unable to go there. One experimental trip only had been accomplished by Mr Soares, who was forced to pay the Makŭa chiefs 120 dollars footing, to reach a small hill in view of the sea, about twenty-five miles off.

Leaving Mozambique on the 9th August, bound for Johanna, we came the next day, at 11.30 a.m. in sight of a slaver, ship-rigged, bearing on us full sail, but so distant from us that her mast-tops were only just visible. As quick as ourselves, she saw who we were and tried to escape by retreating. This manoeuvre left no doubt what she was, and the Brisk, all full of excitement, gave chase at full speed, and in four hours more drew abreast of her. A great commotion ensued on board the slaver. The sea-pirates threw overboard their colours, bags, and numerous boxes, but would not heave-to, although repeatedly challenged, until a gun was fired across her bows. Our boats were then lowered, and in a few minutes more the 'prize' was taken, by her crew being exchanged for some of our men, and we learnt all about her from accurate reports furnished by Mr Frere, the Cape Slave Commissioner. Cleared from Havannah as 'the Sunny South,' professing to be destined for Hong-Kong, she changed her name to the Manuela, and came slave-hunting in these regions. The slaver's crew consisted of a captain, doctor, and several sailors, mostly Spaniards. The vessel was well stored with provisions and medicines; but there was scarcely enough room in her, though she was said to be only half freighted, for the 544 creatures they were transporting. The next morning, as we entered Pamoni harbour by an intricate approach to the rich little island hill Johanna, the slaver, as she followed us, stranded, and for a while caused considerable alarm to everybody but her late captain. He thought his luck very bad, after escaping so often, to be taken thus; for his vessel's powers of sailing were so good, that, had she had the wind in her favour, the Brisk, even with the assistance of steam, could not have come up with her. On going on board her, I found the slaves to be mostly Wahiyow. A few of them were old women, but all the rest children. They had been captured during wars in their own country, and sold to Arabs, who brought them to the coast, and kept them half-starved until the slaver arrived, when they were shipped in dhows and brought off to the slaver, where, for nearly a week, whilst the bargains were in progress, they were kept entirely without food. It was no wonder, then, every man of the Brisk who first looked upon them did so with a feeling of loathing and abhorrence of such a trade. All over the vessel, but more especially below, old women, stark naked, were dying in the most disgusting 'ferret-box' atmosphere; while all those who had sufficient strength were pulling up the hatches, and tearing at the salt fish they found below, like dogs in a kennel.

On the 15th the Manuela was sent to the Mauritius, and we, after passing the Comoro Islands, arrived at our destination, Zanzibar – called Lungŭja by the aborigines, the Wakhadim – and Ungtŭja by the present Wastŭhili.

On the 17th, after the anchor was cast, without a moment's delay I went off to the British Consulate to see my old friend Colonel Rigby. He was delighted to see us; and, in anticipation of our arrival, had prepared rooms for our reception, that both Captain Grant and myself might enjoy his hospitality until arrangements could be made for our final start into the interior. The town, which I had left in so different a condition sixteen months before, was in a state of great tranquillity, brought about by the energy of the Bombay Government on the Muscat side, and Colonel Rigby's exertions on this side, in preventing an insurrection Sultan Majid's brothers had created with a view of usurping his government.

The news of the place was as follows: in addition to the formerly constituted consulates – English, French, and American – a fourth one, representing Hamburg, had been created. Dr Roscher, who during my absence had made a successful journey to the N'yinyézi N'yassa, or Star Lake, was afterwards murdered by some natives in Uhiyow; and Lieutenant-Colonel Baron van der Decken, another enterprising German, was organising an expedition with a view to search for the relics of his countryman, and, if possible, complete the project poor Roscher had commenced.

Slavery had received a severe blow by the sharp measures Colonel Rigby had taken in giving tickets of emancipation to all those slaves whom our Indian subjects the Banyans had been secretly keeping, and by fining the masters and giving the money to the men to set them up in life. The interior of the continent had been greatly disturbed, owing to constant war between the natives and Arab ivory merchants. Mgŭrŭ Mfŭpi (or Short-legs), the chief of Khoko in Ugogo, for instance, had been shot, and Manŭa Séra (the Tippler), who succeeded the old Sultan Fŭndi Kira, of Unyanyembé, on his death, shortly after the late expedition left Kazé, was out in the field fighting the Arabs. Recent letters from the Arabs in the interior, however, gave hopes of peace being shortly restored. Finally, in compliance with my request – and this was the most important item of news to myself – Colonel Rigby had sent on, thirteen days previously, fifty-six loads of cloth and beads, in charge of two of Ramji's men, consigned to Mŭsa at Kazé.

To call on the Sultan, of course, was our first duty. He received us in his usually affable manner; made many trite remarks concerning our plans; was surprised, if my only object in view was to see the great river running out of the lake, that I did not go by the more direct route across the Masai country and Usoga; and then, finding I wished to see Karagŭé, as well as to settle many other great points of interest, he offered to assist me with all the means in his power.

The Hottentots, the mules, and the baggage having been landed, our preparatory work began in earnest. It consisted in proving the sextants; rating the watches; examining the compasses and boiling thermometers; making tents and packsaddles; ordering supplies of beads, cloth, and brass wire; and collecting servants and porters.

Sheikh Said bin Salem, our late Cafila Bashi, or caravan captain, was appointed to that post again, as he wished to prove his character for honour and honesty; and it now transpired that he had been ordered not to go with me when I discovered the Victoria N'yanza. Bombay and his brother Mabrŭki were bound to me of old, and the first to greet me on my arrival here; while my old friends the Belŭchs begged me to take them again. The Hottentots, however, had usurped their place. I was afterwards sorry for this, though, if I ever travel again, I shall trust to none but natives, as the climate of Africa is too trying to foreigners. Colonel Rigby, who had at heart as much as anybody the success of the expedition, materially assisted me in accomplishing my object – that men accustomed to discipline and a knowledge of English honour and honesty should be enlisted, to give confidence to the rest of the men; and he allowed me to select from his boat's crew any men I could find who had served in men-of-war, and had seen active service in India.

For this purpose my factotum, Bombay, prevailed on Baraka, Frij, and Rahan – all of them old sailors, who, like himself, knew Hindŭstani – to go with me. With this nucleus to start with, I gave orders that they should look out for as many Wangŭana (freed men – i.e., men emancipated from slavery) as they could enlist, to carry loads, or do any other work required of them, and to follow me in Africa wherever I wished, until our arrival in Egypt, when I would send them back to Zanzibar. Each was to receive one year's pay in advance, and the remainder when their work was completed.

While this enlistment was going on here, Ladha Damji, the customs' master, was appointed to collect a hundred pagazis (Wanyamŭézi porters) to carry each a load of cloth, beads, or brass wire to Kazé, as they do for the ivory merchants. Meanwhile, at the invitation of the Admiral, and to show him some sport in hippopotamus-shooting, I went with him in a dhow over to Kŭsiki, near which there is a tidal lagoon, which at high tide is filled with water, but at low water exposes sand islets covered with mangrove shrub. In these islets we sought for the animals, knowing they were given to lie wallowing in the mire, and we bagged two. On my return to Zanzibar, the Brisk sailed for the Mauritius, but fortune sent Grant and myself on a different cruise. Sultan Majid, having heard that a slaver was lying at Pangani, and being anxious to show his good faith with the English, begged me to take the command of one of his vessels of war and run her down. Accordingly, embarking at noon, as soon as the vessel could be got ready, we lay-to that night at Tombat, with a view of surprising the slaver next morning; but next day, on our arrival at Pangani, we heard that she had merely put in to provision there three days before, and had left immediately afterwards. As I had come so far, I thought we might go ashore and look at the town, which was found greatly improved since I last saw it, by the addition of several coralline houses and a dockyard. The natives were building a dhow with Lindi and Madagascar timber. On going ashore, I might add, we were stranded on the sands, and, coming off again, nearly swamped by the increasing surf on the bar of the river; but this was a trifle; all we thought of was to return to Zanzibar, and hurry on our preparations there. This, however, was not so easy: the sea current was running north, and the wind was too light to propel our vessel against it; so, after trying in vain to make way in her, Grant and I, leaving her to follow, took to a boat, after giving the captain, who said we would get drowned, a letter, to say we left the vessel against his advice.

We had a brave crew of young negroes to pull us; but, pull as they would, the current was so strong that we feared, if we persisted, we should be drawn into the broad Indian Ocean; so, changing our line, we bore into the little coralline island, Maziwa, where, after riding over some ugly coral surfs, we put in for the night. There we found, to our relief, some fishermen, who gave us fish for our dinner, and directions how to proceed.

Next morning, before daylight, we trusted to the boat and our good luck. After passing, without landmarks to guide us, by an intricate channel, through foaming surfs, we arrived at Zanzibar in the night, and found that the vessel had got in before us.

Colonel Rigby now gave me a most interesting paper, with a map attached to it, about the Nile and the Mountains of the Moon. It was written by Lieutenant Wilford, from the 'Pŭrans' of the ancient Hindis. As it exemplifies, to a certain extent, the supposition I formerly arrived at concerning the Mountains of the Moon being associated with the country of the Moon, I would fain draw the attention of the reader of my travels to the volume of the 'Asiatic Researches' in which it was published. It is remarkable that the Hindŭs have christened the source of the Nile *Amara*, which is the name of a country at the north-east corner of the Victoria N'yanza. This, I think, shows clearly that the ancient Hindŭs must have had some kind of communication with both the northern and southern ends of the Victoria N'yanza.

Having gone to work again, I found that Sheikh Said had brought ten men, four of whom were purchased for one hundred dollars, which I had to pay; Bombay, Baraka, Frij, and Rahan had brought twenty-six more, all freed men; while the Sultan Majid, at the suggestion of Colonel Rigby, gave me thirty-four men more, who were all raw labourers taken from his gardens. It was my intention to have taken one hundred of this description of men throughout the whole journey; but as so many could not be found in Zanzibar, I still hoped to fill up the complement in Unyamŭézi, the land of the Moon, from the large establishments of the Arab merchants residing there. The payment of these men's wages for the first year, as well as the terms of the agreement made with them, by the kind consent of Colonel Rigby were now entered in the Consular Office books, as a security to both parties, and a precaution against disputes on the way. Any one who saw the grateful avidity with which they took the money, and the warmth with which they pledged themselves to serve me faithfully through all dangers and difficulties, would, had he had no dealings with such men before, have thought that I had a first-rate set of followers. I lastly gave Sheikh Said a double-barrelled rifle by Blissett, and distributed fifty carbines among the seniors of the expedition, with the condition that they would forfeit them to others more worthy if they did not behave well, but would retain possession of them for ever if they carried them through the journey to my satisfaction.

On the 21st, as everything was ready on the island, I sent Sheikh Said and all the men, along with the Hottentots, mules, and baggage, off in dhows to Bagamoyo, on the opposite mainland. Colonel Rigby, with Captain Grant and myself, then called on the Sultan, to bid him adieu, when he graciously offered me, as a guard of honour to escort me through Uzaramo, one jemadar and twenty-five Belŭch soldiers. These I accepted, more as a government security in that country against the tricks of the natives, than for any accession they made to our strength. His highness then placed his 22-gun corvette, 'Secundra Shah,' at our disposal, and we went all three over to Bagamoyo, arriving on the 25th. Immediately on landing, Ladha and Sheikh Said showed us into a hut prepared for us, and all things looked pretty well. Ladha's hundred loads of beads, cloths, and brass wire were all tied up for the march, and seventy-five pagazis (porters from the Moon country) had received their hire to carry these loads to Kazé, in the land of the Moon. Competition, I found, had raised these men's wages, for I had to pay, to go even as far as Kazé, nine and a quarter dollars a-head! – as Masŭdi and some other merchants were bound on the same line as myself, and all were equally in a hurry to be off and avoid as much as possible the famine we knew we should have to fight through at this late season. Little troubles, of course, must always be expected, else these blacks would not be true negroes. Sheikh Said now reported it quite impossible to buy anything at a moderate rate; for, as I was a 'big man,' I ought to 'pay a big price' and my men had all been obliged to fight in the bazaar before they could get even tobacco at the same rate as other men, because they were the servants of the big man, who could afford to give higher wages than any one else. The Hottentots, too, began to fall sick, which my Wangŭana laughingly attributed to want of grog to keep their spirits up, as these little creatures, the 'Tots,' had frequently at Zanzibar, after heavy potations, boasted to the more sober free men, that they 'were strong, because they could stand plenty drink.' The first step now taken was to pitch camp under large shady mango-trees, and to instruct every man in his particular duty. At the same time, the Wangŭana, who had carbines, were obliged to be drilled in their use and formed into companies, with captains of ten, headed by General Baraka, who was made commander-in-chief.

Bagamoyo to Ugéni: On the 30th September, as things were looking more orderly, I sent forward half of the property, and all the men I had then collected, to Ugéni, a shamba, or garden, two miles off; and on the 2d October, after settling with Ladha for my 'African money,' as my pagazis were completed to a hundred and one, we wished Rigby adieu, and all assembled together at Ugéni, which resembles the richest parts of Bengal.

CHAPTER II

Uzaramo

WE were now in U-zà-Rāmo, which may mean the country of Ramo, though I have never found any natives who could enlighten me on the derivation of this obviously triple word. The extent of the country, roughly speaking, stretches from the coast to the junction or bifurcation of the Kingani and its upper branch the Mgéta river, westwards; and from the Kingani, north, to the Lŭfigi river, south; though in the southern portions several subtribes have encroached upon the lands. There are no hills in Uzaramo; but the land in the central line, formed like a ridge between the two rivers, furrow fashion, consists of slightly elevated flats and terraces, which, in the rainy season, throw off their surplus waters to the north and south by nullahs into these rivers. The country is uniformly well covered with trees and large grasses, which, in the rainy season, are too thick, tall, and green to be pleasant; though in the dry season, after the grasses have been burnt, it is agreeable enough, though not pretty, owing to the flatness of the land. The villages are not large or numerous, but widely spread, consisting generally of conical grass huts, while others are gable-ended, after the coast-fashion – a small collection of ten or twenty comprising one village. Over these villages certain headmen, titled Phanzé, hold jurisdiction, who take black-mail from travellers with high presumption when they can. Generally speaking, they live upon the coast and call themselves Diwans headmen, and subjects of the Sultan Majid; but they no sooner hear of the march of a caravan than they transpose their position, become sultans in their own right and levy taxes accordingly.

The Wazaramo are strictly agriculturists; they have no cows, and but few goats. They are of low stature and thick set, and their nature tends to the boisterous. Expert slave-hunters, they mostly clothe themselves by the sale of their victims on the coast, though they do business by the sale of goats and grain as well. Nowhere in the interior are natives so well clad as these creatures. In dressing up their hair, and otherwise smearing their bodies with ochreish clay, they are great dandies. They always keep their bows and arrows, which form their national arm, in excellent order, the latter well poisoned, and carried in quivers nicely carved. To intimidate a caravan and extort a hongo or tax, I have seen them drawn out in line as if prepared for battle; but a few soft words were found sufficient to make them all withdraw and settle the matter at issue by arbitration in some appointed place. A few men without property can cross their lands fearlessly, though a single individual with property would stand no chance, for they are insatiable thieves. But little is seen of these people on the journey, as the chiefs take their taxes by deputy, partly out of pride, and partly because they think they can extort more by keeping in the mysterious distance. At the same time, the caravan prefers camping in the jungles beyond the villages to mingling with the inhabitants, where rows might be engendered. We sometimes noticed Albinos, with greyish-blue eyes and light straw-coloured hair. Not unfrequently we would pass on the track-side small heaps of white ashes, with a calcined bone or two among them. These, we were told, were the relics of burnt witches. The caravan track we had now to travel on leads along the right bank of the Kingani valley, overlooking Uzégŭra, which, corresponding with Uzaramo, only on the other side of the Kingani, extends northwards to the Pangani river, and is intersected in the centre by the Wami river, of which more hereafter.

To Bomani, 3d: Starting on a march with a large mixed caravan, consisting of 1 corporal and 9 privates, Hottentots – 1 jemadar and 25 privates, Belŭchs – 1 Arab Cafila Bashi and 75 freed slaves – 1 kirangozi, or leader, and 100 negro porters – 12 mules untrained, 3 donkeys, and 22 goats – one could hardly expect to find everybody in his place at the proper time for breaking ground; but, at the same time, it could hardly be expected that ten men, who had actually received their bounty money, and had sworn fidelity, should give one the slip the very first day. Such, however, was the case. Ten out of the thirty-six given by the Sultan ran away, because they feared that the white men, whom they believed to be cannibals, were only taking them into the interior to eat them; and one pagazi, more honest than the freed men, deposited his pay upon the ground, and ran away too. Go we must, however; for one desertion is sure to lead to more; and go we did. Our procession was in this fashion: The kirangozi, with a load on his shoulder, led the way, flag in hand, followed by the pagazis carrying spears or bows and arrows in their hands, and bearing their share of the baggage in the shape either of bolster-shaped loads of cloth and beads covered with matting, each tied into the fork of a three-pronged stick, or else coils of brass or copper wire tied in even weights to each end of sticks which they laid on the shoulder; then helter-skelter came the Wangŭana, carrying carbines in their hands, and boxes, bundles, tents, cooking-pots – all the miscellaneous property – on their heads; next the Hottentots, dragging the refractory mules laden with ammunition-boxes, but very lightly, to save the animals for the future; and, finally, Sheikh Said and the Belŭch escort; while the goats, sick women, and stragglers, brought up the rear. From first to last, some of the sick Hottentots rode the hospital donkeys, allowing the negroes to tug their animals; for the smallest ailment threw them broadcast on their backs.

In a little while we cleared from the rich gardens, mango clumps, and cocoa-nut trees, which characterise the fertile coast-line. After traversing fields of grass well clothed with green trees, we arrived at the little settlement of Bomani, where camp was formed, and everybody fairly appointed to his place. The process of camp-forming would be thus: Sheikh Said, with Bombay under him, issues cloths to the men for rations at the rate of one-fourth load a-day (about 15 lb) amongst 165; the Hottentots cook our dinners and their own, or else lie rolling on the ground overcome by fatigue; the Belŭchs are supposed to guard the camp, but prefer gossip and brightening their arms. Some men are told off to look after the mules, donkeys, and goats, whilst out grazing; the rest have to pack the kit, pitch our tents, cut boughs for huts and for fencing in the camp – a thing rarely done, by the by. After cooking, when the night has set in, the everlasting dance begins, attended with clapping of hands and jingling small bells strapped to the legs – the whole being accompanied by a constant repetition of senseless words, which stand in place of the song to the negroes; for song they have none, being mentally incapacitated for musical composition, though as timists they are not to be surpassed.

What remains to be told is the daily occupation of Captain Grant, myself, and our private servants. Beginning at the foot: Rahan, a very peppery little negro, who had served in a British man-of-war at the taking of Rangoon, was my valet; and Baraka, who had been trained much in the same manner, but had seen engagements at Multan, was Captain Grant's. They both knew Hindŭstani; but while Rahan's services at sea had been short, Baraka had served nearly all his life with Englishmen – was the smartest and most intelligent negro I ever saw – was invaluable to Colonel Rigby as a detector of slave-traders, and enjoyed his confidence completely – so much so, that he said, on parting with him, that he did not know where he should be able to find another man to fill his post. These two men had now charge of our tents and personal kit, while Baraka was considered the general of the Wangŭana forces, and Rahan a captain of ten.

My first occupation was to map the country. This is done by timing the rate of march with a watch, taking compass-bearings along the road, or on any conspicuous marks – as, for instance, hills off it – and by noting the watershed – in short, all topographical objects. On arrival in camp every day came the ascertaining, by boiling a thermometer, of the altitude of the station above the sea-level; of the latitude of the station by the meridian altitude of a star taken with a sextant; and of the compass variation by azimuth. Occasionally there was the fixing of certain crucial stations, at intervals of sixty miles or so, by lunar observations, or distances of the moon either from the sun or from certain given stars, for determining the longitude, by which the original-timed course can be drawn out with certainty on the map by proportion. Should a date be lost, you can always discover it by taking a lunar distance and comparing it with the Nautical Almanac, by noting the time when a star passes the meridian if your watch is right, or by observing the phases of the moon, or her rising or setting, as compared with the Nautical Almanac. The rest of my work, besides sketching and keeping a diary, which was the most troublesome of all, consisted in making geological and zoological collections. With Captain Grant rested the botanical collections and thermometrical registers. He also boiled one of the thermometers, kept the rain-gauge, and undertook the photography; but after a time I sent the instruments back, considering this work too severe for the climate, and he tried instead sketching with watercolours – the results of which form the chief part of the illustrations in this book. The rest of our day went in breakfasting after the march was over – a pipe, to prepare us for rummaging the fields and villages to discover their contents for scientific purposes – dinner close to sunset, and tea and pipe before turning in at night.

To Ikambŭrŭ 4th: A short stage brought us to Ikambŭrŭ, included in the district of Nzasa, where there is another small village presided over by Phanzé Khombé la Simba, meaning Claw of Lion. He, immediately after our arrival, sent us a present of a basket of rice, value one dollar, of course expecting a return – for absolute generosity is a thing unknown to the negro. Not being aware of the value of the offering, I simply requested the Sheikh to give him four yards of American sheeting, and thought no more about the matter, until presently I found the cloth returned. The 'Sultan' could not think of receiving such a paltry present from me, when on the former journey he got so much; if he showed this cloth at home, nobody would believe him, but would say he took much more and concealed it from his family, wishing to keep all his goods to himself. I answered that my footing in the country had been paid for on the last journey, and unless he would accept me as any other common traveller, he had better walk away; but the little Sheikh, a timid, though very gentlemanly creature, knowing the man, and dreading the consequences of too high a tone, pleaded for him, and proposed as a fitting hongo, one dubŭani, one sahari, and eight yards merikani, as the American sheeting is called here. This was pressed by the jemadar, and acceded to by myself, as the very utmost I could afford. Lion's Claw, however, would not accept it; it was too far below the mark of what he got last time. He therefore returned the cloths to the Sheikh, as he could get no hearing from myself, and retreated in high dudgeon, threatening the caravan with a view of his terrible presence on the morrow. Meanwhile the little Sheikh, who always earned a sword fully two-thirds the length of himself, commenced casting bullets for his double-barrelled rifle, ordered the Wangŭana to load their guns, and came wheedling up to me for one more cloth, as it was no use hazarding the expedition's safety for four yards of cloth. This is a fair specimen of tax-gathering, within twelve miles of the coast, by a native who claims the protection of Zanzibar. We shall soon see what they are further on. The result of experience is, that, ardent as the traveller is to see the interior of Africa, no sooner has he dealings with the natives, than his whole thoughts tend to discovering some road where he won't be molested, or a short cut, but long march, to get over the ground.

To Kizoto, 5th: Quite undisturbed, we packed and marched as usual, and soon passed Nzasa close to the river, which is only indicated by a line ot trees running through a rich alluvial valley. We camped at the little settlement of Kizoto, inhospitably presided over by Phanzé Mŭkia ya Nyani, or Monkey's Tail, who no sooner heard of our arrival than he sent a demand for his 'rights.' One dubŭani was issued, with orders that no one need approach me again, unless he wanted to smell my powder. Two taxes in five miles was a thing unheard of; and I heard no more about the matter, until Bombay in the evening told me how Sheikh Said, fearing awkward consequences, had settled to give two dubhani, one being taken from his own store. Lion's Claw also turned up again, getting his cloths of yesterday – one more being added from the Sheikh's stores – and he was then advised to go off quietly, as I was a fire-eater whom nobody dared approach after my orders had been issued. This was our third march in Uzaramo; we had scarcely seen a man of the country, and had no excessive desire to do so.

To Kiranga Ranga, 6th: Deflecting from the serpentine course of the Kingani a little, we crossed a small bitter rivulet, and entered on the elevated cultivation of Kiranga Banga, under Phanzé Mkungŭ-paré, a very mild man, who, wishing to give no offence, begged for a trifling present. He came in person, and his manner having pleased us, I gave him one sahari, four yards merikani, and eight yards kiniki, which pleased our friend so much that he begged us to consider his estate our own, even to the extent of administering his justice, should any Mzaramo be detected stealing from us. Our target-practice, whilst instructing the men, astonished him not a little, and produced an exclamation that, with so many guns, we need fear nothing, go where we would. From this place a good view is obtained of Uzégŭra. Beyond the flat alluvial valley of the Kingani, seven to eight miles broad, the land rises suddenly to a table-land of no great height, on which trees grow in profusion. In fact it appeared, as far as the eye could reach, the very counterpart of that where we stood, with the exception of a small hill, very distant, called Phongŭé.

A very welcome packet of quinine and other medicines reached us here from Rigby, who, hearing our complaints that the Hottentots could only be kept alive by daily potions of brandy and quinine, feared our supplies were not enough, and sent us more.

To Thŭmba Lhéré, 7th: Skirting along the margin of the rising ground over-looking the river, through thick woods, cleared in places for cultivation, we arrived at Thŭmba Lhéré. The chief here took a hongo of three yards merikani and two yards kiniki without much fuss, for he had no power. The pagazis struck, and said they would not move from this unless I gave them one fundo or ten necklaces of beads each daily, in lieu of rations, as they were promised by Ladha on the coast that I would do so as soon as they had made four marches. This was an obvious invention, concocted to try my generosity, for I had given the kirangozi a goat, which is customary, to 'make the journey prosperous' – had suspended a dollar to his neck in recognition of his office, and given him four yards merikani, that he might have a grand feast with his brothers; while neither the Sheikh, myself, nor any one else in the camp, had heard of such a compact. With high words the matter dropped, African fashion.

To Mŭhŭgŭé, 8th: The pagazis would not start at the appointed time, hoping to enforce their demands of last night; so we took the lead and started, followed by the Wangŭana. Seeing this, the pagazis cried out with one accord: 'The master is gone, leaving the responsibility of his property in our hands; let us follow, let us follow, for verily he is our father' and all came hurrying after us. Here the river, again making a bend, is lost to sight, and we marched through large woods and cultivated fields to Mŭhŭgŭé, observing, as we passed along, the ochreish colour of the earth, and numerous pits which the copal-diggers had made searching for their much-valued gum. A large coast-bound caravan, carrying ivory tusks with double-toned bells suspended to them, ting-tonging as they moved along, was met on the way; and as some of the pagazis composing it were men who had formerly taken me to the Victoria N'yanza, warm recognitions passed between us. The water found here turned our brandy and tea as black as ink. The chief, being a man of small pretensions, took only one sahari and four yards merikani.

To Mŭhonyéra, 9th: Instead of going on to the next village we halted in this jungly place for the day, that I might comply with the desire of the Royal Geographical Society to inspect Mŭhonyéra, and report if there were really any indications of a 'raised sea-beach' there, such as their maps indicate. An inspection brought me to the conclusion that no mind but one prone to discovering sea-beaches in the most unlikely places could have supposed for a moment that one existed here. The form and appearance of the land are the same as we have seen everywhere since leaving Bomani – a low plateau subtended by a bank cut down by the Kingani river, and nothing more. There are no pebbles; the soil is rich reddish loam, well covered with trees, bush, and grass, in which some pigs and antelopes are found. From the top of this embankment we gain the first sight of the East Coast Range, due west of us, represented by the high elephant's-back hill, Mkambakŭ, in Usagara, which, joining Uragŭrŭ, stretches northwards across the Pangani river to Usŭmbara and the Kilimandjaro, and southwards, with a westerly deflection, across the Lŭfiji to Southern N'yassa. What course the range takes beyond those two extremes, the rest of the world knows as well as I. Another conspicuous landmark here is Kidŭnda (the little hill), which is the southernmost point of a low chain of hills, also tending northwards, and representing an advance-guard to the higher East Coast Range in its rear. At night, as we had no local 'sultans' to torment us, eight more men of Sultan Majid's donation ran away, and, adding injury to injury, took with them all our goats, fifteen in number. This was a sad loss. We could keep ourselves on guinea-fowls or green pigeons, doves, etc; but the Hottentots wanted nourishment much more than ourselves, and as their dinners always consisted of what we left, 'short-commons' was the fate in store for them. The Wangŭana, instead of regarding these poor creatures as soldiers, treated them like children; and once, as a diminutive Tot – the common name they go by – was exerting himself to lift his pack and place it on his mule, a fine Herculean Mgŭana stepped up behind, grasped Tot, pack and all, in his muscular arms, lifted the whole over his head, paraded the Tot about, struggling for release, and put him down amidst the laughter of the camp, then saddled his mule and patted him on the back.

To Sagéséra, 10th: After sending a party of Belŭch to track down the deserters and goats, in which they were not successful, we passed through the village of Sagéséra, and camped one mile beyond, close to the river. Phanzé Kirongo (which means Mr Pit) here paid us his respects, with a presentation of rice. In return he received four yards merikani and one dubŭani, which Bombay settled, as the little Sheikh, ever done by the sultans, pleaded indisposition, to avoid the double fire he was always subjected to on these occasions, by the sultans grasping on the one side, and my resisting on the other; for I relied on my strength, and thought it very inadvisable to be generous with my cloth to the prejudice of future travellers, by decreasing the value of merchandise, and increasing proportionately the expectations of these negro chiefs. From the top of the bank bordering on the valley, a good view was obtainable of the Uragŭrŭ hills, and the top of a very distant cone to its northward; but I could see no signs of any river joining the Kingani on its left, though on the former expedition I heard that the Mŭkondokŭa river, which was met with in Uzégŭra, joined the Kingani close to Sagéséra, and actually formed its largest head branch. Neither could Mr Pit inform me what became of the Mŭkondokŭa, as the Wazaramo are not given to travelling. He had heard of it from the traders, but only knew himself of one river beside the Kingani. It was called Wami in Uzégéra, and mouths at Utondŭé, between the ports of Whindi and Saadani. To try and check the desertions of Sultan Majid's men, I advised – ordering was of no use – that their camp should be broken up, and they should be amalgamated with the Wangŭana; but it was found that the two would not mix. In fact, the whole native camp consisted of so many clubs of two, four, six, or ten men, who originally belonged to one village or one master, or were united by some other family tie which they preferred keeping intact; so they cooked together, ate together, slept together, and sometimes mutinied together. The amalgamation having failed, I wrote some emancipation tickets, called the Sultan's men all up together, selected the best, gave them these tickets, announced that their pay and all rewards would be placed for the future on the same conditions as those of the Wangŭana, and as soon as I saw any signs of improvement in the rest, they would all be treated in the same manner; but should they desert, they would find my arm long enough to arrest them on the coast and put them into prison.

To Makŭtaniro, 11th: During this march we crossed three deep nullahs which drain the Uzaramo plateau, and arrived at the Makŭtaniro, or junction of this line with those of Mboamaji and Kondŭchi, which traverse central Uzaramo, and which, on my former return journey, I went down. The gum-copal diggings here cease. The Dŭm palm is left behind; the large rich green-leaved trees of the low plateau give place to the mimosa; and now, having ascended the greater decline of the Kingani liver, instead of being confined by a bank, we found ourselves on flat open park-land, where antelopes roam at large, buffalo and zebra are sometimes met with, and guinea-fowl are numerous. The water for the camp is found in the river, but supplies of grain come from the village of Kipora farther on.

To Matamombo, 12th: A march through the park took us to a camp by a pond, from which, by crossing the Kingani, rice and provisions for the men were obtained on the opposite bank. One can seldom afford to follow wild animals on the line of march, otherwise we might have bagged some antelopes to-day, which, scared by the interminable singing, shouting, bell-jingling, horn-blowing, and other such merry noises of the moving caravan, could be seen disappearing in the distance.

To Dégé la Mhora, 13th: Leaving the park, we now entered the richest part of Uzaramo, affording crops as fine as any part of India. Here it was, in the district of Dégé la Mhora, that the first expedition to this country, guided by a Frenchman, M. Maizan, came to a fatal termination, that gentleman having been barbarously murdered by the sub-chief Hembé. The cause of the affair was distinctly explained to me by Hembé himself, who, with his cousin Darŭnga, came to call upon me, presuming, as he was not maltreated by the last expedition, that the matter would now be forgotten. The two men were very great friends of the little Sheikh, and as a present was expected, which I should have to pay, we all talked cheerfully and confidentially, bringing in the fate of Maizan for no other reason than to satisfy curiosity. Hermbé, who lives in the centre of an almost impenetrable thicket, confessed that he was the murderer, but said the fault did not rest with him, as he merely carried out the instructions of his father, Mzŭngéra, who, a Diwan on the coast sent him a letter directing his actions. Thus it is proved that the plot against Maizan was concocted on the coast by the Arab merchants – most likely from the same motive which has induced one rival merchant to kill another as the best means of checking rivalry or competition. When Arabs – and they are the only class of people who would do such a deed – found a European going into the very middle of their secret trading-places, where such large profits were to be obtained, they would never suppose that the scientific Maizan went for any other purpose than to pry into their ivory stores, bring others into the field after him, and destroy their monopoly. The Sultan of Zanzibar, in those days, was our old ally Said Said, commonly called the Emam of Muscat; and our Consul, Colonel Hamerton, had been M. Maizan's host as long as he lived upon the coast. Both the Emam and Consul were desirous of seeing the country surveyed, and did everything in their power to assist Maizan, the former even appointing the Indian Mŭsa to conduct him safely as far as Unyamŭézi; but their power was not found sufficient to damp the raging fire of jealousy in the ivory-trader's heart. Mŭsa commenced the journey with Maizan, and they travelled together a march or two, when one of Maizan's domestic establishment fell sick and stopped his progress. Mŭsa remained with him eight or ten days, to his own loss in trade and expense in keeping up a large establishment, and then they parted by mutual consent, Maizan thinking himself quite strong enough to take care of himself. This separation was, I believe, poor Maizan's death-blow. His power, on the Emam's side, went with Mŭsa's going, and left the Arabs free to carry out their wicked wills.

The presents I had to give here were one sahari and eight yards merikani to Hembé, and the same to Darŭnga, for which they gave a return in grain.

To Kidŭnda, 14th: Still following close to the river – which, unfortunately led with thick bush that we could seldom see it – a few of the last villages in Uzaramo were passed. Here antelopes reappear amongst the tall mimosa, but we let them alone in prosecution of the survey, and finally encamped opposite the little hill of Kidtinda, which, lying on the left bank of the Kingani, stretches north, a little east, into Uzégŭra. The hill crops out through pisolitic limestone, in which marine fossils were observable. It would be interesting to ascertain whether this lime formation extends down the east coast of

Africa from the Somali country, where also, on my first expedition, I found marine shells in the limestone, especially as a vast continuous band of limestone is known to extend from the Tagus, through Egypt and the Somali country, to the Burrumputra. To obtain food it was necessary here to ferry the river and purchase from the Wazaramo, who, from fear of the passing caravans, had left their own bank and formed a settlement immediately under this pretty little hill – rendered all the more enchanting to our eyes, as it was the first we had met since leaving the sea-coast. The Diwan, or head man, was a very civil creature; he presented us freely with two fine goats – a thing at that time we were very much in want of – and took, in return, without any comments, one dubŭani and eight yards merikani.

Halt, 15th: The next day, as we had no further need of our Belŭch escort, a halt was made to enable me to draw up a 'Progress Report,' and pack all the specimens of natural history collected on the way, for the Royal Geographical Society. Captain Grant, taking advantage of the spare time, killed for the larder two buck antelopes, and the Tots brought in, in high excited triumph, a famous pig.

To the Mgéta River, 16th: This march, which declines from the Kingani a little, leads through rolling, jungly ground, full of game, to the tributary stream Mgéta. It is fordable in the dry season, but has to be bridged by throwing a tree across it in the wet one. Rising in the Usagara hills to the west of the hog-backed Mkambakti, this branch intersects the province of Ukhtitii in the centre, and circles round until it unites with the Kingani about four miles north of the ford. Where the Kingani itself rises, I never could find out; though I have heard that its source lies in a gurgling spring on the eastern face of the Mkambakŭ, by which account the Mgéta is made the longer branch of the two.

CHAPTER III

Usagara

UNDER U-Sagara, or, as it might be interpreted, U-sa-Gara – country of Gara – is included all the country lying between the bifurcation of the Kingani and Mgéta rivers east, and Ugogo, the first country on the interior plateau west, a distance of a hundred miles. On the north it is bounded by the Mŭkondokŭa, or upper course of the Wami river, and on the south by the Rŭaha, or northern great branch of the Lŭfiji river. It forms a link of the great East Coast Range; but though it is generally comprehended under the single name Usagara, many sub-tribes occupy and apply their own names to portions of it; as, for instance, the people on whose ground we now stood at the foot of the hills, are Wa-Khŭtŭ, and their possessions consequently are U-Khŭtŭ, which is by far the best producing land hitherto alluded to since leaving the sea-coast line. Our ascent by the river, though quite imperceptible to the eye, has been 500 feet. From this level the range before us rises in some places to 5000 or 6000 feet, not as one grand mountain, but in two detached lines, lying at an angle of 45 degrees from N.E. to S.W., and separated one from the other by elevated valleys, tables, and crab-claw spurs of hill which incline towards the flanking rivers. The whole having been thrown up by volcanic action, is based on a strong foundation of granite and other igneous rocks, which are exposed in many places in the shape of massive blocks; otherwise the hill-range is covered in the upper part with sandstone, and in the bottoms with alluvial clay. This is the superficial configuration of the land as it strikes the eye; but, knowing the elevation of the interior plateau to be only 2500 feet above the sea immediately on the western flank of these hills, whilst the breadth of the chain is 100 miles, the mean slope or incline of the basal surface must be on a gradual rise of twenty feet per mile. The hill tops and sides, where not cultivated, are well covered with bush and small trees, amongst which the bamboo is conspicuous; whilst the bottoms, having a soil deeper and richer, produce fine large fig-trees of exceeding beauty, the huge calabash, and a variety of other trees. Here, in certain places where water is obtainable throughout the year, and wars, or slave-hunts more properly speaking, do not disturb the industry of the people, cultivation thrives surprisingly; but such a boon is rarely granted them. It is in consequence of these constantly-recurring troubles that the majority of the Wasagara villages are built on hill-spurs, where the people can the better resist attack, or, failing, disperse and hide effectually. The normal habitation is the small conical hut of grass. These compose villages, varying in number according to the influence of their head men. There are, however, a few mud villages on the table-lands, each built in a large irregular square of chambers with a hollow yard in the centre, known as tembé.

As to the people of these uplands, poor, meagre-looking wretches, they contrast unfavourably with the lowlanders on both sides of them. Dingy in colour, spiritless, shy, and timid, they invite attack in a country where every human being has a market value, and are little seen by the passing caravan. In habits they are semi-pastoral agriculturists, and would be useful members of society were they left alone to cultivate their own possessions, rich and beautiful by nature, but poor and desolate by force of circumstance. Some of the men can afford a cloth, but the greater part wear an article which I can only describe as a grass kilt. In one or two places throughout the passage of these hills a caravan may be taxed, but if so, only to a small amount; the villagers more frequently fly to the hill-tops as soon as the noise of the advancing caravan is heard, and no persuasions will bring them down again, so much ground have they, from previous experience, to fear treachery. It is such sad sights, and the obvious want of peace and prosperity, that weary the traveller, and make him ever think of pushing on to his journey's end from the instant he enters Africa until he quits the country.

Halt, 17th and 18th: Knowing by old experience that the beautiful green park in the fork of these rivers abounded in game of great variety and in vast herds, where no men are ever seen except some savage hunters sitting in the trees with poisoned arrows, or watching their snares and pitfalls, I had all along determined on a hunt myself, to feed and cheer the men, and also to collect some specimens for the home museums. In the first object we succeeded well, as 'the bags' we made counted two brindled gnŭ, four water-boc, one pallah-boc, and one pig – enough to feed abundantly the whole camp round. The feast was all the better relished as the men knew well that no Arab master would have given them what he could sell; for if a slave shot game, the animals would be the master's, to be sold bit by bit among the porters, and compensated from the proceeds of their pay. In the variety and number of our game we were disappointed, partly because so many wounded got away, and partly because we could not find what we knew the park to contain, in addition to what we killed – namely, elephants, rhinoceros, giraffes, buffaloes, zebra, and many varieties of antelopes, besides lions and hyenas. In fact, 'the park,' as well as all the adjacent land at the foot of the hills, is worth thinking of, with a view to a sporting tour as well as scientific investigation.

To Kirŭrŭ, 19th and 20th: Our halt at the ford here was cut short by the increasing sickness of the Hottentots, and the painful fact that Captain Grant was seized with fever. We had to change camp to the little village of Kirŭrŭ, where, as rice was grown – an article not to be procured again on this side of Unyamŭézi – we stopped a day to lay in supplies of this most valuable of all travelling food. Here I obtained the most consistent accounts of the river system which, within five days' journey, trends through Uzégŭra; and I concluded, from what I heard, that there is no doubt of the Mŭkondokŭa and Wami rivers being one and the same stream. My informants were the natives of the settlement, and they all concurred in saying that the Kingani above the junction is called the Rŭfŭ, meaning the parent stream. Beyond it, following under the line of the hills, at one day's journey distant, there is a smaller river called Msongé. At an equal distance beyond it, another of the same size is known as Lŭngérengéri; and a fourth river is the Wami, which mouths in the sea at Utondŭé, between the ports of Whindi and Saadani. In former years, the ivory-merchants, ever seeking for an easy road for their trade, and knowing they would have no hills to climb if they could only gain a clear passage by this river from the interior plateau to the sea, made friends with the native chiefs of Uzégŭra, and succeeded in establishing it as a thoroughfare.

Avarice, however, that fatal enemy to the negro chiefs, made them overreach themselves by exorbitant demands of taxes. Then followed contests for the right of appropriating the taxes, and the whole ended in the closing of the road, which both parties were equally anxious to keep open for their mutual gain. This foolish disruption having at first only lasted for a while, the road was again opened and again closed, for the merchants wanted an easy passage, and the native chiefs desired cloths. But it was shut again; and now we heard of its being for a third time opened, with what success the future only can determine – for experience *will* not teach the negro, who thinks only for the moment. Had they only sense to see, and patience to wait, the whole trade of the interior would inevitably pass through their country instead of Uzaramo; and instead of being poor in cloths, they would be rich and well dressed like their neighbours. But the curse of Noah sticks to these his grandchildren by Ham, and no remedy that has yet been found will relieve them. They require a government like ours in India; and without it, the slave-trade will wipe them off the face of the earth.

To Dŭthŭmi, 21st: Now leaving the open parks of pretty acacias, we followed up the Mgazi branch of the Mgéta, traversed large tree-jungles, where the tall palm is conspicuous, and drew up under the lumpy Mkambakŭ, to find a residence for the day. Here an Arab merchant, Khamis, bound for Zanzibar, obliged us by agreeing for a few dollars to convey our recent spoils in natural history to the coast.

To Hozŭ, 22d: My plans for the present were to reach Zungoméro as soon as possible, as a few days' halt would be required there to fix the longitude of the eastern flank of the East Coast Range by astronomical observation; but on ordering the morning's march, the porters – too well fed and lazy – thought our marching-rate much too severe, and resolutely refused to move. They ought to have made ten miles a-day, but preferred doing five. Argument was useless, and I was reluctant to apply the stick, as the Arabs would have done when they saw their porters trifling with their pockets. Determining, however, not to be frustrated in this puerile manner, I ordered the bugler to sound the march, and started with the mules and coast-men, trusting to Sheikh and Baraka to bring on the Wanyamŭdzi as soon as they could move them. The same day we crossed the Mgazi, where we found several Wakhŭtŭ spearing fish in the muddy hovers of its banks.

Zungoméro, 23d: We slept under a tree, and this morning found a comfortable residence under the eaves of a capacious hut. The Wanyamŭézi porters next came in at their own time, and proved to us how little worth arc orders in a land where every man, in his own opinion, is a lord, and no laws prevail. Zungoméro, bisected by the Mgéta, lies on flat ground, in a very pretty amphitheatre of hills, S. lat 7° 26' 53', and E. long. 37° 36' 45'. It is extremely fertile, and very populous, affording everything that man can wish, even to the cocoa and papwa fruits; but the slave trade has almost depopulated it, and turned its once flourishing gardens into jungles. As I have already said, the people who possess these lands are cowardly by nature, and that is the reason why they are so much oppressed. The Wasŭahili, taking advantage of their timidity, flock here in numbers to live upon the fruits of their labours. The merchants on the coast, too, though prohibited by their Sultan from interfering with the natural course of trade, send their hungry slaves, as touters, to entice all approaching caravans to trade with their particular ports, authorising the touters to pay such premiums as may be necessary for the purpose. Where they came from we could not ascertain; but during our residence, a large party of the Wasŭahili marched past, bound for the coast, with one hundred head of cattle, fifty slaves in chains, and as many goats. Halts always end disastrously in Africa, giving men time for mischief; and here was an example of it. During the target-practice, which was always instituted on such occasions to give confidence to our men, the little pepper-box Rahan, my head valet, challenged a comrade to a duel with carbines. Being stopped by those around him, he vented his wrath in terrible oaths, and swung about his arms, until his gun accidentally went off, and blew his middle finger off.

Zungomdro is a terminus or junction of two roads leading to the interior – one, the northern, crossing over the Goma Pass, and trenching on the Mŭkondokŭa river, and the other crossing over the Mabrŭki Pass, and edging on the Rŭaha river. They both unite again at Ugogi, the western terminus on the present great Unyamŭézi line. On the former expedition I went by the northern line and returned by the southern, finding both equally easy, and, indeed, neither is worthy of special and permanent preference. In fact, every season makes a difference in the supply of water and provisions; and with every year, owing to incessant wars, or rather slave-hunts, the habitations of the wretched inhabitants become constantly changed – generally speaking, for the worse. Our first and last object, therefore, as might be supposed, from knowing these circumstances, was to ascertain, before mounting the hill-range, which route would afford us the best facilities for a speedy march now. No one, however, could or would advise us. The whole country on ahead, especially Ugogo, was oppressed by drought and famine. To avoid this latter country, then, we selected the southern route, as by doing so it was hoped we might follow the course of the Rǔaha river from Maroro to Usénga and Usanga, and thence strike across to Unyanyembé, sweeping clear of Ugogo.

To Kirengǔé, 27th: With this determination, after despatching a third set of specimens, consisting of large game animals, birds, snakes, insects, land and freshwater shells, and a few rock specimens, of which one was fossiliferous, we turned southwards, penetrating the forests which lie between the greater range and the little outlying one. At the foot of this is the Maji ya Whéta, a hot, deep-seated spring of fresh water, which bubbles up through many apertures in a large dome-shaped heap of soft lime – an accumulation obviously thrown up by the force of the spring, as the rocks on either side of it are of igneous character. We arrived at the deserted village of Kirengǔé. This was not an easy go-ahead march, for the halt had disaffected both men and mules. Three of the former bolted, leaving their loads upon the ground; and on the line of march, one of the mules, a full-conditioned animal, gave up the ghost after an eighteen hours' sickness. What his disease was I never could ascertain; but as all the remaining animals died afterwards much in the same manner, I may state for once and for all, that these attacks commenced with general swelling, at first on the face, then down the neck, along the belly and down the legs. It proved so obstinate that fire had no effect upon it; and although we cut off the tails of some to relieve them by bleeding, still they died.

Halt, 28th: In former days Kirengǔé was inhabited, and we reasonably hoped to find some supplies for the jungly march before us. But we had calculated without our host, for the slave-hunters had driven every vestige of humanity away; and now, as we were delayed by our three loads behind, there was nothing left but to send back and purchase more grain. Such was one of the many days frittered away in do-nothingness.

To camp, 29th: This day, all together again, we rose the first spurs of the well-wooded Usagara hills, amongst which the familiar bamboo was plentiful, and at night we bivouacked in the jungle.

To E. Mbŭiga, 30th: Rising betimes in the morning, and starting with a good will, we soon reached the first settlements of Mbŭiga, from which could be seen a curious blue mountain, standing up like a giant overlooking all the rest of the hills. The scenery here formed a strong and very pleasing contrast to any we had seen since leaving the coast. Emigrant Waziraha, who had been driven from their homes across the Kingani river by the slave-hunters, had taken possession of the place, and disposed their little conical-hut villages on the heights of the hill-spurs in such a picturesque manner, that one could not help hoping they would here at least be allowed to rest in peace and quietness. The valleys, watered by little brooks, are far richer, and even prettier, than the high lands above, being lined with fine trees and evergreen shrubs; while the general state of prosperity was such, that the people could afford, even at this late season of the year, to turn their corn into malt to brew beer for sale; and goats and fowls were plentiful in the market.

To W. Mbŭiga, 31st: Passing by the old village of Mbŭiga, which I occupied on my former expedition, we entered some huts on the western flank of the Mbŭiga district; and here, finding a coast-man, a great friend of the little sheikh's, willing to take back to Zanzibar anything we might give him, a halt was made, and I drew up my reports. I then consigned to his charge three of the most sickly of the Hottentots in a deplorable condition – one of the mules, that they might ride by turns – and all the specimens that had been collected. With regret I also sent back the camera; because I saw, had I allowed my companion to keep working it, the heat he was subjected to in the little tent whilst preparing and fixing his plates would very soon have killed him. The number of guinea-fowl seen here was most surprising.

To Kikobogo, 2d: A little lighter and much more comfortable for the good riddance of those grumbling 'Tots,' we worked up to and soon breasted the stiff ascent of the Mabrŭki Pass, which we surmounted without much difficulty. This concluded the first range of these Usagara hills; and once over, we dropped down to the elevated valley of Makata, where we halted two days to shoot.

As a travelling Arab informed me that the whole of the Maroro district had been laid waste by the marauding Wahéhé, 1 changed our plans again, and directed our attention to a middle and entirely new line, which in the end would lead us to Ugogi. The first and only giraffe killed upon the journey was here shot by Grant, with a little 40-gauge Lancaster rifle, at 200 yards' distance. Some smaller animals were killed; but I wasted all my time in fruitlessly stalking some wounded striped eland – magnificent animals, as large as Delhi oxen – and some other animals, of which I wounded three, about the size of hartebeest, and much their shape, only cream-coloured, with a conspicuous black spot in the centre of each flank. The eland may probably be the animal first mentioned by Livingstone, but the other animal is not known.

To Ngoto, 5th: Though reluctant to leave a place where such rare animals were to be found, the fear of remaining longer on the road induced us to leave Kikobogo, and at a good stride we crossed the flat valley of Makata, and ascended the higher lands beyond, where we no sooner arrived than we met the last down trader from Unyamŭézi, well known to all my men as the great Mamba or Crocodile. Mamba, dressed in a dirty Arab gown, with coronet of lion's nails decorating a threadbare cutch cap, greeted us with all the dignity of a savage potentate surrounded by his staff of half-naked officials. As usual, he had been the last to leave the Unyamŭézi, and so purchased all his stock of ivory at a cheap rate, there being no competitors left to raise the value of that commodity; but his journey had been a very trying one. With a party, at his own estimate, of two thousand souls – we did not see anything like that number – he had come from Ugogo to this, by his own confession, living on the products of the jungle, and by boiling down the skin aprons of his porters occasionally for a soup. Famines were raging throughout the land, and the Arabs preceding him had so harried the country, that every village was deserted. On hearing our intention to march upon the direct line, he frankly said he thought we should never get through, for my men could not travel as his had done, and therefore he advised our deflecting northwards from New Mbŭmi to join the track leading from Rŭmŭma to Ugogi. This was a sad disappointment; but, rather than risk a failure, I resolved to follow his advice.

To Mŭhanda and M'yombo, 6th and 7th: After reaching the elevated ground, we marched over rolling tops, covered with small trees and a variety of pretty bulbs, and reached the habitations of Mŭhanda, where we no sooner appeared than the poor villagers, accustomed only to rough handling, immediately dispersed in the jungles. By dint of persuasion, however, we induced them to sell us provisions, though at a monstrous rate, such as no merchant could have afforded; and having spent the night quietly, we proceeded on to the upper courses of the M'yombo river, which trends its way northwards to the Mŭkondokŭa river. The scenery was most interesting, with every variety of hill, roll, plateau, and ravine, wild and prettily wooded; but we saw nothing of the people. Like frightened rats, as soon as they caught the sound of our advancing march, they buried themselves in the jungles, carrying off their grain with them. Foraging parties, of necessity, were sent out as soon as the camp was pitched, with cloth for purchases, and strict orders not to use force; the upshot of which was, that my people got nothing but a few arrows fired at them by the lurking villagers, and I was abused for my squeamishness. Moreover, the villagers, emboldened by my lenity, vauntingly declared they would attack the camp by night, as they could only recognise in us such men as plunder their houses and steal their children. This caused a certain amount of alarm among my men, which induced them to run up a stiff bush-fence round the camp, and kept them talking all night.

To New Mbŭmi, 8th: This morning we marched on as usual, with one of the Hottentots lashed on a donkey; for the wretched creature, after lying in the sun asleep, became so sickly that he could not move or do anything for himself, and nobody else would do anything for him. The march was a long one, but under ordinary circumstances would have been very interesting, for we passed an immense lagoon, where hippopotami were snorting as if they invited an attack. In the larger tree-jungles the traces of elephants, buffaloes, rhinoceros, and antelopes were very numerous; while a rich variety of small birds, as often happened, made me wish I had come on a shooting rather than on a long exploring expedition. Towards sunset we arrived at New Mbŭmi, a very pretty and fertile place, lying at the foot of a cluster of steep hills, and pitched camp for three days to lay in supplies for ten, as this was reported to be the only place where we could buy corn until we reached Ugogo, a span of 140 miles. Mr Mbŭmi, the chief of the place, a very affable negro, at once took us by the hand, and said he would do anything we desired, for he had often been to Zanzibar. He knew that the English were the ruling power in that land, and that they were opposed to slavery, the terrible effects of which had led to his abandoning Old Mbŭmi, on the banks of the Mŭkondokŭa river, and residing here.

Halt, 9th, 10th and 11th: The sick Hottentot died here, and we buried him with Christian honours. As his comrades said, he died because he had determined to die, an instance of that obstinate fatalism in their mulish temperament which no kind words or threats can cure. This terrible catastrophe made me wish to send all the remaining Hottentots back to Zanzibar; but as they all preferred serving with me to returning to duty at the Cape, I selected two of the *most* sickly, put them under Tabib, one of Rigby's old servants, and told him to remain with them at Mbŭmi until such time as he might find some party proceeding to the coast; and, in the meanwhile, for board and lodgings I gave Mbŭmi beads and cloth. The prices of provisions here being a good specimen of what one has to pay at this season of the year, I give a short list of them: sixteen rations corn, two yards cloth; three fowls, two yards cloth; one goat, twenty yards cloth; one cow, forty yards cloth, the cloth being common American sheeting. Before we left Mbŭmi, a party of forty men and women of the Waquiva tribe, pressed by famine, were driven there to purchase food. The same tribe had, however, killed many of Mbŭmi's subjects not long since, and therefore, in African revenge, the chief seized them all, saying he would send them off for sale to the Zanzibar market unless they could give a legitimate reason for the cruelty they had committed. These Waquiva, I was given to understand, occupied the steep hills surrounding this place. They were a squalid-looking set, like the generality of the inhabitants of this mountainous region.

To Mdŭnhwi, 12th: This march led us over a high hill to the Mdŭnhwi river, another tributary to the Mŭkondokŭa. It is all clad in the upper regions with the slender pole-trees which characterise these hills, intermingled with bamboo; but the bottoms are characterised by a fine growth of fig-trees of great variety, along with high grasses; whilst near the villages were found good gardens of plantains, and numerous Palmyra trees. The rainy season being not far off, the villagers were busy in burning rubble and breaking their ground. Within their reach everywhere is the sarsaparilla vine, but growing as a weed, for they know nothing of its value.

To Tzanzi, 13th: Rising up from the deep valley of Mdŭnhwi, we had to cross another high ridge before descending to the also deep valley of Chongŭé, as picturesque a country as the middle heights of the Himalayas, dotted on the ridges and spur-slopes by numerous small conical-hut villages; but all so poor that we could not, had we wanted it, have purchased provisions for a day's consumption.

To Manyongé, 14th: Leaving this valley, we rose to the table of Manyovi, overhung with much higher hills, looking, according to the accounts of our Hottentots, as they eyed the fine herds of cattle grazing on the slopes, so like the range in Kafraria, that they formed their expectations accordingly, and appeared, for the first time since leaving the coast, happy at the prospect before them, little dreaming that such rich places were seldom to be met with. The Wanyamŭézi porters even thought they had found a paradise, and forthwith threw down their loads as the villagers came to offer them grain for sale; so that, had I not had the Wangtiana a little under control, we should not have completed our distance that day, and so reached Manyongé, which reminded me, by its ugliness, of the sterile Somali land.

To Rŭmŭma, 15th: Proceeding through the semi-desert rolling table-land – one place occupied by men who build their villages in large open squares of flat-topped mud huts, which, when I have occasion to refer to them in future, I shall call by their native name tembé – we could see on the right hand the massive mountains overhanging the Mŭkondokŭa river, to the front the western chain of these hills, and to the left the high crab-claw shaped ridge, which, extending from the western chain, circles round conspicuously above the swelling knolls which lie between the two main rocky ridges. Contorted green thorn-trees, 'elephant-foot' stumps, and aloes, seem to thrive best here, by their very nature indicating what the country is, a poor stony land. Our camp was pitched by the river Rŭmŭma, where, sheltered from the winds, and enriched by alluvial soil, there ought to have been no scarcity; but still the villagers had nothing to sell.

To camp, 16th: On we went again to Marenga Mkhali, the 'Salt Water,' to breakfast, and camped in the crooked green thorns by night, carrying water on for our supper. This kind of travelling – forced marches – hard as it may appear, was what we liked best, for we felt that we were shortening the journey, and in doing so, shortening the risks of failure by disease, by war, by famine, and by mutiny. We had here no grasping chiefs to detain us for presents, nor had our men time to become irritable and truculent, concoct devices for stopping the way, or fight amongst themselves.

To Inengé, 17th: On again, and at last we arrived at the foot of the western chain; but not all together. Some porters, overcome by heat and thirst, lay scattered along the road, while the corporal of the Hottentots allowed his mule to stray from him, never dreaming the animal would travel far from his comrades, and, in following after him, was led such a long way into the bush, that my men became alarmed for his safety, knowing as they did that the 'savages' were out living like monkeys on the calabash fruit, and looking out for any windfalls, such as stragglers worth plundering, that might come in their way. At first the Wangŭana attempted to track down the corporal; but finding he would not answer their repeated shots, and fearful for their own safety, they came into camp and reported the case. Losing no time, I ordered twenty men, armed with carbines, to carry water for the distressed porters, and bring the corporal back as soon as possible. They all marched off, as they always do on such exploits, in high good-humour with themselves for the valour which they intended to show; and in the evening came in, firing their guns in the most reckless manner, beaming it with delight; for they had the corporal in tow, two men and two women captives, and a spear as a trophy. Then in high impatience, all in a breath, they began a recital of the great day's work. The corporal had followed the spoor of the mule, occasionally finding some of his things that had been torn from the beast's back by the thorns, and, picking up these one by one, had become so burdened with the weight of them, that he could follow no farther. In this fix the twenty men came up with him, but not until they had had a scrimmage with the 'savages,' had secured four, and taken the spear that had been thrown at them. Of the mule's position no one could give an opinion, save that they imagined, in consequence of the thickness of the bush, he would soon become irretrievably entangled in the thicket, where the savages would find him, and bring him in as a ransom for the prisoners.

Halt, 18th: What with the diminution of our supplies, the famished state of the country, and the difficulties which frowned upon us in advance, together with unwillingness to give up so good a mule, with all its gear and ammunition, I must say I felt doubtful as to what had better be done, until the corporal, who felt confident he would find the beast, begged so hard that I sent him in command of another expedition of sixteen men, ordering him to take one of the prisoners with him to proclaim to his brethren that we would give up the rest if they returned us the mule. The corporal then led off his band to the spot where he last saw traces of the animal, and tracked on till sundown; while Grant and myself went out pot-hunting, and brought home a bag consisting of one striped eland, one saltiana antelope, four guinea-fowl, four ringdoves, and one partridge – a welcome supply, considering we were quite out of flesh.

Halt, 19th: Next day, as there were no signs of the trackers, I went again to the place of the elands, wounded a fine male, but gave up the chase, as I heard the unmistakable gun-firing return of the party, and straightway proceeded to camp. Sure enough, there they were; they had tracked the animal back to Marenga Mkhali, through jungle – for he had not taken to the footpath. Then finding he had gone on, they returned quite tired and famished. To make the most of a bad job, I now sent Grant on to the Robého (or windy) Pass, on the top of the western chain, with the mules and heavy baggage, and directions to proceed thence across the brow of the hill the following morning, while I remained behind with the tired men, promising to join him by breakfast-time. I next released the prisoners, much to their disgust, for they had not known such good feeding before, and dreaded being turned adrift again in the jungles to live on calabash seeds; and then, after shooting six guinea-fowl, turned in for the night.

To camp, 20th: Betimes in the morning we were off, mounting the Robého, a good stiff ascent, covered with trees and large blocks of granite, excepting only where cleared for villages; and on we went rapidly, until at noon the advance party was reached, located in a village overlooking the great interior plateau – a picture, as it were, of the common type of African scenery. Here, taking a hasty meal, we resumed the march all together, descended the great western chain, and, as night set in, camped in a ravine at the foot of it, not far from the great junction-station Ugogi, where terminate the hills of Usagara.

CHAPTER IV

Ugogo, and the Wilderness of Mgunda Mkhali

To camp in the Bush, 21st and 22d: This day's work led us from the hilly Usagara range into the more level lands of the interior. Making a double march of it, we first stopped to breakfast at the quiet little settlement of Inengé, where cattle were abundant, but grain so scarce that the villagers were living on calabash seeds. Proceeding thence across fields delightfully checkered with fine calabash and fig trees, we marched, carrying water through thorny jungles, until dark, when we bivouacked for the night, only to rest and push on again next morning, arriving at Marenga Mkhali (the saline water) to breakfast. Here a good view of the Usagara hills is obtained. Carrying water with us, we next marched half-way to the first settlement of Ugogo, and bivouacked again, to eat the last of our store of Mbŭmi grain.

To E. Ugogo, 23d: At length the greater famine lands had been spanned; but we were not in lands of plenty – for the Wagogo we found, like their neighbours Wasagara, eating the seed of the calabash, to save their small stores of grain.

Halt, 24th and 25th: The East Coast Range having been passed, no more hills had to be crossed, for the land we next entered on is a plateau of rolling ground, sloping southward to the Rŭaha river, which forms a great drain running from west to east, carrying off all the rainwaters that fall in its neighbourhood through the East Coast Range to the sea. To the northward can be seen some low hills, which are occupied by Wahŭmba, a subtribe of the warlike Masai; and on the west is the large forest-wilderness of Mgŭnda Mkhali. Ugogo, lying under the lee side of the Usagara hills, is comparatively sterile. Small outcrops of granite here and there poke through the surface, which, like the rest of the rolling land, being covered with bush, principally acacias, have a pleasing appearance after the rains have set in, but are too brown and desert-looking during the rest of the year. Large prairies of grass also are exposed in many places, and the villagers have laid much ground bare for agricultural purposes.

Altogether, Ugogo has a very wild aspect, well in keeping with the natives who occupy it, who, more like the Wazaramo than the Wasagara, carry arms, intended for use rather than show. The men, indeed, are never seen without their usual arms – the spear, the shield, and the assagé. They live in flat-topped, square, tembé villages, wherever springs of water are found, keep cattle in plenty, and farm enough generally to supply not only their own wants, but those of the thousands who annually pass in caravans. They are extremely fond of ornaments, the most common of which is an ugly tube of the gourd thrust through the lower lobe of the ear. Their colour is a soft ruddy brown, with a slight infusion of black, not unlike that of a rich plum. Impulsive by nature, and exceedingly avaricious, they pester travellers beyond all conception, by thronging the road, jeering, quizzing, and pointing at them; and in camp, by intrusively forcing their way into the midst of the kit, and even into the stranger's tent Caravans, in consequence, never enter their villages, but camp outside, generally under the big 'gouty-limbed' trees – encircling their entire camp sometimes with a ring-fence of thorns to prevent any sudden attack.

To resume the thread of the journey: we found, on arrival in Ugogo, very little more food than in Usagara, for the Wagogo were mixing their small stores of grain with the monkey-bread seeds of the gouty-limbed tree. Water was so scarce in the wells at this season that we had to buy it at the normal price of country beer; and, as may be imagined where such distress in food was existing, cows, goats, sheep, and fowls were also selling at high rates.

Our mules here gave us the slip again, and walked all the way back to Marenga Mkhali, where they were found and brought back by some Wagogo, who took four yards of merikani in advance, with a promise of four more on return, for the job – their chief being security for their fidelity. This business detained us two days, during which time I shot a new variety of florikan, peculiar in having a light blue band stretching from the nose over the eye to the occiput. Each day, while we resided here, cries were raised by the villagers that the Wahŭmba were coming, and then all the cattle out in the plains, both far and near, were driven into the village for protection.

To camp in Bush, 26th: At last, on the 26th, as the mules were brought in, To camp in I paid a hongo or tax of four barsati and four yards of chintz to the chief, and departed, but not until one of my porters, a Mhéhé, obtained a fat dog for his dinner; he had set his heart on it, and would not move until he had killed it, and tied it on to his load for the evening's repast. Passing through the next villages – a collection called Kifŭkŭro – we had to pay another small tax of two barsati and four yards of chintz to the chief. There we breakfasted, and pushed on, carrying water to a bivouac in the jungles, as the famine precluded our taking the march more easily.

To Magomba's Palace, 29th: We were still in great want of men; but rather than stop a day, as all delays only lead to more difficulties, I pushed on to Magomba's palace with the assistance of some Wagogo carrying our baggage, each taking one cloth as his hire. The chief wazir at once came out to meet me on the way, and in an apparently affable manner, as an old friend, begged that I would live in the palace – a bait which I did not take, as I knew my friend by experience a little too well. He then, in the politest possible manner, told me that a great dearth of food was oppressing the land – so much so, that pretty cloths only would purchase grain. I now wished to settle my hongo, but the great chief could not hear of such indecent haste.

Halt, 30th, 1st and 2d: The next day, too, the chief was too drunk to listen to any one, and I must have patience. I took out this time in the jungles very profitably, killing a fine buck and doe antelope, of a species unknown. These animals are much about the same size and shape as the common Indian antelope, and, like them, roam about in large herds. The only marked difference between the two is in the shape of their horns, as may be seen by the woodcut; and in their colour, in which, in both sexes, the Ugogo antelopes resemble the picticandata gazelle of Tibet, except that the former have dark markings on the face.

To camp in Bush, 3d: At last, after thousands of difficulties much like those I encountered in Uzaramo, the hongo was settled by a payment of one kisŭtŭ, one dubŭani, four yards bendéra, four yards kiniki, and three yards merikani. The wazir then thought he would do some business on his own account, and commenced work by presenting me with a pot of ghee and flour, saying at the same time 'empty words did not show true love,' and hoping that I would prove mine by making some slight return. To get rid of the animal, I gave him the full value of his present in cloth, which he no sooner pocketed than he had the audacity to accuse Grant of sacrilege for having shot a lizard on a holy stone, and demanded four cloths to pay atonement for this offence against the 'church.' As yet, he said, the chief was not aware of the damage done, and it was well he was not; for he would himself, if I only paid him the four cloths, settle matters quietly, otherwise there would be no knowing what demands might be made on my cloth. It was necessary to get up hot temper, else there was no knowing how far he would go; so I returned him his presents, and told the sheikh, instead of giving four, to fling six cloths in his face, and tell him that the holy-stone story was merely a humbug, and I would take care no more white men ever came to see him again.

Some Wanyamŭézi porters, who had been left sick here by former caravans, now wished to take service with me as far as Kazé; but the Wagogo, hearing of their desire, frightened them off it. A report also at this time was brought to us, that a caravan had just arrived at our last ground, having come up from Whindi, direct by the line of the Wami river, in its upper course called Mŭkondokŭa, without crossing a single hill all the way; I therefore sent three men to see if they had any porters to spare, as it was said they had; but the three men, although they left their bows and arrows behind, never came back.

Another mule died to-day. This was perplexing indeed, but to stop longer was useless; so we pushed forward as best we could to a pond at the western end of the district, where we found a party of Makŭa sportsmen who had just killed an elephant. They had lived in Ugogo one year and a half, and had killed in all seventeen elephants; half the tusks of which, as well as some portion of the flesh, they gave to Magomba for the privilege of residing there. There were many antelopes there, some of which both Grant and I shot for the good of the pot, and he also killed a crocuta hyena. From the pond we went on to the middle of a large jungle, and bivouacked for the night in a shower of rain, the second of the season.

To Usekhé, 4th: During a fierce down-pour of rain, the porters all quivering and quaking with cold, we at length emerged from the jungle, and entered the prettiest spot in Ugogo – the populous district of Usekhé – where little hills and huge columns of granite crop out. Here we halted.

Next day came the hongo business, which was settled by paying one dubŭani, one kitambi, one msŭtŭ, four yards merikani, and two yards kiniki; but whilst we were doing it eight porters ran away, and four fresh ones were engaged (Wanyamŭézi) who had run away from Kanyenyé.

To Khoko, 6th: With one more march from this we reached the last district in Ugogo, Khoko. Here the whole of the inhabitants turned out to oppose us, imagining we had come there to revenge the Arab, Mohinna, because the Wagogo attacked him a year ago, plundered his camp, and drove him back to Kazé, for having shot their old chief 'Short-legs.' They, however, no sooner found out who we were than they allowed us to pass on and encamp in the outskirts of the Mgŭnda Mkhali wilderness. To this position in the bush I strongly objected, on the plea that guns could be best used against arrows in the open; but none would go out in the field, maintaining that the Wagogo would fear to attack us so far from their villages as we now were, lest we might cut them off in their retreat.

Hori Hori was now chief in Short-legs's stead, and affected to be much pleased that we were English, and not Arabs. He told us we might, he thought, be able to recruit all the men that we were in want of, as many Wanyamŭézi who had been left there sick wished to go to their homes; and I would only, in addition to their wages, have to pay their 'hotel bills' to the Wagogo. This, of course, I was ready to do, though I knew the Wanyamŭézi had paid for themselves, as is usual, by their work in the fields of their hosts. Still, as I should be depriving these of hands, I could scarcely expect to get off for less than the value of a slave for each, and told Sheikh Said to look out for some men at once, whilst at the same time he laid in provisions of grain to last us eight days in the wilderness, and settle the hongo.

Change ground, 10th: At last the tax having been settled by the payment of one dubŭani, two barsati, one sahari, six yards of merikani, and three yards kiniki (not, however, until I had our tents struck, and threatened to march away if the chief would not take it), I proposed going on with the journey, for our provisions were stored. But when the loads were being lifted, I found ten more men were missing; and as nothing now could be done but throw ten loads away, which seemed too great a sacrifice to be made in a hurry, I simply changed ground to show we were ready to march, and sent my men about, either to try to induce the fugitive Wanyamŭézi to take service with me, or else to buy donkeys, as the chief said he had some to sell.

Halt, 11th and 12th: We had already been here too long. A report was now spread that a lion had killed one of the chief's cows; and the Wagogo, suspecting that our being here was the cause of this ill luck, threatened to attack us. This no sooner got noised over the camp than all my Wanyamŭézi porters, who had friends in Ugogo, left to live with them, and would not come back again even when the 'storm had blown over,' because they did not like the incessant rains that half deluged the camp. The chief, too, said he would not sell us his donkeys, lest we should give them back to Mohinna, from whom they were taken during his fight here. Intrigues of all sorts I could see were brewing, possibly at the instigation of the fugitive Wanyamŭézi, who suspected we were bound to side with the Arabs – possibly from some other cause, I could not tell what; so, to clear out of this pandemonium as soon as possible, I issued cloths to buy double rations, intending to cross the wilderness by successive relays in double the ordinary number of days. I determined at the same time to send forward two freed men to Kazéto ask Mŭsa and the Arabs to send me out some provisions and men to meet us half-way.

Matters grew worse and worse. The sultan, now finding me unable to move, sent a message to say if I would not give him some better cloths to make his hongo more respectable, he would attack my camp; and advised all the Wanyamŭézi who regarded their lives not to go near me if I resisted. This was by no means pleasant; for the porters showed their uneasiness by extracting their own cloths from my bundles, under the pretext that they wished to make some purchases of their own. I ought, perhaps, to have stopped this; but I thought the best plan was to show total indifference; so, at the same time that they were allowed to take their cloths, I refused to comply with the chief's request, and begged them to have no fear so long as they saw I could hold my own ground with my guns.

The Wanyamŭézi, however, were panic-stricken, and half of them bolted, with the kirangozi at their head, carrying off all the double-ration cloths as well as their own. At this time, the sultan, having changed tactics, as he saw us all ready to stand on the defensive, sent back his hongo; but, instead of using threats, said he would oblige us with donkeys or anything else if we would only give him a few more pretty cloths. With this cringing, perfidious appeal I refused to comply, until the sheikh, still more cringing, implored me to give way, else not a single man would remain with me. I then told him to settle with the chief himself, and give me the account, which amounted to three barsati, two sahari, and three yards merikani; but the donkeys were never alluded to.

To camp, 13th: With half my men gone, I still ordered the march, though strongly opposed to the advice of one of old Mamba's men, who was then passing by on his way to the coast, in command of his master's rear detachment. He thought it impossible for us to pull through the wilderness, with its jungle grasses and roots, depending for food only on Grant's gun and my own; still we made half-way to the Mdabŭrŭ nullah, taking some of Mamba's out to camp with us, as he promised to take letters and specimens down to the coast for us, provided I paid him some cloths as ready money down, and promised some more to be paid at Zanzibar. These letters eventually reached home, but not the specimens.

To camp, 14th: The rains were so heavy that the whole country was now flooded, but we pushed on to the nullah by relays and pitched on its left bank. In the confusion of the march, however, we lost many more porters, who at the same time relieved us of their loads, by slipping off stealthily into the bush.

Halt five days: The fifteenth was a forced halt, as the stream was so deep and so violent we could not cross it. To make the best of this very unfortunate interruption, I now sent on two men to Kazé, with letters to Mŭsa and Sheikh Snay, both old friends on the former expedition, begging them to send me sixty men, each carrying thirty rations of grain, and some country tobacco. The tobacco was to gratify my men, who said of all things they most wanted to cheer them was something to smoke. At the same time I sent back some other men to Khoko, with cloth to buy grain for present consumption, as some of my porters were already reduced to living on wild herbs and white ants. I then set all the remaining men, under the directions of Bombay and Baraka, to fell a tall tree with hatchets, on the banks of the nullah, with a view to bridging it; but the tree dropped to the wrong side, and thwarted the plan. The rain ceased on the 17th, just as we put the rain-gauge out, which was at once interpreted to be our Uganga, or religious charm, and therefore the cause of its ceasing. It was the first fine day for a fortnight, so we were only too glad to put all our things out to dry, and rejoiced to think of the stream's subsiding. My men who went back to Khoko for grain having returned with next to nothing – though, of course, they had spent all the cloths – I sent back another batch with pretty cloths, as it was confidently stated that grain was so scarce there, nothing but the best fabrics would buy it. This also proved a dead failure; but although animals were very scarce, Grant relieved our anxiety by shooting a zebra and an antelope.

Eight successive marches in the wilderness: After five halts, we forded the stream, middle deep, and pushed forward again, doing short stages of four or five miles a-day, in the greatest possible confusion; for, whilst Grant and I were compelled to go out shooting all day for the pot, the sheikh and Bombay went on with the first half of the property, and then, keeping guard over it, sent the men back again to Baraka, who kept rear-guard, to have the rest brought on. Order there was none; the men hated this 'double work' the Wanyamŭézi but three deserted, with the connivance of the coast-men, carrying off their loads with them, under a mutual understanding, as I found out afterwards, that the coast-men were to go shares in the plunder as soon as we reached Unyamŭézi.

The next great obstacle in this tug-and-pull wilderness-march presented itself on the 24th, when, after the first half of the property had crossed the Mabungŭrŭ nullah, it rose in flood and cut off the rear half. It soon, however, subsided; and the next day we reached 'the Springs,' where we killed a pig and two rhinoceros. Not content, however, with this fare – notwithstanding the whole camp had been living liberally on zebra's and antelope's flesh every day previously – some of my coast-men bolted on to the little settlement of Jiwa la Mkoa, contrary to orders, to purchase some grain; and in doing so, increased our transport difficulties.

Pulling on in the same way again – when not actually engaged in shooting, scolding and storming at the men, to keep them up to the mark, and prevent them from shirking their work, which they were for ever trying to do –. we arrived on the 28th at the 'Boss,' a huge granite block, from the top of which the green foliage of the forest-trees looked like an interminable cloud, soft and waving, fit for fairies to dwell upon. Here the patience of my men fairly gave way, for the village of Jiwa la Mkoa was only one long march distance from us; and they, in consequence, smelt food on in advance much sweeter than the wild game and wild grasses they had been living on; and many more of them could not resist deserting us, though they might, had we all pulled together, have gone more comfortably in, as soon as the rear property arrived next day with Baraka.

Halt three days: All the men who deserted on the 25th, save Johur and Mŭtwana came into camp, and told us they had heard from travellers that those men who had been sent on for reliefs to Kazé were bringing us a large detachment of slaves to help us on. My men had brought no food either for us or their friends, as the cloths they took with them, 'which were their own,' were scarcely sufficient to purchase a meal – famines being as bad where they had been as in Ugogo. To try and get all the men together again, I now sent off a party loaded with cloths to see what they could get for us; but they returned on the 30th grinning and joking, with nothing but a small fragment of goat-flesh, telling lies by the dozens. Johur then came into camp, unconscious that Baraka by my orders had, during his absence, been inspecting his kit, where he found concealed seventy-three yards of cloth, which could only have been my property, as Johur had brought no akaba or reserve fund from the coast.

To Jiwa la Mkoa, 1st: As nearly all the men had now returned, Grant and I spent New Year's Day with the first detachment at Jiwa la Mkoa, or Round Rock – a single tembé village occupied by a few Wakimbŭ settlers, who, by their presence and domestic habits, made us feel as though we were well out of the wood. So indeed we found it; for although this wilderness was formerly an entire forest of trees and wild animals, numerous Wakimbŭ, who formerly occupied the banks of the Rŭaha to the southward, had been driven to migrate here, wherever they could find springs of water, by the boisterous naked pastorals the Warori.

At night three slaves belonging to Sheikh Salem bin Saif stole into our camp, and said they had been sent by their master to seek for porters at Kazé, as all the Wanyamŭézi porters of four large caravans had deserted in Ugogo, and they could not move. I was rather pleased by this news, and thought it served the merchants right, knowing, as I well did, that the Wanyamŭézi, being naturally honest, had they not been defrauded by foreigners on the down march to the coast, would have been honest still. Some provisions were now obtained by sending men out to distant villages; but we still supplied the camp with our guns, killing rhinoceros, wild boar, antelope, and zebras. The last of our property did not come up till the 5th, when another thief being caught, got fifty lashes, under the superintendence of Baraka, to show that punishment was only inflicted to prevent further crime.

Halt seven days: The next day my men came from Kazé with letters from Sheikh Snay and Mŭsa. They had been there some days after arrival, as those merchants' slaves had gone to Utambara to settle some quarrel there; but as soon as they returned, Mŭsa ordered them to go and assist us, giving them beads to find rations for themselves on the way, as the whole country about Kazé had been half-starved by famines, though he did send a little rice and tobacco for me. The whole party left Kazé together; but on arrival at Tŭra the slaves said they had not enough beads and would return for some more, when they would follow my men. This bit of news was the worst that could have befallen us; my men were broken-hearted enough before, and this drove the last spark of spirit out of them. To make the best of a bad job, I now sent Bombay with two other men off to Mŭsa to see what he could do, and ordered my other men to hire Wakimbŭ from village to village. On the 7th, a nervous excitement was produced in the camp by some of my men running in and calling all to arm, as the fugitive chief Manŭa Séra was coming, with thirty armed followers carrying muskets. Such was the case: and by the time my men were all under arms, with their sword-bayonets fixed, drawn up by my tent, the veritable 'Tippler' arrived; but, not liking the look of such a formidable array as my men presented, he passed on a short way, and then sent back a deputation to make known his desire of calling on me, which was no sooner complied with than he came in person, attended by a body-guard. On my requesting him to draw near and sit, his wooden stool was placed for him. He began the conversation by telling me he had heard of my distress from want of porters, and then offered to assist me with some, provided I would take him to Kazé, and mediate between him and the Arabs; for, through their unjustifiable interference in his government affairs, a war had ensued, which terminated with the Arabs driving him from his possessions a vagabond. Manŭa Séra, I must say, was as fine a young man as ever I looked upon. He was very handsome, and looked as I now saw him the very picture of a captain of the banditti of the romances. I begged him to tell me his tale, and, in compliance, he gave me the following narrative:

Shortly after you left Kazé for England, my old father, the late chief Fŭndi Kira, died, and by his desire I became lawful chief; for, though the son of a slave girl, and not of Fŭndi Kira's wife, such is the law of inheritance – a constitutional policy established to prevent any chance of intrigues between the sons born in legitimate wedlock. Well, after assuming the title of chief, I gave presents of ivory to all the Arabs with a liberal hand, but most so to Mŭsa, which caused great jealousy amongst the other merchants. Then after this I established a property tax on all merchandise that entered my country. Fŭndi Kira had never done so, but I did not think that any reason why I should not, especially as the Arabs were the only people who lived in my country exempt from taxation. This measure, however, exasperated the Arabs, and induced them to send me hostile messages, to the effect that, if I ever meddled with them, they would dethrone me, and place Mkisiwa, another illegitimate son, on the throne in my stead. This, [Manŭa Séra continued] I could not stand; the merchants were living on sufferance only in my country. I told them so, and defied them to interfere with my orders, for I was not a 'woman' to be treated with contempt; and this got up a quarrel. Mkisiwa, seizing at the opportunity of the prize held out to him by the Arabs as his supporters, then commenced a system of bribery. Words led to blows; we had a long and tough fight; I killed many of their number, and they killed mine. Eventually they drove me from my palace, and placed Mkisiwa there as chief in my stead. My faithful followers, however, never deserted me; so I went to Rŭbŭga, and put up with old Maŭla there. The Arabs followed – drove me to Ngŭrŭ, and tried to kill Maŭla for having fostered me. He, however, escaped them; but they destroyed his country, and then followed me down to Ngŭrŭ. There we fought for many months, until all provisions were exhausted, when I defied them to catch me, and forced my way through their ranks. It is needless to say I have been a wanderer since; and though I wish to make friends, they will not allow it, but do all they can to hunt me to death. Now, as you were a friend of my father, I do hope you will patch up this war for me, which you must think is unjust.

I told Manŭa Séra I felt very much for him, and I would do my best if he would follow me to Kazé; but I knew that nothing could ever be done unless he returned to the free-trade principles of his father. He then said he had never taken a single tax from the Arabs, and would gladly relinquish his intention to do so. The whole affair was commenced in too great a hurry; but whatever happened he would gladly forgive all if I would use my influence to reinstate him, for by no other means could he ever get his crown back again. I then assured him that I would do what I could to restore the ruined trade of his country, observing that, as all the ivory that went out of his country came to ours, and all imports were productions of our country also, this war injured us as well as himself. Manŭa Séra seemed highly delighted, and said he had a little business to transact in Ugogo at present, but he would overtake me in a few days. He then sent me one of my runaway porters, whom he had caught in the woods making off with a load of my beads. We then separated; and Baraka, by my orders, gave the thief fifty lashes for his double offence of theft and desertion.

To Garaéswi, 9th. Halt, 10th. To Zimbo, 11th. Halt, 12th and 13th: On the 9th, having bought two donkeys and engaged several men, we left Jiwa la Mkoa, with half our traps, and marched to Garaéswi, where, to my surprise, there were as many as twenty tembés – a recently-formed settlement of Wakimbŭ. Here we halted a day for the rear convoy, and then went on again by detachments to Zimbo, where, to our intense delight, Bombay returned to us on the 13th, triumphantly firing guns, with seventy slaves accompanying him, and with letters from Snay and Mŭsa, in which they said they hoped, if I met with Manŭa Séra, that I would either put a bullet through his head, or else bring him in a prisoner, that they might do for him, for the scoundrel had destroyed all their trade by cutting off caravans. Their fights with him commenced by his levying taxes in opposition to their treaties with his father, Fŭndi Kira, and then preventing his subjects selling them grain.

To Mgongo Thembo, 14th: Once more the whole caravan moved on; but as I had to pay each of the seventy slaves sixteen yards of cloth, by order of their masters, in the simple matter of expenditure it would have been better had I thrown ten loads away at Ugogo, where my difficulties first commenced. On arrival at Mgongo Thembo – the Elephant's Back – called so in consequence of a large granitic rock, which resembles the back of that animal, protruding through the ground – we found a clearance in the forest, of two miles in extent, under cultivation. Here the first man to meet me was the fugitive chief of Rŭbŭga, Maŭla. This poor old man – one of the honestest chiefs in the country – had been to the former expedition a host and good friend. He now gave me a cow as a present, and said he would give me ten more if I would assist him in making friends with the Arabs, who had driven him out of his country, and had destroyed all his belongings, even putting a slave to reign in his stead, though he had committed no fault or intentional injury towards them. It was true Manŭa Séra, their enemy, had taken refuge in his palace, but that was not his fault; for, anticipating the difficulties that would arise, he did his best to keep Manŭa Séra out of it, but Manŭa Séra, being too strong for him, forced his way in. I need not say I tried to console this unfortunate victim of circumstances as best I could, inviting him to go with me to Kazé, and promising to protect him with my life if he feared the Arabs; but the old man, being too feeble to travel himself, said he would send his son with me.

To camp, 15th. To E. Tŭra, 16th: Next day we pushed on a double march through forest, and reached a nullah. As it crosses the track in a southernly direction, this might either be the head of the Kŭlŭlŭ mongo or river, which, passing through the district of Kiwélé, drains westward into the Malagarazi river, and thence into the Tanganyika, or else the most westerly tributary to the Rŭaha river, draining eastward into the sea. The plateau, however, is apparently so flat here, that nothing but a minute survey, or rather following the watercourse, could determine the matter. Then emerging from the wilderness, we came into the open cultivated district of Tŭra, or 'put down' – called so by the natives because it was, only a few years ago, the first cleared space in the wilderness, and served as a good halting-station, after the normal ten days' march in the jungles, where we had now been struggling more than a month.

To camp, 19th. To E. Rŭbŭga, 20th: By a double march, Sheikh Said riding in a hammock slung on a pole, we now made Kŭalé, or 'Partridge' nullah, which, crossing the road to the northward, drains these lands to the Malagarazi river, and thence into the Tanganyika lake. Thence, having spent the night in the jungle, we next morning pushed into the cultivated district of Rŭbŭga, and put up in some half-deserted tembés, where the ravages of war were even more disgusting to witness than at Tŭra. The chief, as I have said, was a slave, placed there by the Arabs on the condition that he would allow all traders and travellers to help themselves without payment as long as they chose to reside there. In consequence of this wicked arrangement, I found it impossible to keep my men from picking and stealing. They looked upon plunder as their fortune and right, and my interference as unjustifiable.

To W. Rŭbŭga, 21st. To Kigŭé, 22d. To E. Unyanyembé, 23d. By making another morning and evening march, we reached the western extremity of this cultivated opening; where, after sleeping the night, we threaded through another forest to the little clearance of Kigŭé, and in one more march through forest arrived in the large and fertile district of Unyanyembé, the centre of Unyamŭézi – the Land of the Moon – within five miles of Kazé, which is the name of a well in the village of Tabora, now constituted the great central slave and ivory merchants' depot. My losses up to this date (23d) were as follows: One Hottentot dead and five returned; one freeman sent back with the Hottentots, and one flogged and turned off; twenty-five of Sultan Majids gardeners deserted; ninety-eight of the original Wanyamŭézi porters deserted; twelve mules and three donkeys dead. Besides which, more than half of my property had been stolen; whilst the travelling expenses had been unprecedented, in consequence of the severity of the famine throughout the whole length of the march.

CHAPTER V

Unyamŭézi

U-N-YA-MŬÉZI – Country of Moon – must have been one of the
largest kingdoms in Africa. It is little inferior in size to England,
and of much the same shape, though now, instead of being united,
it is cut up into petty states. In its northern extremities it is known
by the appellation U-sŭkŭma – country north; and in the southern,
U-takama – country south. There are no historical traditions known
to the people; neither was anything ever written concerning their
country, as far as we know, until the Hindŭs, who traded with the
east coast of Africa, opened commercial dealings with its people in
slaves and ivory, possibly some time prior to the birth of our Saviour,
when, associated with their name, Men of the Moon, sprang into
existence the Mountains of the Moon. These Men of the Moon are
hereditarily the greatest traders in Africa, and are the only people
who, for love of barter and change, will leave their own country as
porters and go to the coast, and they do so with as much zest as our
country-folk go to a fair. As far back as we can trace they have done
this, and they still do it as heretofore. The whole of their country
ranges from 3000 to 4000 feet above the sea-level – a high plateau,
studded with little outcropping hills of granite, between which, in
the valleys, there are numerous fertilising springs of fresh water,
and rich iron ore is found in sandstone. Generally industrious –
much more so than most other negroes – they cultivate extensively,
make cloths of cotton in their own looms, smelt iron and work it up
very expertly, build tembés to live in over a large portion of their
country, but otherwise live in grass huts, and keep flocks and herds
of considerable extent.

The Wanyamŭezi, however, are not a very well-favoured
people in physical appearance, and are much darker than either
the Wazaramo or the Wagogo, though many of their men

are handsome and their women pretty; neither are they well dressed or well armed, being wanting in pluck and gallantry. Their women, generally, are better dressed than the men. Cloths fastened round under the arms are their national costume, along with a necklace of beads, large brass or copper wire armlets, and a profusion of thin circles, called sambo, made of the giraffe's tail-hairs bound round by the thinnest iron or copper wire; whilst the men at home wear loin-cloths, but in the field, or whilst travelling, simply hang a goat-skin over their shoulders, exposing at least three-fourths of their body in a rather indecorous manner. In all other respects they ornament themselves like the women, only, instead of a long coil of wire wound up the arm, they content themselves with having massive rings of copper or brass on the wrist; and they carry for arms a spear and bow and arrows. All extract more or less their lower incisors, and cut a /\ between their two upper incisors. The whole tribe are desperate smokers, and greatly given to drink.

To Kazé, 24th: On the 24th, we all, as many as were left of us, marched into the merchants' depot, S. lat. 5° 0' 52', " and E. long. 33° 1' 34', escorted by Mŭsa, who advanced to meet us, and guided us into his tembé, where he begged we would reside with him until we could find men to cany our property on to Karagŭé. He added that he would accompany us; for he was on the point of going there when my first instalment of property arrived, but deferred his intention out of respect to myself. He had been detained at Kazé ever since I last left it in consequence of the Arabs having provoked a war with Manŭa Séra, to which he was adverse. For a long time also he had been a chained prisoner; as the Arabs, jealous of the favour Manŭa Séra had shown to him in preference to themselves, basely accused him of supplying Manŭa Séra with gunpowder, and bound him hand and foot 'like a slave.' It was delightful to see old Mŭsa's face again, and the supremely hospitable, kind, and courteous manner in which he looked after us, constantly bringing in all kind of small delicacies, and seeing that nothing was wanting to make us happy. All the property I had sent on in advance he had stored away; or rather, I should say, as much as had reached him, for the road expenses had eaten a great hole in it.

Once settled down into position, Sheikh Snay and the whole
conclave of Arab merchants came to call on me. They said they had
an army of four hundred slaves armed with muskets ready to take
the field at once to hunt down Manŭa Séra, who was cutting their
caravan road to pieces, and had just seized, by their latest reports, a
whole convoy of their ammunition. I begged them strongly to listen
to reason, and accept my advice as an old soldier, not to carry on
their guerilla warfare in such a headlong hurry, else they would be
led a dance by Manŭa Séra, as we had been by Tantia Topee in India.
I advised them to allow me to mediate between them, after telling
them what a favourable interview I had had with Manŭa Séra and
Matila, whose son was at that moment concealed in Mtisa's tembé.
My advice, however, was not wanted. Snay knew better than any one
how to deal with savages, and determined on setting out as soon as
his, army had 'eaten their beef-feast of war.'

On my questioning him about the Nile, Snay still thought the
N'yanza was the source of the Jub river, as he did in our former
journey, but gave way when I told him that vessels frequented the
Nile, as this also coincided with his knowledge of navigators in
vessels appearing on some waters to the northward of Unyoro. In
a great hurry he then bade me good-bye; when, as he thought it
would be final, I gave him, in consideration for his former good
services to the last expedition, one of the gold watches given me
by the Indian Government. I saw him no more, though he and all
the other Arabs sent me presents of cows, goats, and rice, with a
notice that they should have gone on their war-path before, only,
hearing of my arrival, out of due respect to my greatness, they
waited to welcome me in. Further, after doing for Manŭa Séra,
they were determined to go on to Ugogo to assist Salem bin Saif
and the other merchants on, during which, at the same time, they
would fight all the Wagogo who persisted in taking taxes and in
harassing their caravans. At the advice of Mŭsa, I sent Maŭla's
son off at night to tell the old chief how sorry I was to find the
Arabs so hot-headed I could not even effect an arrangement
with them. It was a great pity; for Manŭa Séra was so much liked
by the Wanyamŭézi, they would, had they been able, have done
anything to restore him.

25th and 26th: Next day the non-belligerent Arabs left in charge of the station, headed by my old friends Abdŭlla and Mohinna, came to pay their respects again, recognising in me, as they said, a 'personification of their sultan,' and therefore considering what they were doing only due to my rank. They regretted with myself that Snay was so hot-headed; for they themselves thought a treaty of peace would have been the best thing for them, for they were more than half-ruined already, and saw no hope for the future. Then, turning to geography, I told Abdŭlla all I had written and lectured in England concerning his stories about navigators on the N'yanza, which I explained must be the Nile, and wished to know if I should alter it in any way: but he said, 'Do not; you may depend it will all turn out right' which Mŭsa added, all the people in the north told him that when the N'yanza rose, the stream rushed with such violence it tore up islands and floated them away.

I was puzzled at this announcement, not then knowing that both the lake and the Nile, as well as all ponds, were called N'yanza: but we shall see afterwards that he was right; and it was in consequence of this confusion in the treatment of distinctly different geographical features under one common name by these people, that in my former journey I could not determine where the lake ended and the Nile began. Abdŭlla again – he had done so on the former journey – spoke to me of a wonderful mountain to the northward of Karagŭé, so high and steep no one could ascend it. It was, he said, seldom visible, being up in the clouds, where white matter, snow or hail, often fell. Mŭsa said this hill was in Rŭanda, a much larger country than Urŭndi; and further, both men said, as they had said before, that the lands of Usoga and Unyoro were islands, being surrounded by water; and a salt lake, which was called N'yanza, though not the great Victoria N'yanza, lay on the other side of Unyoro, from which direction Rŭmanika, king of Karagŭé, sometimes got beads forwarded to him by Kamrasi, king of Unyoro, of a different sort from any brought from Zanzibar. Moreover, these beads were said to have been plundered from white men by the Wakidi, – a stark-naked people who live up in trees – have small stools fixed on behind, always ready for sitting – wear their hair hanging down as far as the rump, all covered with cowrie-shells – suspend beads from wire attached to their ears and their lower lips – and wear strong iron collars and bracelets.

This people, I was told, are so fierce in war that no other tribe can stand against them, though they only fight with short spears. When this discourse was ended, ever perplexed about the Tanganyika being a still lake, I inquired of Mohinna and other old friends what they thought about the Marŭngŭ river: did it run into or out of the lake? and they all still adhered to its running into the lake – which, after all, in my mind, is the most conclusive argument that it does run out of the lake, making it one of a chain of lakes leading to the N'yassa, and through it by the Zambézi into the sea; for all the Arabs on the former journey said the Rŭsizi river ran out of the Tanganyika, as also the Kitangŭlé ran out of the N'yanza, and the Nile ran into it, even though Snay said he thought the Jub river drained the N'yanza. All these statements were, when literally translated into English, the reverse of what the speakers, using a peculiar Arab idiom, meant to say; for all the statements made as to the flow of rivers by the negroes – who apparently give the same meaning to 'out' and 'in' as we do – contradicted the Arabs in their descriptions of the direction of the flow of these rivers.

The change that had taken place in Unyanyembé since I last left it was quite surprising. Instead of the Aralis appearing merchants, as they did formerly, they looked more like great farmers, with huge stalls of cattle attached to their houses; whilst the native villages were all in ruins – so much so that, to obtain corn for my men, I had to send out into the district several days' journey off, and even then had to pay the most severe famine prices for what I got. The Wanyamŭézi, I was assured, were dying of starvation in all directions; for, in addition to the war, the last rainy season had been so light, all their crops had failed.

27th and 28th. – I now gave all my men presents for the severe trials they had experienced in the wilderness, forgetting, as I told them, the merciless manner in which they had plundered me; but as I gave a trifle more, in proportion, to the three sole remaining pagazis, because they had now finished their work, my men were all discontented, and wished to throw back their presents, saying I did not love them, although they were 'perminents,' as much as the 'temporaries.' They, however, gave in, after some hours of futile arguments, on my making them understand, through Baraka, that what they saw me give to the pagazis would, if they reflected, only tend to prove to them that I was not a bad master who forgot his obligations when he could get no more out of his servants.

I then went into a long inquiry with Mŭsa about our journey northward to Karagŭé; and as he said there were no men to be found in or near Unyanyembé, for they were either all killed or engaged in the war, it was settled he should send some of his head men on to Rungŭa, where he had formerly resided, trading for some years, and was a great favourite with the chief of the place, by name Kiringŭana. He also settled that I might take out of his establishment of slaves as many men as I could induce to go with me, for he thought them more trouble than profit, hired porters being more safe; moreover, he said the plan would be of great advantage to him, as I offered to pay, both man and master, each the same monthly stipend as I gave my present men. This was paying double, and all the heavier a burden, as the number I should require to complete my establishment to one hundred armed men would be sixty. He, however, very generously advised me not to take them, as they would give so much trouble; but finally gave way when I told him I felt I could not advance beyond Karagŭe unless I was quite independent of the natives there – a view in which he concurred.

29th and 30th. – Jafŭ, another Indian merchant here, and co-partner of Mŭsa, came in from a ten days' search after grain, and described the whole country to be in the most dreadful state of famine. Wanyamŭézi were lying about dead from starvation in all directions, and he did not think we should ever get through Usŭi, as Sŭwarora, the chief, was so extortionate he would 'tear us to pieces' but advised our waiting until the war was settled, when all the Arabs would combine and go with us. Mŭsa even showed fear, but arranged, at my suggestion, that he should send some men to Rŭmanika, informing him of our intention to visit him, and begging, at the same time, he would use his influence in preventing our being detained in Usŭi.

Mŭsa, I must say, was most loud in his praises of Rŭmanika; and on the other hand, as Mŭsa, eight years ago, had saved Rŭmanika's throne for him against an insurrection got up by his younger brother Rogéro, Rŭmanika, always regarding Mŭsa as his saviour, never lost an opportunity to show his gratitude, and would have done anything that Mŭsa might have asked him. Of this matter, however, more in Karagŭé.

31st. – To-day, Jafŭ, who had lost many ivories at Khoko when Mohinna was attacked there, prepared 100 slaves, with Said bin Osman, Mohinna's brother, with a view to follow down Snay, and, combining forces, attack Hori Hori, hoping to recover their losses; for it appeared to them the time had now come when their only hope left in carrying their trade to a successful issue, lay in force of arms. They would therefore not rest satisfied until they had reduced Khoko and Usekhé both, by actual force, to acknowledge their superiority, 'feeding on them' until the Ramazan, when they would return with all the merchants detained in Ugogo, and, again combining their forces, they would fall on Ustii, to reduce that country also.

1st. – Mŭsa's men now started for Rungŭa, and promised to bring all the porters we wanted by the first day of the next moon. We found that this would be early enough, for all the members of the expedition, excepting myself, were suffering from the effects of the wilderness life – some with fever, some with scurvy, and some with ophthalmia – which made it desirable they should all have rest. Little now was done besides counting out my property, and making Sheikh Said, who became worse and worse, deliver his charge of Cafila Bashi over to Bombay for good. When it was found so much had been stolen, especially of the best articles, I was obliged to purchase many things from Mŭsa, paying 400 per cent, which he said was their value here, over the market price of Zanzibar. I also got him to have all my coils of brass and copper wire made into bracelets, as is customary, to please the northern people.

7th. – To-day information was brought here that whilst Manŭa Séra was on his way from Ugogo to keep his appointment with me, Sheikh Snay's army came on him at Tŭra, where he was ensconced in a tembé. Hearing this, Snay, instead of attacking the village at once, commenced negotiations with the chief of the place by demanding him to set free his guest, otherwise they, the Arabs, would storm the tembé. The chief, unfortunately, did not comply at once, but begged grace for one night, saying that if Manŭa Séra was found there in the morning they might do as they liked. Of course Manŭa bolted; and the Arabs, seeing the Tŭra people all under arms ready to defend themselves the next morning, set at them in earnest, and shot, murdered, or plundered the whole of the district. Then, whilst

Arabs were sending in their captures of women, children, and cattle, Manŭa Séra made off to a district called Dara, where he formed an alliance with its chief, Kifŭnja, and boasted he would attack Kazé as soon as the travelling season commenced, when the place would be weakened by the dispersion of the Arabs on their ivory excursions.

This startling news set the place in a blaze, and brought all the Arabs again to seek my advice; for they condemned what Snay had done in not listening to me before, and wished to know if I could not now treat for them with Manŭa Séra, which they thought could be easily managed, as Manŭa Séra himself was not only the first to propose mediation, but was actually on his way here for the purpose when Snay opposed him. I said nothing could give me greater pleasure than mediating for them, to put a stop to these horrors, but it struck me the case had now gone too far. Snay, in opposition to my advice, was bent on fighting; he could not be recalled; and unless all the Arabs were of one mind, I ran the risk of committing myself to a position I could not maintain. To this they replied that the majority were still at Kazé, all wishing for peace at any price, and that whatever terms I might wish to dictate they would agree to. Then I said, 'What would you do with Mkisiwa? you have made him chief, and cannot throw him over.' 'Oh, that,' they said, 'can be easily managed; for formerly, when we confronted Manŭa Séra at Ngŭrŭ, we offered to give him as much territory as his father governed, though not exactly in the same place; but he treated our message with disdain, not knowing then what a fix he was in. Now, however, as he has seen more, and wishes for peace himself, there can be no difficulty.' I then ordered two of my men to go with two of Mŭsa's to acquaint Manŭa Séra with what we were about, and to know his views on the subject; but these men returned to say Manŭa Séra could not be found, for he was driven from 'pillar to post' by the different native chiefs, as, wherever he went, his army ate up their stores, and brought nothing but calamities with them. Thus died this second attempted treaty. Mŭsa then told me it was well it turned out so; for Manŭa Séra would never believe the Arabs, as they had broken faith so often before, even after exchanging blood by cutting incisions in one another's legs – the most sacred bond or oath the natives know of.

25th to 13th. – We all went back to Kazé, arriving there on the 24th. Days rolled on, and nothing was done in particular – beyond increasing my stock of knowledge of distant places and people, enlarging my zoological collection, and taking long series of astronomical observations – until the 13th, when the whole of Kazé was depressed by a sad scene of mourning and tears. Some slaves came in that night – having made their way through the woods from Ugogo, avoiding the track to save themselves from detection – and gave information that Snay, Jafŭ, and five other Arabs, had been killed, as well as a great number of slaves. The expedition, they said, had been defeated, and the positions were so complicated nobody knew what to do. At first the Arabs achieved two brilliant successes, having succeeded in killing Hori Hori of Khoko, when they recovered their ivory, made slaves of all they could find, and took a vast number of cattle; then attacking Usekhé, they reduced that place to submission by forcing a ransom out of its people. At this period, however, they heard that a whole caravan, carrying 5000 dollars' worth of property, had been cut up by the people of Mzanza, a small district ten miles north of Usekhé; so, instead of going on to Kanyenyé to relieve the caravans which were waiting there for them, they foolishly divided their forces into three parts. Of these they sent one to take their loot, back to Kazé, another to form a reserve force at Mdabŭrŭ, on the east flank of the wilderness, and a third, headed by Snay and Jafŭ, to attack Mzanza. At the first onset Snay and Jafŭ carried everything before them, and became so excited over the amount of their loot that they lost all feelings of care or precaution.

In this high exuberance of spirits, a sudden surprise turned their momentary triumph into a total defeat; for some Wahŭmba, having heard the cries of the Wagogo, joined in their cause, and both together fell on the Arab force with such impetuosity that the former victors were now scattered in all directions. Those who could run fast enough were saved – the rest were speared to death by the natives. Nobody knew how Jafŭ fell; but Snay, after running a short distance, called one of his slaves, and begged him to take his gun, saying, 'I am too old to keep up with you; keep this gun for my sake, for I will lie down here and take my chance.' He never was seen again. But this was not all their misfortunes; for the slaves who brought in this information had met the first detachment, sent with the Khoko loot, at Kigŭa, where, they said, the detachment had been surprised by Manŭa Séra, who, having fortified a village with four hundred men, expecting this sort of thing, rushed out upon them, and cut them all up.

The Arabs, after the first burst of their grief was over, came to me again in a body, and begged me to assist them, for they were utterly undone. Manŭa Séra prevented their direct communication with their detachment at Mdabŭrŭ, and that again was cut off from their caravans at Kanyenyé by the Mzanza people, and in fact all the Wagogo; so they hoped at least I would not forsake them, which they heard I was going to do, as Manŭa Séra had also threatened to attack Kazé. I then told them, finally, that their proposals were now beyond my power, for I had a duty to perform as well as themselves, and in a day or two I should be off.

14th to 17th. – On the 14th thirty-nine porters were brought in from Rungŭa by Mŭsa's men, who said they had collected one hundred and twenty, and brought them to within ten miles of this, when some travellers frightened all but thirty-nine away, by telling them, 'Are you such fools as to venture into Kazé now? all the Arabs have been killed, or were being cut up and pursued by Manŭa Séra.' This sad disappointment threw me on my 'beam-ends.' For some reason or other none of Mŭsa's slaves would take service, and the Arabs prevented theirs from leaving the place, as it was already too short of hands. To do the best under these circumstances, I determined on going to Rungŭa with what kit could be carried, leaving Bombay behind with Mŭsa until such time as I should arrive there, and, finding more men, could send them back for the rest. I then gave Mŭsa the last of the gold watches the Indian Government had given me and, bidding Sheikh Said take all our letters and specimens back to the coast as soon as the road was found practicable, set out on the march northwards with Grant and Baraka, and all the rest of my men who were well enough to carry loads, as well as some of Mŭsa's head men, who knew where to get porters.

Break ground, 17th. To Masangé, 18th. To Iviri, 19th. Enter Usagari, 20th. Cross Gombé nullah, 21st: After passing Masangé and Zimbili, we put up a in the village of Iviri, on the northern border of Unyanyembé, and found several officers there, sent by Mkisiwa, to enforce a levy of soldiers to take the field with the Arabs at Kazé against Manŭa Séra; to effect which, they walked about ringing bells, and bawling out that if a certain percentage of all the inhabitants did not muster, the village chief would be seized, and their plantations confiscated. My men all mutinied here for increase of ration allowances. To find themselves food with, I had given them all one necklace of beads each per diem since leaving Kazé, in lieu of cloth, which hitherto had been served out for that purpose. It was a very liberal allowance, because the Arabs never gave more than one necklace to every three men, and that, too, of inferior quality to what I served. I brought them to at last by starvation, and then we went on. Dipping down into a valley between two clusters of granitic hills, beautifully clothed with trees and grass, studded here and there with rich plantations, we entered the district of Usagari, and on the second day forded the Gombé nullah again – in its upper course, called Kŭalé.

To Ungŭgŭ's Palace, 22d: Rising again up to the main level of the plantation, we walked into the boma of the chief of Unyambéwa, Singinya, whose wife was my old friend the late sultana Ungŭgŭ's lady's-maid. Immediately on our entering her palace, she came forward to meet me with the most affable air of a princess, begged I would always come to her as I did then, and sought to make everyone happy and comfortable. Her old mistress, she said, died well stricken in years; and, as she had succeeded her, the people of her country invited Singinya to marry her, because feuds had arisen about the rights of succession; and it was better a prince, whom they thought best suited by birth and good qualities, should head their warriors, and keep all in order. At that moment Singinya was out in the field fighting his enemies; and she was sure, when he heard I was here, that he would be very sorry he had missed seeing me.

To Usenda, 23d: We next went on to the district of Ukŭmbi, and put up in a village there, on approaching which all the villagers turned out to resist us, supposing we were an old enemy of theirs. They flew about brandishing their spears, and pulling their bows in the most grotesque attitudes, alarming some of my porters so much that they threw down their loads and bolted. All the country is richly cultivated, though Indian corn at that time was the only grain ripe. The square, flat-topped tembés had now been left behind, and instead the villagers lived in small collections of grass huts, surrounded by palisades of tall poles.

Proceeding on we put up at the small settlement of Usenda, the proprietor of which was a semi-negro Arab merchant called Sangoro. He had a large collection of women here, but had himself gone north with a view to trade in Karagŭé. Report, however, assured us that he was then detained in Ustŭ by Sŭwarora, its chief, on the plea of requiring his force of musketeers to prevent the Watŭta from pillaging his country, for these Watŭta lived entirely on plunder of other people's cattle.

To Mininga, 24th: With one move, by alternately crossing strips of forest and cultivation, studded here and there with small hills of granite, we forded the Quandé nullah – a tributary to the Gombé – and entered the rich flat district of Mininga, where the gingerbread-palm grows abundantly. The greatest man we found here was a broken-down ivory-merchant called Sirboko, who gave us a good hut to live in. Next morning, I believe at the suggestion of my Wangŭana, with Baraka at their head, he induced me to stop there; for he said Rungŭa had been very recently destroyed by the Watŭta, and this place could afford porters better than it. To all appearance this was the case, for this district was better cultivated than any place I had seen. I also felt a certain inclination to stop, as I was dragging on sick men, sorely against my feelings; and I also thought I had better not go farther away from my rear property; but, afraid of doing wrong in not acting up to Mŭsa's directions, I called up his head men who were with me, and asked them what they thought of the matter, as they had lately come from Rungŭa. On their confirming Sirboko's story, and advising my stopping, I acceded to their recommendation, and immediately gave Mŭsa's men orders to look out for porters.

Hearing this, all my Wangŭana danced with delight; and I, fearing there was some treachery, called Mŭsa's men again, saying I had changed my mind, and wished to go on in the afternoon; but when the time came, not one of our porters could be seen. There was now no help for it; so, taking it coolly, I gave Mŭsa's men presents, begged them to look sharp in getting the men up, and trusted all would end well in the long-run. Sirboko's attentions were most warm and affecting. He gave us cows, rice, and milk, with the best place he had to live in, and looked after us as constantly and tenderly as if he had been our father. It seemed quite unjust to harbour any suspicion against him.

25th to 2d. – I now set to work, collecting, stuffing, and drawing, until the 2d, when Mŭsa's men came in with three hundred men, whom I sent on to Kazé at once with my specimens and letters, directing Mŭsa and Bombay to come on and join us immediately. Whilst waiting for these men's return, one of Sirboko's slaves, chained up by him, in the most piteous manner cried out to me: 'Hai Bana wangi, Bana wangi (Oh, my lord, my lord), take pity on me! When I was a free man I saw you at Uvira, on the Tanganyika lake, when you were there; but since then the Watŭta, in a fight at Ujiji, speared me all over and left me for dead, when I was seized by the people, sold to the Arabs, and have been in chains ever since. Oh, I say, Bana wangi, if you would only liberate me I would never run away, but would serve you faithfully all my life.' This touching appeal was too strong for my heart to withstand, so I called up Sirboko, and told him, if he would liberate this one man to please me he should be no loser; and the release was effected. He was then christened Farhan (Joy), and was enrolled in my service with the rest of my freed men. I then inquired if it was true the Wabembé were cannibals, and also circumcised. In one of their slaves the latter statement was easily confirmed. I was assured that he was a cannibal; for the whole tribe of Wabembé, when they cannot get human flesh otherwise, give a goat to their neighbours for a sick or dying child, regarding such flesh as the best of all. No other cannibals, however, were known of; but the Masai, and their cognates, the Wahŭmba, Watatŭrŭ, Wakasangé, Wanyaramba, and even the Wagogo and Wakimbŭ, circumcise.

On the 15th I was surprised to find Bombay come in with all my rear property and a great quantity of Mŭsa's, but without the old man. By a letter from Sheikh Said I then found that, since my leaving Kazé, the Arabs had, along with Mkisiwa, invested the position of Manŭa Séra at Kigŭé, and forced him to take flight again. Afterwards the Arabs, returning to Kazé, found Mŭsa preparing to leave. Angry at this attempt to desert them, they persuaded him to give up his journey north for the present; so that at the time Bombay left, Mŭsa was engaged as public auctioneer in selling the effects of Snay, Jafŭ, and others, but privately said he would follow me on to Karagŭé as soon as his rice was cut. Adding a little advice of his own, Sheikh

Said pressed me to go on with the journey as fast as possible, because all the Arabs had accused me of conspiring with Manŭa Séra, and would turn against me unless I soon got away.

2d to 30th – Disgusted with Mŭsa's vacillatory conduct, on the 22d I sent him a letter containing a bit of my mind. I had given him, as a present, sufficient cloth to pay for his porters, as well as a watch and a good sum of money, and advised his coming on at once, for the porters who had just brought in my rear property would not take pay to go on to Karagŭé; and so I was detained again, waiting whilst his head man went to Rungŭa to look for more. Five days after this, a party of Sangoros arrived from Karagŭé, saying they had been detained three months in Usŭi by Sŭwarora, who had robbed them of an enormous quantity of property, and oppressed them so that all their porters ran away. Now, slight as this little affair might appear, it was of vital importance to me, as I found all my men shaking their heads and predicting what might happen to us when wo got there; so, as a forlorn hope, I sent Baraka with another letter to Mŭsa, offering to pay as much money for fifty men carrying muskets as would buy fifty slaves, and, in addition to that, I offered to pay them what my men were receiving as servants. Next day (23d) the chief Ugali came to pay his respects to us. He was a fine-looking young man, about thirty years old, the husband of thirty wives, but he had only three children. Much surprised at the various articles composing our kit, he remarked that our 'sleeping-clothes' – blankets – were much better than his royal robes; but of all things that amused him most were our picture-books, especially some birds drawn by Wolf.

Everything still seemed going against me; for on the following day (24th) Mŭsa's men came in from Rungŭa to say the Watŭta were 'out.' They had just seized fifty head of cattle from Rungŭa, and the people were in such a state of alarm they dared not leave their homes and families. I knew not what to do, for there was no hope left but in what Baraka might bring; and as that even would be insufficient, I sent Mŭsa's men into Kazé, to increase the original number by thirty men more.

Patience, thank God, I had a good stock of, so I waited quietly until the 30th, when I was fairly upset by the arrival of a letter from Kazé, stating that Baraka had arrived, and had been very insolent both to Mŭsa and to Sheikh Said. The bearer of the letter was at once to go and search for porters at Rungŭa, but not a word was said about the armed men I had ordered. At the same time reports from the other side came in, to the effect that the Arabs at Kazé and Mséné had bribed the Watŭta to join them, and overrun the whole country from Ugogo to Usŭi; and, in consequence of this, all the natives on the line I should have to take were in such dread of that terrible wandering race of savages, who had laid waste in turn all the lands from N'yassa to Ustŭ on their west flank, that not a soul dared leave his home. I could now only suppose that this foolish and hasty determination of the Arabs, who, quite unprepared to carry out their wicked alliance to fight, still had set every one against their own interests as well as mine, had not reached Mŭsa, so I made up my mind at once to return to Kazé, and settle all matters I had in heart with himself and the Arabs in person.

This settled, I next, in this terrible embarrassment, determined on sending back the last of the Hottentots, as all four of them, though still wishing to go on with me, distinctly said they had not the power to continue the march, for they had never ceased suffering from fever and jaundice, which had made them all yellow as guineas, save one, who was too black to change colour. It felt to me as if I were selling my children, having once undertaken to lead them through the journey; but if I did not send them back then, I never could afterwards, and therefore I allowed the more substantial feelings of humanity to overcome these compunctions.

March back to Kazé, 1st and 2d: Next morning, then, after giving the Tots over in charge of some men to escort them on to Kazé quietly, I set out myself with a dozen men, and the following evening I put up with Mŭsa, who told me Baraka had just left without one man – all his slaves having become afraid to go, since the news of the Arab alliance had reached Kazé. Sŭwarora had ordered his subjects to run up a line of bomas to protect his frontier, and had proclaimed his intention to kill every coast-man who dared attempt to enter Usŭi. My heart was ready to sink as I turned into bed, and I was driven to think of abandoning everybody who was not strong enough to go on with me carrying a load.

3d to 13th. – Baraka, hearing I had arrived, then came back to me, and confirmed Mŭsa's words. The Arabs, too, came flocking in to beg, nay implore, me to help them out of their difficulties. Many of them were absolutely ruined, they said; others had their houses full of stores unemployed. At Ugogo those who wished to join them were unable to do so, for their porters, what few were left, were all dying of starvation; and at that moment Manŭa Séra was hovering about, shooting, both night and day, all the poor villagers in the district, or driving them away. Would to God, they said, I would mediate for them with Manŭa Séra – they were sure I would be successful – and then they would give me as many armed men as I liked. Their folly in all their actions, I said, proved to me that anything I might attempt to do would be futile, for their alliance with the Watŭta, when they were not prepared to act, at once damned them in my eyes as fools. This they in their terror acknowledged, but said it was not past remedy, if I would join them, to counteract what had been done in that matter. Suffice it now to say, after a long conversation, arguing all the pros and cons over, I settled I would write out all the articles of a treaty of peace, by which they should be liable to have all their property forfeited on the coast if they afterwards broke faith; and I begged them to call the next day and sign it.

They were no sooner gone, however, than Mŭsa assured me they had killed old Maŭla of Rŭbŭga in the most treacherous manner, as follows: Khamis, who is an Arab of most gentlemanly aspect, on returning from Ugogo attended by slaves, having heard that Maŭla was desirous of adjusting a peace, invited him with his son to do so. When old Maŭla came as desired, bringing his son with him, and a suitable offering of ivory and cattle, the Arab induced them both to kneel down and exchange blood with him, when, by a previously concerted arrangement, Khamis had them shot down by his slaves. This disgusting story made me quite sorry, when next day the Arabs arrived, expecting that I should attempt to help them; but as the matter had gone so far, I asked them, in the first place, how they could hope Manŭa Séra would have any faith in them when they were so treacherous, or trust to my help, since they had killed Maŭla, who was my *protegé*. They all replied in a breath, 'Oh, let the past be forgotten, and assist us now! for in you alone we can look for a preserver.'

At length an armistice was agreed to; but as no one dared go to negotiate it but my men, I allowed them to take pay from the Arabs, which was settled on the 4th by ten men taking four yards of cloth each, with a promise of a feast on sweetmeats when they returned. Ex Mrs Mŭsa, who had been put aside by her husband because she was too fat for her lord's taste, then gave me three men of her private establishment, and abused Mŭsa for being wanting in 'brains.' She had repeatedly advised him to leave this place and go with me, lest the Arabs, who were all in debt to him, should put him to death; but he still hung on to recover his remaining debts, a portion having been realised by the sale of Snay's and Jafŭ's effects; for everything in the shape of commodities had been sold at the enormous price of 500 per cent – the male slaves even fetching 100 dollars per head, though the females went for less. The Hottentots now arrived, with many more of my men, who, seeing their old 'flames,' Snay's women, sold off by auction, begged me to advance them money to purchase them with, for they could not bear to see these women, who were their own when they formerly stayed here, go off like cattle no one knew where. Compliance, of course, was impossible, as it would have crowded the caravan with women. Indeed, to prevent my men ever thinking of matrimony on the march, as well as to incite them on through the journey, I promised, as soon as we reached Egypt, to give them all wives and gardens at Zanzibar, provided they did not contract marriages on the road.

On the 6th, the deputation, headed by Baraka, returned triumphantly into Kazé, leading in two of Manŭa Séra's ministers – one of them a man with one eye, whom I called Cyclops – and two others, ministers of a chief called Kitambi, or Little Blue Cloth. After going a day's journey, they said they came to where Manŭa Séra was residing with Kitambi, and met with a most cheerful and kind reception from both potentates, who, on hearing of my proposition, warmly acceded to it, issued orders at once that hostilities should cease, and, with one voice, said they were convinced that, unless through my instrumentality, Manŭa Séra would never regain his possessions. Kitambi was quite beside himself, and wished my men to stop one night to enjoy his hospitality. Manŭa Séra, after reflecting seriously about the treacherous murder of old Maŭla, hesitated, but gave way when it had been explained away by my men, and said, 'No; they shall go at once, for my kingdom depends on the issue, and Bana Mzungŭ (the White Lord) may get anxious if they do not return promptly.' One thing, however, he insisted on, and that was, the only place he would meet the Arabs in was Unyanyembé, as it would be beneath his dignity to settle matters anywhere else. And further, he specified that he wished all the transactions to take place in Mŭsas house.

Next day, 7th, I assembled all the Arabs at Mŭsa's 'court,' with all my men and the two chiefs, four men attending, when Baraka, 'on his legs,' told them all I proposed for the treaty of peace. The Arabs gave their assent to it; and Cyclops, for Manŭa Séra, after giving a full narrative of the whole history of the war, in such a rapid and eloquent manner as would have done justice to our Prime Minister, said his chief was only embittered against Snay, and now Snay was killed, he wished to make friends with them. To which the Arabs made a suitable answer, adding, that all they found fault with was an insolent remark which, in his wrath, Manŭa Séra had given utterance to, that their quarrel with him was owing chiefly to a scurvy jest which he had passed on them, and on the characteristic personal ceremony of initiation to their Mussulman faith. Now, however, as Manŭa Séra wished to make friends, they would abide by anything that I might propose. Here the knotty question arose again, what territory they, the Arabs, would give to Manŭa Séra? I thought he would not be content unless he got the old place again; but as Cyclops said no, that was not in his opinion absolutely necessary, as the lands of Unyanyembé had once before been divided, the matter was settled on the condition that another conference should be held with Manila Séra himself on the subject.

I now (8th and 9th) sent these men all off again, inviting Manŭa Séra to come over and settle matters at once, if he would, otherwise I should go on with my journey, for I could not afford to wait longer here. Then, as soon as they left, I made Mŭsa order some of his men off to Rungŭa, requesting the chief of the place to send porters to Mininga to remove all our baggage over to his palace; at the same time I begged him not to fear the Watŭta's threat to attack him, as Mŭsa would come as soon as the treaty was concluded, in company with me, to build a boma alongside his palace, as he did in former years, to be nearer his trade with Karagŭé. I should have mentioned, by the way, that Mŭsa had now made up his mind not to go further than the borders of Usŭi with me, lest I should be 'torn to pieces,' and he would be 'held responsible on the coast.' Mŭsa's men, however, whom he selected for this business, were then engaged making Mussulmans of all the Arab slave boys, and said they would not go until they had finished, although I offered to pay the 'doctor's bill,' or allowance they expected to get. The ceremony, at the same time that it helps to extend their religion, as christening does ours, also stamps the converts with a mark effective enough to prevent desertion; because, after it has been performed, their own tribe would not receive them again. At last, when they did go, Mŭsa, who was suffering from a sharp illness, to prove to me that he was bent on leaving Kazé the same time as myself, began eating what he called his training pills – small dried buds of roses with alternate bits of sugar-candy. Ten of these buds, he said, eaten dry, were sufficient for ordinary cases, and he gave a very formidable description of the effect likely to follow the use of the same number boiled in rice-water or milk.

Fearful stories of losses and distress came constantly in from Ugogo by small bodies of men, who stole their way through the jungles. To-day a tremendous commotion took place in Mŭsa's tembé amongst all the women, as one had been delivered of still-born twins. They went about in procession, painted and adorned in the most grotesque fashion, bewailing and screeching, singing and dancing, throwing their arms and legs about as if they were drunk, until the evening set in, when they gathered a huge bundle of bulrushes, and, covering it over with a cloth, carried it up to the door of the bereaved on their shoulders, as though it had been a coffin. Then setting it down on the ground, they planted some of the rushes on either side of the entrance, and all kneeling together, set to bewailing, shrieking, and howling incessantly for hours together.

After this (10th to 12th), to my great relief, quite unexpectedly, a man arrived from Usŭi conveying a present of some ivories from a great mganga or magician, named Dr Kyengo, who had sent them to Mŭsa as a recollection from an old friend, begging at the same time for some pretty cloths, as he said he was then engaged as mtongi or caravan director, collecting together all the native caravans desirous of making a grand march to Uganda. This seemed to me a heaven-born opportunity of making friends with one who could help me so materially, and I begged Mŭsa to seal it by sending him something on my account, as I had nothing by me; but Mŭsa objected, thinking it better simply to say I was coming, and if he, K'yengo, would assist me in Usŭi, I would then give him some cloths as he wanted; otherwise, Mŭsa said, the man who had to convey it would in all probability make away with it, and then do his best to prevent my seeing K'yengo. As soon as this was settled, against my wish and opinion, a special messenger arrived from Sŭwarora to inquire of Mŭsa what truth there was in the story of the Arabs having allied themselves to the Watŭta. He had full faith in Mŭsa, and hoped, if the Arabs had no hostile intentions towards him, he, Mŭsa, would send him two men of his own, and prevail on the Arabs to send two of theirs; further, Sŭwarora wished Mŭsa would send him a cat. A black cat was then given to the messenger for Sŭwarora, and Mŭsa sent an account of all that I had done towards effecting a peace, saying that the Arabs had accepted my views, and if he would have patience until I arrived in Usŭi, the four men required would be sent with me.

In the evening my men returned again with Cyclops, who said, for his master, that Manŭa Séra desired nothing more than peace, and to make friends with the Arabs; but as nothing was settled about deposing Mkisiwa, he could not come over here. Could the Arabs, was Manŭa Séra's rejoinder, suppose for a moment that he would voluntarily divide his dominion with one whom he regarded as his slave! Death would be preferable; and although he would trust his life in the Mzungŭ's hands if he called him again, he must know it was his intention to hunt Mkisiwa down like a wild animal, and would never rest satisfied until he was dead. The treaty thus broke down; for the same night Cyclops decamped like a thief, after brandishing an arrow which Manŭa Séra had given him to throw down as a gauntlet of defiance to fight Mkisiwa to death. After this the Arabs were too much ashamed of themselves to come near me, though invited by letter, and Mŭsa became so ill he would not take my advice and ride in a hammock, the best possible cure for his complaint; so, after being humbugged so many times by his procrastinations, I gave Sheikh Said more letters and specimens, with orders to take the Tots down to the coast as soon as practicable, and started once more for the north, expecting very shortly to hear of Mŭsa's death, though he promised to follow me the very next day or die in the attempt, and he also said he would bring on the four men required by Sŭwarora; for I was fully satisfied in my mind that he would have marched with me then had he had the resolution to do so at all.

To Mininga, 13th and 14th: Before I had left the district I heard that Manŭa Séra had collected a mixed force of Warori, Wagogo, and Wasakŭma, and had gone off to Kigŭé again, whilst the Arabs and Mkisiwa were feeding their men on beef before setting out to fight him. Manŭa Séra, it was said, had vast resources. His father, Fŭndi Kira, was a very rich man, and had buried vast stores of property, which no one knew of but Manŭa Séra, his heir. The Wanyamŭézi all inwardly loved him for his great generosity, and all alike thought him protected by a halo of charm-power so effective against the arms of the Arabs that he could play with them just as he liked.

On crossing Unyambéwa (14th), when I a third time put up with my old friend the sultana, her chief sent word to say he hoped I would visit him at his fighting boma to eat a cow which he had in store for me, as he could not go home and enjoy the society of his wife whilst the war was going on; since, by so doing, it was considered he 'would lose strength.'

15th to 19th: On arriving at Mininga, I was rejoiced to see Grant greatly recovered. After waiting two days, as no men came from Rungŭa, I begged Grant to push ahead on to Ukŭni, just opposite Rungŭa, with all my coast-men, whilst I remained behind for the arrival of Mŭsa's men and porters to carry on the rest of the kit – for I had now twenty- two in addition to men permanently enlisted, who took service on the same rate of pay as my original coast-men; though, as usual, when the order for marching was issued, a great number were found to be either sick or malingering.

To Mbisŭ, 20th and 21st: Two days afterwards, Mŭsa's men came in with porters, who would not hire themselves for more than two marches, having been forbidden to do so by their chief on account of the supposed Watŭta invasion; and for these two marches they required a quarter of the whole customary hire to Karagŭé Mŭsa's traps, too, I found, were not to be moved, so I saw at once Mŭsa had not kept faith with me, and there would be a fresh set of difficulties; but as every step onwards was of the greatest importance – for my men were consuming my stores at a fearful pace – I paid down the beads they demanded, and next day joined Grant at Mbisŭ, a village of Uktini held by a small chief called Mchiméka, who had just concluded a war of two years' standing with the great chief Ukŭlima (the Digger), of Ntinda (the Hump). During the whole of the two years' warfare the loss was only three men on each side. Meanwhile Mtisa's men bolted like thieves one night, on a report coming that the chief of Unyambdwa, after concluding the war, whilst amusing himself with his wife, had been wounded on the foot by an arrow that fell from her hand. The injury had at once taken a mortal turn, and the chief sent for his magicians, who said it was not the fault of the wife – somebody else must have charmed the arrow to cause such a deadly result. They then seized hold of their magic horn, primed for the purpose, and allowed it to drag them to where the culprits dwelt. Four poor men, who were convicted in this way, were at once put to death, and the chief from that moment began to recover.

Mbisŭ, 22d to 31st: After a great many perplexities, I succeeded in getting a kirangozi, or leader, by name Ungŭrŭé (the Pig). He had several times taken caravans to Karagŭé, and knew all the languages well, but unfortunately he afterwards proved to be what his name implied. That, however, I could not foresee; so, trusting to him and good-luck, I commenced making fresh enlistments of porters; but they came and went in the most tantalising manner, notwithstanding I offered three times the hire that any merchant could afford to give. Every day seemed to be worse and worse. Some of Mŭsa's men came to get palm-toddy for him, as he was too weak to stand, and was so cold nothing would warm him. There was, however, no message brought for myself; and as the deputation did not come to me, I could only infer that I was quite forgotten, or that Mŭsa, after all, had only been humbugging me. I scarcely knew what to do. Everybody advised me to stop where I was until the harvest was over, as no porters could be found on ahead, for Ukŭni was the last of the fertile lands on this side of Usŭé.

Stopping, however, seemed endless; not so my supplies. I therefore tried advancing in detachments again, sending the free men off under Grant to Ukŭlima's, whilst I waited behind, keeping ourselves divided in the hopes of inducing all hands to see the advisability of exerting themselves for the general good – as my men, whilst we were all together, showed they did not care how long they were kept doing no more fatiguing work than chaffing each other, and feeding at my expense.

In the meanwhile the villagers were very merry, brewing and drinking their pombé (beer) by turns, one house after the other providing the treat. On these occasions the chief – who always drank freely, and more than any other – heading the public gatherings of men and women, saw the large earthen pots placed all in a row, and the company taking long draughts from bowls made of plaited straw, laughing as they drank, until, half-screwed, they would begin bawling and shouting. To increase the merriment, one or two jackanapes, with zebras' manes tied over their heads, would advance with long tubes like monster bassoons, blowing with all their might, contorting their faces and bodies, and going through the most obscene and ridiculous motions to captivate their simple admirers. This, however, was only the feast; the ball then began, for the pots were no sooner emptied than five drums at once, of different sizes and tones, suspended in a line from a long horizontal bar, were beaten with fury, and all the men, women, and children, singing and clapping their hands in time, danced for hours together.

A report reached me, by some of Sirboko's men, whom he had sent to convey to us a small present of rice, that an Arab, who was crossing Msalala to our northward, had been treacherously robbed of all his arms and guns by a small district chief, whose only excuse was that the Wanyamŭézi had always traded very well by themselves until the Arabs came into the country; but now, as they were robbed of their property, on account of the disturbances caused by these Arabs, they intended for the future to take all they could get, and challenged the Arabs to do the same.

My patience was beginning to suffer again, for I could not help thinking that the chiefs of the place were preventing their village men going with me in order that my presence here might ward off the Watŭta; so I called up the kirangozi, who had thirteen 'Watoto,' as they are called, or children of his own, wishing to go, and asked him if he knew why no other men could be got. As he could not tell me, saying some excused themselves on the plea they were cutting their corn, and others that they feared the Watŭta, I resolved at once to move over to Nŭnda; and if that place also failed to furnish men, I would go on to Usŭi or Karagŭé with what men I had, and send back for the rest of my property; for though I could not bear the idea of separating from Grant, still the interests of old England were at stake, and demanded it.

To Nŭnda, 31st: This resolve being strengthened by the kirangozi's assurance that the row in Msalala had shaken the few men who had half dreaded to go with me, I marched over to Nŭnda, and put up with Grant in Uktilima's boma, when Grant informed me that the chief had required four yards of cloth from him for having walked round a dead lioness, as he had thus destroyed a charm that protected his people against any more of these animals coming, although, fortunately, the charm could be restored again by paying four yards of cloth. Ukŭlima, however, was a very kind and good man, though he did stick the hands and heads of his victims on the poles of his boma as a warning to others. He kept five wives, of whom the rest paid such respect to the elder one, it was quite pleasing to see them. A man of considerable age, he did everything the state or his great establishment required himself. All the men of his district clapped their hands together as a courteous salutation to him, and the women curtsied as well as they do at our court – a proof that they respected him as a great potentate – a homage rarely bestowed on the chiefs of other small states. Ukŭlima was also hospitable; for on one occasion, when another chief came to visit him, he received his guest and retainers with considerable ceremony, making all the men of the village get up a dance; which they did, beating the drums and firing off guns, like a lot of black devils let loose.

Halt at Nŭnda, 1st and 3d: We were not the only travellers in misfortune here, for Masŭdi, with several other Arabs, all formed in one large caravan, had arrived at Mchiméka's, and could not advance for want of men. They told me it was the first time they had come on this line, and they deeply regretted it, for they had lost 5000 dollars' worth of beads by their porters running away with their loads, and now they did not know how to proceed. Indeed, they left the coast and arrived at Kazé immediately in rear of us, and had, like ourselves, found it as much as they could do even to reach this, and now they were at a standstill for want of porters.

As all hopes of being able to get any more men were given up, I called on Bombay and Baraka to make arrangements for my going ahead with the best of my property as I had devised. They both shook their heads, and advised me to remain until the times improved, when the Arabs, being freed from the pressure of war, would come along and form with us a 'sŭfari kŭ' or grand march, as Ukŭlima and every one else had said we should be torn to pieces in Usŭi if we tried to cross that district with so few men. I then told them again and again of the messages I had sent on to Rŭmanika in Karagŭé, and to Sŭwarora in Usŭi, and begged them to listen to me, instancing as an example of what could be done by perseverance the success of Columbus, who, opposed by his sailors' misgivings, still went on and triumphed, creating for himself immortal renown.

From camp in Phŭnzé, 3d: They gave way at last; so, after selecting all the best of my property, I formed camp at Phŭnzé, left Bombay with Grant behind, as I thought Bombay the best and most honest man I had got, from his having had so much experience, and then went ahead by myself, with the Pig as my guide and interpreter, and Baraka as my factotum. The Wagŭana then all mutinied for a cloth apiece, saying they would not lift a load unless I gave it. Of course a severe contest followed; I said, as I had given them so much before, they could not want it, and ought to be ashamed of themselves. They urged, however, they were doing double work, and would not consent to carry loads as they had done at Mgŭnda Mkhali again.

Halt in Phŭnzé three days: Arguments were useless, for, simply because they were tired of going on, they *would* not see that as they were receiving pay every day, they therefore ought to work every day. However, as they yielded at last, by some few leaning to my side, I gave what they asked for, and went to the next village, still inefficient in men, as all the Pig's Watoto could not be collected together. This second move brought us into a small village, of which Ghiya, a young man, was chief.

To Ghiya's 7th: He was very civil to me, and offered to sell me a most charming young woman, quite the belle of the country; but as he could not bring me to terms, he looked over my picture-books with the greatest delight, and afterwards went into a discourse on geography with considerable perspicacity, seeming fully to comprehend that if I got down the Nile it would afterwards result in making the shores of the N'yanza like that of the coast at Zanzibar, where the products of his country could be exchanged, without much difficulty, for cloths, beads, and brass wire. I gave him a present; then a letter was brought to me from Sheikh Said, announcing Mŭsa's death, and the fact that Manŭa Séra was still holding out at Kigŭé; in answer to which I desired the sheikh to send me as many of Mŭsa's slaves as would take service with me, for they ought now, by the laws of the Koran, to be all free.

To Ungŭrŭé's, 8th: On packing up to leave Ghiya's, all the men of the village shut the bars of the entrance, wishing to extract some cloths from me, as I had not given enough, they said, to their chief. They soon, however, saw that we, being inside their own fort, had the best of it, and they gave way. We then pushed on to Ungŭrŭé's, another chief of the same district. Here the men and women of the place came crowding to see me, the fair sex all playfully offering themselves for wives, and wishing to know which I admired most. They were so importunate, after a time, that I was not sorry to hear an attack was made on their cattle because a man of the village would not pay his dowry-money to his father-in-law, and this set everybody flying out to the scene of action.

After this, as Bombay brought up the last of my skulking men, I bade him good-bye again, and made an afternoon - march on to Takina, in the district of Msalala, which we no sooner approached than all the inhabitants turned out and fired their arrows at us. They did no harm, however, excepting to create a slight alarm, which some neighbouring villagers took advantage of to run off with two of my cows. My men followed after the thieves until these entered a boma and shut the gate in their faces. They called out for the cows to be returned to them, but called in vain, as the scoundrels said, 'Findings are keepings, by the laws of our country; and as we found your cows, so we will keep them.' For my part I was glad they were gone, as the Wangŭana never yet kept anything I put under their charge; so, instead of allowing them to make a fuss the next morning, I marched straight on for M'yonga's, the chief of the district, who was famed for his infamy and great extortions, having pushed his exactions so far as to close the road.

To M'yonga's, 9th: On nearing his palace, we heard war-drums beat in every surrounding village, and the kirangozi would go no farther until permission was obtained from Myonga. This did not take long, as the chief said he was most desirous to see a white man, never having been to the coast, though his father-in-law had, and had told him that the Wazŭngŭ were even greater people than the sultan reigning there. On our drawing near the palace, a small, newly-constructed boma was shown for my residence; but as I did not wish to stop there, knowing how anxious Grant would be to have his relief, I would not enter it, but instead sent Baraka to pay the hongo as quickly as possible, that we might move on again; at the same time ordering him to describe the position both Grant and myself were in, and explain that what I paid now was to frank both of us, as the whole of the property was my own. Should he make any remarks about the two cows that were stolen, I said he must know that I could not wait for them, as my brother would die of suspense if we did not finish the journey and send back for him quickly. Off went Baraka with a party of men, stopping hours, of course, and firing volleys of ammunition away. He did not return again until the evening, when the palace-drums announced that the hongo had been settled for one barsati, one lŭgoi, and six yards merikani. Baraka approached me triumphantly, saying how well he had managed the business. M'yonga did not wish to see me, because he did not know the coast language. He was immensely pleased with the present I had given him, and said he was much and very unjustly abused by the Arabs, who never came this way, saying he was a bad man. He should be very glad to see Grant, and would take nothing from him; and, though he did not see me in person, he would feel much affronted if I did not stop the night there. In the meanwhile he would have the cows brought in, for he could not allow any one to leave his country abused in any way.

My men had greatly amused him by firing their guns off and showing him the use of their sword-bayonets. I knew, as a matter of course, that if I stopped any longer I should be teased for more cloths, and gave orders to my men to march the same instant, saying, if they did not – for I saw them hesitate – I would give the cows to the villagers, since I knew that was the thing that weighed on their minds. This raised a mutiny. No one would go forward with the two cows behind; besides which, the day was far spent, and there was nothing but jungle, they said, beyond. The kirangozi would not show the way, nor would any man lift a load. A great confusion ensued. I knew they were telling lies, and would not enter the village, but shot the cows when they arrived, for the villagers to eat, to show them I cared for nothing but making headway, and remained out in the open all night. Next morning, sure enough, before we could get under way, M'yonga sent his prime minister to say that the king's sisters and other members of his family had been crying and tormenting him all night for having let me off so cheaply – they had got nothing to cover their nakedness, and I must pay something more. This provoked fresh squabbles. The drums had beaten and the tax was settled; I could not pay more. The kirangozi, however, said he would not move a peg unless I gave something more, else he would be seized on his way back. His 'children' all said the same; and as I thought Grant would only be worsted if I did not keep friends with the scoundrel, I gave four yards more merikani, and then went on my way.

For the first few miles there were villages, but after that a long tract of jungle, inhabited chiefly by antelopes and rhinoceros. It was wilder in appearance than most parts of Unyamŭézi. In this jungle a tributary nullah to the Gombé, called Nŭrhŭngŭré, is the boundary-line between the great Country of the Moon and the kingdom of Uzinza.

CHAPTER VI

Uzinza

CROSS Unyamŭézi frontier, 10th and enter Uzinza: Unzinza, which we now entered, is ruled by two Wahŭma chieftains of foreign blood, descended from the Abyssmian stock, of whom we saw specimens scattered all over Unyamŭézi, and who extended even down south as far as Fipa. Travellers see very little, however, of these Wahŭma, because, being pastorals, they roam about with their flocks and build huts as far away as they can from cultivation. Most of the small district chiefs, too, are the descendants of those who ruled in the same places before the country was invaded, and with them travellers put up and have their dealings. The dress of the Wahŭma is very simple, composed chiefly of cow-hide tanned black – a few magic ornaments and charms, brass or copper bracelets, and immense numbers of sambo for stockings, which looked very awkward on their long legs. They smear themselves with rancid butter instead of macassar, and are, in consequence, very offensive to all but the negro, who seems, rather than otherwise, to enjoy a good sharp nose-tickler. For arms, they carry both bow and spear; more generally the latter. The Wazinza in the southern parts are so much like the Wanyamŭézi, as not to require any especial notice; but in the north, where the country is more hilly, they are much more energetic and actively built. All alike live in grass-hut villages, fenced round by bomas in the south, but open in the north. Their country rises in high rolls, increasing in altitude as it approaches the Mountains of the Moon, and is generally well cultivated, being subjected to more of the periodical rains than the regions we have left, though springs are not so abundant, I believe, as they are in the Land of the Moon, where they ooze out by the flanks of the little granitic hills.

After tracking through several miles of low bush-jungle, we came to the sites of some old bomas that had been destroyed by the Watŭta not long since. Farther on, as we wished to enter a newly-constructed

boma, the chief of which was Mafŭmbŭ Wantŭ (a Mr Balls), we felt
the effects of those ruthless marauders; for the villagers, thinking us
Watŭta in disguise, would not let us in; for those savages, they said,
had once tricked them by entering their village, pretending to be
traders carrying ivory and merchandise, whilst they were actually
spies. This was fortunate for me, however, as Mr Balls, like M'yonga,
was noted for his extortions on travellers. We then went on and put
up in the first large village of Bogŭé, where I wished to get porters
and return for Grant, as the place seemed to be populous. Finding,
however, that I could not get a sufficient number for that purpose,
I directed those who wished for employment to go off at once and
take service with Grant.

To Rŭhé's. 11th: I found many people assembled here from all
parts of the district, for the purpose of fighting M'yonga; but the
chief Rŭhé, having heard of my arrival, called me to his palace,
which, he said, was on my way, that he might see me, for he never in
all his life had a white man for his guest, and was so glad to hear of
my arrival that he would give orders for the dispersing of his forces.
I wished to push past him, as I might be subjected to such calls every
day; but Ungŭrŭé, in the most piggish manner – for he was related
to Rŭhé – insisted that neither himself nor any of his children would
advance one step farther with me unless I complied with their wish,
which was a simple conformity with the laws of their country, and
therefore absolute. At length giving in, I entered Rŭhé's boma, the
poles of which were decked with the skulls of his enemies stuck
upon them. Instead, however, of seeing him myself, as he feared
my evil eye, I conducted the arrangements for the hongo through
Baraka, in the same way as I did at M'yonga's, directing that it should
be limited to the small sum of one barsati and four yards kiniki.

To Mihambo, 12th: The drum was beaten, as the public intimation
of the payment of the hongo, and consequently of our release, and
we went on to Mihambo, on the west border of the eastern division
of Uzinza, which is called Ukhanga. It overlooks the small district
of Sorombo, belonging to the great western division, known as
Usŭi, and is presided over, by a Sorombo chief, named Makaka,
whose extortions had been so notorious that no Arabs now ever
went near him. I did not wish to do so either, though his palace lay

in the direct route. It was therefore agreed we should skirt round by the east of this district, and I even promised the Pig I would give him ten necklaces a-day in addition to his wages, if he would avoid all the chiefs, and march steadily ten miles every day. By doing so, we should have avoided the wandering Watŭta, whose depredations had laid waste nearly all of this country; but the designing blackguard, in opposition to my wishes, to accomplish some object of his own, chose to mislead us all, and quietly took us straight into Sorombo to Kagŭé, the boma of a sub-chief, called Mfŭmbi, where we no sooner arrived than the inhospitable brute forbade any one of his subjects to sell us food until the hongo was paid, for he was not sure that we were not allied with the Watŭta to rob his country. After receiving what he called his dues – one barsati, two yards merikani, and two yards kiniki – the drums beat, and all was settled with him; but I was told the head chief Makaka, who lived ten miles to the west, and so much out of my road, had sent expressly to invite me to see him. He said it was his right I should go to him as the principal chief of the district. Moreover, he longed for a sight of a white man; for though he had travelled all across Uganda and Usoga into Masawa, or the Masai country, as well as to the coast, where he had seen both Arabs and Indians, he had never yet seen an Englishman. If I would oblige him, he said he would give me guides to Sŭwarora, who was his mkama or king. Of course I knew well what all this meant; and at the same time that I said I could not comply, I promised to send him a present of friendship by the hands of Baraka.

This caused a halt. Makaka would not hear of such an arrangement. A present, he said, was due to him of course, but of more importance than the present was his wish to see me. Baraka and all the men begged I would give in, as they were sure he must be a good man to send such a kind message. I strove in vain, for no one would lift a load unless I complied; so, perforce, I went there, in company, however, with Mfŭmbi, who now pretended to be great friends; but what was the result? On entering the palace we were shown into a cowyard without a tree in it, or any shade; and no one was allowed to sell us food until a present of friendship was paid, after which the hongo would be discussed.

The price of friendship was not settled that day, however, and my men had to go supperless to bed. Baraka offered him one common cloth, and then another – all of which he rejected with such impetuosity that Baraka said his head was all on a whirl. Makaka insisted he would have a déolé, or nothing at all. I protested I had no déolés I could give him; for all the expensive cloths which I had brought from the coast had been stolen in Mgŭnda Mkhali. I had three, however, concealed at the time – which I had bought from Mŭsa, at forty dollars each – intended for the kings of Karagŭé and Uganda.

Incessant badgering went on for hours and hours, until at last Baraka, clean done with the incessant worry of this hot-headed young chief, told him, most unfortunately, he would see again if he could find a déolé, as he had one of his own. Baraka then brought one to my tent, and told me of his having bought it for eight dollars at the coast; and as I now saw I was let in for it, I told him to give it. It was given, but Makaka no sooner saw it than he said he must have another one; for it was all nonsense saying a white man had no rich cloths. Whenever he met Arabs, they all said they were poor men, who obtained all their merchandise from the white men on credit, which they refunded afterwards, by levying a heavy percentage on the sale of their ivory.

Halt, 16th: I would not give way that night; but next day, after fearful battling, the present of friendship was paid by Baraka's giving first a dubŭani, then one sahari, then one barsati, then one kisŭtŭ, and then eight yards of merikani – all of which were contested in the most sickening manner – when Baraka, fairly done up, was relieved by Makaka's saying, 'That will do for friendship ; if you had given the déolé quietly, all this trouble would have been saved; for I am not a bad man, as you will see.' My men then had their first dinner here, after which the hongo had to be paid. This for the time was, however, more easily settled; because Makaka at once said he would never be satisfied until he had received, if I had really not got a déolé, exactly double in equivalents of all I had given him. This was a fearful drain on my store; but the Pig, seeing my concern, merely laughed at it, and said, 'Oh, these savage chiefs are all alike here; you will have one of these taxes to pay every stage to Uyofti, and then the heavy work will begin; for all these men, although they assume the dignity of chief to themselves, are mere officers, who have to pay tribute to Sǔwarora, and he would be angry if they were shortcoming.'

The drums as yet had not beaten, for Makaka said he would not be satisfied until we had exchanged presents, to prove that we were the best of friends. To do this last act properly, I was to get ready whatever I wished to give him, whilst he would come and visit me with a bullock; but I was to give him a royal salute, or the drums would not beat. I never felt so degraded as when I complied, and gave orders to my men to fire a volley as he approached my tent; but I ate the dirt with a good grace, and met the young chief as if nothing had happened. My men, however, could not fire the salute fast enough for him; for he was one of those excitable impulsive creatures who expect others to do everything in as great a hurry as their minds wander. The moment the first volley was fired, he said, 'Now, fire again, fire again; be quick, be quick! What's the use of those things?' (meaning the guns.) 'We could spear you all whilst you are loading: be quick, be quick, I tell you.' But Baraka, to give himself law, said, 'No; I must ask Bana' (master) 'first, as we do everything by order; this is not fighting at all.'

The men being ready, file-firing was ordered, and then the young chief came into my tent. I motioned him to take my chair, which, after he sat down upon it, I was very sorry for, as he stained the seat all black with the running colour of one of the new barsati cloths he had got from me, which, to improve its appearance, he had saturated with stinking butter, and had tied round his loins. A fine-looking man of about thirty, he wore the butt-end of a large sea-shell cut in a circle, and tied on his forehead, for a coronet, and sundry small saltiana antelope horns, stuffed with magic powder, to keep off the evil eye. His attendants all fawned on him, and snapped their fingers whenever he sneezed. After passing the first compliment, I gave him a barsati, as my token of friendship, and asked him what he saw when he went to the Masai country. He assured me 'that there were two lakes, and not one' for, on going from Usoga to the Masai country, he crossed over a broad strait, which connected the big N'yanza with another one at its north-east comer. Fearfully impetuous, as soon as this answer was given, he said, 'Now I have replied to your questions, do you show me all the things you have got, for I want to see everything, and be very good friends. I did not see you the first day, because you being a stranger, it was necessary I should first look into the magic horn to see if all was right and safe; and now I can assure you that, whilst I saw I was safe, I also saw that your road would be prosperous. I am indeed delighted to see you, for neither my father, nor any of my forefathers, ever were honoured with the company of a white man in all their lives.'

My guns, clothes, and everything were then inspected, and begged for in the most importunate manner. He asked for the picture-books, examined the birds with intense delight – even trying to insert under their feathers his long royal finger-nails, which are grown like a Chinaman's by these chiefs, to show they have a privilege to live on meat. Then turning to the animals, he roared over each one in turn as he examined them, and called out their names. My bull's-eye lantern he coveted so much, I had to pretend exceeding anger to stop his further importunities. He then began again begging for lucifers, which charmed him so intensely I thought I should never get rid of him. He would have one box of them. I swore I could not part with them. He continued to beg, and I to resist. I offered a knife instead, but this he would not have, because the lucifers would be so valuable for his magical observances. On went the storm, till at last I drove him off with a pair of my slippers, which he had stuck his dirty feet into without my leave. I then refused to take his bullock, because he had annoyed me. On his part he was resolved not to beat the drum; but he graciously said he would think about it if I paid another lot of cloth equal to the second déolé I ought to have given him.

I began seriously to consider whether I should have this chief shot, as a reward for his oppressive treachery, and a warning to others; but the Pig said it was just what the Arabs were subjected to in Ubéna, and they found it best to pay down at once, and do all they were ordered. If I acted rightly, I would take the bullock, and then give the cloth; whilst Baraka said, 'We will shoot him if you give the order, only remember Grant is behind, and if you commence a row you will have to fight the whole way, for every chief in the country will oppose you.'

I then told the Pig and Baraka to settle at once. They no sooner did so than the drums beat, and Makaka, in the best humour possible, came over to say I had permission to go when I liked, but he hoped I would give him a gun and a box of lucifers. This was too provoking. The perpetual worry had given Baraka a fever, and had made me feel quite sick; so I said, if he ever mentioned a gun or lucifers again, I would fight the matter out with him, for I had not come there to be bullied. He then gave way, and begged I would allow my men to fire a volley outside his boma, as the Watŭta were living behind a small line of granitic hills flanking the west of his district, and he wished to show them what a powerful force he had got with him. This was permitted; but his wisdom in showing off was turned into ridicule; for the same evening the Watŭta made an attack on his villages and killed three of his subjects, but were deterred from committing further damage by coming in contact with my men, who, as soon as they saw the Watŭta fighting, fired their muskets off in the air and drove them away, they themselves at the same time bolting into my camp, and as usual vaunting their prowess.

I then ordered a march for the next morning, and went out in the fields to take my regular observations for latitude. Whilst engaged in this operation, Baraka, accompanied by Wadimoyo (Heart's-stream), another of my freemen, approached me in great consternation, whispering to themselves. They said they had some fearful news to communicate, which, when I heard it, they knew would deter our progress: it was of such great moment and magnitude, they thought they could not deliver it then. I said, 'What nonsense! out with it at once. Are we such chickens that we cannot speak about matters like men? out with it at once.'

Then Baraka said, 'I have just heard from Makaka, that a man who arrived from Usŭi only a few minutes ago has said Sŭwarora is so angry with the Arabs that he has detained one caravan of theirs in his country, and, separating the whole of their men, has placed each of them in different bomas, with orders to his village officers that, in case the Watŭta came into his country, without further ceremony they were to be all put to death.' I said, 'Oh, Baraka, how can you be such a fool? Do you not see through this humbug? Makaka only wishes to keep us here to frighten away the Watŭta;

for Godsake be a man, and don't be alarmed at such phantoms as these. You always are nagging at me that Bombay is the 'big' and you are the 'small' man. Bombay would never be frightened in this silly way. Now, do you reflect that I have selected you for this journey, as it would, if you succeed with me in carrying out our object, stamp you for ever as a man of great fame. Pray, don't give way, but do your best to encourage the men, and let us march in the morning.' On this as on other occasions of the same kind, I tried to impart confidence, by explaining, in allusion to Petherick's expedition, that I had arranged to meet white men coming up from the north. Baraka at last said, 'All right – I am not afraid; I will do as you desire.' But as the two were walking off, I heard Wadimoyo say to Baraka, 'Is he not afraid now? won't he go back?' – which, if anything, alarmed me more than the first intelligence; for I began to think that they, and not Makaka, had got up the story.

All night Makaka's men patrolled the village, drumming and shouting to keep off the Watŭta, and the next morning, instead of a march, after striking my tent I found that the whole of my porters, the Pig's children, were not to be found. They had gone off and hidden themselves, saying they were not such fools as to go any farther, as the Watŭta were out, and would cut us up on the road. This was sickening indeed.

I knew the porters had not gone far, so I told the Pig to bring them to me, that we might talk the matter over; but say what I would, they all swore they would not advance a step farther. Most of them were formerly men of Utămbara. The Watŭta had invaded their country and totally destroyed it, killing all their wives and their children, and despoiling everything they held dear to them. They did not wish to rob me, and would give up their hire, but not one step more would they advance. Makaka then came forward and said, 'Just stop here with me until this ill wind blows over' but Baraka, more in a fright at Makaka than at any one else, said, No – he would do anything rather than that; for Makaka's bullying had made him quite ill. I then said to my men, 'If nothing else will suit you, the best plan I can think of is to return to Mihambo in Bogŭé, and there form a depot, where, having stored my property, I shall give the Pig a whole load, or 63 lb., of Mzizima beads if he will take Baraka in disguise on to Sŭwarora, and ask him to send me eighty men, whilst I go back to Unyanyembé to see what men I can get from the late Mŭsa's establishment, and then we might bring on Grant, and move in a body together.' At first Baraka said, 'Do you wish to have us killed? Do you think if we went to Sŭwarora's you would ever see us back again? You would wait and wait for us, but we should never return.' To which I replied, 'Oh, Baraka, do not think so! Bombay, if he were here, would go in a minute. Sŭwarora by this time knows I am coming, and you may depend on it he will be just as anxious to have us in Usŭi as Makaka is to keep us here, and he cannot hurt us, as Rŭmanika is over him, and also expects us.' Baraka then, in the most doleful manner, said he would go if the Pig would. The Pig, however, did not like it either, but said the matter was so important he would look into the magic horn all night, and give his answer next morning as soon as we arrived at Mihambo.

Return to Mihambo, 19th: On arrival at Mihambo next day, all the porters brought their pay to me, and said they would not go, for nothing would induce them to advance a step farther. I said nothing; but, with 'my heart in my shoes,' I gave what I thought their due for coming so far, and motioned them to be off; then calling on the Pig for his decision, I tried to argue again, though I saw it was no use, for there was not one of my own men who wished to go. They were unanimous in saying Usŭi was a 'fire,' and I had no right to sacrifice them. The Pig then finally refused, saying three loads even would not tempt him, for all were opposed to it. Of what value, he observed, would the beads be to him if his life was lost? This was crushing; the whole camp was unanimous in opposing me. I then made Baraka place all my kit in the middle of the boma, which was a very strong one, keeping out only such beads as I wished him to use for the men's rations daily, and ordered him to select a few men who would return with me to Kazé; when I said, if I could not get all the men I wanted, I would try and induce some one, who would not fear, to go on to Usŭi; failing which, I would even walk back to Zanzibar for men, as nothing in the world would ever induce me to give up the journey.

This appeal did not move him; but, without a reply, he sullenly commenced collecting some men to accompany me back to Kazé. At first no one would go; they then mutinied for more beads, announcing all sorts of grievances, which they said they were always talking over to themselves, though I did not hear them. The greatest, however, that they could get up was, that I always paid the Wanyamŭézi 'temporaries' more than they got, though 'permanents.' 'They were the flesh, and I was the knife' I cut and did with them just as I liked, and they could not stand it any longer. However, they had to stand it; and next day, when I had brought them to reason, I gave over the charge of my tent and property to Baraka, and commenced the return with a bad hitching cough, caused by those cold easterly winds that blow over the plateau during the six dry months of the year, and which are, I suppose, the Harmattan peculiar to Africa.

Next day I joined Grant once more, and found he had collected a few Sorombo men, hoping to follow after me. I then told him all my mishaps in Sorombo, as well as of the 'blue-devil' frights that had seized all my men. I felt greatly alarmed about the prospects of the expedition, scarcely knowing what I should do. I resolved at last, if everything else failed, to make up a raft at the southern end of the N'yanza, and try to go up to the Nile in that way. My cough daily grew worse. I could not lie or sleep on either side. Still my mind was so excited and anxious that, after remaining one day here to enjoy Grant's society, I pushed ahead again, taking Bombay with me, and had breakfast at Mchiméka's.

There I found the Pig, who now said he wished he had taken my offer of beads, for he had spoken with his chief, and saw that I was right. Baraka and the Wangŭana were humbugs, and had they not opposed his going, he would have gone then; even now, he said, he wished I would take him again with Bombay. Though half inclined to accept his offer, which would have saved a long trudge to Kazé, yet as he had tricked me so often, I felt there would be no security unless I could get some coast interpreters, who would not side with the chiefs against me as he had done. From this I went on to Sirboko's, and spent the next day with him talking over my plans. The rafting up the lake he thought a good scheme; but he did not think I should ever get through Usŭi until all the Kazé merchants went north in a body, for it was no use trying to force my men against their inclinations; and if I did not take care how I handled them, he thought they would all desert.

8th. – As I had no interpreters, and could not go forward myself, I made up my mind at once to send back all my men, with Bombay, to Grant; after joining whom, Bombay would go back to Kazé again for other interpreters, and on his return would pick up Grant, and bring him on here. This sudden decision set all my men up in a flame; they swore it was no use my trying to go on to Karagŭé; they would not go with me; they did not come here to be killed. If I chose to lose my life, it was no business of theirs, but they would not be witness to it. They all wanted their discharge at once; they would not run away, but must have a letter of satisfaction, and then they would go back to their homes at Zanzibar. But when they found they lost all their arguments and could not move me, they said they would go back for Grant, but when they had done that duty, then they would take their leave.

10th to 15th. – This business being at last settled, I wrote to Grant on the subject, and sent all the men off who were not sick. Thinking then how I could best cure the disease that was keeping me down, as I found the blister of no use, I tried to stick a packing needle, used as a seton, into my side; but finding it was not sharp enough, in such weak hands as mine, to go through my skin, I got Baraka to try; and he failing too, I then made him fire me, for the coughing was so incessant I could get no sleep at night. I had now nothing whatever to think of but making dodges for lying easy, and for relieving my pains, or else for cooking strong broths to give me strength, for my legs were reduced to the appearance of pipe-sticks, until the 15th, when Baraka, in the same doleful manner as in Sorombo, came to me and said he had something to communicate, which was so terrible, if I heard it I should give up the march. Lŭmérési was his authority, but he would not tell it until Grant arrived. I said to him, 'Let us wait till Grant arrives; we shall then have some one with us who won't shrink from whispers' – meaning Bombay; and so I let the matter drop for the time being. But when Grant came, we had it out of him, and found this terrible mystery all hung on Lŭmérési's prognostications that we never should get through Usŭi with so little cloth.

16th to 19th. – At night, I had such a terrible air-catching fit, and made such a noise whilst trying to fill my lungs, that it alarmed all the camp, so much so that my men rushed into my tent to see if I was dying. Lŭmérési, in the morning, then went on a visiting excursion into the district, but no sooner left than the chief of Isamiro, whose place lies close to the N'yanza, came here to visit him (17th); but after waiting a day to make friends with me, he departed (18th), as I heard afterwards, to tell his great Mhŭma chief, Rohinda, the ruler of Ukhanga, to which district this state of Bogŭé belongs, what sort of presents I had given to Lŭmérési. He was, in fact, a spy whom Rohinda had sent to ascertain what exactions had been made from me, as he, being the great chief, was entitled to the most of them himself. On Lŭmérési's return, all the men of the village, as well as mine, set up a dance, beating the drums all day and all night.

20th to 21st. – Next night they had to beat their drums for a very different purpose, as the Watŭta, after lifting all of Makaka's cattle in Sorombo, came hovering about, and declared they would never cease fighting until they had lifted all those that Lŭmérési harboured round his boma; for it so happened that Lŭmérési allowed a large party of Watosi, alias Wahŭma, to keep their cattle in large stalls all round his boma, and these the Watŭta had now set their hearts upon. After a little reflection, however, they thought better of it, as they were afraid to come in at once on account of my guns.

Most gladdening news this day came in to cheer me. A large mixed caravan of Arabs and coast-men, arriving from Karagŭé, announced that both Rŭmanika and Sŭwarora were anxiously looking out for us, wondering why we did not come. So great, indeed, was Sŭwaroras desire to see us, that he had sent four men to invite us, and they would have been here now, only that one of them fell sick on the way, and the rest had to stop for him. I cannot say what pleasure this gave me; my fortune, I thought, was made; and so I told Baraka, who, instead of rejoicing with me, only shook his head at it, and pretended he did not believe the news to be true. Without loss of time I wrote off to Grant, and got these men to carry the letter.

Next day (22d) the Wasŭi from Sŭwarora arrived. They were a very gentle, nice-dispositioned-looking set of men – small, but well knit together. They advanced to my tent with much seeming grace; then knelt at my feet, and began clapping their hands together, saying, at the same time, 'My great chief, my great chief, I hope you are well; for Sŭwarora, having heard of your detention here, has sent us over, to assure you that all those reports that have been circulated regarding his ill-treatment of caravans are without foundation; he is sorry for what has happened to deter your march, and hopes you will at once come to visit him.' I then told them all that had happened – how Grant and myself were situated – and begged them to assist me by going off to Grant's camp to inspire all the men there with confidence, and bring my rear property to me – saying, as they agreed to do so, 'Here are some cloths and some beads for your expenses, and when you return I will give you more.' Baraka at once, seeing this, told me they were not trustworthy, for at Mihambo an old man had come there and tried to inveigle him in the same manner, but he kicked him out of the camp, because he knew he was a touter, who wished merely to allure him with sweet words to fleece him afterwards. I then wrote to Grant another letter to be delivered by these men.

Lŭmérési no sooner heard of the presents I had given them, than he flew into a passion, called them impostors, abused them for not speaking to him before they came to me, and said he would not allow them to go. High words then ensued. I said the business was mine, and not his; he had no right to interfere, and they should go. Still Lŭmérési was obstinate, and determined they should not, for I was his guest; he would not allow any one to defraud me. It was a great insult to himself, if true, that Sŭwarora should attempt to snatch me out of his house; and he could not bear to see me take these strangers by the hand, when, as we have seen, it took him so long to entice me to his den, and he could not prevail over me until he actually sent his copper hatchet

When this breeze blew over, by Lŭmérési's walking away, I told the Wasŭi not to mind him, but to do just as I bid them. They said they had their orders to bring me, and if Lŭmérési would not allow them to go for Grant, they would stop where they were, for they knew that if Sŭwarora found them delaying long, he would send more, men to look after them. There was no peace yet, however; for Lŭmérési, finding them quietly settled down eating with my men, ordered them out of his district, threatening force if they did not comply at once. I tried my best for them, but the Wasŭi, fearing to stop any longer, said they would take leave to see Sŭwarora, and in eight days more they would come back again, bringing something with them, the sight of which would make Lŭmérési quake. Further words were now useless, so I gave them more cloth to keep them up to the mark, and sent them off. Baraka, who seemed to think this generosity a bit of insanity, grumbled that if I had cloths to throw away it would have been better had I disposed of them to my own men.

Next day (26th), as I was still unwell, I sent four men to Grant with inquiries how he was getting on, and a request for medicines. The messengers took four days to bring back the information that Bombay had not returned from Kazé, but that Grant, having got assistance, hoped to break ground about the 5th of next month. They brought me at the same time information that the Watŭta had invested Rŭhé's, after clearing off all the cattle in the surrounding villages, and had proclaimed their intention of serving out Lŭmérési next. In consequence of this, Lŭmérési daily assembled his grey-beards and had councils of war in his drum-house; but though his subjects sent to him constantly for troops, he would not assist them.

Another caravan then arrived (31st) from Karagŭé, in which I found an old friend, of half Arab breed, called Saim, who, whilst I was residing with Sheikh Snay at Kazé on my former expedition, taught me the way to make plantain-wine. He, like the rest of the porters in the caravan, wore a shirt of fig-tree bark called mbŭgŭ. As I shall have frequently to use this word in the course of the Journal, I may here give an explanation of its meaning. The porter here mentioned told me that the people about the equator all wore this kind of covering, and made it up of numerous pieces of bark sewn together, which they stripped from the trees after cutting once round the trunk above and below, and then once more down the tree from the upper to the lower circular cutting. This operation did not kill the trees, because, if they covered the wound, whilst it was fresh, well over with plantain-leaves, shoots grew down from above, and a new bark came all over it. The way they softened the bark, to make it like cloth, was by immersion in water, and a good strong application of a mill-headed mallet, which ribbed it like corduroy. Saim told me he had lived ten years in Uganda, had crossed the Nile, and had traded eastward as far as the Masai country. He thought the N'yanza was the source of the Rŭvŭma river; as the river which drained the Nyanza, after passing between Uganda and Usoga, went through Unyoro, and then all round the Tanganyika lake into the Indian Ocean, south of

Zanzibar. Kiganda, he also said, he knew as well as his own tongue; and as I wanted an interpreter, he would gladly take service with me. This was just what I wanted – a heaven-born stroke of luck. I seized at his offer with avidity, gave him a new suit of clothes, which made him look quite a gentleman, and arranged to send him next day with a letter to Grant.

1st and 2d. – A great hubbub and confusion now seized all the place, for the Watŭta were out, and had killed a woman of the place who had formerly been seized by them in war, but had since escaped and resided here. To avenge this, Lŭmérési headed his host, and was accompanied by my men; but they succeeded in nothing save in frightening off their enemies, and regaining possession of the body of the dead woman. Then another hubbub arose, for it was discovered that three Wahŭma women were missing (2d); and, as they did not turn up again, Lŭmérési suspected the men of the caravan, which left with Saim, must have taken them off as slaves. He sent for the chief of the caravan, and had him brought back to account for this business. Of course the man swore he knew nothing about the matter, whilst Lŭmérési swore he should stop there a prisoner until the women were freed, as it was not the first time his women had been stolen in this manner. About the same time a man of this place, who had been to Sorombo to purchase cows, came in with a herd, and was at once seized by Lŭmérési; for, during his absence, one of Lŭmérési's daughters had been discovered to be with child, and she, on being asked who was the cause of it, pointed out that man. To compensate for damage done to himself, as his daughter by this means had become reduced to half her market-value, Lŭmérési seized all the cattle this man had brought with him.

3d to 10th. – When two days had elapsed, one of the three missing Wahŭma women was discovered in a village close by. As she said she had absconded because her husband had ill-treated her, she was flogged, to teach her better conduct. It was reported they had been seen in M'yongas establishment; and I was at the same time informed that the husbands who were out in search of them would return, as M'yonga was likely to demand a price for them if they were claimed, in virtue of their being his rightful property under the acknowledged law of bŭni, or findings-keepings.

For the next four days nothing but wars and rumours of wars could be heard. The Watŭta were out in all directions plundering cattle and burning villages, and the Wahŭma of this place had taken such fright, they made a stealthy march with all their herds to a neighbouring chief, to whom it happened that one of Lŭmérési's grey-beards was on a visit. They thus caught a Tartar; for the grey-beard no sooner saw them than he went and flogged them all back again, rebuking them on the way for their ingratitude to their chief, who had taken them in when they sought his shelter, and was now deserted by them on the first alarm of war.

10th. – Wishing now to gain further intelligence of Grant, I ordered some of my men to carry a letter to him; but they all feared the Watŭta meeting them on the way, and would not. Just then a report came in that one of Lŭmérési's sons, who had gone near the capital of Ukhanga to purchase cows, was seized by Rohinda in consequence of the Isamiro chief telling him that Lŭmérési had taken untold wealth from me, and he was to be detained there a prisoner until Lŭmérési either disgorged, or sent me on to be fleeced again. Lŭmérési, of course, was greatly perplexed at this, and sought my advice, but could get nothing out of me, for I laughed in my sleeve, and told him such was the consequence of his having been too greedy.

11th to 15th. – Masŭdi with his caravan arrived from Mchiméka – Ungŭrŭé 'the Pig,' who had led me astray, was, by the way, his kirangozi or caravan-leader. Masŭdi told us he had suffered most severely from losses by his men running away, one after the other, as soon as they received their pay. He thought Grant would soon join me, as, the harvest being all in, the men about Rŭngŭa would naturally be anxious for service. He had had fearful work with M'yonga, having paid him a gun, some gunpowder, and a great quantity of cloth; and he had to give the same to Rŭhé, with the addition of twenty brass wires, one load of mzizima, and one load of red coral beads. This was startling, and induced me to send all the men I could prudently spare off to Grant at once, cautioning him to avoid Rŭhé's, as Lŭmérési had promised me he would not allow one other thing to be taken from me. Lŭmérési by this time was improving, from lessons on the policy of moderation which I had been teaching him; for when he tried to squeeze as much more out of Masŭdi as Rŭhé had taken, he gave way, and let him off cheaply at my intercession. He had seen enough to be persuaded that this unlimited taxation or plunder system would turn out a losing game, such as Unyamyembé and Ugogo were at that time suffering from. Moreover, he was rather put to shame by my saying, 'Pray, who now is biggest – Rŭhé or yourself? for any one entering this country would suspect that he was, as he levies the first tax, and gives people to understand that, by their paying it, the whole district will be free to them; such at any rate he told me, and so it appears he told Masŭdi. If you are the sultan, and will take my advice, I would strongly recommend your teaching Rŭhé a lesson, by taking from him what the Arabs paid, and giving it back to Masŭdi.

At midnight (16th) I was startled in my sleep by the hurried tramp of several men, who rushed in to say they were Grant's porters – Bogŭé men who had deserted him. Grant, they said, in incoherent, short, rapid, and excited sentences, was left by them standing under a tree, with nothing but his gun in his hand. All the Wangŭana had been either killed or driven away by M'yonga's men, who all turned out and fell upon the caravan, shooting, spearing, and plundering, until nothing was left. The porters then, seeing Grant all alone, unable to help him, bolted off to inform me and Lŭmérési, as the best thing they could do. Though disbelieving the story in all its minutiae, I felt that something serious must have happened; so, without a moments delay, I sent off the last of my men strong enough to walk to succour Grant, carrying with them a bag of beads. Baraka then stepped outside my tent, and said in a loud voice, purposely for my edification, 'There, now, what is the use of thinking any more about going to Karagŭé? I said all along it was impossible upon hearing which I had him up before all the remaining men, and gave him a lecture, saying, happen what would, I must die or go on with the journey, for shame would not allow me to give way as Baraka was doing. Baraka replied, he was not afraid – he only meant to imply that men could not act against impossibilities. 'Impossibilities!' I said; 'what is impossible? Could I not go on as a servant with the first caravan, or buy up a whole caravan if I liked? What is impossible? For Godsake don't try any more to frighten my men, for you have nearly killed me already in doing so.'

Next day (17th) I received a letter from Grant, narrating the whole of his catastrophes:

In the Jungles Near M'Yonga's 16 Sept. 1861
My dear Speke, – The caravan was attacked, plundered, and the men driven to the winds, while marching this morning into M'yonga's country.

Awaking at cock-crow, I roused the camp, all anxious to rejoin you; and while the loads were being packed, my attention was drawn to an angry discussion between the head men and seven or eight armed fellows sent by Sultan M'yonga, to insist on my putting up for the day in his village. They were summarily told that as *you* had already made him a present, he need not expect a visit from *me*. Adhering, I doubt not, to their master's instructions, they officiously constituted themselves our guides till we chose to strike off their path, when, quickly heading our party, they stopped the way, planted their spears, and *dared* our advance!

This menace made us firmer in our determination, and we swept past the spears. After we had marched unmolested for some seven miles, a loud yelping from the woods excited our attention, and a sudden rush was made upon us by, say, two hundred men, who came down *seemingly* in great glee. In an instant, at the caravan's centre, they fastened upon the poor porters. The struggle was short; and with the threat of an arrow or spear at their breasts, men were robbed of their cloths and ornaments, loads were yielded and run away with before resistance could be organised; only three men of a hundred stood by me, the others, whose only *thought* was their lives, fled into the woods, where I went shouting for them. One man, little Rahan – rip as he is – stood with cocked gun, defending his load, against five savages with uplifted spears. No one else could be seen. Two or three were reported killed; some were wounded. Beads, boxes, cloths, etc, lay strewed about the woods. In fact, I felt wrecked. My attempt to go and demand redress from the sultan was resisted, and, in utter despair, I seated myself among a mass of rascals jeering round me, and insolent after the success of the day. Several were dressed in the very cloths, etc, they had stolen from my men.

In the afternoon, about fifteen men and loads were brought me, with a message from the sultan, that the attack had been a *mistake* of his subjects – that one man had had a hand cut off for it, and that all the property would be restored! Yours sincerely,
J. W. GRANT.

Now, judging from the message sent to Grant by M'yonga, it appeared to me that his men had mistaken their chief's orders, and had gone one step beyond his intentions. It was obvious that the chief merely intended to prevent Grant from passing through or evading his district without paying a hongo, else he would not have sent his men to invite him to his palace, doubtless with instructions, if necessary, to use force. This appears the more evident from the fact of his subsequent contrition, and finding it necessary to send excuses when the property was in his hands: for these chiefs, grasping as they are, know they must conform to some kind of system, to save themselves from a general war, or the avoidance of their territories by all travellers in future. To assist Grant, I begged Lŭmérési to send him some aid in men at once; but he refused, on the plea that M'yonga was at war with him, and would kill them if they went. This was all the more provoking, as Grant, in a letter next evening, told me he could not get all his men together again, and wished to know what should be done. He had recovered all the property except six loads of beads, eighty yards of American sheeting, and many minor articles, besides what had been rifled more or less from every load. I now proposed to Grant that, as Lŭmérési's territories extended to within eight miles of M'yonga's, he should try to move over the Msalala border by relays, when I would send some Bogŭé men to meet him; for though Lŭmérési would not risk sending his men into the clutches of M'yonga, he was most anxious to have another white visitor.

20th and 21st – I again urged Lŭmérési to help on Grant, saying it was incumbent on him to call M'yonga to account for maltreating Grant's porters, who were his own subjects, else the road would be shut up – he would lose all the hongos he laid on caravans – and he would not be able to send his own ivory down to the coast. This appeal had its effect: he called on his men to volunteer, and twelve porters came forward, who no sooner left, than in came another letter from Grant, informing me that he had collected almost enough men to march with, and that M'yonga had returned one of the six missing loads, and promised to right him in everything.

Next day, however, I had from Grant two very opposite accounts – one, in the morning, full of exultation, in which he said he hoped to reach Rŭhé's this very day, as his complement of porters was then completed; while by the other, which came in the evening, I was shocked to hear that M'yonga, after returning all the loads, much reduced by rifling, had demanded as a hongo two guns, two boxes ammunition, forty brass wires, and 160 yards of American sheeting, in default of which he, Grant, must lend M'yonga ten Wangŭana to build a boma on the west of his district, to enable him to fight some Wasonga who were invading his territory, otherwise he would not allow Grant to move from his palace. Grant knew not what to do. He dared not part with the guns, because he knew it was against my principle, and therefore deferred the answer until he heard from me, although all his already collected porters were getting fidgety, and two had bolted In this fearful fix I sent Baraka off with strict orders to bring Grant away at any price, except the threatened sacrifice of men, guns, and ammunition, which I would not listen to, as one more day's delay might end in further exactions; at the same time, I cautioned him to save my property as far as he could, for it was to him that M'yonga had formerly said that what I paid him should do for all.

Some of M'yonga's men who had plundered Grant now 'caught a Tartar.' After rifling his loads of a kilyndo, or bark box of beads, they, it appeared, received orders from M'yonga to sell a lot of female slaves, amongst whom were the two Wahŭma women who had absconded from this. The men in charge, not knowing their history, brought them for sale into this district, where they were instantly recognised by some of Lŭmérési's men, and brought in to him. The case was not examined at once, Lŭmérési happening to be absent; so, to make good their time, the men in charge brought their beads to me to be exchanged for something else, not knowing that both camps were mine, and that they held my beads and not Grants. Of course I took them from them, but did not give them a flogging, as I knew if I did so they would at once retaliate upon

Grant. The poor Wahŭma women, as soon as Lŭmérési arrived, were put to death by their husbands, because, by becoming slaves, they had broken the laws of their race.

22d to 24th – At last I began to recover. All this exciting news, with the prospect of soon seeing Grant, did me a world of good, – so much so, that I began shooting small birds for specimens – watching the blacksmiths as they made tools, spears, and bracelets – and doctoring some of the Wahtima women who came to be treated for ophthalmia, in return for which they gave me milk. The milk, however, I could not boil excepting in secrecy, else they would have stopped their donations on the plea that this process would be an incantation or bewitchment, from which their cattle would fall sick and dry up. I now succeeded in getting Lŭmérési to send his Wanyapara to go and threaten M'yonga, that if he did not release Grant at once, we would combine to force him to do so. They, however, left too late, for the hongo had been settled, as I was informed by a letter from Grant next day, brought to me by Bombay, who had just returned from Kazé after six weeks' absence. He brought with him old Nasib and another man, and told me both Bŭi and Nasib had hidden themselves in a boma close to Lŭmérési's the day when my hongo was settled; but they bolted the instant the drums beat, and my men fired guns to celebrate the event, supposing that the noise was occasioned by our fighting with Lŭmérési. These cowards then made straight for Kazé, when Fŭndi Sangoro gave Nasib a flogging for deserting me, and made him so ashamed of his conduct that he said he would never do it again. Bŭi also was flogged, but, admitting himself to be a coward, was sent to the 'right-about'. With him Bombay also brought three new déolés, for which I had to pay 160 dollars, and news that the war with Manŭa Séra was not then over. He had effected his escape in the usual manner, and was leading the Arabs another long march after him.

Expecting to meet Grant this morning (25th), I strolled as far as my strength and wind would allow me towards Rŭhé's; but I was sold, for Rŭhé had detained him for a hongo. Lŭmérési also having heard of it, tried to interpose, according to a plan arranged between us in case of such a thing happening, by sending his officers to Rŭhé, with an order not to check my 'brother's' march, as I had settled accounts for all. Later in the day, however, I heard from Grant that Rŭhé would not let him go until he paid sixteen pretty cloths, six wires, one gun, one box of ammunition, and one load of mzizima beads, coolly saying I had only given him a trifle, under the condition that, when the big caravan arrived, Grant would make good the rest. I immediately read this letter to Lŭmérési, and asked him how I should answer it, as Grant refused to pay anything until I gave the order.

To which Lŭmérési replied, Rŭhé, 'my child,' could not dare to interfere with Grant after his officers arrived, and advised me to wait until the evening. At all events, if there were any further impediments, he himself would go over there with a force and release Grant. In the evening another messenger arrived from Grant, giving a list of his losses and expenses at M'yonga's. They amounted to an equivalent of eight loads, and were as follows: 100 yards cloth, and 4600 necklaces of beads (these had been set aside as the wages paid to the porters, but being in my custody, I had to make them good); 300 necklaces of beads stolen from the loads; one brass wire stolen; one sword-bayonet stolen; Grant's looking-glass stolen; one saw stolen; one box ammunition stolen. Then paid in hongo, 160 yards cloth; 150 necklaces; one scarlet blanket, double; one case ammunition; ten brass wires. Lastly, there was one donkey beaten to death by the savages. This was the worst of all; for this poor brute carried me on the former journey to the southern end of the N'yanza, and in consequence was a great pet.

As nothing further transpired, and I was all in the dark (26th), I wrote to Grant telling him of my interviews with Lŭmérési, and requesting him to pay nothing; but it was too late, for Grant, to my inexpressible delight, was the next person I saw; he walked into camp, and then we had a good laugh over all our misfortunes. Poor Grant, he had indeed had a most troublesome time of it. The scoundrel Rŭhé, who only laughed at Lŭmérési's orders, had stopped his getting supplies of food for himself and his men; told him it was lucky that he came direct to the palace, for full preparations had been made for stopping him had he attempted to avoid it; would not listen to any reference being made to myself; badgered and bullied over every article that he extracted; and, finally, when he found compliance with his extortionate requests was not readily granted, he beat the war-drums to frighten the porters, and ordered the caravan out of his palace, to where he said they would find his men ready to fight it put with them. It happened that Grant had just given Rŭhé a gun when my note arrived, on which they made an agreement that it was to be restored, provided that, after the full knowledge of all these transactions had reached us, it was both Lŭmérési's and my desire that it should be so.

I called Lŭmérési (27th), and begged he would show whether he was the chief or not, by requiring Rŭhé to disgorge the property he had taken from me. His Wanyapara had been despised, and I had been most unjustly treated. Upon this the old chief hung down his head, and said it touched his heart more than words could tell to hear my complaint, for until I came that way no one had come, and I had paid him handsomely. He fully appreciated the good service I had done to him and his country by opening a road which all caravans for the future would follow if properly dealt with. Having two heads in a country was a most dangerous thing, but it could not be helped for the present, as his hands were too completely occupied already. There were Rohinda, the Watŭta, and M'yonga, whom he must settle with before he could attend to Rŭhé; but when he was free, then Rŭhé should know who was the chief. To bring the matter to a climax, Mrs Lŭmérési then said she ought to have something, because Rŭhé was her son, whilst Lŭmérési was only her second husband and consort, for Rŭhé was born to her by her former husband. She therefore was queen.

Meanwhile my Wasŭi friends, who left on the 25th of August, returned, bearing what might he called Sŭwarora's mace – a long rod of brass bound up in stick charms, and called Kaqueuziugiriri, 'the commander of all things.' This they said was their chief's invitation to us; Sŭwarora did not want a hongo – he only wished to see us, and sent this Kaqneuzingiriri, to command us respect wherever we went.

5th. – Without seeing us again, Lŭmérési, evidently ashamed of the power held over him by this rod of Sŭwarora's, walked off in the night, leaving word that he was on his way to Rŭhé's, to get back my gun and all the other things that had been taken from Grant. The same night a large herd of cattle was stolen from the boma without any one knowing it; so next morning, when the loss was discovered, all the Wahŭma set off on the spoor to track them down; but with what effect I never knew.

To Mŭamba, 6th: As I had now men enough to remove half our property, I made a start of it, leaving Grant to bring up the rest. I believe I was a most miserable spectre in appearance, puffing and blowing at each step I took, with shoulder drooping, and left arm hanging like a dead log, which I was unable ever to swing. Grant, remarking this, told me then, although from a friendly delicacy he had abstained from saying so earlier, that my condition, when he first saw me on rejoining, gave him a sickening shock. Next day (7th) he came up with, the rest of the property, carried by men who had taken service for that one march only.

Halt, 8th: Before us now lay a wilderness of five marches' duration, as the few villages that once lined it had all been depopulated by the Sorombo people and the Watŭta. We therefore had to lay in rations for those days, and as no men could be found who would take service to Karagŭé, we filled up our complement with men at exorbitant wages to carry our things on to Usŭi. At this place, to our intense joy, three of Sheikh Said's boys came to us with a letter from Rigby; but, on opening it, our spirits at once fell far below zero, for it only informed us that he had sent us all kinds of nice things, and letters from home, which were packed up in boxes, and despatched from the coast on the 30th October 1860.

The boys then told me that a merchant, nicknamed Msopora, had left the boxes in Ugogo, in charge of some of those Arabs who were detained there, whilst he went rapidly round by the south, following up the Rŭaha river to Usanga and Usenga, whence he struck across to Kazé. Sheikh Said, they said, sent his particular respects to me; he had heard of Grant's disasters with great alarm. If he could be of service, he would readily come to me; but he had dreamed three times that he saw me marching into Cairo, which, as three times were lucky, he was sure would prove good, and he begged I would still keep my nose well to the front, and push boldly on. Manŭa Séra was still in the field, and all was uncertain. Bombay then told me – he had forgotten to do so before – that when he was last at Kazé, Sheikh Said told him he was sure we would succeed if both he and myself pulled together, although it was well known no one else of my party wished to go northwards.

To Kangongo, 9th: With at last a sufficiency of porters, we all set out together, walking over a new style of country. Instead of the constantly-recurring outcrops of granite, as in Unyamŭézi, with valleys between, there were only two lines of little hills visible, one right and one left of us, a good way off; whilst the ground over which we were travelling, instead of being confined like a valley, rose in long high swells of sandstone formation, covered with small forest-trees, among which flowers like primroses, only very much larger, and mostly of a pink colour, were frequently met with. Indeed, wc ought all to have been happy together, for all my men were paid and rationed trebly – far better than they would have been if they had been travelling with any one else; but I had not paid all, as they thought, proportionably, and therefore there were constant heartburnings, with strikes and rows every day. It was useless to tell them that they were all paid according to their own agreements – that all short-service men had a right to expect more in proportion to their work than long-service ones; they called it all love and partiality, and in their envy would think themselves ill-used.

To Kagéra, 10th: At night the kirangozi would harangue the camp, cautioning hands to keep together on the line of march, as the Watŭta were constantly hovering about, and the men should not squabble and fight with their master, else no more white men would come this way again. On the 11th we were out of Bogŭé, in the district of Ugomba, and next march brought us into Ugombé (12th), where we crossed the Ukongo nullah, draining westwards to the Malagarazi river. Here some of the porters, attempting to bolt, were intercepted by my coast-men and had a fight of it, for they fired arrows, and in return the coast-men cut their bows. The whole camp, of course, was in a blaze at this; their tribe was insulted, and they would not stand it, until Bombay put down their pride with a few strings of beads, as the best means of restoring peace in the camp.

Halt, 13th and 14th: At this place we were visited by the chief of the district, Pongo (Bush-boc), who had left his palace to see us and invite us his way, for he feared we might give him the slip by going west into Uyofŭ. He sent us a cow, and said he should like some return; for Masŭdi, who had gone ahead, only gave him a trifle, professing to be our vanguard, and telling him that as soon as we came with the large caravan we would satisfy him to his heart's content. We wished for an interview, but he would not see us, as he was engaged looking into his magic horn, with an endeavour to see what sort of men we were, as none of our sort had ever come that way before.

The old sort of thing occurred again. I sent him one kitambi and eight yards kiniki, explaining how fearfully I was reduced from theft and desertions, and begging he would have mercy; but instead of doing so, he sent the things back in a huff, after a whole day's delay, and said, he required, besides, one sahari, one kitambi, and eight yards kiniki. In a moment I sent them over, and begged he would beat the drums; but no, he thought he was entitled to ten brass wires in addition, and would accept them at his palace the next day, as he could not think of allowing us to leave his country until we had done him that honour, else all the surrounding chiefs would call him inhospitable.

To Ponga's residence, 15th: Too knowing now to be caught with such chaff, I told him, through Bombay, if he would consider the ten brass wires final, I would give them, and then go to his palace, not otherwise. He acceded to this, but no sooner got them, than he broke his faith, and said he must either have more pretty cloths, or five more brass wires, and then, without doubt, he would beat the drums. A long badgering bargain ensued, at which I made all my men be present as witnesses, and we finally concluded the hongo with four more brass wires.

The drums then no sooner beat the satisfaction, than the Wasŭi mace-bearers, in the most feeling and good-mannered possible manner, dropped down on their knees before me, and congratulated me on the cessation of this tormenting business. Feeling much freer, we now went over and put up in Pongo's palace, for we had to halt there a day to collect more porters, as half my men had just bolted. This was by no means an easy job, for all my American sheeting was out, and so was the kiniki. Pongo then for the first time showed himself, sneaking about with an escort, hiding his head in a cloth lest our 'evil eyes' might bewitch him. Still he did us a good turn; for on the 16th he persuaded his men to take service with us at the enormous hire of ten necklaces of beads per man for every day's march – nearly ten times what an Arab pays. Fowls were as plentiful here as elsewhere, though the people only kept them to sell to travellers, or else for cutting them open for divining purposes, by inspection of their blood and bones.

To N'yarŭwamba's, 17th: From the frying-pan we went into the
fire in crossing from Ugombé into the district of Wanga, where we
beat up the chief, N'yarŭwamba, and at once went into the hongo
business. He offered a cow to commence with, which I would not
accept until the tax was paid, and then I made my offering of two
wires, one kitambi, and one kisŭtŭ. Badgering then commenced: I
must add two wires, and six makete or necklaces of mzizima beads,
the latter being due to the chief for negotiating the tax. When this
addition was paid, we should be freed by beat of drum.

I complied at once, by way of offering a special mark of respect
and friendship, and on the reliance that he would keep his word. The
scoundrel, however, no sooner got the articles, than he said a man had
just come there to inform him that I gave Pongo ten wires and ten
cloths; he, therefore, could not be satisfied until I added one more wire,
when, without fail, he would beat the drums. It was given, after many
angry words; but it was the old story over again – he would have one
more wire and a cloth, or else he would not allow us to proceed on the
morrow. My men, this time really provoked, said they would fight it out
– a king breaking his word in that way! But in the end the demand had
to be paid; and at last, at 9 p.m. the drums beat the satisfaction.

To the border of Ukhanga, 18th: From this we went on to the
north end of Wanga, in front of which was a wilderness, separating
the possessions of Rohinda from those of Sŭwarora. We put up in
a boma, but were not long ensconced there when the villagers got
up a pretext for a quarrel, thinking they could plunder us of all our
goods, and began pitching into my men. We, however, proved more
than a match for them. Our show of guns frightened them all out of
the place; my men then gave chase, firing off in the air, which sent
them flying over the fields, and left us to do there as we liked until
night, when a few of the villagers came back and took up their abode
with us quietly. Next, after dark, the little village was on the alert
again. The Watŭta were out marching, and it was rumoured that
they were bound for N'yarŭwamba's. The porters who were engaged
at Pongo's now gave us the slip; we were consequently detained here
next day (19th), when, after engaging a fresh set, we crossed the
wilderness, and in Usŭi put up with Sŭwaroras border officer of this
post, N'yamanira. Here we were again brought to a standstill.

CHAPTER VII

Usŭi

HALT at Usŭi border, 20th and 21st: We were now in Usŭi, and so the mace-bearers, being on their own ground, forgot their manners, and peremptorily demanded their pay before they would allow us to move one step farther. At first I tried to stave the matter off, promising great rewards if they took us quickly on to Sŭwarora; but they would take no alternative – their rights were four wires each. I could not afford such a sum, and tried to beat them down, but without effect; for they said they had it in their power to detain us here a whole month, and they could get us bullied at every stage by the officers of the stations. No threats of reporting them to their chief had any effect, so, knowing that treachery in these countries was a powerful enemy, I ordered them to be paid. N'yamanira, the Mkŭngŭ, then gave us a goat and two pots of pombé, begging, at the same time, for four wires, which I paid, hoping thus to get on in the morning.

I then made friends with him, and found he was a great doctor as well as an officer. In front of his hut he had his church or uganga – a tree, in which was fixed a blaue boc's horn charged with magic powder, and a zebra's hoof, suspended by a string over a pot of water sunk in the earth below it. His badges of office he had tied on his head; the butt of a shell, representing the officer's badge, being fixed on the forehead, whilst a small sheep's horn, fixed jauntily over the temple, denoted that he was a magician. Wishing to try my powers in magical arts, as I laughed at his church, he begged me to produce an everlasting spring of water by simply scratching the ground. He, however, drew short up, to the intense delight of my men, on my promising that I would do so if he made one first.

I wished to move in the morning (23d), and had all hands ready, but was told by Makinga he must be settled with first. His dues for the present were four brass wires, and as many more when we reached the palace. I could not stand this: we were literally, as Mŭsa said we should be, being 'torn to pieces' so I appealed to the mace-bearers, protested that Makinga could have no claims on me, as he was not a man of Usŭi, but a native of Utambara, and brought on a row. On the other hand, as he could not refute this, Makinga swore the mace was all a pretence, and set a-fighting with the Wasŭi and all the men in turn.

To put a stop to this, I ordered a halt, and called on the district officer to assist us, on which he said he would escort us on to Sŭwarora's if we would stop till next morning. This was agreed to; but in the night we were robbed of three goats, which he said he could not allow to be passed over, lest Sŭwarora might hear of it, and he would get into a scrape. He pressed us strongly to stop another day whilst he sought for them, but I told him I would not, as his magic powder was weak, else he would have found the scabbard we lost long before this.

To Virembo's, 24th: At last we got under way, and, after winding through a long forest, we emerged on the first of the populous parts of Ustii, a most convulsed-looking country, of well-rounded hills composed of sandstone. In all the parts not under cultivation they were covered with brushwood. Here the little grass-hut villages were not fenced by a boma, but were hidden in large fields of plantains. Cattle were numerous, kept by the Wahŭma, who would not sell their milk to us because we ate fowls and a bean called maharagŭé.

To Vikora's, 25th: Happily no one tried to pillage us here, so on we went to Vikora's, another officer, living at N'yakasenyé, under a sandstone hill, faced with a dyke of white quartz, over which leaped a small stream of water – a seventy-feet drop – which, it is said, Sŭwarora sometimes paid homage to when the land was oppressed by drought Vikora's father it was whom Sirboko of Miniuga shot. Usually he was very severe with merchants in consequence of that act; but he did not molest us, as the messenger who went on to Sŭwarora returned here just as we arrived, to say we must come on at once, as Sŭwarora was anxious to see us, and had ordered his Wakungŭ not to molest us. Thieves that night entered our ring-fence of thorns, and stole a cloth from off one of my men while he was sleeping.

To Kariwami's, 26th: We set down Sŭwarora, after this very polite message, 'a regular trump', and walked up the hill of N'yakasenyé with considerable mirth, singing his praises; but we no sooner planted ourselves on the summit than we sang a very different tune. We were ordered to stop by a huge body of men, and to pay toll.

Sŭwarora, on second thoughts, had changed his mind, or else he had been overruled by two of his officers – Kariwami, who lived here, and Virembo, who lived two stages back, but were then with their chief. There was no help for it, so I ordered the camp to be formed, and sent Nasib and the mace-bearers at once off to the palace to express to his highness how insulted I felt as his guest, being stopped in this manner, even when I had his Kaquenzingiriri with me as his authority that I was invited there as a guest I was not a merchant who carried merchandise, but a prince like himself, come on a friendly mission to see him and Rŭmanika. I was waiting at night for the return of the messengers, and sitting out with my sextant observing the stars, to fix my position, when some daring thieves, in the dark bushes close by, accosted two of the women of the camp, pretending a desire to know what I was doing. They were no sooner told by the unsuspecting women, than they whipped off their clothes and ran away with them, allowing their victims to pass me in a state of absolute nudity. I could stand this thieving no longer. My goats and other things had been taken away without causing me much distress of mind, but now, after this shocking event I ordered my men to shoot at any thieves that came near them.

Halt, 27th and 28th: This night one was shot, without any mistake about it; for the next morning we tracked him by his blood, and afterwards heard he had died of his wound The Wasŭi elders, contrary to my expectation, then came and congratulated us on our success. They thought us most wonderful men, and possessed of supernatural powers; for the thief in question was a magician, who until now was thought to be invulnerable. Indeed, they said Arabs with enormous caravans had often been plundered by these people; but though they had so many more guns than ourselves, they never succeeded in killing one.

Nasib then returned to inform us that the king had heard our complaint, and was sorry for it, but said he could not interfere with the rights of his officers. He did not wish himself to take anything from us, and hoped we would còme on to him as soon as we had satisfied his officers with the trifle they wanted. Virembo then sent us some pombé by his officers, and begged us to have patience, for he was then fleecing Masŭdi at the encamping-ground near the palace. This place was alive with thieves. During the day they lured my men into their huts by inviting them to dinner; but when they got them they stripped them stark-naked and let them go again; whilst at night they stoned our camp. After this, one more was shot dead and two others wounded.

I knew that Sŭwarora's message was all humbug, and that his officers merely kept about one per cent of what they took from travellers, paying the balance into the royal coffers. Thinking I was now well in for a good fleecing myself, I sent Bombay off to Masŭdi's camp, to tell Insangéz, who was travelling with him on a mission of his master's, old Mŭsa's son, that I would reward him handsomely if he would, on arrival at Karagŭé, get Rŭmanika to send us his mace here in the same way as Sŭwarora had done to help us out of Bogŭé as he knew Mŭsa at one time said he would go with us to Karagŭé in person. When Bombay was gone, Virembo then deputed Kariwami to take the hongo for both at once, mildly requiring 40 wires, 80 cloths, and 400 necklaces of *every* kind of bead we possessed. This was, indeed, too much of a joke. I complained of all the losses I had suffered, and begged for mercy; but all he said, after waiting the whole day, was, 'Do not stick at trifles; for, after settling with us, you will have to give as much more to Vikora, who lives down below.'

Halt, 29th: Next morning, as I said I could not by any means pay such an exorbitant tax as was demanded, Kariwami begged me to make an offer, which I did by sending him four wires. These, of course, were rejected with scorn; so, in addition, I sent an old box. That, too, was thrown back on me, as nothing short of 20 wires, 40 cloths, and 200 necklaces of all sorts of beads, would satisfy him; and this I ought to be contented to pay, as he had been so moderate because I was the king's guest, and had been so reduced by robbery. I now sent six wires more, and said this was the last I could give – they were worth so many goats to me – and now, by giving them away, I should have to live on grain like a poor man, though I was a prince in my own country, just like Sŭwarora. Surely Sŭwarora could not permit this if he knew it; and if they would not suffice, I should have to stop here until called again by Sŭwarora. The ruffian, on hearing this, allowed the wires to lie in his hut, and said he was going away, but hoped, when he returned, I should have, as I had got no cloths, 20 wires, and 1000 necklaces of extra length, strung and all ready for him.

Just then Bombay returned flushed with the excitement of a great success. He had been in Masŭdi's camp, and had delivered my message to Insangéz. Masŭdi, he said, had been there a fortnight unable to settle his hongo, for the great Mkama had not deigned to see him, though the Arab had been daily to his palace requesting an interview. 'Well,' I said, 'that is all very interesting, but what next? – will the big king see us?' 'O no; by the very best good fortune in the world, on going into the palace I saw Sŭwarora, and spoke to him at once; but he was so tremendously drunk, he could not understand me.' 'What luck was there in that?' I asked. On which Bombay said, 'Oh, everybody in the place congratulated me on my success in having obtained an interview with that great monarch the very first day, when Arabs had seldom that privilege under one full month of squatting; even Masŭdi had not yet seen him.' To which Nasib also added, 'Ah, yes – indeed it is so – a monstrous success; there is great ceremony as well as business at these courts; you will better see what I mean when you get to Uganda. These Wahŭma kings are not like those you ever saw in Unyamŭézi or anywhere else; they have officers and soldiers like Said Majid, the Sultan at Zanzibar.' 'Well,' said I to Bombay, 'what was Sŭwarora like?' 'Oh, he is a very fine man – just as tall, and in the face very like Grant; in fact, if Grant were black you would not know the difference.' 'And were his officers drunk too?' 'O yes, they were all drunk together; men were bringing in pombé all day.' 'And did you get drunk?' 'O yes,' said Bombay, grinning, and showing his whole row of sharp-pointed teeth, 'they *would* make me drink; and then they showed me the place they assigned for your camp when you come over there. It was not in the palace, but outside, without a tree near it; anything but a nice-looking residence.' I then sent Bombay to work at the hongo business; but, after haggling till night with Kariwami, he was told he must bring fourteen brass wires, two cloths, and five mukhnai of kanyéra, or white porcelain beads – which, reduced, amounted to three hundred necklaces; else he said I might stop there for a month.

Halt, 30th: At last I settled this confounded hongo, by paying seven additional wires in lieu of the cloth; and, delighted at the termination of this tedious affair, I ordered a march. Like magic, however, Vikora turned up, and said we must wait until he was settled with. His rank was the same as the others, and one bead less than I had given them he would not take. I fought all the day out, but the next morning, as he deputed his officers to take nine wires, these were given, and then we went on with the journey.

To Uthungŭ, 31st: Tripping along over the hill, we descended to a deep miry watercourse, full of bulrushes, then over another hill, from the heights of which we saw Sŭwarora's palace, lying down in the Uthungŭ valley, behind which again rose another hill of sandstone, faced on the top with a dyke of white quartz. The scene was very striking, for the palace enclosures, of great extent, were well laid out to give effect. Three circles of milk bush, one within the other, formed the boma, or ring-fence. The chief's hut (I do not think him worthy the name of king, since the kingdom is divided in two) was three times as large as any of the others, and stood by itself at the farther end; whilst the smaller huts, containing his officers and domestics, were arranged in little groups within the circle, at certain distances apart from one another, sufficient to allow of their stalling their cattle at night.

On descending into the Uthungŭ valley, Grant, who was preceding the men, found Makinga opposed to the progress of the caravan until his dues were paid. He was a stranger like ourselves, and was consequently treated with scorn, until he tried to maintain what he called his right, by pulling the loads off my men's shoulders, whereupon Grant cowed him into submission, and all went on again – not to the palace, as we had supposed, but, by the direction of the mace-bearers, to the huts of Sŭwarora's commander-in-chief, two miles from the palace; and here we found Masŭdi's camp also. We had no sooner formed camp for ourselves and arranged all our loads, than the eternal Vikora, whom I thought we had settled with before we started, made a claim for some more wire, cloth, and beads, as he had not received as much as Kariwami and Virembo. Of course I would not listen to this, as I had paid what his men asked for, and that was enough for me. Just then Masŭdi, with the other Arabs who were travelling with him, came over to pay us a visit, and inquire what we thought of the Usŭi taxes. He had just concluded his hongo to Sŭwarora by paying 80 wires, 120 yards of cloth, and 130 lb of beads, whilst he had also paid to every officer from 20 to 40 wires, as well as cloths and beads. On hearing of my transactions, he gave it as his opinion that I had got off surprisingly well.

Next morning (1st) Masŭdi and his party started for Karagŭé. They had been more than a year between this and Kazé, trying all the time to get along. Provisions here were abundant – hawked about by the people, who wore a very neat skin kilt strapped round the waist, but otherwise were decorated like the Wanyamŭezi. It was difficult to say who were of true breed here, for the intercourse of the natives with the Wahŭma and the Wanyamŭézi produced a great variety of facial features amongst the people. Nowhere did I ever see so many men and women with hazel eyes as at this place.

In the evening, an Uganda man, by name N'yamgundŭ, came to pay his respects to us. He was dressed in a large skin wrapper, made up of a number of very small antelope skins: it was as soft as kid, and just as well sewn as our gloves. To our surprise the manners of the man were quite in keeping with his becoming dress. I was enchanted with his appearance, and so were my men, though no one could speak to him but Nasib, who told us he knew him before. He was the brother of the dowager queen of Uganda, and, along with a proper body of officers, he had been sent by Mŭsa, the present king of Uganda, to demand the daughter of Sŭwarora, as reports had reached his king that she was surprisingly beautiful. They had been here more than a year, during which time this beautiful virgin had died; and now Sŭwarora, fearful of the great king's wrath, consequent on his procrastinations, was endeavouring to make amends for it, by sending, instead of his daughter, a suitable tribute in wires. I thought it not wonderful that we should be fleeced.

Next day (2d) Sirhid paid us a visit, and said he was the first man in the state. He certainly was a nice-looking young man, with a good deal of the Wahŭma blood in him. Flashily dressed in coloured cloths and a turban, he sat down in one of our chairs as if he had been accustomed to such a seat all his life, and spoke with great suavity. I explained our difficulties as those of great men in misfortune; and, after listening to our tale, he said he would tell Sŭwarora of the way we had been plundered, and impress upon him to deal lightly with us. I said I had brought with me a few articles of European manufacture for Sŭwarora, which I hoped would he accepted if I presented them, for they were such things as only great men like his chief ever possessed. One was a five-barrelled pistol, another a large block-tin box, and so forth; but after looking at them, and seeing the pistol fired, he said: 'No; you must not show these things at first, or the Mkama might get frightened, thinking them magic. I might lose my head for presuming to offer them, and then there is no knowing what might happen afterwards.' 'Then can I not see him at once and pay my respects, for I have come a great way to obtain that pleasure?' 'No,' said Sirhid, 'I will see him first; for he is not a man like myself, but requires to be well assured before he sees anybody.' 'Then why did he invite me here?' 'He heard that Makaka, and afterwards Lŭmérési, had stopped your progress; and as he wished to see what you were like, he ordered me to send some men to you, which, as you know, I did twice. He wishes to see you, but does not like doing things in a hurry. Superstition, you know, preys on these men's minds who have not seen the world like you and myself.' Sirhid then said he would ask Sŭwarora to grant us an interview as soon as possible; then, whilst leaving, he begged for the iron chair he had sat upon; but hearing we did not know how to sit on the ground, and therefore could not spare it, he withdrew without any more words about it.

Virembo then said (3d) he must have some more wire and beads, as his proxy Kariwami had been satisfied with too little. I drove him off in a huff, but he soon came back again with half the hongo I had paid to Kariwami, and said he must have some cloths, or he would not have anything. As fortune decreed it, just then Sirhid dropped in, and stopped his importunity for the time by saying that if we had possessed cloths his men must have known it, for they had been travelling with us. No sooner, however, did Virembo turn tail than the Sirhid gave as a broad hint that he usually received a trifle from the Arabs before he made an attempt at arranging the hongo with Sŭwarora. Any trifle would do, but he preferred cloth.

This was rather perplexing. Sirhid knew very well that I had a small reserve of pretty cloths, though all the common ones had been expended; so, to keep in good terms with him who was to be our intercessor, I said I would give him the last I had got, if he would not tell Sŭwarora or any one else what I had done. Of course he was quite ready to undertake the condition, so I gave him two pretty cloths, and he in return gave me two goats. But when this little business had been transacted, to my surprise he said: 'I have orders from Sŭwarora to be absent five days to doctor a sick relation of his, for there is no man in the country so skilled in medicines as myself; but whilst I am gone I will leave Karambŭlé, my brother, to officiate in my stead about taking your hongo; but the work will not commence until to-morrow, for I must see Sŭwarora on the subject myself first'

Irungti, a very fine-looking man of Uganda, now called on me and begged for beads. He said his king had heard of our approach, and was most anxious to see us. Hearing this, I begged him to wait here until my hongo was paid, that we might travel on to Uganda together. He said, No, he could not wait, for he had been detained here a whole year already; but, if I liked, he would leave some of his children behind with me, as their presence would intimidate Sŭwarora, and incite him to let us off quickly.

I then begged him to convey a Colt's six-chamber revolving rifle to his king, Mtésa, as an earnest that I was a prince most desirous of seeing him. No one, I said, but myself could tell what dangers and difficulties I had encountered to come this far for the purpose, and all was owing to his great fame, as the king of kings, having reached me even as far off as Zanzibar. The ambassador would not take the rifle, lest his master, who had never seen such a wonderful weapon before, should think he had brought him a malign charm, and he would be in danger of losing his head. I then tried to prevail on him to take a knife and some other pretty things, but he feared them all; so, as a last chance – for I wished to send some token, by way of card or letter, for announcing my approach and securing the road – I gave him a red sixpenny pocket-handkerchief, which he accepted; and he then told me he was surprised I had come all this way round to Uganda, when the road by the Masai country was so much shorter. He told me how, shortly after the late king of Uganda, Sunna, died, and before Mtésa had been selected by the officers of the country to be their king, an Arab caravan came across the Masai as far as Usoga, and begged for permission to enter Uganda; but as the country was disturbed by the elections, the officers of the state advised the Arabs to wait, or come again when the king was elected. I told him I had heard of this before, but also heard that those Arabs had met with great disasters, owing to the turbulence of the Masai. To which he replied: 'That is true; there were great difficulties in those times, but now the Masai country was in better order; and as Mtésa was most anxious to open that line, he would give me as many men as I liked if I wished to go home that way.'

This was pleasant information, but not quite new, for the Arabs had told me Mtésa was so anxious to open that route, he had frequently offered to aid them in it himself. Still it was most gratifying to myself, as I had written to the Geographical Society, on leaving Bogŭé, that if I found Petherick in Uganda, or on the northern end of the N'yanza, so that the Nile question was settled, I would endeavour to reach Zanzibar *via* the Masai country. In former days, I knew, the kings of Uganda were in the habit of sending men to Karagŭé when they heard that Arabs wished to visit them – even as many as two hundred at a time – to carry their kit; so I now begged Irungti to tell Mtésa that I should want at least sixty men; and then, on his promising he would be my commissioner, I gave him the beads he had begged for himself.

4th to 6th. – Karambŭlé now told us to string our beads on the fibre of the Mwalé tree, which was sold here by the Wasŭi, as he intended to live in the palace for a couple of days, arranging with Sŭwarora what tax we should have to pay, after which he would come and take it from us; but we must mind and be ready, for whatever Sŭwarora said, it must be done instantly. There was no such thing as haggling with him; you must pay and be off at once, failing which, you might be detained a whole month before there would be an opportunity to speak on the subject again. Beads were then served out to all my men to be strung, a certain quantity to every khambi or mess, and our work was progressing; but next day we heard that Karambŭlé was sick, or feigning to be so, and therefore had never gone to the palace at all. On the 6th, provoked at last by the shameful manner in which we were treated, I sent word to him to say, if he did not go at once I would go myself, and force my way in with my guns, for I could not submit to being treated like a slave, stuck out here in the jungle with nothing to do but shoot for specimens, or make collections of rocks, etc. This brought on another row; for he said both Virembo and Vikora had returned their hongos, and until their tongues were quieted he could not speak to Sŭwarora.

To expedite matters (7th), as our daily consumption in camp was a tax of itself, I gave these tormenting creatures one wire, one pretty cloth, and five hundred necklaces of white beads, which were no sooner accepted than Karambŭlé, in the same way as Sirhid had done, said it would be greatly to my advantage if I gave him something worth having before he saw the Mkama. Only too glad to begin work, I gave him a red blanket, called joho, and five strings of mzizima beads, which were equal to fifty of the common white.

Ten days now had elapsed since we came here, still nothing was done (10th), as Karambŭlé said, because Sŭwarora had been so fully occupied collecting an army to punish an officer who had refused to pay his taxes, had ignored his authority, and had set himself up as king of the district he was appointed to superintend. After this, at midnight, Karambŭlé, in an excited manner, said he had seen Sŭwarora, and it then was appointed that, not he, but Virembo should take the royal hongo, as well as the Wahinda, or princes' shares, the next morning – after which, we might go as fast as we liked, for Sŭwarora was so fully occupied with his army, he could not see us this time. Before, however, the hongo could be paid, I must give the Sirhid and himself twenty brass wires, three joho, three barsati, twenty strings of mzizima, and one thousand strings of white beads. They were given.

13th. – In the evening Virembo and Karambŭlé came to receive the hongo for their chief, demanding 60 wires, 160 yards merikani, 300 strings of mzizima, and 5000 strings of white beads; but they allowed themselves to be beaten down to 50 wires, 20 pretty cloths, 100 strings mzizima, and 4000 kŭtŭamnazi, or cocoa-nut-leaf coloured beads, my white being all done. It was too late, however, to count all the things out, so they came the next day and took them. They then said we might go as soon as we had settled with the Wahinda or Wanawami (the king's children), for Sŭwarora could not see us this time, as he was so engaged with his army; but he hoped to see us and pay us more respect when we returned from Uganda, little thinking I had sworn in my mind never to see him, or return that way again. I said to those men, I thought he was ashamed to see us, as he had robbed us so after inviting us into the country, else he was too superstitious, for he ought at least to have given us a place in his palace. They both rebutted the insinuation; and, to change the subject, commenced levying the remaining dues to the princes, which ended by my giving thirty-four wires and six pretty cloths in a lump.

Early in the morning we were on foot again, only too thankful to have got off so cheaply. Then men were appointed as guides and protectors, to look after us as far as the border. What an honour! We had come into the country drawn there by a combination of pride and avarice, and now we were leaving it in hot haste under the guidance of an escort of officers, who were in reality appointed to watch us as dangerous wizards and objects of terror. It was all the same to us, as we now only thought of the prospect of relief before us, and laughed at what we had gone through.

Rising out of the Uthungŭ valley, we walked over rolling ground, drained in the dips by miry rush rivulets. The population was thinly scattered in small groups of grass huts, where the scrub jungle had been cleared away. On the road we passed cairns, to which every passer-by contributed a stone. Of the origin of the cairns I could not gain any information, though it struck me as curious I should find them in the first country we had entered governed by the Wahŭma, as I formerly saw the same thing in the Somali country, which doubtless, in earlier days, was governed by a branch of the Abyssinians. Arrived at our camping, we were immediately pounced upon by a deputation of officers, who said they had been sent by Semamba, the officer of this district. He lived ten miles from the road; but hearing of our approach, he had sent these men to take his dues. At first I objected to pay, lest he should afterwards treat me as Virembo had done; but I gave way in the end, and paid nine wires, two chintz and two bindéra cloths, as the guides said they would stand my security against any further molestation.

To Vihembé, 16th: Rattling on again as merry as larks, over the same red sandstone formation, we entered a fine forest, and trended on through it at a stiff pace until we arrived at the head of a deep valley called Lohŭgati, which was so beautiful we instinctively pulled up to admire it. Deep down its well-wooded side below us was a stream, of most inviting aspect for a trout-fisher, flowing towards the N'yanza. Just beyond it the valley was clothed with fine trees and luxuriant vegetation of all descriptions, amongst which was conspicuous the pretty pandana palm, and rich gardens of plantains; whilst thistles of extraordinary size and wild indigo were the more common weeds. The land beyond that again rolled back in high undulations, over which, in the far distance, we could see a line of cones, red and bare on their tops, guttered down with white streaks, looking for all the world like recent volcanoes; and in the far background, rising higher than all, were the rich grassy hills of Karagŭé and Kishakka.

On resuming our march, a bird, called khongota, flew across our path; seeing which, old Nasib, beaming with joy, in his superstitious belief cried out with delight, 'Ah, look at that good omen! – now our journey will be sure to be prosperous.' After fording the stream, we sat down to rest, and were visited by all the inhabitants, who were more naked than any people we had yet seen. All the maidens, even at the age of puberty, did not hesitate to stand boldly in front of us – for evil thoughts were not in their minds. From this we rose over a stony hill to the settlement of Vihembé, which, being the last on the Usŭi frontier, induced me to give our guides three wires each, and four yards of bindéra, which Nasib said was their proper fee. Here Bombay's would-be, but disappointed, father-in-law sent after us to say that he required a hongo; Sŭwarora had never given his sanction to our quitting his country; his hongo even was not settled. He wished, moreover, particularly to see us; and if we did not return in a friendly manner, an array would arrest our march immediately.

CHAPTER VIII

Karagŭé

To Vigŭra, 17th: This was a day of relief and happiness. A load was removed from us in seeing the Wasŭi protectors depart, with the truly cheering information that we now had nothing but wild animals to contend with before reaching Karagŭé. This land is 'neutral' by which is meant that it is untenanted by human beings; and we might now hope to bid adieu for a time to the scourging system of taxation to which we had been subjected.

Gradually descending from the spur which separates the Lohŭgati valley from the bed of the Lŭérŭ lo Urigi, or Lake of Urigi, the track led us first through a meadow of much pleasing beauty, and then through a passage between the 'saddle-back' domes we had seen from the heights above Lohŭgati, where a new geological formation especially attracted my notice. From the green slopes of the hills, set up at a slant, as if the central line of pressure on the dome top had weighed on the inside plates, protruded soft slabs of argillaceous sandstone, whose laminae presented a beef-sandwich appearance, puce or purple alternating with creamy-white. Quartz and other igneous rocks were also scattered about, lying like superficial accumulations in the dips at the foot of the hills, and red sandstone conglomerates clearly indicated the presence of iron. The soil itself looked rich and red, not unlike our own fine county of Devon.

On arriving in camp we pitched under some trees, and at once were greeted by an officer sent by Rŭmanika to help us out of Usŭi. This was Kachŭchŭ, an old friend of Nasib's, who no sooner saw him than, learning with delight, he said to us, 'Now, was I not right when I told you the birds flying about on Lohŭgati hill were a good omen? Look here what this man says: Rŭmanika has ordered him to bring you on to his palace at once, and wherever you stop a day, the village officers are instructed to supply you with food at the king's expense, for there are no taxes gathered from strangers in the kingdom of Karagŭé. Presents may be exchanged, but the name of tax is ignored.' Grant here shot a rhinoceros, wilich came well into play to mix with the day's flour we had carried on from Vihembé.

To First Urigi, 18th: Deluded yesterday by the sight of the broad waters of the Lŭérŭ lo Urigi, espied in the distance from the top of a hill, into the belief that we were in view of the N'yanza itself, we walked triumphantly along, thinking how well the Arabs at Kazé had described this to be a creek of the great lake; but on arrival in camp we heard from the village officer that we had been misinformed, and that it was a detached lake, but connected with the Victoria N'yanza by a passage in the hills and the Kitangŭlé river. Formerly, he said, the Urigi valley was covered with water, extending up to Uhha, when all the low lands we had crossed from Usŭi had to be ferried, and the saddle-back hills were a mere chain of islands in the water. But the country had dried up, and the lake of Urigi became a small swamp. He further informed us, that even in the late king Dagara's time it was a large sheet of water; but the instant he ceased to exist, the lake shrank to what we now saw.

Our day's march had been novel and very amusing. The hilly country surrounding us, together with the valley, brought back to recollection many happy days I had once spent with the Tartars in the Thibetian valley of the Indus – only this was more picturesque; for though both countries are wild, and very thinly inhabited, this was greened over with grass, and dotted here and there on the higher slopes with thick bush of acacias, the haunts of rhinoceros, both white and black; whilst in the flat of the valley, herds of hartebeests and fine cattle roamed about like the kiyang and tame yâk of Thibet. Then, to enhance all these pleasures, so different from our former experiences, we were treated like guests by the chief of the place, who, obeying the orders of his king, Rŭmanika, brought me presents, as soon as we arrived, of sheep, fowls, and sweet potatoes, and was very thankful for a few yards of red blanketing as a return, without begging for more.

To Second Urigi, 19th: The farther we went in this country the better we liked it, as the people were all kept in good order; and the village chiefs were so civil, that we could do as we liked. After following down the left side of the valley and entering the village, the customary presents and returns were made. Wishing then to obtain a better view of the country, I strolled over the nearest hills, and found the less exposed slopes well covered with trees. Small antelopes occasionally sprang up from the grass. I shot a florikan for the pot; and as I had never before seen white rhinoceros, killed one now; though, as no one would eat him, I felt sorry rather than otherwise for what I had done. When I returned in the evening, small boys brought me sparrows for sale; and then I remembered the stories I had heard from Mŭsa Mzŭri – that in the whole of Karagŭé these small birds were so numerous, the people, to save themselves from starvation, were obliged to grow a bitter corn which the birds disliked; and so I found it. At night, whilst observing for latitude, I was struck by surprise to see a long noisy procession pass by where I sat, led by some men who carried on their shoulders a woman covered up in a blackened skin. On inquiry, however, I heard she was being taken to the hut of her espoused, where, 'bundling fashion,' she would be put in bed; but it was only with virgins they took so much trouble.

A strange but characteristic story now reached my ears. Masŭdi, the merchant who took up Insangéz, had been trying his best to deter Rŭmanika from allowing us to enter his country, by saying we were addicted to sorcery; and had it not been for Insangéz's remonstrances, who said we were sent up by Mŭsa, our fate would have been doubtful. Rŭmanika, it appeared, as I always had heard, considered old Musa his saviour, for having eight years before quelled a rebellion, when his younger brother, Rogéro, aspired to the throne; whilst Mŭsa's honour and honesty were quite unimpeachable. But more of this hereafter.

To Khonzé, 20th: Khonzé, the next place, lying in the bending concave of this swamp lake, and facing Hangiro, was commanded by a fine elderly man called Mŭzégi, who was chief officer during Dagara's time. He told me with the greatest possible gravity, that he remembered well the time when a boat could have gone from this to Vigŭra; as also when fish and crocodiles came up from the Kitangŭlé; but the old king no sooner died than the waters dried up; which showed as plainly as words could tell, that the king had designed it, to make men remember him with sorrow in all future ages. Our presents after this having been exchanged, the good old man, at my desire, explained the position of all the surrounding countries, in his own peculiar manner; by laying a long stick on the ground pointing due north and south, to which he attached shorter ones pointing to the centre of each distant country. He thus assisted me in the protractions of the map, to the countries which lie east and west of the route.

To Uthenga, 22d: Rising out of the bed of the Urigi, we passed over a low spur, of beef-sandwich clay sandstones, and descended into the close, rich valley of Uthenga, bound in by steep hills hanging over us more than a thousand feet high, as prettily clothed as the mountains of Scotland; whilst in the valley there were not only magnificent trees of extraordinary height, but also a surprising amount of the richest cultivation, amongst which the banana may be said to prevail. Notwithstanding this apparent richness in the land, the Wanyambo, living in their small squalid huts, seem poor. The tobacco they smoke is imported from the coffee-growing country of Uhaiya. After arrival in the village, who should we see but the Uganda officer, Irtingti! The scoundrel, instead of going on to Uganda as he had promised to do, conveying my present to Mtdsa, had stopped here plundering the Wanyambo, and getting drunk on their pombé, called, in their language, *marwa* – a delicious kind of wine made from the banana. He, of course, begged for more beads; but, not able to trick me again, set his drummers and fifers at work, in hopes that he would get over our feelings in that way.

To Rozoka, 23d: Henceforth, as we marched, Irŭngŭ's drummers and fifers kept us alive on the way. This we heard was a privilege that Uganda Wakungŭ enjoyed both at home and abroad, although in all other countries the sound of the drum is considered a notice of war, unless where it happens to accompany a dance or festival. Leaving the valley of Uthenga, we rose over the spur of N'yamwara, where we found we had attained the delightful altitude of 5000 odd feet. Oh, how we enjoyed it I every one feeling so happy at the prospect of meeting so soon the good king Rŭnanika. Tripping down the greensward, we now worked our way to the Rozoka valley, and pitched our tents in the village.

Kachŭchŭ here told us he had orders to precede us, and prepare Rŭmanika for our coming, as his king wished to know what place we would prefer to live at – the Arab depôt at Kufro, on the direct line to Uganda, in his palace with himself, or outside his enclosures. Such politeness rather took us aback; so, giving our friend a coil of copper wire to keep him in good spirits, I said all our pleasure rested in seeing the king; whatever honours he liked to confer on us we should take with good grace, but one thing he must understand, we came not to trade, but to see him and great kings, and therefore the Arabs had no relations with us. This little point settled, off started Kachŭchŭ in his usual merry manner, whilst I took a look at the hills, to see their geological formation, and found them much as before, based on streaky clay sandstones, with the slight addition of pure blue shales, and above sections of quartzose sandstone lying in flags, as well as other metamorphic and igneous rocks scattered about.

To Katawanga, 24th: Moving on the next morning over hill and dale, we came to the junction of two roads, where Irungŭ, with his drummers, fifers, and amazon followers, took one way to Kufro, followed by the men carrying Sŭwarora's hongo, and we led off on the other, directed to the palace. The hill-tops in many places were breasted with dykes of pure white quartz, just as we had seen in Usŭi, only that here their direction tended more to the north. It was most curious to contemplate, seeing that the chief substance of the hills was a pure blue, or otherwise streaky clay sandstone, which must have been formed when the land was low, but has now been elevated, making these hills the axis of the centre of the continent, and therefore probably the oldest of all.

When within a few miles of the palace we were ordered to stop and wait for Kachŭchŭ's return; but we no sooner put up in a plantain grove, where pombé was brewing, and our men were all taking a suck at it, than the worthy arrived to call us on the same instant, as the king was most anxious to see us. The love of good beer of course made our men all too tired to march again; so I sent off Bombay with Nasib to make our excuses, and in the evening found them returning with a huge pot of pombé and some royal tobacco, which Rŭmanika sent with a notice that he intended it exclusively for our own use, for though there was abundance for my men, there was nothing so good as what came from the palace; the royal tobacco was as sweet and strong as honey-dew, and the beer so strong it required a strong man to drink it.

To Weranhanjé, 25th: After breakfast next morning, we crossed the hill-spur called Weranhanjé, the grassy tops of which were 5500 feet above the sea. Descending a little, we came suddenly in view of what appeared to us a rich clump of trees, in S. lat. 1° 42' 42', and E. long. 31° 1' 49'; and, 500 feet below it, we saw a beautiful sheet of water lying snugly within the folds of the hills. We were not altogether unprepared for it, as Mŭsa of old had described it, and Bombay, on his return yesterday, told us he had seen a great pond. The clump, indeed, was the palace enclosure. As to the lake, for want of a native name, I christened it the Little Windermere, because Grant thought it so like our own English lake of that name. It was one of many others which, like that of Urigi, drains the moisture of the overhanging hills, and gets drained into the Victoria N'yanza through the Kitangŭlé river.

To do royal honours to the king of this charming land, I ordered my men to put down their loads and fire a volley. This was no sooner done than, as we went to the palace gate, we received an invitation to come in at once, for the king wished to see us before attending to anything else. Now, leaving our traps outside, both Grant and myself, attended by Bombay and a few of the seniors of my Wangŭana, entered the vestibule, and, walking through extensive enclosures studded with huts of kingly dimensions, were escorted to a pent-roofed baraza, which the Arabs had built as a sort of government office, where the king might conduct his state affairs.

Here, as we entered, we saw sitting cross-legged on the ground Rŭmanika the king, and his brother Nuanaji, both of them men of noble appearance and size. The king was plainly dressed in an Arab's black choga, and wore, for ornament, dress stockings of rich-coloured beads, and neatly-worked wristlets of copper. Nuanaji, being a doctor of very high pretensions, in addition to a check cloth wrapped round him, was covered with charms. At their sides lay huge pipes of black clay. In their rear, squatting quiet as mice, were all the king's sons, some six or seven lads, who wore leather middle-coverings, and little dream-charms tied under their chins. The first greetings of the king, delivered in good Kisŭahili, were warm and affecting, and in an instant we both felt and saw we were in the company of men who were as unlike as they could be to the common order of the natives of the surrounding districts. They had fine oval faces, large eyes, and high noses, denoting the best blood of Abyssinia. Having shaken hands in true English style, which is the peculiar custom of the men of this country, the ever-smiling Rŭmanika begged us to be seated on the ground opposite to him, and at once wished to know what we thought of Karagŭé, for it had struck him his mountains were the finest in the world; and the lake, too, did we not admire it? Then laughing, he inquired – for he knew all the story – what we thought of Sŭwarora, and the reception we had met with in Usŭi. When this was explained to him, I showed him that it was for the interest of his own kingdom to keep a check on Sŭwarora, whose exorbitant taxations prevented the Arabs from coming to see him and bringing things from all parts of the world. He made inquiries for the purpose of knowing how we found our way all over the world; for on the former expedition a letter had come to him for Mŭsa, who no sooner read it than he said I had called him and he must leave, as I was bound for Ujiji.

This of course led to a long story, describing the world, the proportions of land and water, and the power of ships, which conveyed even elephants and rhinoceros – in fact, all the animals in the world – to fill our menageries at home, – etc etc; as well as the strange announcement that we lived to the northward, and had only come this way because his friend Mŭsa had assured me without doubt that he would give us the road on through Uganda. Time flew like magic, the king's mind was so quick and inquiring; but as the day was wasting away, he generously gave us our option to choose a place for our residence in or out of his palace, and allowed us time to select one. We found the view overlooking the lake to be so charming, that we preferred camping outside, and set our men at once to work cutting sticks and long grass to erect themselves sheds.

One of the young princes – for the king ordered them all to be constantly in attendance on us – happening to see me sit on an iron chair, rushed back to his father and told him about it. This set all the royals in the palace in a state of high wonder, and ended by my getting a summons to show off the white man sitting on his throne; for of course I could only be, as all of them called me, a king of great dignity, to indulge in such state. Rather reluctantly I did as

I was bid, and allowed myself once more to be dragged into court Rŭmanika, as gentle as ever, then burst into a fresh fit of merriment, and after making sundry enlightened remarks of inquiry, which of course were responded to with the greatest satisfaction, finished off by saying, with a very expressive shake of the head, 'Oh, these Wazungŭ, these Wazungŭ! They know and do everything.'

I then put in a word for myself. Since we had entered Karagŭé we never could get one drop of milk either for love or for money, and I wished to know what motive the Wahŭma had for withholding it. We had heard they held superstitious dreads; that any one who ate the flesh of pigs, fish, or fowls, or the bean called maharagŭé, if he tasted the products of their cows, would destroy their cattle – and I hoped he did not labour under any such absurd delusions. To which he replied, It was only the poor who thought so; and as he now saw we were in want, he would set apart one of his cows expressly for our use. On bidding adieu, the usual formalities of handshaking were gone through; and on entering camp, I found the good thoughtful king had sent us some more of his excellent beer.

The Wangŭana were now all in the highest of good-humour; for time after time goats and fowls were brought into camp by the officers of the king, who had received orders from all parts of the country to bring in supplies for his guests; and this kind of treatment went on for a month, though it did not diminish my daily expenditure of beads, as grain and plantains were not enough thought of. The cold winds, however, made the coast-men all shiver, and suspect, in their ignorance, we must be drawing close to England, the only cold place they had heard of.

26th. – Hearing it would be considered indecent haste to present my tributary offering at once, I paid my morning's visit, only taking my revolving-pistol, as I knew Rŭmanika had expressed a strong wish to see it. The impression it made was surprising – he had never seen such a thing in his life; so, in return for his great generosity, as well as to show I placed no value on property, not being a merchant, I begged him to accept it. We then adjourned to his private hut, which rather surprised me by the neatness with which it was kept. The roof was supported by numerous clean poles, to which he had fastened a large assortment of spears – brass-headed with iron handles, and iron-headed with wooden ones – of excellent workmanship. A large standing-screen, of fine straw-plait work, in elegant devices, partitioned off one part of the room; and on the opposite side, as mere ornaments, were placed a number of brass grapnels and small models of cows, made in iron for his amusement by the Arabs at Kufro. A little later in the day, as soon as we had done breakfast, both Rŭmanika and Nuanaji came over to pay us a visit; for they thought, as we could find our way all over the world, so we should not find much difficulty in prescribing some magic charms to kill his brother, Rogéro, who lived on a hill overlooking the Kitangŭlé. Seating them both on our chairs, which amused them intensely, I asked Rŭmanika, although I had heard before the whole facts of the case, what motives now induced him to wish the committal of such a terrible act, and brought out the whole story afresh.

Before their old father Dagara died, he had unwittingly said to the mother of Rogéro, although he was the youngest born, what a fine king he would make; and the mother, in consequence, tutored her son to expect the command of the country, although the law of the land in the royal family is the primogeniture system, extending, however, only to those sons who are born after the accession of the king to the throne.

As soon, therefore, as Dagara died, leaving the three sons alluded to, all by different mothers, a contest took place with the brothers, which, as Nuanaji held by Rŭmanika, ended in the two elder driving Rogéro away. It happened, however, that half the men of the country, either from fear or love, attached themselves to Rogéro. Feeling his power, he raised an army and attempted to fight for the crown, which it is generally admitted would have succeeded, had not Mŭsa, with unparalleled magnanimity, employed all the ivory merchandise at his command to engage the services of all the Arabs' slaves residing at Kufro, to bring muskets against him. Rogéro was thus frightened away; but he went swearing that he would carry out his intentions at some future date, when the Arabs had withdrawn from the country.

Magic charms, of course, we had none; but the king would not believe it, and, to wheedle some out of us, said they would not kill their brother even if they caught him – for fratricide was considered an unnatural crime in their country – but they would merely gouge out his eyes and set him at large again; for without the power of sight he could do them no harm.

I then recommended, as the best advice I could give him for the time being, to take some strong measures against Sŭwarora and the system of taxation carried on in Usŭi. These would have the effect of bringing men with superior knowledge into the country – for it was only through the power of knowledge that good government could be obtained. Sŭwaroa at present stopped eight-tenths of the ivory-merchants who might be inclined to trade here from coming into the country, by the foolish system of excessive taxation he had established. Next I told him, if he would give me one or two of his children, I would have them instructed in England; for I admired his race, and believed them to have sprung from our old friends the Abyssinians, whose king, Sahéla Sélassié, had received rich presents from our Queen. They were Christians like ourselves, and had the Wahŭma not lost their knowledge of God they would be so also.

A long theological and historical discussion ensued, which so pleased the king, that he said he would be delighted if I would take two of his sons to England, that they might bring him a knowledge of everything. Then turning again to the old point, his utter amazement that we should spend so much property in travelling, he wished to know what we did it for; when men had such means they would surely sit down and enjoy it. 'Oh no,' was the reply; 'we have had our fill of the luxuries of life; eating, drinking, or sleeping have no charms for us now; we are above trade, therefore require no profits, and seek for enjoyment the run of the world. To observe and admire the beauties of creation are worth much more than beads to us. But what led us this way we have told you before; it was to see your majesty in particular, and the great kings of Africa – and at the same time to open another road to the north, whereby the best manufactures of Europe would find their way to Karagüé, and you would get so many more guests.' In the highest good-humour the king said, 'As you have come to see me and see sights, I will order some boats and show you over the lake, with musicians to play before you, or anything else that you like.' Then, after looking over our pictures with intensest delight, and admiring our beds, boxes, and outfit in general, he left for the day.

27th. – Ever anxious to push on with the journey, as I felt every day's delay only tended to diminish my means – that is, my beads and copper wire – I instructed Bombay to take the under-mentioned articles to Rŭmanika as a small sample of the products of my country; to say I felt quite ashamed of their being so few and so poor, but I hoped he would forgive my shortcomings, as he knew I had been so often robbed on the way to him; and I trusted, in recollection of Mŭsa, he would give me leave to go on to Uganda, for every day's delay was consuming my supplies. Nuanaji, however, it was said, should get something; so, in addition to the king's present, I apportioned one out for him, and Bombay took both up to the palace. Everybody, I was pleased to hear, was surprised with both the quantity and quality of what I had been able to find for them; for, after the plundering in Ugogo, the immense consumption caused by such long delays on the road, the fearful prices I had had to pay for my porters' wages, the enormous taxes I had been forced to give both in Msalala and Uzinza, besides the constant thievings in camp, all of which was made public by the constantly-recurring tales of my men, nobody thought I had got anything left.

Rŭmanika, above all, was as delighted as if he had come in for a fortune, and sent to say the Raglan coat was a marvel, and the scarlet broadcloth the finest thing he had ever seen. Nobody but Mŭsa had ever given him such beautiful beads before, and none ever gave with such free liberality. Whatever I wanted I should have in return for it, as it was evident to him I had really done him a great honour in visiting him. Neither his father nor any of his forefathers had had such a great favour shown them. He was alarmed, he confessed, when he heard we were coming to visit him, thinking we might prove some fearful monsters that were not quite human, but now he was delighted beyond all measure with what he saw of us. A messenger should be sent at once to the king of Uganda to inform him of our intention to visit him, with his own favourable report of us. This was necessary according to the etiquette of the country. Without such a recommendation our progress would be stopped by the people, whilst with one word from him all would go straight; for was he not the gatekeeper, enjoying the full confidence of Uganda? A month, however, must elapse, as the distance to the palace of Uganda was great; but, in the mean time, he would give me leave to go about in his country to do and see what I liked, Nuanaji and his sons escorting me everywhere. Moreover, when the time came for my going on to Uganda, if I had not enough presents to give the king, he would fill up the complement from his own stores, and either go with me himself, or send Nuanaji to conduct me as far as the boundary of Uganda, in order that Rogéro might not molest us on the way. In the evening, Masŭdi, with Sangoro and several other merchants, came up from Kufro to pay us a visit of respect.

28th and 29th. – A gentle hint having come to us that the king's brother, Wazézérŭ, expected a trifle in virtue of his rank, I sent him a blanket and seventy-five blue egg-beads. These were accepted with the usual good grace of these people. The king then, ever attentive to our position as guests, sent his royal musicians to give us a tune. The men composing the band were a mixture of Waganda and Wanyambo, who played on reed instruments made telescope fashion, marking time by hand-drums. At first they marched up and down, playing tunes exactly like the regimental bands of the Turks, and then commenced dancing a species of 'hornpipe,' blowing furiously all the while. When dismissed with some beads, Nuanaji dropped in and invited me to accompany him out shooting on the slopes of the hills overlooking the lake. He had in attendance all the king's sons, as well as a large number of beaters, with three or four dogs. Tripping down the greensward of the hills together, these tall, athletic princes every now and then stopped to see who could shoot furthest, and I must say I never witnessed better feats in my life. With powerful six-feet-long bows they pulled their arrows' heads up to the wood, and made wonderful shots in the distance. They then placed me in position, and, arranging the field, drove the covers like men well accustomed to sport – indeed, it struck me they indulged too much in that pleasure, for we saw nothing but two or three montana and some diminutive antelopes, about the size of mouse deer, and so exceedingly shy that not one was bagged.

Returning home to the tents as the evening sky was illumined with the red glare of the sun, my attention was attracted by observing in the distance some bold skyscraping cones situated in the country Rŭanda, which at once brought back to recollection the ill-defined story I had heard from the Arabs of a wonderful hill always covered with clouds, on which snow or hail was constantly falling. This was a valuable discovery, for I found these hills to be the great turn-point of the Central African watershed. Without loss of time I set to work, and, gathering all the travellers I could in the country, protracted, from their descriptions, all the distant topographical features set down in the map, as far north as 3° of north latitude, as far east as 36°, and as far west as 26° of east longitude; only afterwards slightly corrected, as I was better able to connect and clear up some trifling but doubtful points.

Indeed, I was not only surprised at the amount of information about distant places I was enabled to get here from these men, but also at the correctness of their vast and varied knowledge, as I afterwards tested it by observation and the statements of others. I rely so far on the geographical information I thus received, that I would advise no one to doubt the accuracy of these protractions until ho has been on the spot to test them by actual inspection. About the size only of the minor lakes do I feel doubtful, more especially the Little Lŭta Nzigé, which on the former journey I heard was a salt lake, because salt was found on its shores and in one of its islands. Now, without going into any lengthy details, and giving Rŭmanika due credit for everything – for had he not ordered his men to give me every information that lay in their power, they would not have done so – I will merely say for the present that, whilst they conceived the Victoria N'yanza would take a whole month for a canoe to cross it, they thought the Little Lŭta Nzigé might be crossed in a week. The Mfŭmbiro cones in Rŭanda, which I believe reach 10,000 feet, are said to be the highest of the 'Mountains of the Moon.' At their base are both salt and copper mines, as well as hot springs. There are also hot springs in Mpororo, and one in Karagŭé near where Rogéro lived.

30th. – The important business of announcing our approach to Uganda was completed by Rŭmanika appointing Kachŭchŭ to go to king Mtésa as quickly as possible, to say we were coming to visit him. He was told that we were very great men, who only travelled to see great kings and great countries; and, as such, Rŭmanika trusted we should be received with courteous respect, and allowed to roam all over the country wherever we liked, he holding himself responsible for our actions for the time being. In the end, however, we were to be restored to him, as he considered himself our father, and therefore must see that no accident befell us.

To put the royal message in proper shape, I was now requested to send some trifle by way of a letter or visiting card; but, on taking out a Colt's revolving-rifle for the purpose, Rŭmanika advised me not to send it, as Mtésa might take fright, and, considering it a charm of evil quality, reject us as bad magicians, and close his gates on us. Three bits of cotton cloth were then selected as the best thing for the purpose; and, relying implicitly on the advice of Rŭmanika, who declared his only object was to further our views, I arranged accordingly, and off went Kachŭchŭ.

To keep my friend in good-humour, and show him how well the English can appreciate a kindness, I presented him with a hammer, a sailor's knife, a Rodger's three-bladed penknife, a gilt letter-slip with paper and envelopes, some gilt pens, an ivory holder, and a variety of other small articles. Of each of these he asked the use, and then in high glee put it into the big block-tin box, in which he kept his other curiosities, and which I think he felt more proud of than any other possession. After this, on adjourning to his baraza, Ungŭrŭé the Pig, who had floored my march in Sorombo, and Makinga, our persecutor in Usŭi, came in to report that the Watŭta had been fighting in Usŭi, and taken six bomas, upon which Rŭmanika asked me what I thought of it, and if I knew where the Watŭta came from. I said I was not surprised to hear Usŭi had attracted the Watŭta's cupidity, for every one knew of the plundering propensities of the inhabitants, and as they became rich by their robberies, they must in turn expect to be robbed. Where the Watŭta came from, nobody could tell; they were dressed something like the Zŭlŭ Kafirs of the south, but appeared to be now gradually migrating from the regions of Lake Nyassa. To this Dr K'yengo, who was now living with Rŭmanika as his head magician, added that, whilst he was living in Utambara, the Watŭta invested his boma six months; and finally, when all their cows and stores were exhausted, they killed all the inhabitants but himself, and he only escaped by the power of the charms which he earned about him. These were so powerful, that although he lay on the ground, and the Watŭta struck at him with their spears, not one could penetrate his body.

In the evening after this, as the king wished to see all my scientific instruments, we walked down to the camp; and as he did not beg for anything, I gave him some gold and mother-of-pearl shirt-studs to swell up his trinket-box. The same evening I made up my mind, if possible, to purchase a stock of beads from the Arabs, and sent Baraka off to Kufro, to see what kind of a bargain he could make with them; for, whilst I trembled to think what those 'blood-suckers' would have the impudence to demand when they found me at their mercy, I felt that the beads must be bought, or the expedition would certainly come to grief.

1st and 2d. – Two days after this the merchants came in a body to see me, and said their worst beads would stand me 80 dollars per frasala, as they could realise that value in *ivory* on arrival at the coast. Of course no business was done, for the thing was preposterous by all calculation, being close on 2500 per cent above Zanzibar valuation. I was 'game' to give 50 dollars, but as they would not take this, I thought of dealing with Rŭmanika instead. I then gave Nuanaji, who had been constantly throwing out hints that I ought to give him a gun, as he was a great sportsman, a lappet of bead-work to keep his tongue quiet, and he in return sent me a bullock and sundry pots of pombé, which, in addition to the daily allowance sent by Rŭmanika, made all my people drunk.

3d. – At daybreak Rŭmanika sent us word he was off to Moga-Namirinzi, a spur of a hill beyond 'the Little Windermere,' overlooking the Ingézi Kagéra, or river which separates Kishakka from Karagŭé, to show me how the Kitangŭlé river was fed by small lakes and marshes, in accordance with my expressed wish to have a better comprehension of the drainage system of the Mountains of the Moon. He hoped we would follow him, not by the land route he intended to take, but in canoes which he had ordered at the ferry below. Starting off shortly afterwards, I made for the lake, and found the canoes all ready, but so small that, besides two paddlers, only two men could sit down in each. After pushing through the tall reeds with which the end of the lake is covered, we emerged in the clear open, and skirted the farther side of the water until a small strait was gained, which led us into another lake, drained at the northern end into a vast swampy plain, covered entirely with tall rushes, excepting only in a few places where bald patches expose the surface of the water, or where the main streams of the Ingézi and Luchŭro valleys cut a clear drain for themselves.

The whole scenery was most beautiful. Green and fresh, the slopes of the hills were covered with grass, with small clumps of soft cloudy-looking acacias growing at a few feet only above the water, and above them, facing over the hills, fine detached trees, and here and there the gigantic medicinal aloe. Arrived near the end of the Moga-Namiriuzi hill in the second lake, the paddlers splashed into shore, where a large concourse of people, headed by Nuanaji, were drawn up to receive me. I landed with all the dignity of a prince, when the royal band struck up a march, and we all moved on to Rŭmanika's frontier palace, talking away in a very complimentary manner, not unlike the very polite and flowery fashion of educated Orientals.

Rŭmanika we found sitting dressed in a wrapper made of an nzoé antelope's skin, smiling blandly as we approached him. In the warmest manner possible he pressed me to sit by his side, asked how I had enjoyed myself, what I thought of his country, and if I did not feel hungry; when a picnic dinner was spread, aud we all set to at cooked plantains and pombé, ending with a pipe of his best tobacco. Bit by bit Rŭmanika became more interested in geography, and seemed highly ambitious of gaining a world-wide reputation through the medium of my pen. At his invitation we now crossed over the spur to the Ingézi Kagéra side, when, to surprise me, the canoes I had come up the lake in appeared before us. They had gone out of the lake at its northern end, paddled into, and then up the Kagéra to where we stood, showing, by actual navigation, the connection of these highland lakes with the rivers which drain the various spurs of the Mountains of the Moon. The Kagéra was deep and dark, of itself a very fine stream, and, considering it was only one – and that, too, a minor one – of the various affluents which drain the mountain valleys into the Victoria N'yanza through the medium of the Kitangŭlé river, I saw at once there must be water sufficient to make the Kitangŭlé a very powerful tributary to the lake.

On leaving this interesting place, with the widespread information of all the surrounding countries I had gained, my mind was so impressed with the topographical features of all this part of Africa, that in my heart I resolved I would make Rŭmanika as happy as he had made me, and asked K'yengo, his doctor, of all things I possessed what the king would like best. To my surprise I then learnt that Rŭmanika had set his heart on the revolving rifle I had brought for Mtésa – the one, in fact, which he had prevented my sending on to Uganda in the hands of Kachŭchŭ, and he would have begged me for it before had his high-minded dignity, and the principle he had established of never begging for anything, not interfered. I then said he should certainly have it; for as strongly as I had withheld from giving anything to those begging scoundrels who wished to rob me of all I possessed in the lower countries, so strongly now did I feel inclined to be generous with this exceptional man Rŭmanika. We then had another picnic together, and whilst I went home to join Grant, Rŭmanika spent the night doing homage and sacrificing a bullock at the tomb of his father Dagara.

Instead of paddling all down the lake again, I walked over the hill, and, on crossing at its northern end, wished to shoot ducks; but the superstitious boatmen put a stop to my intended amusement by imploring me not to do so, lest the spirit of the lake should be roused to dry up the waters.

4th. – Rŭmanika returned in the morning, walking up the hill, followed by a long train of his officers, and a party of men carrying on their shoulders his state carriage, which consisted of a large open basket laid on the top of two very long poles. After entering his palace, I immediately called on him to thank him for the great treat he had given me, and presented him, as an earnest of what I thought, with the Colt's revolving rifle and a fair allowance of ammunition. His delight knew no bounds on becoming the proprietor of such an extraordinary weapon, and induced him to dwell on his advantages over his brother Rogéro, whose antipathy to him was ever preying on his mind. He urged me again to devise some plan for overcoming him; and, becoming more and more confidential, favoured me with the following narrative, by way of evidence how the spirits were inclined to show all the world that he was the rightful successor to the throne: – When Dagara died, and he, Nuanaji, and Rogéro, were the only three sons left in line of succession to the crown, a small mystic drum of diminutive size was placed before them by the officers of state. It was only feather weight in reality, but, being loaded with charms, became so heavy to those who were not entitled to the crown, that no one could lift it but the one person whom the spirits were inclined towards as the rightful successor.

Now, of all the three brothers, he, Rŭmanika, alone could raise it from the ground; and whilst his brothers laboured hard, in vain attempting to move it, he with his little finger held it up without any exertion.

This little disclosure in the history of Karagŭé led us on to further particulars of Dagara's death and burial, when it transpired that the old king's body, after the fashion of his predecessors, was sewn up in a cow-skin, and placed in a boat floating on the lake, where it remained for three days, until decomposition set in and maggots were engendered, of which three were taken into the palace and given in charge to the heir-elect; but instead of remaining as they were, one worm was transformed into a lion, another into a leopard, and the third into a stick. After this the body of the king was taken up and deposited on the hill Moga-Namirinzi, where, instead of putting him underground, the people erected a hut over him, and, thrusting in five maidens and fifty cows, enclosed the doorway in such a manner that the whole of them subsequently died from starvation.

This, as may naturally be supposed, led into further genealogical disclosures of a similar nature, and I was told by Rŭmanika that his grandfather was a most wonderful man; indeed, Karagŭé was blessed with more supernatural agencies than any other country. Rohinda the Sixth, who was his grandfather, numbered so many years that people thought he never would die; and he even became so concerned himself about it, reflecting that his son Dagara would never enjoy the benefit of his position as successor to the crown of Karagŭé, that he took some magic powders and charmed away his life. His remains were then taken to Moga-Namirinzi, in the same manner as were those of Dagara; but, as an improvement on the maggot story, a young lion emerged from the heart of the corpse and kept guard over the hill, from whom other lions came into existence, until the whole place has become infested by them, and has since made Karagŭé a power and dread to all other nations; for these lions became subject to the will of Dagara, who, when attacked by the countries to the northward, instead of assembling an army of men, assembled his lion force, and so swept all before him.

Another test was then advanced at the instigation of K'yengo, who thought Rŭmanika not quite impressive enough of his right to the throne; and this was, that each heir in succession, even after the drum dodge, was required to sit on the ground in a certain place of the country, where, if he had courage to plant himself, the land would gradually rise up, telescope-fashion, until it reached to the skies, when, if the aspirant was considered by the spirits the proper person to inherit Karagŭé, he would gradually be lowered again without any harm happening; but, otherwise, the elastic hill would suddenly collapse, and he would be dashed to pieces. Now, Rŭmanika, by his own confession, had gone through this ordeal with marked success; so I asked him if he found the atmosphere cold when so far up aloft, and as he said he did so, laughing at the quaintness of the question, I told him I saw he had learnt a good practical lesson on the structure of the universe, which I wished he would explain to me. In a state of perplexity, K'yengo and the rest, on seeing me laughing, thought something was wrong; so, turning about, they thought again, and said, 'No, it must have been hot, because the higher one ascended the nearer he got to the sun.'

This led on to one argument after another, on geology, geography, and all the natural sciences, and ended by Rŭmanika showing me an iron much the shape and size of a carrot. This he said was found by one of his villagers whilst tilling the ground, buried some way down below the surface; but dig as he would, he could not remove it, and therefore called some more men to his help. Still the whole of them united could not lift the iron, which induced them, considering there must be some magic in it, to inform the king. 'Now' says Rŭmanika, 'I no sooner went there and saw the iron, than, without the smallest exertion, I uplifted the iron, and brought it here as you see it. What can such a sign mean?' 'Of course that you are the rightful king,' said his flatterers. 'Then,' said Rŭmanika, in exuberant spirits, 'during Dagara's time, as the king was sitting with many other men outside his hut, a fearful storm of thunder and lightning arose, and a thunderbolt struck the ground in the midst of them, which dispersed all the men but Dagara, who calmly took up the thunderbolt and placed it in the palace. I, however, no sooner came into possession, and Rogéro began to contend with me, than the thunderbolt vanished. How would you account for this?' The flatterers said, 'It is clear as possible;

God gave the thunderbolt to Dagara as a sign he was pleased with him and his rule; but when he found two brothers contending, he withdrew it to show their conduct was wicked.'

5th. – Rŭmanika in the morning sent me a young male nzoé (water-boc) which his canoe-men had caught in the high rushes at the head of the lake, by the king's order, to please me; for I had heard this peculiar animal described in such strange ways at Kazé, both by Mŭsa and the Arabs, I was desirous of having a look at one. It proved to be closely allied to a water-boc found by Livingstone on the Ngami Lake; but, instead of being striped, was very faintly spotted, and so long were its toes, it could hardly walk on the dry ground; whilst its coat, also well adapted to the moist element it lived in, was long, and of such excellent quality that the natives prize it for wearing almost more than any other of the antelope tribe. The only food it would eat were the tops of the tall papyrus rushes; but though it ate and drank freely, and lay down very quietly, it always charged with ferocity any person who went near it

In the afternoon Rŭmanika invited both Grant and myself to witness his New Moon Levée, a ceremony which takes place every month with a view of ascertaining how many of his subjects are loyal. On entering his palace enclosure, the first thing we saw was a blaue boc's horn stuffed full of magic powder, with very imposing effect, by K'yengo, and stuck in the ground, with its mouth pointing in the direction of Rogéro. In the second court, we found thirty-five drums ranged on the ground, with as many drummers standing behind them, and a knot of young princes and officers of high dignity waiting to escort us into the third enclosure, where, in his principal hut, we found Rŭmanika squatting on the ground, half-concealed by the portal, but showing his smiling face to welcome us in. His head was got up with a tiara of beads, from the centre of which, directly over the forehead, stood a plume of red feathers, and encircling the lower face with a fine large white beard set in a stock or band of beads. We were beckoned to squat alongside Nuanaji, the master of ceremonies, and a large group of high officials outside the porch. Then the thirty-five drums all struck up together in very good harmony; and when their deafening noise was over, a smaller band of hand-drums and reed instruments was ordered in to amuse us.

This second performance over, from want of breath only, district officers, one by one, came advancing on tiptoe, then pausing, contorting and quivering their bodies, advancing again with a springing gait and outspread arms, which they moved as if they wished to force them out of their joints, in all of which actions they held drum-sticks or twigs in their hands, swore with a maniacal voice an oath of their loyalty and devotion to their king, backed by the expression of a hope that he would cut off their heads if they ever turned from his enemies, and then, kneeling before him, they held out their sticks that he might touch them. With a constant reiteration of these scenes – the saluting at one time, the music at another – interrupted only once by a number of girls dancing something like a good rough Highland fling whilst the little band played, the day's ceremonies ended.

6th and 7th. – During the next two days, as my men had all worn out their clothes, I gave them each thirty necklaces of beads to purchase a suit of the bark cloth called mbŭgŭ, already described. Finding the flour of the country too bitter to eat by itself, we sweetened it with ripe plantains, and made a good cake of it. The king now, finding me disinclined to fight his brother Rogéro, either with guns or magic horns, asked me to give him a 'doctor' or charm to create longevity and to promote the increase of his family, as his was not large enough to maintain the dignity of so great a man as himself. I gave him a blister, and, changing the subject, told him the history of the creation of man. After listening to it attentively, he asked what thing in creation I considered the greatest of all things in the world; for whilst a man at most could only live one hundred years, a tree lived many; but the earth ought to be biggest, for it never died.

Before breaking up, Rŭmanika wished to give me any number of ivories I might like to mention, even three or four hundred, as a lasting remembrance that I had done him the honour of visiting Karagŭé in his lifetime, for though Dagara had given to coloured merchants, he would be the first who had given to a white man. Of course this royal offer was declined with politeness; he must understand that it was not the custom of big men in my country to accept presents of value when we made visits of pleasure. I had enjoyed my residence in Karagüé, his intellectual conversations and his kind hospitality, all of which I should record in my books to hand down to posterity; but if he would give me a cow's horn, I would keep it as a trophy of the happy days I had spent in his country. He gave me one, measuring 3 feet 5 inches in length, and 18 inches in circumference at the base. He then offered me a large sheet, made up of a patchwork of very small N'yéra antelope skins, most exquisitely cured and sewn. This I rejected, as he told me it had been given to himself, explaining that we prided ourselves on never parting with the gifts of a friend; and this speech tickled his fancy so much, that he said he never would part with anything I gave him.

8th and 9th. – The 8th went off much in the usual way, by my calling on the king, when I gave him a pack of playing-cards, which he put into his curiosity-box. He explained to me, at my request, what sort of things he would like any future visitors to bring him – a piece of gold and silver embroidery; but, before anything else, I found he would like to have toys – such as Yankee clocks with the face in a man's stomach, to wind up behind, his eyes rolling with every beat of the pendulum; or a china-cow milk-pot, a jack-in-the-box, models of men, carriages, and horses – all animals in fact, and railways in particular.

On the 9th I went out shooting, as Rŭmanika, with his usual politeness, on hearing my desire to kill some rhinoceros, ordered his sons to conduct the field for me. Off we started by sunrise to the bottom of the hills overlooking the head of the Little Windermere lake. On arrival at the scene of action – a thicket of acacia shrubs – all the men in the neighbourhood were assembled to beat. Taking post myself, by direction, in the most likely place to catch a sight of the animals, the day's work began by the beaters driving the covers in my direction. In a very short time, a fine male was discovered making towards me, but not exactly knowing where he should bolt to. While he was in this perplexity, I stole along between the bushes, and caught sight of him standing as if anchored by the side of a tree, and gave him a broadsider with Blissett, which, too much for his constitution to stand, sent him off trotting, till exhausted by bleeding he lay down to die, and allowed me to give him a settler.

In a minute or two afterwards, the good young princes, attracted by the sound of the gun, came to see what was done. Their surprise knew no bounds; they could scarcely believe what they saw; and then, on recovering, with the spirit of true gentlemen, they seized both my hands, congratulating me on the magnitude of my success, and pointed out, as an example of it, a bystander who showed fearful scars, both on his abdomen and at the blade of his shoulder, who they declared had been run through by one of these animals. It was, therefore, wonderful to them, they observed, with what calmness I went up to such formidable beasts.

10th and 11th. – The next day, when I called on Rŭmanika, the spoils were brought into court, and in utter astonishment he said, 'Well, this must have been done with something more potent than powder, for neither the Arabs nor Nuanaji, although they talk of their shooting powers, could have accomplished such a great feat as this. It is no wonder the English are the greatest men in the world.'

Neither the Wanyambo nor the Wahŭma would eat the rhinoceros, so I was not sorry to find all the Wanyamŭézi porters of the Arabs at Kufro, on hearing of the sport, come over and carry away all the flesh. They passed by our camp half borne down with their burdens of sliced flesh, suspended from poles which they carried on their shoulders; but the following day I was disgusted by hearing that their masters had forbidden their eating 'the carrion,' as the throats of the animals had not been cut; and, moreover, had thrashed them soundly because they complained they were half starved, which was perfectly true, by the poor food that they got as their pay.

12th. – On visiting Rŭmanika again, and going through my geographical lessons, he told me, in confirmation of Mŭsa's old stories, that in Rŭanda there existed pigmies who lived in trees, but occasionally came down at night, and, listening at the hut doors of the men, would wait until they heard the name of one of its inmates, when they would call him out, and, firing an arrow into his heart, disappear again in the same way as they came. But, more formidable even than these little men, there were monsters who could not converse with men, and never showed themselves unless they saw women pass by; then, in voluptuous excitement, they squeezed them to death. Many other similar stories were then told, when I, wishing to go, was asked if I could kill hippopotami. Having answered that I could, the king graciously said he would order some canoes for me next morning; and as I declined because Grant could not accompany me, as a terrible disease had broken out in his leg, he ordered a pig-shooting party. Agreeably with this, the next day I went out with his sons, numerously attended; but although we beat the covers all day, the rain was so frequent the pigs would not bolt.

14th. – After a long and amusing conversation with Rŭmanika in the morning, I called on one of his sisters-in-law, married to an elder brother who was born before Dagara ascended the throne. She was another of those wonders of obesity, unable to stand excepting on all fours. I was desirous to obtain a good view of her, and actually to measure her, and induced her to give me facilities for doing so, by offering in return to show her a bit of my naked legs and arms. The bait took as I wished it, and after getting her to sidle and wriggle into the middle of the hut, I did as I promised, and then took her dimensions, as noted below. All of these are exact except the height, and I believe I could have obtained this more accurately if I could have had her laid on the floor. Not knowing what difficulties I should have to contend with in such a piece of engineering, I tried to get her height by raising her up. This, after infinite exertions on the part of us both, was accomplished, when she sank down again, fainting, for her blood had rushed into her head. Meanwhile, the daughter, a lass of sixteen, sat stark-naked before us, sucking at a milk-pot, on which the father kept her at work by holding a rod in his hand, for as fattening is the first duty of fashionable female life, it must be duly enforced by the rod if necessary. I got up a bit of flirtation with missy, and induced her to rise and shake hands with me. Her features were lovely, but her body was as round as a ball.

In the evening we had another row with my head men – Baraka having accused Bombay of trying to kill him with magic. Bombay, who was so incessantly bullied by Baraka's officious attempts to form party cliques opposed to the interests of the journey, and get him turned out of the camp, indiscreetly went to one of K'yengo's men, and asked him if he knew of any medicine that would affect the hearts of the Wangŭana so as to incline them towards him; and on the sub-doctor saying Yes, Bombay gave him some beads, and bought the medicine required, which, put into a pot of pombé, was placed by Baraka's side. Baraka in the meanwhile got wind of the matter through K'yengo, who, misunderstanding the true facts of the case, said it was a charm to deprive Baraka of his life. A court of inquiry having been convened, with all the parties concerned in attendance, K'yengo's mistake was discovered, and Bombay was lectured for his folly, as he had a thousand times before abjured his belief in such magical follies; moreover, to punish him for the future, I took Baraka, whenever I could, with me to visit the king, which, little as it might appear to others, was of the greatest consequence to the hostile parties.

15th and 16th. – When I next called on Rŭmanika I gave him a Yautier's binocular and prismatic compass; on which he politely remarked he was afraid he was robbing me of everything. More compliments went round, and then he asked if it was true we could open a man's skull, look at his brains, and close it up again; also if it was true we sailed all round the world into regions where there was no difference between night and day, and how, when we ploughed the seas in such enormous vessels as would carry at once 20,000 men, we could explain to the sailors what they ought to do; for, although he had heard of these things, no one was able to explain them to him.

After all the explanations were given, he promised me a boat-hunt after the nzoé in the morning; but when the time came, as difficulties were raised, I asked him to allow us to anticipate the arrival of Kachŭchŭ, and march on to Kitángŭlé. He answered, with his usual courtesy, That he would be very glad to oblige us in any way that we liked; but he feared that, as the Waganda were such superstitious people, some difficulties would arise, and he must decline to comply with our request. 'You must not,' he added, 'expect ever to find again a reasonable man like myself.' I then gave him a book on 'Kafir laws,' which he said he would keep for my sake, with all the rest of the presents, which he was determined never to give away, though it was usual for him to send novelties of this sort to Mtésa, king of Uganda, and Kamrasi, king of Unyoro, as a friendly recognition of their superior positions in the world of great monarchies.

17th. – Rŭmanika next introduced me to an old woman who came from the island of Gasi, situated in the little Lŭta Nzigé. Both her upper and lower incisors had been extracted, and her upper lip perforated by a number of small holes, extending in an arch from one comer to the other. This interesting but ugly old lady narrated the circumstances by which she had been enslaved, and then sent by Kamrasi as a curiosity to Rŭmanika, who had ever since kept her as a servant in his palace. A man from Rŭanda then told us of the Wilyanwantŭ (men-eaters), who disdained all food but human flesh; and Rŭmanika confirmed the statement. Though I felt very sceptical about it, I could not help thinking it a curious coincidence that the position they were said to occupy agreed with Pethericks Nyam Nyams (men-eaters).

Of far more interest were the results of a conversation which I had with another of Kamrasi's servants, a man of Amara, as it threw some light upon certain statements made by Mr Leon of the people of Amara being Christians. He said they bore single holes in the centres both of their upper and lower lips, as well as in the lobes of both of their ears, in which they wear small brass rings. They live near the N'yanza – where it is connected by a strait with a salt lake, and drained by a river to the northward – in comfortable houses, built like the tembés of Unyamŭézi. When killing a cow, they kneel down in an attitude of prayer, with both hands together, held palm upwards, and utter Zŭ, a word the meaning of which he did not know. I questioned him to try if the word had any trace of a Christian meaning – for instance, as a corruption of Jesu – but without success. Circumcision is not known amongst them, neither have they any knowledge of God or a soul. A tribe called Wakŭavi, who are white, and described as not unlike myself, often came over the water and made raids on their cattle, using the double-edged simé as their chief weapon of war. These attacks were as often resented, and sometimes led the Wamara in pursuit a long way into their enemy's country, where, at a place called Kisigŭisi, they found men robed in red cloths. Beads were imported, he thought, both from the east and from Ukidi. Associated with the countries Masau or Masai, and Usambŭrŭ, which he knew, there was a large mountain, the exact position of which he could not describe.

I took down many words of his language, and found they corresponded with the North African dialects, as spoken by the people of Kidi, Gani, and Madi. The southerners, speaking of these, would call them Wakidi, Wagani, and Wamadi, but among themselves the syllable *wa* is not prefixed, as in the southern dialects, to signify people. Rŭmanika, who appeared immensely delighted as he assisted me in putting the questions I wanted, and saw me note them down in my book, was more confirmed than ever in the truth of my stories that I came from the north, and thought as the beads came to Amara, so should I be able to open the road and bring him more visitors. This he knew was his only chance of ever seeing me any more, for I swore I would never go back through Usŭi, so greatly did I feel the indignities imposed on me by Sŭwarora.

19th to 22d. – On the 19th I went fishing, but without success, for they said the fish would not take in the lake; and on the following day, as Grant's recovery seemed hopeless, for a long time at least, I went with all the young princes to see what I could do with the hippopotami in the lake, said to inhabit the small island of Conty. The party was an exceedingly merry one. We went off to the island in several canoes, and at once found an immense number of crocodiles basking in the sun, but not a single hippopotamus was in sight. The princes then, thinking me 'green' at this kind of sport, said the place was enchanted, but I need not fear, for they would bring them out to my feet by simply calling out certain names, and this was no sooner done than four old and one young one came immediately in front of us. It seemed quite a sin to touch them, they looked all so innocent; but as the king wanted to try me again, I gave one a ball on the head which sent him under, never again to be seen, for on the 22d, by which time I supposed he ought to have risen inflated with gases, the king sent out his men to look out for him; but they returned to say, that whilst all the rest were in the old place, that one, in particular, could not be found.

On this K'yengo, who happened to be present whilst our interview lasted, explained that the demons of the deep were annoyed with me for intruding on their preserves, without having the courtesy to commemorate the event by the sacrifice of a goat or a cow. Rŭmanika then, at my suggestion, gave Nuanaji the revolving pistol I first gave him, but not without a sharp rebuke for his having had the audacity to beg a gun of me in consideration of his being a sportsman.

We then went into a discourse on astrology, when the intelligent Rŭmanika asked me if the same sun we saw one day appeared again, or whether fresh suns came every day, and whether or not the moon made different faces, to laugh at us mortals on earth.

23rd and 24th. – This day was spent by the king introducing me to his five fat wives, to show with what esteem he was held by all the different kings of the countries surrounding. From Mpororo – which,, by the by, is a republic – he was wedded to Kaogéz, the daughter of Kahaya, who is the greatest chief in the country; from Unyoro he received Kaŭyangi, Kamrasi's daughter; from Nkolé, Kambiri, the late Kasiyonga's daughter; from Utŭmbi, Kirangŭ, the late Kitémbŭa's daughter; and lastly, the daughter of Chiŭarŭngi, his head cook.

After presenting Rŭmanika with an india-rubber band – which, as usual, amused him immensely – for the honour he had done me in showing me his wives, a party of Waziwa, who had brought some ivory from Kidi, came to pay their respects to him. On being questioned by me, they said that they once saw some men like my Wangŭana there; they had come from the north to trade, but, though they carried firearms, they were all killed by the people of Kidi. This was famous; it corroborated what I knew, but could not convince others of, – that traders could find their way up to Kidi by the Nile. It in a manner explained also how it was that Kamrasi, some years before, had obtained some pink beads, of a variety the Zanzibar merchants had never thought of bringing into the country. Bombay was now quite convinced, and we all became transported with joy, until Rŭmanika, reflecting on the sad state of Grant's leg, turned that joy into grief by saying that the rules of Uganda are so strict, that no one who is sick could enter the country. 'To show,' he said, 'how absurd they are, your donkey would not be permitted because he has no trousers; and you even will have to put on a gown, as your unmentionables will be considered indecorous.' I now asked Rŭmanika if he would assist me in replenishing my fast-ebbing store of beads, by selling tusks to the Arabs at Kufro, when for every 35 lb weight I would give him 50 dollars by orders on Zanzibar, and would insure him from being cheated, by sending a letter of advice to our Consul residing there.

At first he demurred, on the high-toned principle that he could not have any commercial dealings with myself; but, at the instigation of Bombay and Baraka, who viewed it in its true character, as tending merely to assist my journey in the best manner he could, without any sacrifice to dignity, he eventually yielded, and, to prove his earnestness, sent me a large tusk, with a notice that his ivory was not kept in the palace, but with his officers, and as soon as they could collect it, so soon I should get it.

Christmas Day: Rŭmanika, on hearing that it was our custom to celebrate the birth of our Saviour with a good feast of beef, sent us an ox. I immediately paid him a visit to offer the compliments of the season, and at the same time regretted, much to his amusement, that he, as one of the old stock of Abyssinians, who are the oldest Christians on record, should have forgotten this rite; but I hoped the time would come when, by making it known that his tribe had lapsed into a state of heathenism, white teachers would be induced to set it all to rights again. At this time some Wahaiya traders (who had been invited at my request by Rŭmanika) arrived. Like the Waziwa, they had traded with Kidi, and they not only confirmed what the Waziwa had said, but added that, when trading in those distant parts, they heard of Wangŭana coming in vessels to trade to the north of Unyoro; but the natives there were so savage, they only fought with these foreign traders. A man of Rŭanda now informed us that the cowrie-shells, so plentiful in that country, come there from the other or western side, but he could not tell whence they were originally obtained. Rŭmanika then told me Sŭwarora had been so frightened by the Watŭta, and their boastful threats to demolish Usŭi bit by bit, reserving him only as a tit-bit for the end, that he wanted a plot of ground in Karagŭé to preserve his property in.

26th, 27th, and 28th. – Some other travellers from the north again informed us that they had heard of Wangŭana who attempted to trade in Gani and Chopi, but were killed by the natives. I now assured Rŭmanika that in two or three years he would have a greater trade with Egypt than he ever could have with Zanzibar; for when I opened the road, all those men he heard of would swarm up here to visit him. He, however, only laughed at my folly in proposing to go to a place of which all I heard was merely that every stranger who went there was killed. He began to show a disinclination to allow my going there, and though from the most friendly intention, this view was alarming, for one word from him could have ruined my projects. As it was, I feared my followers might take flight and refuse to advance with me. I thought it good policy to talk of there being many roads leading through Africa, so that Rŭmanika might see he had not got, as he thought, the sole key to the interior. I told him again of certain views I once held of coming to see him from the north up the Nile, and from the east through the Masai. He observed that, 'To open either of those routes, you would require at least two hundred guns.' He would, however, do something when we returned from Uganda; for as Mtésa followed his advice in everything, so did Kamrasi, for both held the highest opinion of him.

The conversation then turning on London, and the way men and carriages moved up the streets like strings of ants on their migrations, Rŭmanika said the villages in Rŭanda were of enormous extent, and the people great sportsmen, for they turned out in multitudes, with small dogs on whose necks were tied bells, and blowing horns themselves, to hunt leopards. They were, however, highly superstitious, and would not allow any strangers to enter their country; for some years ago, when some Arabs went there, a great drought and famine set in, which they attributed to evil influences brought by them, and, turning them out of their country, said they would never admit any of their like amongst them again. I said, in return, I thought his Wanyambo just as superstitious, for I observed, whilst walking one day, that they had placed a gourd on the path, and on inquiry found they had done so to gain the sympathy of all passers-by to their crop close at hand, which was blighted, imagining that the voice of the sympathiser heard by the spirits would induce them to relent, and restore a healthy tone to the crop.

29th and 30th. – On telling Rŭmanika this story next morning, he said, 'Many funny things happen in Karagŭé and related some domestic incidents, concluding with the moral that 'Marriage in Karagŭé was a mere matter of money.' Cows, sheep, and slaves have to be given to the father for the value of his daughter; but if she finds she has made a mistake, she can return the dowry-money, and gain her release. The Wahŭma, although they keep slaves and marry with pure negroes, do not allow their daughters to taint their blood by marrying out of their clan. In warfare it is the rule that the Wahinda, or princes, head their own soldiers, and set them the example of courage, when, after firing a few arrows, they throw their bows away, and close at once with their spears and assagés. Life is never taken in Karagŭé, either for murder or cowardice, as they value so much their Wahŭma breed; but, for all offences, fines of cows are exacted according to the extent of the crime.

31st. – Ever proud of his history since I had traced his descent from Abyssinia and King David, whose hair was as straight as my own, Rŭmanika dwelt on my theological disclosures with the greatest delight, and wished to know what difference existed between the Arabs and ourselves; to which Baraka replied, as the best means of making him understand, that whilst the Arabs had only one Book, we had two; to which I added, Yes, that is true in a sense; but the real merits lie in the fact that we have got the better *book,* as may be inferred from the obvious fact that we are more prosperous, and their superiors in all things, as I would prove to him if he would allow me to take one of his sons home to learn that *book;* for then he would find his tribe, after a while, better off than the Arabs are. Much delighted, he said he would be very glad to give me two boys for that purpose.

Then, changing the subject, I pressed Rŭmanika, as he said he had no idea of a God or future state, to tell me what advantage he expected from sacrificing a cow yearly at his father's grave. He laughingly replied he did not know, but he hoped he might be favoured with better crops if he did so. He also placed pombé and grain, he said, for the same reason, before a large stone on the hillside, although it could not eat, or make any use of it; but the coast-men were of the same belief as himself, and so were all the natives. No one in Africa, as far as he knew, doubted the power of magic and spells; and if a fox barked when he was leading an army to battle, he would retire at once, knowing that this prognosticated evil. There were many other animals, and lucky and unlucky birds, which all believed in.

I then told him it was fortunate he had no disbelievers like us to contend with in battle, for we, instead of trusting to luck and such omens, put our faith only in skill and pluck, which Baraka elucidated from his military experience in the wars in British India. Lastly, I explained to him how England formerly was as unenlightened as Africa, and believing in the same sort of superstitions, and the inhabitants were all as naked as his skin-wearing Wanyambo; but now, since they had grown wiser, and saw through such impostures, they were the greatest men in the world. He said, for the future he would disregard what the Arabs said, and trust to my doctrines, for without doubt he had never seen such a wise man as myself; and the Arabs themselves confirmed this when they told him that all their beads and cloths came from the land of the Wazŭngŭ, or white men.

1st, 2d, and 3d. – The new year was ushered in by the most exciting intelligence, which drove us half wild with delight, for we fully believed Mr. Petherick was indeed on his road up the Nile, endeavouring to meet us. It was this: – An officer of Rŭmanika's, who had been sent four years before on a mission to Kamrasi, had just then returned with a party of Kamrasi's who brought ivory for sale to the Arabs at Kufro, along with a vaunting commission to inform Rŭmanika that Kamrasi had foreign visitors as well as himself. They had not actually come into Unyoro, but were in his dependency, the country of Gani, coming up the Nile in vessels. They had been attacked by the Gani people, and driven back with considerable loss both of men and property, although they were in sailing vessels, and fired guns which even broke down the trees on the banks. Some of their property had been brought to him, and he in return had ordered his subjects not to molest them, but allow them to come on to him. Rŭmanika enjoyed this news as much as myself, especially when I told him of Petherick's promise to meet us, just as these men said he was trying to do; and more especially so, when I told him that if he would assist me in trying to communicate with Petherick, the latter would either come here himself, or send one of his men, conveying a suitable present, whilst I was away in Uganda; and then in the end we would all go off to Kamrasi's together.

4th. – Entering warmly into the spirit of this important intelligence, Rŭmanika inquired into its truth; and, finding no reason to doubt it, said he would send some men back with Kamrasi's men, if I could have patience until they were ready to go. There would be no danger, as Kamrasi was his brother-in-law, and would do all that he told him.

I now proposed to send Baraka, who, ashamed to cry off, said he would go with Rŭmanika's officers if I allowed him a companion of his own choosing, who would take care of him if he got sick on the way, otherwise he should be afraid they would leave him to die, like a dog, in the jungles. We consoled him by assenting to the companion he wished, and making Rŭmanika responsible that no harm should come to him from any of the risks which his imagination conjured up. Rŭmanika then gave him and Ulédi, his selected companion, some sheets of mbŭgŭ, in order that they might disguise themselves as his officers whilst crossing the territories of the king of Uganda. On inquiring as to the reason of this, it transpired that, to reach Unyoro, the party would have to cross a portion of Uddŭ, which the late king Sunna, on annexing that country to Uganda, had divided, not in halves, but by alternate bands running transversely from Nkolé to the Victoria N'yanza.

5th and 6th. – To keep Rŭmanika up to the mark, I introduced to him Saidi, one of my men, who was formerly a slave, captured in Walâmo, on the borders of Abyssinia, to show him, by his similarity to the Wahŭma, how it was I had come to the conclusion that he was of the same race. Saidi told him his tribe kept cattle with the same stupendous horns as those of the Wahŭma; and also that, in the same manner, they all mixed blood with milk for their dinners, which, to his mind, confirmed my statement. At night, as there was a partial eclipse of the moon, all the Wangŭana marched up and down from Rŭmanika's to Nuanaji's huts, singing and beating our tin cooking-pots to frighten off the spirit of the sun from consuming entirely the chief object of reverence, the moon.

7th. – Our spirits were now further raised by the arrival of a semi-Hindŭ-Sŭahili, named Jŭma, who had just returned from a visit to the king of Uganda, bringing back with him a large present of ivory and slaves; for he said he had heard from the king of our intention to visit him, and that he had despatched officers to call us immediately. This intelligence delighted Rŭmanika as much as it did us, and he no sooner heard it than he said, with ecstasies, 'I will open Africa, since the white men desire it; for did not Dagara command us to show deference to strangers?' Then, turning to me, he added, 'My only regret is, you will not take something as a return

for the great expenses you have been put to in coming to visit me.'
The expense was admitted, for I had now been obliged to purchase
from the Arabs upwards of £400 worth of beads, to keep such a
store in reserve for my return from Uganda as would enable me to
push on to Gondokoro. I thought this necessary, as every report that
arrived from Unyamŭézi only told us of further disasters with the
merchants in that country. Sheikh Said was there even then, with my
poor Hottentots, unable to convey my post to the coast.

8th to 10th. – At last we heard the familiar sound of the Uganda
drum. Maŭla, a royal officer, with a large escort of smartly-dressed
men, women, and boys, leading their dogs and playing their reeds,
announced to our straining ears the welcome intelligence that their
king had sent them to call us. N'yamgundti, who had seen us in
Usŭi, had marched on to inform the king of our advance and desire
to see him; and he, intensely delighted at the prospect of having
white men for his guests, desired no time should be lost in our
coming on. Maiila told us that his officers had orders to supply us
with everything we wanted whilst passing through his country, and
that there would be nothing to pay.

One thing only now embarrassed me – Grant was worse, without
hope of recovery for at least one or two months. This large body of
Waganda could not be kept waiting. To get on as fast as possible was
the only chance of ever bringing the journey to a successful issue;
so, unable to help myself, with great remorse at another separation,
on the following day I consigned my companion, with several
Wangŭana, to the care of my friend Rŭmanika. I then separated ten
loads of beads and thirty copper wires for my expenses in Uganda;
wrote a letter to Petherick, which I gave to Baraka; and gave him
and his companion beads to last as money for six months, and also
a present both for Kamrasi and the Gani chief. To Nsangéz I gave
charge of my collections in natural history, and the reports of my
progress, addressed to the Geographical Society, which he was to
convey to Sheikh Said at Kazé, for conveyance as far as Zanzibar.

This business concluded in camp, I started my men and went to
the palace to bid adieu to Rŭmanika, who appointed Rozaro, one
of his officers, to accompany me wherever I went in Uganda, and
to bring me back safely again. At Rŭmanika's request I then gave

Mtésa's pages some ammunition to hurry on with to the great king of Uganda, as his majesty had ordered them to bring him, as quickly as possible, some strengthening powder, and also some powder for his gun. Then, finally, to Maŭla, also under Rŭmanika's instructions, I gave two copper wires and five bundles of beads; and, when all was completed, set out on the march, perfectly sure in my mind that before very long I should settle the great Nile problem for ever; and, with this consciousness, only hoping that Grant would be able to join me before I should have to return again, for it was never supposed for a moment that it was possible I ever could go north from Uganda. Rŭmanika was the most resolute in this belief, as the kings of Uganda, ever since that country was detached from Unyoro, had been making constant raids, seizing cattle and slaves from the surrounding countries.

CHAPTER IX

Karagŭé and Uganda

CROSSING back over the Weranhanjé spur, I put up with the Arabs at Kufro. Here, for the first time in this part of the world, I found good English peas growing. Next day (11th), crossing over a succession of forks, supporters to the main spur, we encamped at Lŭandalo. Here we were overtaken by Rozaro, who had remained behind, as I now found, to collect a large number of Wanyambo, whom he called his children, to share with him the gratuitous living these creatures always look out for on a march of this nature.

To Kisaho, 12th: After working round the end of the great spur, whilst following down the crest of a fork, we found Karagŭé separated by a deep valley from the hilly country of Uhaiya, famous for its ivory and coffee productions. On entering the rich plantain gardens of Kisaho, I was informed we must halt there a day for Maŭla to join us, as he had been detained by Rŭmanika, who, wishing to give him a present, had summoned Rozaro's sister to his palace for that purpose. She was married to another, and had two children by him, but that did not signify, as it was found in time her husband had committed a fault, on account of which it was thought necessary to confiscate all his property.

Halt, 13th: At this place all the people were in a constant state of inebriety, drinking pombé all day and all night. I shot a montana antelope, and sent its head and skin back to Grant, accompanied with my daily report to Rŭmanika.

To Narŭeri, 14th: Maŭla having joined me, we marched down to near the end of the fork overlooking the plain of Kitangŭlé – the Waganda drums beating, and whistles playing all the way as we went along.

To Kitangŭlé, 15th: We next descended from the Mountains of the Moon, and spanned a long alluvial plain to the settlement of the so-long-heard-of Kitangŭlé, where Rŭmanika keeps his thousands and thousands of cows. In former days the dense green forests peculiar to the tropics, which grow in swampy places about this plain, were said to have been stocked by vast herds of elephants; but, since the ivory trade had increased, these animals had all been driven off to the hills of Kisiwa and Uhaiya, or into Uddŭ beyond the river, and all the way down to the N'yanza.

To Ndongo, 16th: To-day we reached the Kitangŭlé Kagéra, or river, which, as I ascertained in the year 1858, falls into the Victoria N'yanza on the west side. Most unfortunately, as we led off to cross it, rain began to pour, so that everybody and everything was thrown into confusion. I could not get a sketch of it, though Grant was more fortunate afterwards; neither could I measure or fathom it; and it was only after a long contest with the superstitious boatmen that they allowed me to cross in their canoe with my shoes on, as they thought the vessel would either upset, or else the river would dry up, in consequence of their Neptune taking offence at me.

Once over, I looked down on the noble stream with considerable pride. About eighty yards broad, it was sunk down a considerable depth below the surface of the land, like a huge canal, and is so deep, it could not be poled by the canoemen; while it runs at a velocity of from three to four knots an hour.

I say I viewed it with pride, because I had formed my judgment of its being fed from high-seated springs in the Mountains of the Moon solely on scientific geographical reasonings; and, from the bulk of the stream, I also believed those mountains must attain an altitude of 8000 feet or more, just as we find they do in Rŭanda. I thought then to myself, as I did at Rŭmanika's, when I first viewed the Mfŭmbiro cones, and gathered all my distant geographical information there, that these highly saturated Mountains of the Moon give birth to the Congo as well as to the Nile, and also to the Shiré branch of the Zambézé.

I came, at the same time, to the conclusion that all our previous information concerning the hydrography of these regions, as well as the Mountains of the Moon, originated with the ancient Hindŭs, who told it to the priests of the Nile; and that all those busy Egyptian geographers, who disseminated *their* knowledge with a view to be famous for *their* long-sightedness, in solving the deep-seated mystery which enshrouded the source of their holy river, were so many hypothetical humbugs. Reasoning thus, the Hindŭ traders alone, in those days, I believed, had a firm basis to stand upon, from their intercourse with the Abyssinians – through whom they must have heard of the country of Amara, which they applied to the N'yanza – and with the Wanyamŭézi or men of the Moon, from whom they heard of the Tanganyika and Karagfid mountains. I was all the more impressed with this belief, by knowing that the two church missionaries, Rebmann and Erhardt, without the smallest knowledge of the Hindŭs' map, constructed a map of their own, deduced from the Zanzibar traders, something on the same scale, by blending the Victoria N'yanza, Tanganyika, and N'yassa into one; whilst to their triuned lake they gave the name Moon, because the men of the Moon happened to live in front of the central lake. And later still, Mr Leon, another missionary, heard of the N'yanza and the country Amara, near which he heard the Nile made its escape.

Going on with the march we next came to Ndongo, a perfect garden of plantains. The whole country was rich – most surprisingly so. The same streaky argillaceous sandstones prevailed as in Karagŭé. There was nothing, in fact, that would not have grown here, if it liked moisture and a temperate heat. It was a perfect paradise for negroes: as fast as they sowed they were sure of a crop without much trouble; though, I must say, they kept their huts and their gardens in excellent order.

17th. – As Maŭla would stop here, I had to halt also. The whole country along the banks of the river, and near some impenetrable forests, was alive with antelopes, principally hartebeests, but I would not fire at them until it was time to return, as the villagers led me to expect buffaloes. The consequence was, as no buffaloes were to be found, I got no sport, though I wounded a hartebeest, and followed him almost into camp, when I gave up the chase to some negroes, and amused myself by writing to Rŭmanika, to say if Grant did not reach me by a certain date, I would try to navigate the N'yanza, and return to him in boats up the Kitangŭlé river.

To Ngambézi, 18th: We crossed over a low spur of hill extending from the mountainous kingdom of Nkolé, on our left, towards the N'yanza. Here I was shown by Nasib a village called Ngandŭ, which was the farthest trading depot of the Zanzibar ivory-merchants. It was established by Mŭsa Mzŭri, by the permission of Rŭmanika; for, as I shall have presently to mention, Sunna, after annexing this part of Uddŭ to Uganda, gave Rŭmanika certain bands of territory in it as a means of security against the possibility of its being wrested out of his hands again by the future kings of Unyoro. Following on Mŭsa's wake, many Arabs also came here to trade; but they were so oppressive to the Waganda that they were recalled by Rŭmanika, and obliged to locate themselves at Kufro. To the right, at the end of the spur, stretching as far as the eye could reach towards the N'yanza, was a rich, well-wooded, swampy plain, containing large open patches of water, which not many years since, I was assured, were navigable for miles, but now, like the Urigi lake, were gradually drying up. Indeed, it appeared to me as if the N'yanza must have once washed the foot of these hills, but had since shrunk away from its original margin.

On arrival at Ngambézi, I was immensely struck with the neatness and good arrangement of the place, as well as its excessive beauty and richness. No part of Bengal or Zauzibar could excel it in either respect; and my men, with one voice, exclaimed, 'Ah, what people these Waganda are!' and passed other remarks, which may be abridged as follows: 'They build their huts and keep their gardens just as well as we do at Ungŭja, with screens and enclosures for privacy, a clearance in front of their establishments, and a baraza or reception-hut facing the buildings. Then, too, what a beautiful prospect it has! – rich marshy plains studded with mounds, on each of which grow the umbrella cactus, or some other evergreen tree; and beyond, again, another hill-spur such as the one we have crossed over.' One of king Mtésa's uncles, who had not been burnt to death by the order of the late king Sunna on his ascension to the throne, was the proprietor of this place, but unfortunately he was from home. However, his substitute gave me his baraza to live in, and brought many presents of goats, fowls, sweet potatoes, yams, plantains, sugar-cane, and Indian corn, and apologised in the end for deficiency in hospitality. I, of course, gave him beads in return.

To Semizabi, 19th: Continuing over the same kind of ground in the next succeeding spurs of the streaky red-clay sandstone hills, we put up at the residence of Isamgévi, a Mkungŭ or district officer of Rŭmanika's. His residence was as well kept as Mtésa's uncle's; but instead of a baraza fronting his house, he had a small enclosure, with three small huts in it, kept apart for devotional purposes, or to propitiate the evil spirits – in Bhort, according to the notions of the place, a church. This officer gave me a cow and some plantains, and I in return gave him a wire and some beads. Many mendicant women, called by some Wichwézi, by others Mabandwa, all wearing the most fantastic dresses of mbŭgŭ, covered with beads, shells, and sticks, danced before us, singing a comic song, the chorus of which was a long shrill rolling Coo-roo-coo-roo, coo-roo-coo-roo, delivered as they came to a standstill. Their true functions were just as obscure as the religion of the negroes generally; some called them devil-drivers, others evil-eye averters; but, whatever it was for, they imposed a tax on the people, whose minds being governed by a necessity for making some self-sacrifice to propitiate something, they could not tell what, for their welfare in the world, they always gave them a trifle in the same way as the East Indians do their fakirs.

To Kisŭéré, 20th: After crossing another low swampy flat, we reached a much larger group, or rather ramification, of hill-spurs pointing to the N'yanza, called Kisŭéré, and commanded by M'yombo, Rŭmanikas frontier officer. Immediately behind this, to the northward, commenced the kingdom of Unyoro; and here it was, they said, Baraka would branch off my line on his way to Kamrasi. Maŭla's home was one march distant from this, so the scoundrel now left me to enjoy himself there, giving as his pretext for doing so, that Mtésa required him, as soon as I arrived here, to send on a messenger that order might be taken for my proper protection on the line of march; for the Waganda were a turbulent set of people, who could only be kept in order by the executioner; and doubtless many, as was customary on such occasions, would be beheaded, as soon as Mtésa heard of my coming, to put the rest in a fright I knew this was all humbug, of course, and I told him so; but it was of no use, and I was compelled to halt.

Halt, 20th to 24th: On the 23d another officer, named Maribŭ, came to me and said, Mtésa, having heard that Grant was left sick behind at Karagŭé, had given him orders to go there and fetch him, whether sick or well, for Mtésa was most anxious to see white men. Hearing this I at once wrote to Grant, begging him to come on if he could do so, and to bring with him all the best of my property, or as much as he could of it, as I now saw there was more cunning humbug than honesty in what Rŭmanika had told me about the impossibility of our going north from Uganda, as well as in his saying sick men could not go into Uganda, and donkeys without trousers would not be admitted there, because they were considered indecent. If he was not well enough to move, I advised him to wait there until I reached Mtésa's, when I would either go up the lake and Kitangŭlé to fetch him away, or would make the king send boats for him, which I more expressly wished, as it would tend to give us a much better knowledge of the lake.

To N'yagussa, 24th: Maŭla now came again, after receiving repeated and angry messages, and I forced him to make a move. He led me straight up to his home, a very nice place, in which he gave me a very large, clean, and comfortable hut – had no end of plantains brought for me and my men – and said, 'Now you have really entered the kingdom of Uganda, for the future you must buy no more food. At every place that you stop for the day, the officer in charge will bring you plantains, otherwise your men can help themselves in the gardens, for such are the laws of the land when a king's guest travels in it. Any one found selling anything to either yourself or your men would be punished.' Accordingly, I stopped the daily issue of beads; but no sooner had I done so, than all my men declared they could not eat plantains. It was all very well, they said, for the Waganda to do so, because they were used to it, but it did not satisfy their hunger.

Halt, 25th: Maŭla, all smirks and smiles, on seeing me order the things out for the march, begged I would have patience, and wait till the messenger returned from the king; it would not take more than ten days at the most. Much annoyed at this nonsense, I ordered my tent to be pitched. I refused all Maŭla's plantains, and gave my men beads to buy grain again with; and, finding it necessary to get up some indignation, said I would not stand being chained like a dog; if he would not go on ahead, I should go without him. Maŭla then said he would go to a friend's and come back again. I said, if he did not, I should go off; and so the conversation ended.

27th. – N'yamgundŭ, my old friend at Usŭi, then came to me, and said he was the first man to tell Mtésa of our arrival in Usŭi, and wish to visit him. The handkerchief I had given Irungŭ at Usŭi to present as a letter to Mtésa he had snatched away from him, and given, himself, to his king, who no sooner received it than he bound it round his head and said, in ecstasies of delight, 'Oh, the Mzungŭ, the Mzungŭ! he does indeed want to see me.' Then giving him four cows as a return letter to take to me, he said, 'Hurry off as quickly as possible and bring him here.' 'The cows,' said N'yamgundŭ, 'have gone on to Kisŭéré by another route, but I will bring them here; and then, as Maŭla is taking you, I will go and fetch Grant.' I then told him not to be in such a hurry. I had turned off Maŭla for treating me like a dog, and I would not be escorted by him again. He replied that his orders would not be fully accomplished as long as any part of my establishment was behind; so he would, if I wished it, leave part of his 'children' to guide me on to Mtésa's, whilst he went to fetch Grant. An officer, I assured him, had just gone on to fetch Grant, so he need not trouble his head on that score; at any rate, he might reverse his plan, and send his children for Grant, whilst he went on with me, by which means he would fully accomplish his mission. Long arguments ensued, and I at length turned the tables by asking who was the greatest – myself or my children; when he said, 'As I see you are the greatest, I will do as you wish; and after fetching the cows from Kisŭéré, we will march to-morrow at sunrise.'

To Mashondé, 28th: The sun rose, but N'yamgundŭ did not appear. I was greatly annoyed lest Maŭla should come and try to drive him away. I waited, restraining my impatience until noon, when, as I could stand it no longer, I ordered Bombay to strike my tent, and commence the march. A scene followed, which brought out my commander-in-chief's temper in a rather surprising shape. 'How can we go?' said Bombay. 'Strike the tent,' said I. 'Who will guide us?' said Bombay. 'Strike the tent,' I said again. 'But Rŭmanika's men have all gone away, and there is no one to show us the way.' 'Never mind; obey my orders, and strike the tent.' Then, as Bombay would not do it, I commenced myself, assisted by some of my other men, and pulled it down over his head, all the women who were assembled under it, and all the property. On this, Bombay flew into a passion, abusing the men who were helping me, as there were fires and powder-boxes under the tent. I of course had to fly into a passion and abuse Bombay. He, in a still greater rage, said he would pitch into the men, for the whole place would be blown up. 'That is no reason why you should abuse my men,' I said, 'who are better than you by obeying my orders. If I choose to blow up my property, that is my look-out; and if you don't do your duty, I will blow you up also.' Foaming and roaring with rage, Bombay said he would not stand being thus insulted. I then gave him a dig on the head with my fist. He squared up, and pouted like an enraged chameleon, looking savagely at me. I gave him another dig, which sent him staggering. He squared again: I gave him another; till at last, as the claret was flowing, he sulked off, and said he would not serve me any more. I then gave Nasib orders to take Bombay's post, and commence the march; but the good old man made Bombay give in, and off we went, amidst crowds of Waganda, who had collected to witness this comedy, and were all digging at one another's heads, showing off in pantomime the strange ways of the white man. N'yamgundŭ then joined us, and begged us to halt only one more day, as some of his women were still at Kistierd; but Bombay, showing his nozzle rather flatter than usual, said, 'No; I got this on account of your lies. I won't tell Bana any more of your excuses for stopping; you may tell him yourself if you like.' N'yamgundŭ, however, did not think this advisable, and so we went on as we were doing. It was the first and last time I had ever occasion to lose my dignity by striking a blow with my own hands; but I could not help it on this occasion without losing command and respect; for although I often had occasion to award 100 and even 150 lashes to my men for stealing, I could not, for the sake of due subordination, allow any inferior officer to strike Bombay, and therefore had to do the work myself.

Skirting the hills on the left, with a large low plain to the right, we soon came on one of those numerous rush-drains that appear to me to be the last waters left of the old bed of the N'yanza. This one in particular was rather large, being 150 yards wide. It was sunk where I crossed it, like a canal, 14 feet below the plain; and what with mire and water combined, so deep, I was obliged to take off my trousers whilst fording it. Once across, we sought for and put up in a village beneath a small hill, from the top of which I saw the Victoria N'yanza for the first time on this march. N'yamgundŭ delighted me much: treating me as a king, he always fell down on his knees to address me, and made all his 'children' look after my comfort in camp.

To Ukara, 29th: We marched on again over the same kind of ground, alternately crossing rush-drains of minor importance, though provokingly frequent, and rich gardens, from which, as we passed, all the inhabitants bolted at the sound of our drums, knowing well that they would be seized and punished if found gazing at the king's visitors. Even on our arrival at Ukara not one soul was visible. The huts of the villagers were shown to myself and my men without any ceremony. The Wanyambo escort stole what they liked out of them, and I got into no end of troubles trying to stop the practice; for they said the Waganda served them the same way when they went to Karagŭé, and they had a right to retaliate now. To obviate this distressing sort of plundering, I still served out beads to my men, and so kept them in hand a little; but they were fearfully unruly, and did not like my interference with what by the laws of the country they considered their right.

Halt, 30th: Here I had to stop a day for some of N'yamgundŭ's women, who, in my hurry at leaving Matŭa's, were left behind. A letter from Grant was now brought to me by a very nice-looking young man, who had the skin of a leopard-cat tied round his neck – a badge which royal personages only were entitled to wear. N'yamgundŭ seeing this, as he knew the young man was not entitled to wear it, immediately ordered his 'children' to wrench it from him. Two ruffianly fellows then seized him by his hands, and twisted his arms round and round until I thought they would come out of their sockets. Without uttering a sound the young man resisted, until N'yamgundŭ told them to be quiet, for he would hold a court on the subject, and see if the young man could defend himself. The ruffians then sat on the ground, but still holding on to him; whilst N'yamgundŭ took up a long stick, and breaking it into sundry bits of equal length, placed one by one in front of him, each of which was supposed to represent one number in line of succession to his forefathers. By this it was proved he did not branch in any way from the royal stock. N'yamgundŭ then turning to the company said, What would he do now to expiate his folly? If the matter was taken before Mtésa he would lose his head; was it not better he should pay one hundred cows? All agreeing to this, the young man said he would do so, and quietly allowed the skin to be untied and taken off by the ruffians.

To Mérŭka, 31st: Next day, after crossing more of those abominable rush-drains, whilst in sight of the Victoria N'yanza, we ascended the most beautiful hills, covered with verdure of all descriptions. At Mérŭka, where I put up, there resided some grandees, the chief of whom was the king's aunt. She sent me a goat, a hen, a basket of eggs, and some plantains, in return for which I sent her a wire and some beads. I felt inclined to stop here a month, everything was so very pleasant. The temperature was perfect. The roads, as indeed they were everywhere, were as broad as our coach-roads, cut through the long grasses, straight over the hills and down through the woods in the dells – a strange contrast to the wretched tracks in all the adjacent countries. The huts were kept so clean and so neat, not a fault could be found with them – the gardens the same. Wherever I strolled I saw nothing but richness, and what ought to be wealth. The whole land was a picture of quiescent beauty, with a boundless sea in the background. Looking over the hills, it struck the fancy at once that at one period the whole land must have been at a uniform level with their present tops, but that, by the constant denudation it was subjected to by frequent rains, it had been cut down and sloped into those beautiful hills and dales which now so much pleased the eye; for there were none of those quartz dykes I had seen protruding through the same kind of aqueous formations in Usŭi and Karagŭé; nor were there any other sorts of volcanic disturbance to distort the calm quiet aspect of the scene.

To Sangŭa, 1st: From this, the country being all hill and dale, with miry rush-drains in the bottoms, I walked, carrying my shoes and stockings in my hands, nearly all the way. Rozaro's 'children' became more and more troublesome, stealing everything they could lay their hands upon out of the village huts we passed on the way. On arrival at Sangŭa, I found many of them had been seized by some men who, bolder than the rest, had overtaken them whilst gutting their huts, and made them prisoners, demanding of me two slaves and one load of beads for their restitution. I sent my men back to see what had happened, and ordered them to bring all the men on to me, that I might see fair play. They, however, took the law into their own hands, drove off the Waganda villagers by firing their muskets, and relieved the thieves. A complaint was then laid against N'yamgundŭ by the chief officer of the village, and I was requested to halt. That I would not do, leaving the matter in the hands of the governor-general, Mr Pokino, whom I heard we should find at the next station, Masaka.

To Masaka, 2d: On arrival there at the government establishment – a large collection of grass huts, separated one from the other within large enclosures, which overspread the whole top of a low hill – I was requested to withdraw and put up in some huts a short distance off, and wait until his excellency, who was from home, could come and see me; which the next day he did, coming in state with a large number of officers, who brought with them a cow, sundry pots of pombé, enormous sticks of sugar-cane, and a large bundle of country coffee. This grows in great profusion all over this land in large bushy trees, the berries sticking on the branches like clusters of holly-berries.

Halt, 3d and 4th: I was then introduced, and told that his excellency was the appointed governer of all the land lying between the Katonga and the Kitangŭlé rivers. After the first formalities were over, the complaint about the officers at Sangŭa was preferred for decision, on which Pokino at once gave it against the villagers, as they had no right, by the laws of the land, to lay hands on a king's guest. Just then Maŭla arrived, and began to abuse N'yamgundŭ. Of course I would not stand this; and, after telling all the facts of the case, I begged Pokino to send Maŭla away out of my camp. Pokino said he could not do this, as it was by the king's order he was appointed; but he put Maŭla in the background, laughing at the way he had 'let the bird fly out of his hands,' and settled that N'yamgundŭ should be my guide. I then gave him a wire, and he gave me three large sheets of mbŭgŭ, which he said I should require, as there were so many watercourses to cross on the road I was going. A second day's halt was necessitated by many of my men catching fever, probably owing to the constant crossing of those abominable rush-drains. There was no want of food here, for I never saw such a profusion of plantains anywhere. They were literally lying in heaps on the ground, though the people were brewing pombé all day, and cooking them for dinner every evening.

To Ugonzi, 5th; to Kituntŭ, 6th: After crossing many more hills and miry bottoms, constantly coming in view of the lake, we reached

Ugonzi, and after another march of the same description, came to Kituntŭ, the last officer's residence in Uddŭ. Formerly it was the property of a Belŭch named Eseau, who came to this country with merchandise, trading on account of Said Said, late Sultan of Zanzibar; but having lost it all on his way here, paying mahongo, or taxes, and so forth, he feared returning, and instead made great friends with the late king Sunna, who took an especial fancy to him because he had a very large beard, and raised him to the rank of Mkungŭ. A few years ago, however, Eseau died, and left all his family and property to a slave named Ulédi, who now, in consequence, is the border officer.

Halt, 7th: I became now quite puzzled whilst thinking which was finest spot I had seen in Uddŭ, so many were exceedingly beautiful; but I think I gave the preference to this, both for its own immediate neighbourhood and the long range of view it afforded of Uganda proper, the lake, and the large island, or group of islands, called Sésé, where the king of Uganda keeps one of his fleets of boats.

To Mbŭlé, 8th: Some little boys came here who had all their hair shaved off excepting two round tufts on either side of the head. They were the king's pages; and, producing three sticks, said they had brought them to me from their king, who wanted three charms or medicines. Then placing one stick on the ground before me, they said, 'This one is a head which, being affected by dreams of a deceased relative, requires relief; the second symbolised the king's desire for the accomplishment of a phenomenon to which the old phalic worship was devoted; 'and this third one,' they said, 'is a sign that the king wants a charm to keep all his subjects in awe of him.' I then promised I would do what I could when I reached the palace, but feared to do anything in the distance. I wished to go on with the march, but was dissuaded by N'yamgundŭ, who said he had received orders to find me some cows here, as his king was most anxious I should be well fed. Next day, however, we descended into the Katonga valley, where, instead of finding a magnificent broad sheet of water, as I had been led to expect by the Arabs' account of it, I found I had to wade through a succession of rush-drains divided one from the other by islands. It took me two hours, with my clothes tucked up under my arms, to get through them all; and many of them were so matted with weeds, that my feet sank down as though I trod in a bog.

The Waganda all said that at certain times in the year no one could ford these drains, as they all flooded; but, strangely enough, they were always lowest when most rain fell in Uganda. No one, however, could account for this singular fact. No one knew of a lake to supply the waters, nor where they came from. That they flowed into the lake there was no doubt – as I could see by the trickling waters in some few places – and they lay exactly on the equator. Rising out of the valley, I found all the country just as hilly as before, but many of the rush-drains going to northward; and in the dells were such magnificent trees, they quite took me by surprise. Clean-trunked, they towered up just as so many great pillars, and then spread out their high branches like a canopy over us. I thought of the blue gums of Australia, and believed these would beat them. At the village of Mbŭlé we were gracefully received by the local officer, who brought a small present, and assured me that the king was in a nervous state of excitement, always asking after me. Whilst speaking he trembled, and he was so restless he could never sit still.

To Nakŭsi, 9th: Up and down we went on again through this wonderful country, surprisingly rich in grass, cultivation, and trees. Watercourses were as frequent as ever, though not quite so troublesome to the traveller, as they were more frequently bridged with poles or palm-tree trunks.

To Kibibi, 10th: This, the next place we arrived at, was N'yamgundŭ's own residence, where I stopped a day to try and shoot buffaloes. Maŭla here had the coolness to tell me he must inspect all the things I had brought for presentation to the king, as he said it was the custom; after which he would hurry on and inform his majesty. Of course I refused, saying it was uncourteous to both the king and myself. Still he persisted, until, finding it hopeless, he spitefully told N'yamgundŭ to keep me here at least two days. N'yamgundŭ, however, very prudently told him he should obey his orders, which were to take me on as fast as he could. I then gave N'yamgundŭ wires and beads for himself and all his family round, which made Maŭla slink farther away from me than ever.

Halt, 11th: The buffaloes were very numerous in the tall grasses that lined the sides and bottoms of the hills; but although I saw some, I could not get a shot, for the grasses being double the height of myself, afforded them means of dashing out of view as soon as seen, and the rustling noise made whilst I followed them kept them on the alert. At night a hyena came into my hut, and carried off one of my goats that was tied to a log between two of my sleeping men.

To Nakatéma, 12th: During the next march, after passing some of the most beautifully-wooded dells, in which lay small rush-lakes on the right of the road, draining, as I fancied, into the Victoria Lake, I met with a party of the king's gamekeepers, staking their nets all along the side of a hill, hoping to catch antelopes by driving the covers with dogs and men. Farther on, also, I came on a party driving one hundred cows, as a present from Mtésa to Rŭmanika, which the officers in charge said was their king's return for the favour Rŭmanika had done him in sending me on to him. It was in this way that great kings sent 'letters' to one another.

To N'yama Goma, 13th: Next day, after going a short distance, we came on the Mwarango river, a broad rush-drain of three hundred yards' span, two-thirds of which was bridged over. Until now I did not feel sure where the various rush-drains I had been crossing since leaving the Katonga valley all went to, but here my mind was made up, for I found a large volume of water going to the northwards. I took off my clothes at the end of the bridge and jumped into the stream, which I found was twelve yards or so broad, and deeper than my height. I was delighted beyond measure at this very surprising fact, that I was indeed on the northern slopes of the continent, and had, to all appearance, found one of the branches of the Nile's exit from the N'yanza. I drew Bombay's attention to the current; and, collecting all the men of the country, inquired of them where the river sprang from. Some of them Baid, in the hills to the southward; but most of them said, from the lake. I argued the point with them; for I felt quite sure so large a body of flowing water could not be collected together in any place but the lake. They then all agreed to this view, and further assured me it went to Kamrasi's palace in Unyoro, where it joined the N'yanza, meaning the Nile.

Pushing on again we arrived at N'yama Goma, where I found Irungŭ – the great ambassador I had first met in Usŭi, with all his 'children' – my enemy Makinga, and Sŭwarora's deputation with wire, – altogether, a collection of one hundred souls. They had been here a month waiting for leave to approach the king's palace. Not a villager was to be seen for miles round; not a plantain remained on the trees, nor was there even a sweet potato to be found in the ground. The whole of the provisions of this beautiful place had been devoured by the king's guests, simply because he had been too proud to see them in a hurry. This was alarming, for I feared I should be served the same trick, especially as all the people said this kind of treatment was a mere matter of custom which those great kings demanded as a respect due to their dignity; and Bombay added, with laughter, they make all manner of fuss to entice one to come when in the distance, but when they have got you in their power they become haughty about it, and think only of how they can best impose on your mind the great consequence which they affect before their own people.

Halt, 14th: Here I was also brought to a standstill, for N'yamgundŭ said I must wait for leave to approach the palace. He wished to have a look at the presents I had brought for Mtésa. I declined to gratify it, taking my stand on my dignity; there was no occasion for any distrust on such a trifling matter as that, for I was not a merchant who sought for gain, but had come, at great expense, to see the king of this region. I begged, however, he would go as fast as possible to announce my arrival, explain my motive for coming here, and ask for an early interview, as I had left my brother Grant behind at Karagŭé, and found my position, for want of a friend to talk to, almost intolerable. It was not the custom of my country for great men to consort with servants, and until I saw him, and made friends, I should not be happy. I had a great deal to tell him about, as he was the father of the Nile, which river drained the N'yanza down to my country to the northward. With this message N'yamgundŭ hurried off as fast as possible.

Next day (15th) I gave each of my men a fez cap, and a piece of red blanket to make up military jackets. I then instructed them how to form a guard of honour when I went to the palace, and taught Bombay the way Nazirs were presented at courts in India. Altogether we made a good show. When this was concluded I went with Nasib up a hill, from which we could see the lake on one side, and on the other a large range of huts said to belong to the kings uncle, the second of the late king Sunna's brothers, who was not burnt to death when he ascended the throne.

I then (16th) very much wished to go and see the escape of the Mwérango river, as I still felt a little sceptical as to its origin, whether or not it came off those smaller lakes I had seen on the road the day before I crossed the river; but no one would listen to my project. They all said I must have the king's sanction first, else people, from not knowing my object, would accuse me of practising witchcraft, and would tell their king so. They still all maintained that the river did come out of the lake, and said, if I liked to ask the king's leave to visit the spot, then they would go and show it me. I gave way, thinking it prudent to do so, but resolved in my mind I would get Grant to see it in boats on his voyage from Karagŭé. There were no guinea-fowls to be found here, nor a fowl, in any of the huts, so I requested Rozaro to hurry off to Mtésa, and ask him to send me something to eat. He simply laughed at my request, and said I did not know what I was doing. It would be as much as his life was worth to go one yard in advance of this until the king's leave was obtained. I said, rather than be starved to death in this ignominious manner, I would return to Karagŭé; to which he replied, laughing, 'Whose leave have you got to do that? Do you suppose you can do as you like in this country?'

Next day (17th), in the evening, N'yamgundŭ returned full of smirks and smiles, dropped on his knees at my feet, and, in company with his 'children,' set to n'yanzigging, according to the form of that state ceremonial already described. In his excitement he was hardly able to say all he had to communicate. Bit by bit, however, I learned that he first went to the palace, and, finding the king had gone off yachting to the Murchison Creek, he followed him there. The king for a long while would not believe his tale that I had come, but, being assured, he danced with delight, and swore he would not taste food until he had seen me. 'Oh,' he said, over and over again and again, according to my informer, 'can this be true? Can the white man have come all this way to see me? What a strong man he must be too, to come so quickly! Here are seven cows, four of them milch ones, as you say he likes milk, which you will give him; and there are three for yourself for having brought him so quickly. Now, hurry off as fast as you can, and tell him I am more delighted at the prospect of seeing him than he can be to see me. There is no place here fit for his reception. I was on a pilgrimage which would have kept me here seven days longer; but as I am so impatient to see him, I will go off to my palace at once, and will send word for him to advance as soon as I arrive there.'

To Sunna's Kibŭga, 18th: About noon the succeeding day, some pages ran in to say we were to come along without a moment's delay, as their king had ordered it. He would not taste food until he saw me, so that everybody might know what great respect he felt for me. In the meanwhile, however, he wished for some gunpowder. I packed the pages off as fast as I could with some, and then tried myself to follow, but my men were all either sick or out foraging, and therefore we could not get under way until the evening. After going a certain distance, we came on a rush-drain, of much greater breadth even than the Mwérango, called the Moga (or river) Myanza, which was so deep I had to take off my trousers and tuck my clothes under my arms. It flowed into the Mwérango, but with scarcely any current at all. This rush-drain, all the natives assured me, rose in the hills to the southward – not in the lake, as the Mwérango did – and it was never bridged over like that river, because it was always fordable. This account seemed to me reasonable; for though so much broader in its bed than the Mwérango, it had no central, deep-flowing current. The time for judging as to their relative size, too, was favourable, as it was the height of the dry season, when most of the long grasses were burnt. When we were across this great rush-drain it was almost dark, so I gave orders to spend the night in the most favourable spot we could find. We had, however, to pass the late king Sunna's kibŭga or palace before this could be done, as no eyes were allowed to dwell on the royal establishments of departed kings.

To Bandawarogo, 19th: One march more and we came in sight of the king's kibŭga or palace, in the province of Bandawarogo, N. lat. 0° 21' 19', and E. long. 32° 44' 30'. It was a magnificent sight. A whole hill was covered with gigantic huts, such as I had never seen in Africa before. I wished to go up to the palace at once, but the officers said, 'No, that would be considered indecent in Uganda; you must draw up your men, and fire your guns off, to let the king know you are here; we will then show you your residence, and to-morrow you will doubtless be sent for, as the king could not now hold a levee whilst it is raining.' I made the men fire, and then was shown into a lot of dirty huts, which, they said, were built expressly for all the king's visitors. The Arabs, when they came on their visits, always put up here, and I must do the same. At first I stuck out on my claims as a foreign prince, whose royal blood could not stand such an indignity. The palace was my sphere, and unless I could get a hut there, I would return without seeing the king.

In a terrible fright at my blustering, N'yamgundŭ fell at my feet, and implored me not to be hasty. The king did not understand who I was, and could not be spoken to then. He implored me to be content with my lot for the present, after which the king, when he knew all about it, would do as I liked, he was sure, though no strangers had ever yet been allowed to reside within the royal enclosures. I gave way to this good man's appeal, and cleaned my hut by firing the ground, for, like all the huts in this dog country, it was full of fleas. Once ensconced there, the king's pages darted in to see me, bearing a message from their master, who said he was sorry the rain prevented him from holding a levee that day, but the next he would be delighted to see me. Irungŭ, with all Sŭwarora's men, then came to a collection of huts near where I was residing; and whilst I lay in bed that night, Irungti with all his wives came in to see me and beg for beads.

CHAPTER X

Palace, Uganda

HALT, from 19th Feb to 7th July: To-day the king sent his pages to announce his intention of holding a levee in my honour. I prepared for my first presentation at court, attired in my best, though in it I cut a poor figure in comparison with the display of the dressy Waganda. They wore neat bark cloaks resembling the best yellow corduroy cloth, crimp and well set, as if stiffened with starch, and over that, as upper-cloaks, a patchwork of small antelope skins, which I observed were sewn together as well as any English glovers could have pieced them; whilst their head-dresses, generally, were abrus turbans, set off with highly-polished boar-tusks, stick-charms, seeds, beads, or shells; and on their necks, arms, and ankles they wore other charms of wood, or small horns stuffed with magic powder, and fastened on by strings generally covered with snake-skin. N'yamgundŭ and Maŭla demanded, as their official privilege, a first peep; and this being refused, they tried to persuade me that the articles comprising the present required to be covered with chintz, for it was considered indecorous to offer anything to his majesty in a naked state. This little interruption over, the articles enumerated below were conveyed to the palace in solemn procession thus: With N'yamgundŭ, Maŭla, the pages, and myself on the flanks, the Union-Jack carried by the kirangozi guide led the way, followed by twelve men as a guard of honour, dressed in red flannel cloaks, and carrying their arms sloped, with fixed bayonets; whilst in their rear were the rest of my men, each carrying some article as a present.

On the march towards the palace, the admiring courtiers, wonder-struck at such an unusual display, exclaimed, in raptures of astonishment, some with both hands at their mouths, and others clasping their heads with their hands, 'Irungi! irungi!' which may be translated 'Beautiful! beautiful!' I thought myself everything was going on as well as could be wished; but before entering the royal enclosures, I found, to my disagreeable surprise, that the men with Sŭwarora's hongo or offering, which consisted of more than a hundred coils of wire, were ordered to lead the procession, and take precedence of me. There was something specially aggravating in this precedence; for it will be remembered that these very brass wires which they saw, I had myself intended for Mtésa, that they were taken from me by Sŭwarora as far back as Usŭi, and it would never do, without remonstrance, to have them boastfully paraded before my eyes in this fashion. My protests, however, had no effect upon the escorting Wakungŭ. Resolving to make them catch it, I walked along as if ruminating in anger up the broad high road into a cleared square, which divides Mtésa's domain on the south from his Kamraviona's, or commander-in-chief, on the north, and then turned into the court. The palace or entrance quite surprised me by its extraordinary dimensions, and the neatness with which it was kept. The whole brow and sides of the hill on which we stood were covered with gigantic grass huts, thatched as neatly as so many heads dressed by a London barber, and fenced all round with the tall yellow reeds of the common Uganda tiger-grass whilst within the enclosure, the lines of huts were joined together, or partitioned off into courts, with walls of the same grass. It is here most of Mtésa's three or four hundred women are kept, the rest being quartered chiefly with his mother, known by the title of N'yamasoré, or queen-dowager. They stood in little groups at the doors, looking at us, and evidently passing their own remarks, and enjoying their own jokes, on the triumphal procession. At each gate as we passed, officers on duty opened and shut it for us, jingling the big bells which are hung upon them, as they sometimes are at shop-doors, to prevent silent, stealthy entrance.

The first court passed, I was even more surprised to find the unusual ceremonies that awaited me. There courtiers of high dignity stepped forward to greet me, dressed in the most scrupulously neat fashions. Men, women, bulls, dogs, and goats, were led about by strings; cocks and hens were carried in men's arms; and little pages, with rope-turbans, rushed about, conveying messages, as if their lives depended on their swiftness, every one holding his skin-cloak tightly round him lest his naked legs might by accident be shown.

This, then, was the ante-reception court; and I might have taken possession of the hut, in which musicians were playing and singing on large nine-stringed harps, like the Nubian tambira, accompanied by harmonicons. By the chief officers in waiting, however, who thought fit to treat us like Arab merchants, I was requested to sit on the ground outside in the sun with my servants. Now, I had made up my mind never to sit upon the ground as the natives and Arabs are obliged to do, nor to make my obeisance in any other manner than is customary in England, though the Arabs had told me that from fear they had always complied with the manners of the court. I felt that if I did not stand up for my social position at once, I should be treated with contempt during the remainder of my visit, and thus lose the vantage-ground I had assumed of appearing rather as a prince than a trader, for the purpose of better gaining the confidence of the king. To avert over-hastiness, however – for my servants began to be alarmed as I demurred against doing as I was bid – I allowed five minutes to the court to give me a proper reception, saying, if it were not conceded I would then walk away.

Nothing, however, was done. My own men, knowing me, feared for me, as they did not know what a 'savage' king would do in case I carried out my threat; whilst the Waganda, lost in amazement at what seemed little less than blasphemy, stood still as posts. The affair ended by my walking straight away home, giving Bombay orders to leave the present on the ground, and to follow me.

Although the king is said to be unapproachable, excepting when he chooses to attend court – a ceremony which rarely happens – intelligence of my hot wrath and hasty departure reached him in an instant. He first, it seems, thought of leaving his toilet-room to follow me, but, finding I was walking fast and had gone far, changed his mind, and sent Wakungŭ running after me. Poor creatures! they caught me up, fell upon their knees, and implored I would return at once, for the king had not tasted food, and would not until he saw me. I felt grieved at their touching appeals; but, as I did not understand all they said, I simply replied by patting my heart and shaking my head, walking if anything all the faster.

On my arrival at my hut, Bombay and others came in, wet through with perspiration, saying the king had heard of all my grievances.

Sŭwarora's hongo was turned out of court, and, if I desired it, I might bring my own chair with me, for he was very anxious to show me great respect – although such a seat was exclusively the attribute of the king, no one else in Uganda daring to sit on an artificial seat.

My point was gained, so I cooled myself with coffee and a pipe, and returned rejoicing in my victory, especially over Sŭwarora. After returning to the second tier of huts from which I had retired, everybody appeared to be in a hurried, confused state of excitement, not knowing what to make out of so unprecedented an exhibition of temper. In the most polite manner, the officers in waiting begged me to be seated on my iron stool, which I had brought with me, whilst others hurried in to announce my arrival. But for a few minutes only I was kept in suspense, when a band of music, the musicians wearing on their backs long-haired goat-skins, passed me, dancing as they went along, like bears in a fair, and playing on reed instruments worked over with pretty beads in various patterns, from which depended leopard-cat skins – the time being regulated by the beating of long hand-drums.

The mighty king was now reported to be sitting on his throne in the state hut of the third tier. I advanced, hat in hand, with my guard of honour following, formed in 'open ranks,' who in their turn were followed by the bearers carrying the present. I did not walk straight up to him as if to shake hands, but went outside the ranks of a three-sided square of squatting Wakungŭ, all habited in skins, mostly cow-skins; some few of whom had, in addition, leopard-cat skins girt round the waist, the sign of royal blood. Here I was desired to halt and sit in the glaring sun; so I donned my hat, mounted my umbrella, a phenomenon which set them all a-wondering and laughing, ordered the guard to close ranks, and sat gazing at the novel spectacle. A more theatrical sight I never saw. The king, a good-looking, well-figured, tall young man of twenty-five, was sitting on a red blanket spread upon a square platform of royal grass, encased in tiger-grass reeds, scrupulously well dressed in a new mbŭgŭ. The hair of his head was cut short, excepting on the top, where it was combed up into a high ridge, running from stem to stern like a cockscomb. On his neck was a very neat ornament – a large ring, of beautifully-worked small beads, forming elegant patterns by their various colours. On one arm was another bead ornament, prettily devised; and on the other a wooden charm, tied by a string covered with snake-skin. On every finger and every toe he had alternate brass and copper rings; and above the ankles, half-way up to the calf, a stocking of very pretty beads. Everything was light, neat, and elegant in its way; not a fault could be found with the taste of his 'getting up.' For a handkerchief he held a well-folded piece of bark, and a piece of gold-embroidered silk, which he constantly employed to hide his large mouth when laughing, or to wipe it after a drink of plantain-wine, of which he took constant and copious draughts from neat little gourd-cups, administered by his ladies-in-waiting, who were at once his sisters and wives. A white dog, spear, shield, and woman – the Uganda cognisance – were by his side, as also a knot of staff officers, with whom he kept up a brisk conversation on one side; and on the other was a band of Wichwézi, or lady-sorcerers, such as I have already described.

I was now asked to draw nearer within the hollow square of squatters, where leopard-skins were strewed upon the ground, and a large copper kettledrum, surmounted with brass bells on arching wires, along with two other smaller drums covered with cowrie-shells, and beads of colour worked into patterns, were placed. I now longed to open conversation, but knew not the language, and no one near me dared speak, or even lift his head from fear of being accused of eyeing the women; so the king and myself sat staring at one another for full an hour – I mute, but he pointing and remarking with those around him on the novelty of my guard and general appearance, and even requiring to see my hat lifted, the umbrella shut and opened, and the guards face about and show off their red cloaks – for such wonders had never been seen in Uganda.

Then, finding the day waning, he sent Maŭla on an embassy to ask me if I had seen him; and on receiving my reply, 'Yes, for full one hour,' I was glad to find him rise, spear in hand, lead his dog, and walk unceremoniously away through the enclosure into the fourth tier of huts; for this being a pure levée day, no business was transacted.

The king's gait in retiring was intended to be very majestic, but did not succeed in conveying to me that impression. It was the traditional walk of his race, founded on the step of the lion; but the outward sweep of the legs, intended to represent the stride of the noble beast, appeared to me only to realise a very ludicrous kind of waddle, which made me ask Bombay if anything serious was the matter with the royal person.

I had now to wait for some time, almost as an act of humanity; for I was told the state secret, that the king had retired to break his fast and eat for the first time since hearing of my arrival; but the repast was no sooner over than he prepared for the second act, to show off his splendour, and I was invited in, with all my men, to the exclusion of all his own officers save my two guides. Entering as before, I found him standing on a red blanket, leaning against the right portal of the hut, talking and laughing, handkerchief in hand, to a hundred or more of his admiring wives, who, all squatting on the ground outside, in two groups, were dressed in new mbŭgŭs. My men dared not advance upright, nor look upon the women, but, stooping, with lowered heads and averted eyes, came cringing after me. Unconscious myself, I gave loud and impatient orders to my guard, rebuking them for moving like frightened geese, and, with hat in hand, stood gazing on the fair sex till directed to sit and cap.

Mtésa then inquired what messages were brought from Rŭmanika; to which Maŭla, delighted with the favour of speaking to royalty, replied by saying, Rŭmanika had gained intelligence of Englishmen coming up the Nile to Gani and Kidi. The king acknowledged the truthfulness of their story, saying he had heard the same himself; and both Wakungŭ, as is the custom in Uganda, thanked their lord in a very enthusiastic manner, kneeling on the ground – for no one can stand in the presence of his majesty – in an attitude of prayer, and throwing out their hands as they repeated the words N'yanzig, N'yanzig, ai N'yanzig Mkahma wangi, etc. etc., for a considerable time; when, thinking they had done enough of this, and heated with the exertion, they threw themselves flat upon their stomachs, and, floundering about like fish on land, repeated the same words over again and again, and rose doing the same, with their faces covered with earth; for majesty in Uganda is never satisfied till subjects have grovelled before it like the most abject worms. This conversation over, after gazing at me, and chatting with his women for a considerable time, the second scene ended. The third scene was more easily arranged, for the day was fast declining. He simply moved with his train of women to another hut, where, after seating himself upon his throne, with his women around him, he invited me to approach the nearest limits of propriety, and to sit as before. Again he asked me if I had seen him – evidently desirous of indulging in his regal pride; so I made the most of the opportunity thus afforded me of opening a conversation by telling him of those grand reports I had formerly heard about him, which induced me to come all this way to see him, and the trouble it had cost me to reach the object of my desire; at the same time taking a gold ring from off my finger, and presenting it to him, I said, 'This is a small token of friendship; if you will inspect it, it is made after the fashion of a dog-collar, and, being the king of metals, gold, is in every respect appropriate to your illustrious race.'

He said, in return, 'If friendship is your desire, what would you say if I showed you a road by which you might reach your home in one month?' Now everything had to be told to Bombay, then to Nasib, my Kiganda interpreter, and then to either Maŭla or N'yamgundŭ, before it was delivered to the king, for it was considered indecorous to transmit any message to his majesty excepting through the medium of one of his officers. Hence I could not get an answer put in; for as all Waganda are rapid and impetuous in their conversation, the king, probably forgetting he had put a question, hastily changed the conversation and said, 'What guns have you got? Let me see the one you shoot with.' I wished still to answer the first question first, as I knew he referred to the direct line to Zanzibar across the Masai, and was anxious, without delay, to open the subject of Petherick and Grant; but no one dared to deliver my statement. Much disappointed, I then said, 'I had brought the best shooting-gun in the world – Whitworth's rifle – which I begged he would accept, with a few other trifles; and, with his permission, I would lay them upon a carpet at his feet, as is the custom of my country when visiting sultans.' He assented, sent all his women away, and had an mbŭgŭ spread for the purpose, on which Bombay, obeying my order, first spread a red blanket, and then opened each article one after the other, when Nasib, according to the usage already mentioned, smoothed them down with his dirty hands, or rubbed them against his sooty face, and handed them to the king to show there was no poison or witchcraft in them. Mtésa appeared quite confused with the various wonders as he handled them, made silly remarks, and pondered over them like a perfect child, until it was quite dark. Torches were then lit, and guns, pistols, powder, boxes, tools, beads – the whole collection, in short – were tossed together topsy-turvy, bundled into mbŭgŭs, and carried away by the pages. Mtésa now said, 'It is late, and time to break up; what provisions would you wish to have ?' I said, 'A little of everything, but no one thing constantly.' 'And would you like to see me to-morrow ?' 'Yes, every day.' 'Then you can't to-morrow, for I have business; but the next day come if you like. You can now go away, and here are six pots of plantain-wine for you; my men will search for food to-morrow.'

21st. – In the morning, whilst it rained, some pages drove in twenty cows and ten goats, with a polite metaphorical message from their king, to the effect that I had pleased him much, and he hoped I would accept these few 'chickens' until he could send more, – when both Maŭla and N'yamgundŭ, charmed with their success in having brought a welcome guest to Uganda, never ceased showering eulogiums on me for my fortune in having gained the countenance of their king. The rain falling was considered at court a good omen, and everybody declared the king mad with delight. Wishing to have a talk with him about Petherick and Grant, I at once started off the Wakungŭ to thank him for the present, and to beg pardon for my apparent rudeness of yesterday, at the same time requesting I might have an early interview with his majesty, as I had much of importance to communicate; but the solemn court formalities which these African kings affect as much as Oriental emperors, precluded my message from reaching the king. I heard, however, that he had spent the day receiving Sŭwarora's hongo of wire, and that the officer who brought them was made to sit in an empty court, whilst the king sat behind a screen, never deigning to show his majestic person. I was told, too, that he opened conversation by demanding to know how it happened that Sŭwarora became possessed of the wires, for they were made by the white men to be given to himself, and Sŭwarora must therefore have robbed me of them; and it was by such practices he, Mtésa, never could see any visitors. The officer's reply was, Sŭwarora would not show the white men any respect, because they were wizards who did not sleep in houses at night, but flew up to the tops of hills, and practised sorcery of every abominable kind. The king to this retorted, in a truly African fashion, 'That's a lie; I can see no harm in this white man; and if he had been a bad man, Rǔmanika would not have sent him on to me.' At night, when in bed, the king sent his pages to say, if I desired his friendship I would lend him one musket to make up six with what I had given him, for he intended visiting his relations the following morning. I sent three, feeling that nothing would be lost by being 'open-handed.'

22d – To-day the king went the round of his relations, showing the beautiful things given him by the white man – a clear proof that he was much favoured by-the 'spirits,' for neither his father nor any of his forefathers had been so recognised and distinguished by any 'sign' as a rightful inheritor to the Uganda throne: an anti-Christian interpretation of omens, as rife in these dark regions now as it was in the time of King Nebuchadnezzar. At midnight the three muskets were returned, and I was so pleased with the young king's promptitude and honesty, I begged he would accept them.

23d. – At noon Mtésa sent his pages to invite me to his palace. I went, with my guard of honour and my stool, but found I had to sit waiting in an ante-hut three hours with his commander-in-chief and other high officers before he was ready to see me. During this time Wasoga minstrels, playing on tambira, and accompanied by boys playing on a harmonicon, kept us amused; and a small page, with a large bundle of grass, came to me and said, 'The king hopes you won't be offended if required to sit on it before him; for no person in Uganda, however high in office, is ever allowed to sit upon anything raised above the ground, nor can anybody but himself sit upon such grass as this; it is all that his throne is made of. The first day he only allowed you to sit on your stool to appease your wrath.'

On consenting to do in 'Rome as the Romans do,' when my position was so handsomely acknowledged, I was called in, and found the court sitting much as it was on the first day's interview, only that the number of squatting Wakungǔ was much diminished; and the king, instead of wearing his ten brass and copper rings, had my gold one on his third finger. This day, however, was cut out for business, as, in addition to the assemblage of officers, there were women, cows, goats, fowls, confiscations, baskets of fish, baskets of small antelopes, porcupines, and curious rats caught by his gamekeepers, bundles of mbŭgŭ, etc. etc., made by his linen-drapers, coloured earths and sticks by his magician, all ready for presentation; but, as rain fell, the court broke up, and I had nothing for it but to walk about under my umbrella, indulging in angry reflections against the haughty king for not inviting me into his hut.

When the rain had ceased, and we were again called in, he was found sitting in state as before, but this time with the head of a black bull placed before him, one horn of which, knocked off, was placed alongside, whilst four living cows walked about the court.

I was now requested to shoot the four cows as quickly as possible; but having no bullets for my gun, I borrowed the revolving pistol I had given him, and shot all four in a second of time; but as the last one, only wounded, turned sharply upon me, I gave him the fifth and settled him. Great applause followed this *wonderful* feat, and the cows were given to my men. The king now loaded one of the carbines I had given him with his own hands, and giving it full-cock to a page, told him to go out and shoot a man in the outer court; which was no sooner accomplished than the little urchin returned to announce his success, with a look of glee such as one would see in the face of a boy who had robbed a bird's nest, caught a trout, or done any other boyish trick. The king said to him, 'And did you do it well?' 'Oh yes, capitally.' He spoke the truth, no doubt, for he dared not have trifled with the king; but the affair created hardly any interest. I never heard, and there appeared no curiosity to know, what individual human being the urchin had deprived of life.

The Wakungŭ were now dismissed, and I asked to draw near, when the king showed me a book I had given to Rŭmanika, and begged for the inspiring medicine which he had before applied for through the mystic stick. The day was now gone, so torches were lit, and we were ordered to go, though as yet I had not been able to speak one word I wished to impart about Petherick and Grant; for my interpreters were so afraid of the king they dared not open their mouths until they were spoken to. The king was now rising to go, when, in great fear and anxiety that the day would be lost, I said, in Kisŭahili, 'I wish you would send a letter by post to Grant, and also send a boat up the Kitangŭlé, as far as Rŭmanika's palace, for him, for he is totally unable to walk.' I thus attracted his notice, though he did not understand one word I uttered. The result was, that he waited for the interpretation, and replied that a post would be no use, for no one would be responsible for the safe delivery of the message; he would send N'yamgundŭ to fetch him, but he thought Rŭmanika would not consent to his sending boats up the Kitangŭlé as far as the Little Windermere; and then, turning round with true Mganda impetuosity, he walked away without taking a word from me in exchange.

24th. – Early this morning the pages came to say Mtésa desired I would send him three of my Wangŭana to shoot cows before him. This was just what I wanted. It had struck me that personal conferences with me so roused the excitable king, that there was no bringing plain matters of business home to him; so, detaching seven men with Bombay, I told him, before shooting, to be sure and elicit the matter I wanted – which was, to excite the king's cupidity by telling him I had a boat full of stores with two white men at Gani, whom I wished to call to me if he would furnish some guides to accompany my men; and farther, as Grant could not walk, I wished boats sent for him, at least as far as the ferry on the Kitangŭlé, to which place Rŭmanika, at any rate, would slip him down in canoes. At once, on arriving, Mtésa admitted the men, and ordered them to shoot at some cows; but Bombay, obeying my orders to first have his talk out, said, No – before he could shoot he must obey master and deliver his message; which no sooner was told than the king, in a hurry, excited by the prospects of sport, impatiently said, 'Very good; I will send men either by water or overland through Kidi, just as your master likes; only some of his men had better go with mine: but now shoot cows, shoot cows; for I want to see how the Wangŭana shoot.' They shot seven, and all were given to them when they were dismissed. In the evening the pages came to ask me if I would like to shoot kites in the palace with their king; but I declined shooting anything less than elephants, rhinoceros, or buffaloes; and even for these I would not go out unless the king went with me; a dodge I conceived would tend more than any other to bring us together, and so break through those ceremonial restraints of the court, which at present were stopping all plans of progression.

25th. – The king invited me to shoot with him – really buffaloes – close to the palace; but as the pages had been sent off in a hurry, without being fully instructed, I declined, on the plea that I had always been gulled and kept waiting, or treated with incivility, for hours before I obtained an interview; and as I did not wish to have any more. ruptures in the palace, I proposed Bombay should go to make proper arrangements for my reception on the morrow – as, anyhow, at present I felt indisposed. The pages dreaded their master's wrath, departed for a while, and then sent another lad to tell me he was sorry to hear I felt unwell, but he hoped I would come if only for a minute, bringing my medicines with me, for he himself felt pain. That this second message was a forged one I had no doubt, for the boys had not been long enough gone; still, I packed up my medicines and went, leaving the onus, should any accident happen, upon the mischievous story-bearers.

As I anticipated, on arrival at the palace I found the king was not ready to receive me, and the pages desired me to sit with the officers in waiting until he might appear. I found it necessary to fly at once into a rage, called the pages a set of deceiving young blackguards, turned upon my heel, and walked straight back through the courts, intending to leave the palace. Everybody was alarmed; information of my retreat at once reached the king, and he sent his Wakungŭ to prevent my egress. These officers passed me, as I was walking hurriedly along under my umbrella, in the last court, and shut the entrance-gate in front of me. This was too much, so I stamped, and, pointing my finger, swore in every language I knew, that if they did not open the gate again, as they had shut it at once, and that, too, before my face, I would never leave the spot I stood upon alive. Terror-stricken, the Wakungŭ fell on their knees before me, doing as they were bid; and, to please them, I returned at once and went up to the king, who, now sitting on his throne, asked the officers how they had managed to entice me back; to which they all replied in a breath, n'yanzigging heartily, 'Oh, we were so afraid – he was so terrible! but he turned at once as soon as we opened the gate.' 'How? what gate? tell us all about it.' And when the whole story was fully narrated, the matter was thought a good joke. After pausing a little, I asked the king what ailed him, for I was sorry to hear he had been sick; but instead of replying, he shook his head, as much as to say, I had put a very uncouth question to his majesty – and ordered some men to shoot cows.

Instead of admiring this childish pastime, which in Uganda is considered royal sport, I rather looked disdainful, until, apparently disappointed at my indifference, he asked what the box I had brought contained. On being told it was the medicine he desired, he asked me to draw near, and sent his courtiers away. When only the interpreters and one confidential officer were left, besides myself, he wished to know if I could apply the medicine without its touching the afflicted part. To give him confidence in my surgical skill, I moved my finger, and asked if he knew what gave it action; and on his replying in the negative, I gave him an anatomical lecture, which so pleased him, he at once consented to be operated on, and I applied a blister to him accordingly. The whole operation was rather ridiculous; for the blister, after being applied, had to be rubbed in turn on the hands and faces of both Bombay and Nasib, to show there was no evil spirit in the 'doctor.' Now, thought I to myself, is the right time for business; for I had the king all to myself, then considered a most fortunate occurrence in Uganda, where every man courts the favour of a word with his king, and adores him as a deity, and he in turn makes himself as distant as he can, to give greater effect to his exalted position. The matter, however, was merely deferred; for I no sooner told him my plans for communicating quickly with Petherick and Grant, than, after saying he desired their coming even more than myself, he promised to arrange everything on the morrow.

26th. – In the morning, as agreed, I called on the king, and found the blister had drawn nicely; so I let off the water, which Bombay called the malady, and so delighted the king amazingly. A basket of fruit, like Indian loquots, was then ordered in, and we ate them together, holding a discussion about Grant and Petherick, which ended by the king promising to send an officer by water to Kitangŭlé, and another, with two of my men, *viâ* Usoga and Kidi, to Gani; but as it was necessary my men should go in disguise, I asked the king to send me four mbŭgŭ and two spears; when, with the liberality of a great king, he sent me twenty sheets of the former, four spears, and a load of sun-dried fish strung on a stick in shape of a shield.

27th. – At last something was done. One Uganda officer and one Kidi guide were sent to my hut by the king, as agreed upon yesterday, when I detached Mabrŭki and Bilal from my men, gave them letters and maps addressed to Petherick; and giving the officers a load of Mtendé to pay their hotel bills on the way, I gave them, at the same time, strict orders to keep by the Nile; then, having dismissed them, I called on the king to make arrangements for Grant, and to complain that my residence in Uganda was anything but cheerful, as my hut was a mile from the palace, in an unhealthy place, where he kept his Arab visitors. It did not become my dignity to live in houses appropriated to persons in the rank of servants, which I considered the ivory-merchants to be; and as I had come only to see him and the high officers of Uganda, not seeking for ivory or slaves, I begged he would change my place of residence to the west end, when I also trusted his officers would not be ashamed to visit me, as appeared to be the case at present. Silence being the provoking resort of the king, when he did not know exactly what to say, he made no answer to my appeal, but instead, he began a discourse on geography, and then desired me to call upon his mother, N'yamasoré, at her palace Masorisori, vulgarly called Soli Soli, for she also required medicine; and, moreover, I was cautioned that for the future the Uganda court etiquette required I should attend on the king two days in succession, and every third day on his mother the queen-dowager, as such were their respective rights.

Till now, owing to the strict laws of the country, I had not been able to call upon anybody but the king himself. I had not been able to send presents or bribes to any one, nor had any one, except the cockaded pages, by the king's order, visited me; neither was anybody permitted to sell me provisions, so that my men had to feed themselves by taking anything they chose from certain gardens pointed out by the king's officers, or by seizing pombé or plantains which they might find Waganda carrying towards the palace. This non-interventive order was part of the royal policy, in order that the king might have the full fleecing of his visitors.

To call upon the queen-mother respectfully, as it was the opening visit, I took, besides the medicine-chest, a present of eight brass and copper wire, thirty blue-egg beads, one bundle of diminutive beads, and sixteen cubits of chintz, a small guard, and my throne of royal grass. The palace to be visited lay half a mile beyond the king's, but the highroad to it was forbidden me, as it is considered uncourteous to pass the king's gate without going in. So after winding through back-gardens, the slums of Bandowaroga, I struck upon the highroad close to her majesty's, where everything looked like the royal palace on a miniature scale. A large cleared space divided the queen's residence from her Kamraviona's. The outer enclosures and courts were fenced with tiger-grass; and the huts, though neither so numerous nor so large, were constructed after the same fashion as the king's. Guards also kept the doors, on which large bells were hung to give alarm, and officers in waiting watched the throne-rooms. All the huts were full of women, save those kept as waiting-rooms, where drums and harmonicons were placed for amusement. On first entering, I was required to sit in a waiting-hut till my arrival was announced; but that did not take long, as the queen was prepared to receive me; and being of a more affable disposition than her son, she held rather a levee of amusement than a stiff court of show. I entered the throne-hut as the gate of that court was thrown open, with my hat off, but umbrella held over my head, and walked straight towards her till ordered to sit upon my bundle of grass.

Her majesty – fat, fair, and forty-five – was sitting, plainly garbed in mbŭgŭ, upon a carpet spread upon the ground within a curtain of mbŭgŭ, her elbow resting on a pillow of the same bark material; the only ornaments on her person being an abrus necklace, and a piece of mbŭgŭ tied round her head, whilst a folding looking-glass, much the worse for wear, stood open by her side. An iron rod like a spit, with a cup on the top, charged with magic powder, and other magic wands, were placed before the entrance; and within the room, four Mabandwa sorceresses or devil-drivers, fantastically dressed, as before described, and a mass of other women, formed the company. For a short while we sat at a distance, exchanging inquiring glances at one another, when the women were dismissed, and a band of music, with a court full of Wakungŭ, was ordered in to change the scene. I also got orders to draw near and sit fronting her within the hut. Pombé, the best in Uganda, was then drunk by the queen, and handed to me and to all the high officers about her, when she smoked her pipe, and bade me smoke mine. The musicians, dressed in long-haired Usoga goat-skins, were now ordered to strike up, which they did, with their bodies swaying or dancing like bears in a fair. Different drums were then beat, and I was asked if I could distinguish their different tones.

The queen, full of mirth, now suddenly rose, leaving me sitting, whilst she went to another hut, changed her mbŭgŭ for a déolé, and came back again for us to admire her, which was no sooner done to her heart's content, than a second time, by her order, the court was cleared, and, when only three or four confidential Wakungŭ were left, she took up a small faggot of well-trimmed sticks, and, selecting three, told me she had three complaints. 'This stick,' she says, 'represents my stomach, which gives me much uneasiness; this second stick my liver, which causes shooting pains all over my body; and this third one my heart, for I get constant dreams at night about Sunna, my late husband, and they are not pleasant.' The dreams and sleeplessness I told her was a common widow's complaint, and could only be cured by her majesty making up her mind to marry a second time; but before I could advise for the bodily complaints, it would be necessary for me to see her tongue, feel her pulse, and perhaps, also, her sides. Hearing this, the Wakungŭ said, 'Oh, that can never be allowed without the sanction of the king;' but the queen, rising in her seat, expressed her scorn at the idea of taking advice from a mere stripling, and submitted herself for examination.

I then took out two pills, the powder of which was tasted by the Wakungŭ to prove that there was no devilry in 'the doctor,' and gave orders for them to be eaten at night, restricting her pombé and food until I saw her again. My game was now advancing, for I found through her I should get the key to an influence that might bear on the king, and was much pleased to hear her express herself delighted with me for everything I had done except stopping her grog, which, naturally enough in this great pombé-drinking country, she said would be a very trying abstinence.

The doctoring over, her majesty expressed herself ready to inspect the honorarium I had brought for her, and the articles were no sooner presented by Bombay and Nasib, with the usual formalities of stroking to insure their purity, than she, boiling with pleasure, showed them all to her officers, who declared, with a voice of most exquisite triumph, that she was indeed the most favoured of queens. Then, in excellent good taste, after saying that nobody had ever given her such treasures, she gave me, in return, a beautifully-worked pombé sucking-pipe, which was acknowledged by every one to be the greatest honour she could pay me.

Not satisfied with this, she made me select, though against my desire, a number of sambo, called here gundu, rings of giraffe hair wound round with thin iron or copper wire, and worn as anklets; and crowned all with sundry pots of pombé, a cow, and a bundle of dried fish, of the description given in the woodcut, called by my men Samaki Kambari. This business over, she begged me to show her my picture-books, and was so amused with them that she ordered her sorceresses and all the other women in again to inspect them with her. Then began a warm and complimentary conversation, which ended by an inspection of my rings and all the contents of my pockets, as well as of my watch, which she called Lŭbari – a term equivalent to a place of worship, the object of worship itself or the iron horn or magic pan. Still she said I had not yet satisfied her; I must return again two days hence, for she liked me much – excessively – she could not say how much; but now the day was gone, I might go. With this queer kind of adieu she rose and walked away, leaving me with my servants to carry the royal present home.

28th – My whole thoughts were now occupied in devising some scheme to obtain a hut in the palace, not only the better to maintain my dignity, and so gain superior influence in the court, but also that I might have a better insight into the manners and customs of these strange people. I was not sorry to find the king attempting to draw me to court, daily to sit in attendance on him as his officers are obliged to do all day long, in order that he might always have a full court or escort whenever by chance he might emerge from his palace, for it gave me an opening for asserting a proper position.

Instead, therefore, of going at the call of his pages this morning, I sent Bombay with some men to say that although I was desirous of seeing him daily, I could not so expose myself to the sun. In all other countries I received, as my right, a palace to live in when I called on the king of the country, and unless he gave one now I should feel slighted; moreover, I should like a hut in the same enclosure as himself, when I could sit and converse with him constantly, and teach him the use of the things I had given him. By Bombay's account, the king was much struck with the force of my humble request, and replied that he should like to have Bana, meaning myself, ever by his side, but his huts were all full of women, and therefore it could not be managed; if, however, Bana would but have patience for a while, a hut should be built for him in the environs, which would be a mark of distinction he had never paid to any visitor before. Then changing the subject by inspecting my men, he fell so much in love with their little red 'fez' caps, that he sent off his pages to beg me for a specimen, and, on finding them sent by the boys, he remarked, with warm approbation, how generous I was in supplying his wishes, and then, turning to Bombay, wished to know what sort of return-presents would please me best. Bombay, already primed, instantly said, 'Oh, Bana, being a great man in his own country, and not thirsting for gain in ivory or slaves, would only accept such things as a spear, shield, or drum, which he could take to his own country as a specimen of the manufactures of Uganda, and a pleasing recollection of his visit to the king.'

'Ah,' says Mtésa, 'if that is all he wants, then indeed will I satisfy him, for I will give him the two spears with which I took all this country, and, when engaged in so doing, pierced three men with one stab.

'But, for the present, is it true what I have heard, that Bana would like to go out with me shooting?' 'Oh, yes, he is a most wonderful sportsman – shoots elephants and buffaloes, and birds on the wing. He would like to go out on a shooting excursion and teach you the way.'

Then turning the subject, in the highest good-humour the king made centurions of N'yamgundŭ and Maŭla, my two Wakungŭ, for their good service, he said, in bringing him such a valuable guest. This delighted them so much that as soon as they could they came back to my camp, threw themselves at my feet, and n'yanzigging incessantly, narrated their fortunes, and begged, as a great man, I would lend them some cows to present to the king as an acknowledgment for the favour he had shown them. The cows, I then told them, had come from the king, and could not go back again, for it was not the habit of white men to part with their presents; but as I felt their promotion redounded on myself, and was certainly the highest compliment their king could have paid me, I would give them each a wire to make their salaam good.

This was enough; both officers got drunk, and, beating their drums, serenaded the camp until the evening set in, when, to my utter surprise, an elderly Mganda woman was brought into camp with the commander-in-chief's metaphorical compliments, hoping I would accept her 'to carry my water;' with this trifling addition, that in case I did not think her pretty enough, he hoped I would not hesitate to select which I liked from ten others, of 'all colours,' Wahǔma included, who, for that purpose, were then waiting in his palace.

Unprepared for this social addition in my camp, I must now confess I felt in a fix, knowing full well that nothing so offends as rejecting an offer at once, so I kept her for the time being, intending in the morning to send her back with a string of blue beads on her neck; but during the night she relieved me of my anxieties by running away, which Bombay said was no wonder, for she had obviously been seized as part of some confiscated estate, and without doubt knew where to find some of her friends.

To-day, for the first time since I have been here, I received a quantity of plantains. This was in consequence of my complaining that the king's orders to my men to feed themselves at others' expense was virtually making them a pack of thieves.

1st – I received a letter from Grant, dated 10th February, reporting Baraka's departure for Unyoro on the 30th January, escorted by Kamrasi's men on their return, and a large party of Rǔmanika's bearing presents as a letter from their king; whilst Grant himself hoped to leave Karagǔé before the end of the month. I then sent Bombay to see the queen, to ask after her health, beg for a hut in the palace enclosures, and say I should have gone myself, only I feared her gate might be shut, and I cannot go backwards and forwards so far in the sun without a horse or an elephant to ride upon. She begged I would come next morning. A wonderful report came that the king put two tops of powder into his Whitworth rifle to shoot a cow, and the bullet not only passed through the cow, but through the court fence, then through the centre of a woman, and, after passing the outer fence, flew whizzing along no one knew where.

2d. – Calling on the queen early, she admitted me at once, scolding me severely for not having come or sent my men to see her after she had taken the pills. She said they did her no good, and prevailed on me to give her another prescription. Then sending her servant for a bag full of drinking-gourds, she made me select six of the best, and begged for my watch. That, of course, I could not part with; but I took the opportunity of telling her I did not like my residence; it was not only far away from everybody, but it was unworthy of my dignity. I came to Uganda to see the king and queen, because the Arabs said they were always treated with great respect; but now I could perceive those Arabs did not know what true respect means. Being poor men, they thought much of a cow or goat given gratis, and were content to live in any hovels. Such, I must inform her, was not my case. I could neither sit in the sun nor live in a poor man's hut. When I rose to leave for breakfast, she requested me to stop, but I declined, and walked away. I saw, however, there was something wrong; for Maŭla, always ordered to be in attendance when anybody visits, was retained by her order to answer why I would not stay with her longer. If I wanted food or pombé, there was plenty of it in her palace, and her cooks were the cleverest in the world; she hoped I would return to see her in the morning.

3d. – Our cross purposes seemed to increase; for, while I could not get a satisfactory interview, the king sent for N'yamgundŭ to ascertain why I never went to see him. I had given him good guns and many pretty things which he did not know the use of, and yet I would not visit him to explain their several uses. N'yamgundŭ told him I lived too far off, and wanted a palace. After this I walked off to see N'yamasoré, taking my blankets, a pillow, and some cooking-pots to make a day of it, and try to win the affections of the queen with sixteen cubits bindéra, three pints péké, and three pints mtendé beads, which, as Waganda are all fond of figurative language, I called a trifle for her servants.

I was shown in at once, and found her majesty sitting on an Indian carpet, dressed in a red linen wrapper with a gold border, and a box, in shape of a lady's work-box, prettily coloured in divers patterns with minute beads, by her side. Her councillors were in attendance; and in the yard a band of music, with many minor Wakungŭ squatting in a semicircle, completed her levee. Maŭla on my behalf opened conversation, in allusion to her yesterday's question, by saying I had applied to Mtésa for a palace, that I might be near enough both their majesties to pay them constant visits. She replied, in a good hearty manner, that indeed was a very proper request, which showed my good sense, and ought to have been complied with at once; but Mtésa was only a Kijana or stripling, and as she influenced all the government of the country, she would have it carried into effect. Compliments were now passed, my presents given and approved of; and the queen, thinking I must be hungry, for she wanted to eat herself, requested me to refresh myself in another hut. I complied, spread my bedding, and ordered in my breakfast; but as the hut was full of men, I suspended a Scotch plaid, and quite eclipsed her mbŭgŭ curtain.

Reports of this magnificence at once flew to the queen, who sent to know how many more blankets I had in my possession, and whether, if she asked for one, she would get it. She also desired to see my spoons, fork, and pipe – an English meerschaum, mounted with silver; so, after breakfast, I returned to see her, showed her the spoons and forks, and smoked my pipe, but told her I had no blankets left but what formed my bed. She appeared very happy and very well, did not say another word about the blankets, but ordered a pipe for herself, and sat chatting, laughing, and smoking in concert with me.

I told her I had visited all the four quarters of the globe, and had seen all colours of people, but wondered where she got her pipe from, for it was much after the Rŭmish (Turkish) fashion, with a long stick. Greatly tickled at the flattery, she said, 'We hear men like yourself come to Amara from the other side, and drive cattle away.' 'The Gallas, or Abyssinians, who are tall and fair, like Rŭmanika,' I said, 'might do so, for they live not far off on the other side of Amara, but we never fight for such paltry objects. If cows fall into our hands when fighting, we allow our soldiers to eat them, while we take the government of the country into our own hands.' She then said, 'We hear you don't like the Unyamŭézi route, we will open the Ukori one for you.' 'Thank your majesty,' said I, in a figurative kind of speech to please Waganda ears; and turning the advantage of the project on her side, 'You have indeed hit the right nail on the head. I do not like the Unyamŭézi route, as you may well imagine when I tell you I have lost so much property there by mere robbery of the people and their kings. The Waganda do not see me in a true light; but if they have patience for a year or two, until the Ukori road is open, and trade between our respective countries shall commence, they will then see the fruits of my advent; so much so, that every Mganda will say the first Uganda year dates from the arrival of the first Mzungŭ (white) visitor. As one coffee-seed sown brings forth fruit in plenty, so my coming here may be considered.' All appreciated this speech, saying, 'The white man, he even speaks beautifully! beautifully! beautifully! beautifully!' and, putting their hands to their mouths, they looked askance at me, nodding their admiring approval.

The queen and her ministers then plunged into pombé and became uproarious, laughing with all their might and main. Small bugu cups were not enough to keep up the excitement of the time, so a large wooden trough was placed before the queen and filled with liquor. If any was spilt, the Wakungŭ instantly fought over it, dabbing their noses on the ground, or grabbing it with their hands, that not one atom of the queen's favour might be lost; for everything must be adored that comes from royalty, whether by design or accident The queen put her head to the trough and drank like a pig from it, and was followed by her ministers. The band, by order, then struck up a tune called the Milélé, playing on a dozen reeds, ornamented with beads and cow-tips, and five drums, of various tones and sizes, keeping time. The musicians dancing with zest, were led by four bandmasters, also dancing, but with their backs turned to the company to show off their long, shaggy, goat-skin jackets, sometimes upright, at other times bending and on their heels, like the hornpipe-dancers of western countries.

It was a merry scene, but soon became tiresome; when Bombay, by way of flattery, and wishing to see what the queen's wardrobe embraced, told her, Any woman, however ugly, would assume a goodly appearance if prettily dressed; upon which her gracious majesty immediately rose, retired to her toilet-hut, and soon returned attired in a common check cloth, an abrus tiara, a bead necklace, and with a folding looking-glass, when she sat, as before, and was handed a blown-glass cup of pombé, with a cork floating on the liquor, and a napkin mbŭgŭ covering the top, by a naked virgin. For her kind condescension in assuming plain raiment, everybody, of course, n'yanzigged. Next she ordered her slave girls to bring a large number of sambo (anklets), and begged me to select the best, for she liked me much. In vain I tried to refuse them: she had given more than enough for a keepsake before, and I was not hungry for property; still I had to choose some, or I would give offence. She then gave me a basket of tobacco, and a nest of hen eggs for her 'son's' breakfast When this was over, the Mŭkondéri, another dancing-tune, with instruments something like clarionets, was ordered; but it had scarcely been struck up, before a drenching rain, with strong wind, set in and spoilt the music, though not the playing – for none dared stop without an order; and the queen, instead of taking pity, laughed most boisterously over the exercise of her savage power as the unfortunate musicians were nearly beaten down by the violence of the weather.

When the rain ceased, her majesty retired a second time to her toilet-hut, and changed her dress for a puce-coloured wrapper, when I, ashamed of having robbed her of so many sambo, asked her if she would allow me to present her with a little English 'wool' to hang up instead of her mbŭgŭ curtain on cold days like this. Of course she could not decline, and a large double scarlet blanket was placed before her. 'Oh, wonder of wonders!' exclaimed all the spectators, holding their mouths in both hands at a time – such a 'pattern' had never been seen here before. It stretched across the hut, was higher than the men could reach – indeed it was a perfect marvel; and the man must be a good one who brought such a treasure as this to Uddŭ. 'And why not say Uganda?' I asked. 'Because all this country is called Uddŭ. Uganda is personified by Mtésa; and no one can say he has seen Uganda until he has been presented to the king.'

As I had them all in a good humour now, I complained I did not see enough of the Waganda – and as every one dressed so remarkably well, I could not discern the big men from the small; could she not issue some order by which they might call on me, as they did not dare do so without instruction, and then I, in turn, would call on them? Hearing this, she introduced me to her prime minister, chancellor of exchequer, women-keepers, hangmen, and cooks, as the first nobles in the land, that I might recognise them again if I met them on the road. All n'yanzigged for this great condescension, and said they were delighted with their guest; then producing a strip of common joho to compare it with my blanket, they asked if I could recognise it. Of course, said I, it is made in my country, of the same material, only of coarser quality, and everything of the same sort is made in Uzungŭ. Then, indeed, said the whole company, in one voice, we do like you, and your cloth too – but you most. I modestly bowed my head, and said their friendship was my chief desire.

This speech also created great hilarity; the queen and councillors all became uproarious. The queen began to sing, and the councillors to join in chorus; then all sang and all drank, and drank and sang, till, in their heated excitement, they turned the palace into a pandemonium; still there was not noise enough, so the band and drums were called again, and tomfool – for Uganda, like the old European monarchies, always keeps a jester – was made to sing in the gruff, hoarse, unnatural voice which he ever affects to maintain his character, and furnished with pombé when his throat was dry.

Now all of a sudden, as if a devil had taken possession of the company, the prime minister with all the courtiers jumped upon their legs, seized their sticks, for nobody can carry a spear when visiting, swore the queen had lost her heart to me, and running into the yard, returned, charging and jabbering at the queen; retreated and returned again, as if they were going to put an end to her for the guilt of loving me, but really to show their devotion and true love to her. The queen professed to take this ceremony with calm indifference, but her face showed that she enjoyed it. I was now getting very tired of sitting on my low stool, and begged for leave to depart, but N'yamasoré would not hear of it; she loved me a great deal too much to let me go away at this time of day, and forthwith ordered in more pombé. The same roystering scene was repeated; cups were too small, so the trough was employed; and the queen graced it by drinking, pig-fashion, first, and then handing it round to the company.

Now, hoping to produce gravity and then to slip away, I asked if my medicines had given her any relief, that I might give her more to strengthen her. She said she could not answer that question just yet; for though the medicine had moved her copiously, as yet she had seen no snake depart from her. I told her I would give her some strengthening medicine in the morning: for the present, however, I would take my leave, as the day was far gone, and the distance home very great; but though I dragged my body away, my heart would still remain here, for I loved her much.

This announcement took all by surprise; they looked at me and then at her, and looked again and laughed, whilst I rose, waved my hat, and said, 'Kŭa héri, Bibi' (good-bye, madam). On reaching home I found Maribŭ, a Mkungŭ, with a gang of men sent by Mtésa to fetch Grant from Kitangŭlé by water. He would not take any of my men with him to fetch the kit from Karagŭé, as Mtésa, he said, had given him orders to find all the means of transport; so I gave him a letter to Grant, and told him to look sharp, else Grant would have passed the Kitangŭlé before he arrived there. 'Never mind,' says Maribti, 'I shall walk to the mouth of the Katonga, boat it to Sésé island, where Mtésa keeps all his large vessels, and I shall be at Kitangŭlé in a very short time."

4th. – I sent Bombay off to administer quinine to the queen; but the king's pages, who watched him making for her gateway, hurried up to him, and turned him back by force. He pleaded earnestly that I would flog him if he disobeyed my orders, but they would take all the responsibility – the king had ordered it; and then they, forging a lie, bade him run back as fast as he could, saying I wanted to see the king, but could not till his return. In this way poor Bombay returned to me half-drowned in perspiration. Just then another page hurried in with orders to bring me to the palace at once, for I had not been there these four days; and while I was preparing to express the proper amount of indignation at this unceremonious message, the last impudent page began rolling like a pig upon my mbŭgŭed or carpeted floor, till I stormed and swore I would turn him out unless he chose to behave more respectfully before my majesty, for I was no peddling merchant, as he had been accustomed to see, and would not stand it; moreover, I would not leave my hut at the summons of the king or anybody else, until I chose to do so.

This expression of becoming wrath brought every one to a sense of his duty; and I then told them all I was excessively angry with Mtésa for turning back my messenger; nobody had ever dared do such a thing before, and I would never forgive the king until my medicines had been given to the queen. As for my going to the palace, it was out of the question, as I had repeatedly before told the king, unless it pleased him to give me a fitting residence near himself. In order now that full weight should be given to my expressions, I sent Bombay with the quinine to the king, in company with the boys, to give an account of all that had happened; and further, to say I felt exceedingly distressed I could not go to see him constantly – that I was ashamed of my domicile – the sun was hot to walk in; and when I went to the palace, his officers in waiting always kept me waiting like a servant – a matter hurtful to my honour and dignity. It now rested with himself to remove these obstacles. Everybody concerned in this matter left for the palace but Maŭla, who said he must stop in camp to look after Bana. Bombay no sooner arrived in the palace, and saw the king upon his throne, than Mtésa asked him why he came? 'By the instructions of Bana,' was his reply – 'for Bana cannot walk in the sun; no white man of the sultan's breed can do so.'

Hearing this, the king rose in a huff, without deigning to reply, and busied himself in another court Bombay, still sitting, waited for hours till quite tired, when he sent a boy in to say he had not delivered half my message; he had brought medicine for the queen, and as yet he had no reply for Bana. Either with haughty indifference, or else with injured pride at his not being able to command me at his pleasure, the king sent word, if medicine is brought for the queen, then let it be taken to her; and so Bombay walked off to the queen's palace. Arrived there, he sent in to say he had brought medicine, and waited without a reply till nightfall, when, tired of his charge, he gave the quinine into N'yamgundŭ's hands for delivery, and returned home. Soon after, however, N'yamgundŭ also returned to say the queen would not take the dose to-day, but hoped I would administer it personally in the morning.

Whilst all this vexatious business had been going on in court – evidently dictated by extreme jealousy, because I showed, as they all thought, a preference for the queen – Maŭla, more than tipsy, brought a Mkungŭ of some standing at court before me, contrary to all law – for as yet no Mganda, save the king's pages, had ever dared enter even the precincts of my camp. With a scowling, determined, hang-dog-looking countenance, he walked impudently into my hut, and, taking down the pombé-suckers the queen had given me, showed them with many queer gesticulations, intended to insinuate there was something between the queen and me. Among his jokes were, that I must never drink pombé excepting with these sticks; if I wanted any when I leave Uganda, to show my friends, she would give me twenty more sticks of that sort if I liked them; and, turning from verbal to practical jocularity, the dirty fellow took my common sucker out of the pot, inserted one of the queen's, and sucked at it himself, when I snatched and threw it away.

Maŭla's friend, who, I imagined, was a spy, then asked me whom I liked most – the mother or the son; but, without waiting to hear me, Maŭla hastily said, 'The mother, the mother, of course! he does not care for Mtésa, and won't go to see him.' The friend coaxingly responded, 'Oh no; he likes Mtésa, and will go and see him too; won't you?' I declined, however, to answer, from fear of mistake, as both interpreters were away. Still the two went on talking to themselves, Maŭla swearing that I loved the mother most, whilst the friend said, No, he loves the son, and asking me with anxious looks, till they found I was not to be caught by chaff, and then, both tired, walked away – the friend advising me, next time I went to court, to put on an Arab's gown, as trousers are indecent in the estimation of every Mganda.

5th. – Alarmed at having got involved in something that looked like court intrigues, I called up N'yamgundŭ; told him all that happened yesterday, both at the two courts and with Maŭla at home; and begged him to apply to the king for a meeting of five elders, that a proper understanding might be arrived at; but instead of doing as I desired, he got into a terrible fright, calling Maŭla, and told me if I pressed the matter in this way men would lose their lives. Meanwhile the cunning blackguard Maŭla begged for pardon; said I quite misunderstood his meaning; all he had said was that I was very fortunate, being in such favour at court, for the king and queen both equally loved me.

N'yamgundŭ now got orders to go to Karagŭé overland for Dr K'yengo; but, dreading to tell me of it, as I had been so kind to him, he forged a falsehood, said he had leave to visit his home for six days, and begged for a wire to sacrifice to his church. I gave him what he wanted, and away he went. I then heard his servants had received orders to go overland for Grant and K'yengo; so I wrote another note to Grant, telling him to come sharp, and bring all the property by boat that he could carry, leaving what he could not behind in charge of Rŭmanika.

At noon, the plaguy little imps of pages hurried in to order the attendance of all my men fully armed before the king, as he wished to seize some refractory officer. I declined this abuse of my arms, and said I should first go and speak to the king on the subject myself, ordering the men on no account to go on such an errand; and saying this, I proceeded towards the palace, leaving instructions for those men who were not ready to follow. As the court messengers, however, objected to our going in detachments, I told Bombay to wait for the rest, and hurry on to overtake me. Whilst lingering on the way, every minute expecting to see my men, the Wazinza, who had also received orders to seize the same officer, passed me, going to the place of attack, and, at the same time, I heard my men firing in a direction exactly opposite to the palace. I now saw I had been duped, and returned to my hut to see the issue. The boys had deceived us all. Bombay, tricked on the plea of their taking him by a short cut to the palace, suddenly found himself with all the men opposite the fenced gardens that had to be taken – the establishment of the recusant officer – and the boys, knowing how eager all blacks are to loot, said, 'Now, then, at the houses; seize all you can, sparing nothing – men, women, or children, mbŭgŭs or cowries, all alike – for it is the order of the king' and in an instant my men surrounded the place, fired their guns, and rushed upon the inmates. One was speared forcing his way through the fence, but the rest were taken and brought triumphantly into my camp. It formed a strange sight in the establishment of an English gentleman, to see my men flushed with the excitement of their spoils, staggering under loads of mbŭgŭ, or leading children, mothers, goats, and dogs off in triumph to their respective huts. Bombay alone, of all my men, obeyed my orders, touching nothing; and when remonstrated with for having led the men, he said he could not help it – the boys had deceived him in the same way as they had tricked me.

It was now necessary that I should take some critical step in African diplomacy; so, after ordering all the seizures to be given up to Maŭla on behalf of the king, and threatening to discharge any of my men who dared retain one item of the property, I shut the door of my hut to do penance for two days, giving orders that nobody but my cook Ilmas, not even Bombay, should come near me; for the king had caused my men to sin – had disgraced their red cloth – and had inflicted on me a greater insult than I could bear. I was ashamed to show my face. Just as the door was closed, other pages from the king brought the Whitworth rifle to be cleaned, and demanded an admittance; but no one dared approach me, and they went on their way again.

6th. – I still continued to do penance. Bombay, by my orders, issued from within, prepared for a visit to the king, to tell him all that had happened yesterday, and also to ascertain if the orders for sending my men on a plundering mission had really emanated from himself, when the bothering pages came again, bringing a gun and knife to be mended. My door was found shut, so they went to Bombay, asked him to do it, and told him the king desired to know if I would go shooting with him in the morning. The reply was, 'No; Bana is praying to-day that Mtésa's sins might be forgiven him for having committed such an injury to him, sending his soldiers on a mission that did not become them, and without his sanction too. He is very angry about it, and wishes to know if it was done by the king's orders.' The boys said, 'Nothing can be done without the king's orders.' After further discussion, Bombay intimated that I wished the king to send me a party of five elderly officers to counsel with, and set all disagreeables to rights, or I would not go to the palace again; but the boys said there were no elderly gentlemen at court, only boys such as themselves. Bombay now wished to go with them before the king, to explain matters to him, and to give him all the red cloths of my men, which I took from them, because they defiled their uniform when plundering women and children; but the boys said the king was unapproachable just then, being engaged shooting cows before his women. He then wished the boys to carry the cloth; but they declined, saying it was contrary to orders for anybody to handle cloth, and they could not do it.

CHAPTER XI

March Down the Northern Slopes of Africa

To Nanavundŭ, Nasirié, Namarya, Baja and Kari, 7th to 11th. – WITH Budja appointed as the general director, a lieutenant of the Sakibobo's to furnish us with sixty cows in his division at the first halting-place, and Kasoro (Mr Cat), a lieutenant of Jumba's, to provide the boats at Urondogani, we started at 1 P.M. on the journey northwards. The Wangŭana still grumbled, swearing they would carry no loads, as they got no rations, and threatening to shoot us if we pressed them, forgetting that their food had been paid for to the king in rifles, chronometers, and other articles, costing about 2000 dollars, and, what was more to the point, that all the ammunition was in our hands. A judicious threat of the stick, however, put things right, and on we marched five successive days to Kari – as the place was afterwards named, in consequence of the tragedy mentioned below – the whole distance accomplished being thirty miles from the capital, through a fine hilly country, with jungles and rich cultivation alternating. The second march, after crossing the Katawana river with its many branches flowing north-east into the huge rush-drain of Lŭajerri, carried us beyond the influence of the higher hills, and away from the huge grasses which characterise the southern boundary of Uganda bordering on the lake.

Each day's march to Kari was directed much in the same manner. After a certain number of hours' travelling, Budja appointed some village of residence for the night, avoiding those which belonged to the queen, lest any rows should take place in them, which would create disagreeable consequences with the king, and preferring those the heads of which had been lately seized by the orders of the king. Nevertheless, wherever we went, all the villagers forsook their homes, and left their houses, property, and gardens an easy prey to the thieving propensities of the escort. To put a stop to this vile practice was now beyond my power; the king allowed it, and his men were the first in every house, taking goats, fowls, skins, mbŭgŭs, cowries, beads, drums, spears, tobacco, pombé – in short, everything they could lay their hands on – in the most ruthless manner. It was a perfect marauding campaign for them all, and all alike were soon laden with as much as they could carry.

A halt of some days had become necessary at Kari to collect the cows given by the king; and, as it is one of his most extensive pasture-grounds, I strolled with my rifle (11th) to see what new animals could be found; but no sooner did I wound a zebra than messengers came running after me to say Kari, one of my men, had been murdered by the villagers three miles off; and such was the fact. He, with others of my men, had been induced to go plundering, with a few boys of the Waganda escort, to a certain village of potters, as pots were required by Budja for making plantain-wine, the first thing ever thought of when a camp is formed. On nearing the place, however, the women of the village, who were the only people visible, instead of running away, as our braves expected, commenced hullalooing, and brought out their husbands. Flight was now the only thought of our men, and all would have escaped had Kari not been slow and his musket empty. The potters overtook him, and, as he pointed his gun, which they considered a magic-horn, they speared him to death, and then fled at once. Our survivors were not long in bringing the news into camp, when a party went out, and in the evening brought in the man's corpse and everything belonging to him, for nothing had been taken.

12th. – To enable me at my leisure to trace up the Nile to its exit from the lake, and then go on with the journey as quickly as possible, I wished the cattle to be collected and taken by Budja and some of my men with the heavy baggage overland to Kamrasi's. Another reason for doing so was, that I thought it advisable Kamrasi should be forewarned that we were coming by the water route, lest we should be suspected and stopped as spies by his officers on the river, or regarded as enemies, which would provoke a fight Budja, however, objected to move until a report of Kari's murder had been forwarded to the king, lest the people, getting bumptious, should try the same trick again; and Kasoro said he would not go up the river, as he had received no orders to do so.

In this fix I ordered a march back to the palace, mentioning the king's last words, and should have gone, had not Budja ordered Kasoro to go with me. A page then arrived from the king to ask after Sana's health, carrying the Whitworth rifle as his master's card, and begging for a heavy double-barrelled gun to be sent him from Gani. I called this lad to witness the agreement I had made with Budja, and told him, if Kasoro satisfied me, I would return by him, in addition to the heavy gun, a Massey's patent log. I had taken it for the navigation of the lake, and it was now of no further use to me, but, being an instrument of complicated structure, it would be a valuable addition to the king's museum of magic charms. I added I should like the king to send me the robes of honour and spears he had once promised me, in order that I might, on reaching England, be able to show my countrymen a specimen of the manufactures of his country. The men who were with Kari were now sent to the palace, under accusation of having led him into ambush, and a complaint was made against the villagers, which we waited the reply to. As Budja forbade it, no men would follow me out shooting, saying the villagers were out surrounding our camp, and threatening destruction on any one who dared show his face; for this was not the highroad to Uganda, and therefore no one had a right to turn them out of their houses and pillage their gardens.

13th. – Budja lost two cows given to his party last night, and seeing ours securely tied by their legs to trees, asked by what spells we had secured them; and would not believe our assurance that the ropes that bound them were all the medicines we knew of. One of the queen's sisters, hearing of Kari's murder, came on a visit to condole with us, bringing a pot of pombé, for which she received some beads. On being asked how many sisters the queen had, for we could not help suspecting some imposition, she replied she was the only one, till assured ten other ladies had presented themselves as the queen's sisters before, when she changed her tone, and said, 'That is true, I am not the only one; but if I had told you the truth I might have lost my head.' This was a significant expression of the danger of telling court secrets.

15th. – In the morning, when our men went for water to the springs, some Waganda in ambush threw a spear at them, and this time caught a Tartar, for the 'horns,' as they called their guns, were loaded, and two of them received shot-wounds. In the evening, whilst we were returning from shooting, a party of Waganda, also lying in the bush, called out to know what we were about; saying, 'Is it not enough that you have turned us out of our homes and plantations, leaving us to live like animals in the wilderness?' and when told we were only searching for sport, would not believe that our motive was any other than hostility to themselves.

At night one of Budja's men returned from the palace, to say the king was highly pleased with the measures adopted by his Wakungŭ, in prosecution of Kari's affair. He hoped now, as we had cows to eat, there would be no necessity for wandering for food, but all would keep together 'in one garden.' At present no notice would be taken of the murderers, as all the culprits would have fled far away in their fright to escape chastisement. But when a little time had elapsed, and all would appear to have been forgotten, officers would be sent and the miscreants apprehended, for it was impossible to suppose anybody could be ignorant of the white men being the guests of the king, considering they had lived at the palace so long. The king took this opportunity again to remind me that he wanted a heavy solid double gun, such as would last him all his life; and intimated that in a few days the arms and robes of honour were to be sent.

16th. – Most of the cows for ourselves and the guides – for the king gave them also a present, ten each – were driven into camp. We also got 50 lb. of butter, the remainder to be picked up on the way. I strolled with the gun, and shot two zebras, to be sent to the king, as, by the constitution of Uganda, he alone can keep their royal skins.

17th. – We had to halt again, as the guides had lost most of their cows, so I strolled with my rifle and shot a ndjezza doe, the first I had ever seen. It is a brown animal, a little smaller than the leucotis, and frequents much the same kind of ground.

18th. – We had still to wait another day for Budja's cows, when, as it appeared all-important to communicate quickly with Petherick, and as Grant's leg was considered too weak for travelling fast, we took counsel together, and altered our plans. I arranged that Grant should go to Kamrasi's direct with the property, cattle, and women, taking my letters and a map for immediate despatch to Petherick at Gani, whilst I should go up the river to its source or exit from the lake, and come down again navigating as far as practicable.

At night the Waganda startled us by setting fire to the huts our men were sleeping in, but providentially did more damage to themselves than to us, for one sword only was buried in the fire, whilst their own huts, intended to be vacated in the morning, were burnt to the ground. To fortify ourselves against another invasion, we cut down all their plantains to make a boma or fence.

Cross the Lŭajerri, 19th. To Kiwŭkéri, 20th: We started all together on our respective journeys; but, after the third mile, Grant turned west, to join the highroad to Kamrasi's, whilst I went east for Urondogani, crossing the Lŭajerri, a huge rush-drain three miles broad, fordable nearly to the right bank, where we had to ferry in boats, and the cows to be swum over with men holding on to their tails. It was larger than the Katonga, and more tedious to cross, for it took no less than four hours, mosquitoes in myriads biting our bare backs and legs all the while. The Lŭajerri is said to rise in the lake and fall into the Nile, due south of our crossing-point. On the right bank wild buffalo are described to be as numerous as cows, but we did not see any, though the country is covered with a most inviting jungle for sport, with intermediate lays of fine grazing grass. Such is the nature of the country all the way to Urondogani, except in some favoured spots, kept as tidily as in any part of Uganda, where plantains grow in the utmost luxuriance. From want of guides, and misguided by the exclusive ill-natured Wahŭma, who were here in great numbers tending their king's cattle, we lost our way continually, so that we did not reach the boat-station until the morning of the 21st.

To Urondogandi, 21st: Here at last I stood on the brink of the Nile; most beautiful was the scene, nothing could surpass it! It was the very perfection of the kind of effect aimed at in a highly kept park; with a magnificent stream from 600 to 700 yards wide, dotted with islets and rocks, the former occupied by fishermen's huts, the latter by stems and crocodiles basking in the sun, – flowing between fine high grassy banks, with rich trees and plantains in the background, where herds of the nsunnŭ and hartebeest could be seen grazing, while the hippopotami were snorting in the water, and florikan and guinea-fowl rising at our feet. Unfortunately, the chief district officer, Mlondo, was from home, but we took possession of his huts – clean, extensive, and tidily kept – facing the river, and felt as if a residence here would do one good. Delays and subterfuges, however, soon came to damp our spirits. The acting officer was sent for, and asked for the boats; they were all scattered, and could not be collected for a day or two; but, even if they were at hand, no boat ever went up or down the river. The chief was away and would be sent for, as the king often changed his orders, and, after all, might not mean what had been said. The district belonged to the Sakibobo, and no representative of his had come here. These excuses, of course, would not satisfy us. The boats must be collected, seven, if there are not ten, for we must try them, and come to some understanding about them, before we march up stream, when, if the officer values his life, he will let us have them, and acknowledge Kasoro as the king's representative, otherwise a complaint will be sent to the palace, for we won't stand trifling.

We were now confronting Usoga, a country which may be said to be the very counterpart of Uganda in its richness and beauty. Here the people use such huge iron-headed spears with short handles, that, on seeing one to-day, my people remarked that they were better fitted for digging potatoes than piercing men. Elephants, as we had seen by their devastations during the last two marches, were very numerous in this neighbourhood. Till lately, a party from Unyoro, ivory-hunting, had driven them away. Lions were also described as very numerous and destructive to human life. Antelopes were common in the jungle, and the hippopotami, though frequenters of the plantain-garden and constantly heard, were seldom seen on land in consequence of their unsteady habits.

The king's page again came, begging I would not forget the gun and stimulants, and bringing with him the things I asked for – two spears, one shield, one dirk, two leopard-cat skins, and two sheets of small antelope skins. I told my men they ought to shave their heads and bathe in the holy river, the cradle of Moses – the waters of which, sweetened with sugar, men carry all the way from Egypt to Mecca, and sell to the pilgrims. But Bombay, who is a philosopher of the Epicurean school, said, 'We don't look on those things in the same fanciful manner that you do; we are contented with all the common-places of life, and look for nothing beyond the present. If things don't go well, it is God's will; and if they do go well, that is His will also.'

22d. – The acting chief brought a present of one cow, one goat, and pombé, with a mob of his courtiers to pay his respects. He promised that the seven boats, which are all the station could muster, would be ready next day, and in the meanwhile a number of men would conduct me to the shooting-ground. He asked to be shown the books of birds and animals, and no sooner saw some specimens of Wolf's handiwork, than, in utter surprise, he exclaimed, 'I know how these are done; a bird was caught and stamped upon the paper,' using action to his words, and showing what he meant, while all his followers n'yanzigged for the favour of the exhibition.

23d. – Three boats arrived, like those used on the Murchison Creek, and when I demanded the rest, as well as a decisive answer about going to Kamrasi's, the acting Mkungŭ said he was afraid accidents might happen, and he would not take me. Nothing would frighten this pigheaded creature into compliance, though I told him I had arranged with the king to make the Nile the channel of communication with England. I therefore applied to him for guides to conduct me up the river, and ordered Bombay and Kasoro to obtain fresh orders from the king, as all future Wazungŭ, coming to Uganda to visit or trade, would prefer the passage by the river. I shot another buck in the evening, as the Waganda love their skins, and also a load of guinea-fowl – three, four, and five at a shot – as Kasoro and his boys prefer them to anything.

24th. – The acting officer absconded, but another man came in his place, and offered to take us on the way up the river to-morrow, humbugging Kasoro into the belief that his road to the palace would branch off from the first stage, though in reality it was here. The Mkungŭ's women brought pombé, and spent the day gazing at us, till, in the evening, when I took up my rifle, one ran after Bana to see him shoot, and followed like a man; but the only sport she got was on an ant-hill, where she fixed herself some time, popping into her mouth and devouring the white ants as fast as they emanated from their cells – for, disdaining does, I missed the only pongo buck I got a shot at in my anxiety to show the fair one what she came for.

To Isamba Rapids, 25th: I marched up the left bank of the Nile at a considerable distance from the water, to the Isamba Rapids, passing through rich jungle and plantain-gardens. Nango, an old friend, and district officer of the place, first refreshed us with a dish of plantain-squash and dried fish, with pombé. He told us he is often threatened by elephants, but he sedulously keeps them off with charms; for if they ever tasted a plantain they would never leave the garden until they had cleared it out. He then took us to see the nearest falls of the Nile – extremely beautiful, but very confined. The water ran deep between its banks, which were covered with fine grass, soft cloudy acacias, and festoons of lilac convolvuli; whilst here and there, where the land had slipped above the rapids, bared places of red earth could be seen, like that of Devonshire; there, too, the waters, impeded by a natural dam, looked like a huge mill-pond, sullen and dark, in which two crocodiles, laving about, were looking out for prey. From the high banks we looked down upon a line of sloping wooded islets lying across the stream, which divide its waters, and, by interrupting them, cause at once both dam and rapids. The whole was more fairy-like, wild, and romantic than – I must confess that my thoughts took that shape – anything I ever saw outside of a theatre. It was exactly the sort of place, in fact, where, bridged across from one side-slip to the other, on a moon-light night, brigands would assemble to enact some dreadful tragedy. Even the Wangŭana seemed spellbound at the novel beauty of the sight, and no one thought of moving till hunger warned us night was setting in, and we had better look out for lodgings.

To Kirindi, 26th: Start again, and after drinking pombé with Nango, when we heard that three Wakungŭ had been seized at Kari, in consequence of the murder, the march was recommenced, but soon after stopped by the mischievous machinations of our guide, who pretended it was too late in the day to cross the jungles on ahead, either by the road to the source or the palace, and therefore would not move till the morning; then, leaving us, on the pretext of business, he vanished, and was never seen again. A small black fly, with thick shoulders and bullet-head, infests the place, and torments the naked arms and legs of the people with its sharp stings to an extent that must render life miserable to them.

To Church Estate, 27th: After a long struggling march, plodding through huge grasses and jungle, we reached a district which I cannot otherwise describe than by calling it a 'Church Estate.' It is dedicated in some mysterious manner to Lŭbari (Almighty), and although the king appeared to have authority over some of the inhabitants of it, yet others had apparently a sacred character, exempting them from the civil power, and he had no right to dispose of the land itself. In this territory there are small villages only at every fifth mile, for there is no road, and the lands run high again, whilst, from want of a guide, we often lost the track. It now transpired that Budja, when he told at the palace that there was no road down the banks of the Nile, did so in consequence of his fear that if he sent my whole party here they would rob these church lands, and so bring him into a scrape with the wizards or ecclesiastical authorities. Had my party not been under control, we could not have put up here; but on my being answerable that no thefts should take place, the people kindly consented to provide us with board and lodgings, and we found them very obliging. One elderly man, half-witted – they said the king had driven his senses from him by seizing his house and family – came at once on hearing of our arrival, laughing and singing in a loose jaunty maniacal manner, carrying odd sticks, shells, and a bundle of mbŭgŭ rags, which he deposited before me, dancing and singing again, then retreating and bringing some more, with a few plantains from a garden, which I was to eat, as kings lived upon flesh, and 'poor Tom' wanted some, for he lived with lions and elephants in a hovel beyond the gardens, and his belly was empty. He was precisely a black specimen of the English parish idiot.

To Ripon Falls, 28th: At last, with a good push for it, crossing hills and threading huge grasses, as well as extensive village plantations lately devastated by elephants – they had eaten all that was eatable, and what would not serve for food they had destroyed with their trunks, not one plantain or one hut being left entire – we arrived at the extreme end of the journey, the farthest point ever visited by the expedition on the same parallel of latitude as king Mtésa's palace, and just forty miles east of it.

We were well rewarded; for the 'stones,' as the Waganda call the falls, was by far the most interesting sight I had seen in Africa. Everybody ran to see them at once, though the march had been long and fatiguing, and even my sketch-block was called into play. Though beautiful, the scene was not exactly what I expected; for the broad surface of the lake was shut out from view by a spur of hill, and the falls, about 12 feet deep, and 400 to 500 feet broad, were broken by rocks. Still it was a sight that attracted one to it for hours – the roar of the waters, the thousands of passenger-fish, leaping at the falls with all their might, the Wasoga and Waganda fishermen coming out in boats and taking post on all the rocks with rod and hook, hippopotami and crocodiles lying sleepily on the water, the ferry at work above the falls, and cattle driven down to drink at the margin of the lake, – made, in all, with the pretty nature of the country – small hills, grassy-topped, with trees in the folds, and gardens on the lower slopes – as interesting a picture as one could wish to see.

The expedition had now performed its functions. I saw that old father Nile without any doubt rises in the Victoria N'yanza, and, as I had foretold, that lake is the great source of the holy river which cradled the first expounder of our religious belief. I mourned, however, when I thought how much I had lost by the delays in the journey having deprived me of the pleasure of going to look at the north-east comer of the N'yanza to see what connection there was, by the strait so often spoken of, with it and the other lake where the Waganda went to get their salt, and from which another river flowed to the north, making 'Usoga an island.' But I felt I ought to be content with what I had been spared to accomplish; for I had seen full half of the lake, and had information given me of the other half, by means of which I knew all about the lake, as far, at least, as the chief objects of geographical importance were concerned.

Let us now sum up the whole and see what it is worth. Comparative information assured me that there was as much water on the eastern side of the lake as there is on the western – if anything, rather more. The most remote waters, *or top head of the Nile*, is the southern end of the lake, situated close on the third degree of south latitude, which gives to the Nile the surprising length, in direct measurement, rolling over thirty-four degrees of latitude, of above 2300 miles, or more than one-eleventh of the circumference of our globe. Now from this southern point, round by the west, to where the *great* Nile stream issues, there is only one feeder of any importance, and that is the Kitangŭlé river; whilst from the southernmost point, round by the east, to the strait, there are no rivers at all of any importance; for the travelled Arabs one and all aver, that from the west of the snow-clad Kilimandjaro to the lake where it is cut by the second degree, and also the first degree of south latitude, there are salt lakes and salt plains, and the country is hilly, not unlike Unyamŭézi; but they said there were no great rivers, and the country was so scantily watered, having only occasional runnels and rivulets, that they always had to make long marches in order to find water when they went on their trading journeys: and further, those Arabs who crossed the strait when they reached Usoga, as mentioned before, during the late interregnum, crossed no river either.

There remains to be disposed of the 'salt lake,' which I believe is not a salt, but a fresh-water lake; and my reasons are, as before stated, that the natives call all lakes salt, if they find salt beds or salt islands in such places. Dr Krapf, when he obtained a sight of the Kenia mountain, heard from the natives there that there was a salt lake to its northward, and he also heard that a river ran from Kenia towards the Nile. If his information was true on this latter point, then, without doubt, there must exist some connection between his river and the salt lake I have heard of, and this in all probability would also establish a connection between my salt lake and his salt lake which he heard was called Baringo. In no view that can be taken of it, however, does this unsettled matter touch the established fact that the head of the Nile is in 3° south latitude, where, in the year 1858, I discovered the head of the Victoria N'yanza to be.

I now christened the 'stones.' Ripon Falls, after the nobleman who presided over the Royal Geographical Society when my expedition was got up; and the arm of water from which the Nile issued, Napoleon Channel, in token of respect to the French Geographical Society, for the honour they had done me, just before leaving England, in presenting me with their gold medal for the discovery of the Victoria N'yanza. One thing seemed at first perplexing – the volume of water in the Kitangŭlé looked as large as that of the Nile; but then the one was a slow river and the other swift, and on this account I could form no adequate judgment of their relative values.

Ripon Falls, 29th: Not satisfied with my first sketch of the falls, I could not resist sketching them again; and then, as the cloudy state of the weather prevented my observing for latitude, and the officer of the place said a magnificent view of the lake could be obtained from the hill alluded to as intercepting the view from the falls, we proposed going there; but Kasoro, who had been indulged with nsunnŭ antelope skins, and with guinea-fowl for dinner, resisted this, on the plea that I never should be satisfied. There were orders given only to see the 'stones,' and if he took me to one hill I should wish to see another and another, and so on. It made me laugh, for that had been my nature all my life; but, vexed at heart, and wishing to trick the young tyrant, I asked for boats to shoot hippopotami, in the hope of reaching the hills to picnic; but boating had never been ordered, and he would not listen to it. 'Then bring fish,' I said, that I might draw them: no, that was not ordered. 'Then go you to the palace, and leave me to go to Urondogani to-morrow, after I have taken a latitude' but the wilful creature would not go until he saw me under way. And as nobody would do anything for me without Kasoro's orders, I amused the people by firing at the ferry-boat upon the Usoga side, which they defied me to hit, the distance being 500 yards; but nevertheless a bullet went through her, and was afterwards brought by the Wasoga nicely folded up in a piece of mbŭgŭ. Bombay then shot a sleeping crocodile with his carbine, whilst I spent the day out watching the falls.

Ripon Falls, 30th: This day also I spent watching the fish flying at the falls, and felt as if I only wanted a wife and family, garden and yacht, rifle and rod, to make me happy here for life, so charming was the place. What a place, I thought to myself, this would be for missionaries! They never could fear starvation, the land is so rich; and, if farming were introduced by them, they might have hundreds of pupils. I need say no more.

Return, 31st: Church Estate again. As the clouds and Kasoro's wilfulness were still against me, and the weather did not give hopes of a change, I sacrificed the taking of the latitude to gain time. I sent Bombay with Kasoro to the palace, asking for the Sakibobo himself to be sent with an order for five boats, five cows, and five goats, and also for a general order to go where I like, and do what I like, and have fish supplied me; 'for, though I know the king likes me, his officers do not and then on separating I retraced my steps to the Church Estate.

1st. – To-day, after marching an hour, as there was now no need for hurrying, and a fine pongo buck, the Ngubbi of Uganda, offered a tempting shot, I proposed to shoot it for the men, and breakfast in a neighbouring village. This being agreed to, the animal was despatched, and we no sooner entered the village than we heard that nsamma, a magnificent description of antelope, abound in the long grasses close by, and that a rogue elephant frequents the plantains every night. This tempting news created a halt. In the evening I killed a nsamma doe, an animal very much like the Kobus Ellipsiprymnus, but without the lunated mark over the rump; and at night, about 1 A.M., turned out to shoot an elephant, which we distinctly heard feasting on plantains; but rain was falling, and the night so dark, he was left till the morning.

2d. – I followed up the elephant some way, till a pongo offering an irresistible shot I sent a bullet through him, but he was lost after hours' tracking in the interminable large grasses. An enormous snake, with fearful mouth and fangs, was speared by the men. In the evening I wounded a buck nsamma, which, after tracking till dark, was left to stiffen ere the following morning; and just after this, on the way home, we heard the Hogue elephant crunching the branches not far off from the track; but as no one would dare follow me against the monster at this late hour, he was reluctantly left to do more injury to the gardens.

3d. – After a warm search in the morning we found the nsamma buck lying in some water; the men tried to spear him, but he stood at bay, and took another bullet. This was all we wanted, affording one good specimen; so, after breakfast, we marched to Kirindi, where the villagers, hearing of the sport we had had, and excited with the hopes of getting flesh, begged us to halt a day.

4th. – Not crediting the stories told by the people about the sport here, we packed to leave, but were no sooner ready than several men ran hastily in to say some fine bucks were waiting to be shot close by. This was too powerful a temptation to be withstood, so, shouldering the rifle, and followed by half the village, if not more, women included, we went to the place, but, instead of finding a buck – for the men had stretched a point to keep me at their village – we found a herd of does, and shot one at the people's urgent request.

Urondogani again, 5th: We reached this in one stretch, and put up in our old quarters, where the women of Mlondo provided pombé, plantains, and potatoes, as before, with occasional fish, and we lived very happily till the 10th, shooting buck, guinea-fowl, and florikan, when, Bombay and Kasoro arriving, my work began again. These two worthies reached the palace, after crossing twelve considerable streams, of which one was the Lŭajerri, rising in the lake. The evening of the next day after leaving me at Kira, they obtained an interview with the king immediately; for the thought flashed across his mind that Bombay had come to report our death, the Waganda having been too much for the party. He was speedily undeceived by the announcement that nothing was the matter, excepting the inability to procure boats, because the officers at Urondogani denied all authority but the Sakibobo's, and no one would show Bana anything, however trifling, without an express order for it.

Irate at this announcement, the king ordered the Sakibobo, who happened to be present, to be seized and bound at once, and said warmly, 'Pray, who is the king, that the Sakibobo's orders should be preferred to mine?' and then, turning to the Sakibobo himself, asked what he would pay to be released? The Sakibobo, alive to his danger, replied at once, and without the slightest hesitation, Eighty cows, eighty goats, eighty slaves, eighty mbŭgŭ, eighty butter, eighty coffee, eighty tobacco, eighty jowari, and eighty of all the produce of Uganda. He was then released. Bombay said Bana wished the Sakibobo to come to Urondogani, and give him a start with five boats, five cows, and five goats; to which the king replied, 'Bana shall have all he wants, nothing shall be denied him, not even fish; but it is not necessary to send the Sakibobo, as boys carry all my orders to kings as well as subjects. Kasoro will return again with you, fully instructed in everything, and, moreover, both he and Budja will follow Bana to Gani.' Four days, however, my men were kept at the palace ere the king gave them the cattle and leave to join me, accompanied with one more officer, who had orders to find the boats at once, see us off, and report the circumstance at court. Just as at the last interview, the king had four women, lately seized and condemned to execution, squatting in his court. He wished to send them to Bana, and when Bombay demurred, saying he had no authority to take women in that way, the king gave him one, and asked him if he would like to see some sport, as he would have the remaining women cut to pieces before him. Bombay, by his own account, behaved with great propriety, saying Bana never wished to see sport of that cruel kind, and it would ill become him to see sights which his master had not. Viarŭngi sent me some tobacco, with kind regards, and said he and the Wazinza had just obtained leave to return to their homes, K'yengo alone, of all the guests, remaining behind as a hostage until Mtésa's powder-seeking Wakungŭ returned. Finally, the little boy Lŭgoi had been sent to his home. Such was the tenor of Bombay's report.

11th. – The officer sent to procure boats, impudently saying there were none, was put in the stocks by Kasoro, whilst other men went to Kirindi for sailors, and down the stream for boats. On hearing the king's order that I was to be supplied with fish, the fishermen ran away, and pombé was no longer brewed from fear of Kasoro.

CHAPTER XII

Bahr El Abiad

To N'yassi, 13th: In five boats of five planks each, tied together and caulked with mbŭgŭ rags, I started with twelve Wangŭana, Kasoro and his page-followers, and a small crew, to reach Kamrasi's palace in Unyoro – goats, dogs, and kit, besides grain and dried meat, filling up the complement – but how many days it would take nobody knew. Paddles propelled these vessels, but the lazy crew were slow in the use of them, indulging sometimes in racing spurts, then composedly resting on their paddles whilst the gentle current drifted us along. The river, very unlike what it was from the Ripon Falls downward, bore at once the character of river and lake – clear in the centre, but fringed in most places with tall rush, above which the green banks sloped back like park lands. It was all very pretty and very interesting, and would have continued so, had not Kasoro disgraced the Union Jack, turning it to piratical purposes in less than one hour.

A party of Wanyoro, in twelve or fifteen canoes, made of single tree trunks, had come up the river to trade with the Wasoga, and having stored their vessels with mbŭgŭ, dried fish, plantains cooked and raw, pombé, and other things, were taking their last meal on shore before they returned to their homes. Kasoro seeing this, and bent on a boyish spree, quite forgetting we were bound for the very ports they were bound for, ordered our sailors to drive in amongst them, landed himself, and sent the Wanyoro flying before I knew what game was up, and then set to pillaging and feasting on the property of those very men whom it was our interest to propitiate, as we expected them shortly to be our hosts.

The ground we were on belonged to king Mtésa, being a dependency of Uganda, and it struck me as singular that Wanyoro should be found here; but I no sooner discovered the truth than I made our boatmen disgorge everything they had taken, called back the Wanyoro to take care of their things, and extracted a promise from Kasoro that he would not practise such wicked tricks again, otherwise we could not travel together. Getting to boat again, after a very little paddling we pulled in to shore, on the Uganda side, to stop for the night, and thus allowed the injured Wanyoro to go down the river before us. I was much annoyed by this interruption, but no argument would prevail on Kasoro to go on. This was the last village on the Uganda frontier, and before we could go any farther in boats it would be necessary to ask leave of Kamrasi's frontier officer, N'yamyonjo, to enter Unyoro. The Wangŭana demanded ammunition in the most imperious manner, whilst I, in the same tone, refused to issue any lest a row should take place and they then would desert, alluding to their dastardly desertion in Msalala, when Grant was attacked. If a fight should take place, I said they must flock to me at once, and ammunition, which was always ready, would be served out to them.

They laughed at this, and asked, Who would stop with me when the fight began? This was making a jest of what I was most afraid of – that they would all run away.

Down to the Nile and back again, 14th: I held a levee to decide on the best manner of proceeding. The Waganda wanted us to stop for the day and feel the way gently, arguing that etiquette demands it. Then, trying to terrify me, they said, N'yamyonjo had a hundred boats, and would drive us back to a certainty if we tried to force past them, if he were not first spoken with, as the Waganda had often tried the passage and been repulsed. On the other hand, I argued that Grant must have arrived long ago at Kamrasi's, and removed all these difficulties for us; but, I said, if they would send men, let Bombay start at once by land, and we will follow in boats, after giving him time to say we are coming. This point gained after a hot debate, Bombay started at 10 A.M., and we not till 5 P.M., it being but one hour's journey by water. The frontier line was soon crossed; and then both sides of the river, Usoga as well as Unyoro, belong to Kamrasi.

I flattered myself all my walking this journey was over, and there was nothing left but to float quietly down the Nile, for Kidgwiga had promised boats, on Kamrasi's account, from Unyoro to Gani, where Petherick's vessels were said to be stationed; but this hope shared the fate of so many others in Africa. In a little while an enormous canoe, full of well-dressed and well-armed men, was seen approaching us. We worked on, and found they turned, as if afraid. Our men paddled faster, they did the same, the pages keeping time playfully by beat of drum, until at last it became an exciting chase, won by the Wanyoro by their superior numbers. The sun was now setting as we approached N'yamyonjo's. On a rock by the river stood a number of armed men, jumping, jabbering, and thrusting with their spears, just as the Waganda do. I thought, indeed, they were Waganda doing this to welcome us; but a glance at Kasoro's glassy eyes told me such was not the case, but, on the contrary, their language and gestures were threats, defying us to land.

The bank of the river, as we advanced, then rose higher, and was crowned with huts and plantations, before which stood groups and lines of men, all fully armed. Further, at this juncture, the canoe we had chased turned broadside on us, and joined in the threatening demonstrations of the people on shore. I could not believe them to be serious – thought they had mistaken us – and stood up in the boat to show myself, hat in hand. I said I was an Englishman going to Kamrasi's, and did all I could, but without creating the slightest impression. They had heard a drum beat, they said, and that was a signal of war, so war it should be; and Kamrasi's drums rattled up both sides the river, preparing everybody to arm. This was serious. Further, a second canoe full of armed men issued out from the rushes behind us, as if with a view to cut off our retreat, and the one in front advanced upon us, hemming us in. To retreat together seemed our only chance, but it was getting dark, and my boats were badly manned. I gave the order to close together and retire, offering ammunition as an incentive, and all came to me but one boat, which seemed so paralysed with fright, it kept spinning round and round like a crippled duck.

The Wanyoro, as they saw us retreating, were now heard to say, 'They are women, they are running, let us at them' whilst I kept roaring to my men, 'Keep together – come for powder' and myself loaded with small shot, which even made Kasoro laugh and inquire if it was intended for the Wanyoro. 'Yes, to shoot them like guinea-fowl; and he laughed again. But confound my men! they would not keep together, and retreat with me. One of those served with ammunition went as hard as he could go up stream to be out of harm's way, and another preferred hugging the dark shade of the rushes to keeping the clear open, which I desired for the benefit of our guns. It was now getting painfully dark, and the Wanyoro were stealing on us, as we could hear, though nothing could be seen. Presently the shade-seeking boat was attacked, spears were thrown, fortunately into the river instead of into our men, and grappling-hooks were used to link the boats together. My men cried, 'Help, Bana! they are killing us' whilst I roared to my crew, 'Go in, go in, and the victory will be ours' but not a soul would – they were spell-bound to the place; we might have been cut up in detail, it was all the same to those cowardly Waganda, whose only action consisted in crying, 'N'yawo! n'yawo!' – mother, mother, help us!

Three shots from the hooked boat now finished the action. The Wanyoro had caught a Tartar. Two of their men fell – one killed, one wounded. They were heard saying their opponents were not Waganda, it were better to leave them alone; and retreated, leaving us, totally uninjured, a clear passage up the river. But where was Bombay all this while? He did not return till after us, and then, in considerable excitement, he told his tale. He reached N'yamyonjo's village before noon, asked for the officer, but was desired to wait in a hut until the chief should arrive, as he had gone out on business; the villagers inquired, however, why we had robbed the Wanyoro yesterday, for they had laid a complaint against us. Bombay replied it was no fault of Bana's, he did everything he could to prevent it, and returned all that the boatmen took.

These men then departed, and did not return until evening, when they asked Bombay, impudently, why he was sitting there, as he had received no invitation to spend the night; and unless he walked off soon they would set fire to his hut. Bombay, without the smallest intention of moving, said he had orders to see N'yamyonjo, and until he did so he would not budge. 'Well,' said the people, 'you have got your warning, now look out for yourselves; and Bombay, with his Waganda escort, was left again. Drums then began to beat, and men to hurry to and fro with spears and shields, until at last our guns were heard, and, guessing the cause, Bombay with his Waganda escort rushed out of the hut into the jungle, and, without daring to venture on the beaten track, through thorns and thicket worked his way back to me, lame, and scratched all over with thorns.

Return to Kiwŭkéri, 15th: Crowds of Waganda, all armed as if for war, came to congratulate us in the morning, jumping, jabbering, and shaking their spears at us, denoting a victory gained – for we had shot Wanyoro and no harm had befallen us. 'But the road,' I cried, 'has that been gained? I am not going to show my back. We must go again, for there is some mistake; Grant is with Kamrasi, and N'yamyonjo cannot stop us. If you won't go in boats, let us go by land to N'yamyonjo's, and the boats will follow after.' Not a soul, however, would stir. N'yamyonjo was described as an independent chief, who listened to Kamrasi only when he liked. He did not like strange eyes to see his secret lodges on the N'yanza; and if he did not wish us to go down the river, Kamrasi's orders would go for nothing. His men had now been shot; to go within his reach would be certain death. Argument was useless, boating slow, to send messages worse; so I gave in, turned my back on the Nile, and the following day (16th) came on the Lŭajerri.

Here, to my intense surprise, I heard that Grant's camp was not far off, on its return from Kamrasi's. I could not, rather would not, believe it, suspicious as it now appeared after my reverse. The men, however, were positive, and advised my going to king Mtésa's – a ridiculous proposition, at once rejected; for I had yet to receive Kamrasi's answer to our Queen, about opening a trade with England. I must ascertain why he despised Englishmen without speaking with them, and I could not believe Kamrasi would prove less avaricious than either Rŭmanika or Mtésa, especially as Rŭmanika had made himself responsible for our actions. We slept that night near Kari, the Waganda eating two goats which had been drowned in the Lŭajerri; and the messenger-page, having been a third time to the palace and back again, called to ask after our welfare, on behalf of his king, and remind us about the gun and brandy promised.

17th and 18th. – The two following days were spent wandering about without guides, trying to keep the track Grant had taken after leaving us, crossing at first a line of small hills, then traversing grass and jungle, like the dâk of India. Plantain-gardens were frequently met, and the people seemed very hospitably inclined, though they complained sadly of the pages rudely rushing into every hut, seizing everything they could lay their hands on, and even eating the food which they had just prepared for their own dinners, saying, in a mournful manner, 'If it were not out of respect for you we should fight those little rascals, for it is not the king's guest nor his men who do us injury, but the king's own servants, without leave or licence.' I observed that special bomas or fences were erected to protect these villages against the incursions of lions. Buffaloes were about, but the villagers cautioned us not to shoot them, holding them as sacred animals; and, to judge from the appearance of the country, wild animals should abound, were it not for the fact that every Mganda seems by instinct to be a sportsman.

To N'yakinyama, 19th: At last, after numerous and various reports about Grant, we heard his drums last night, but we arrived this morning just in time to be too late. He was on his march back to the capital of Uganda, as the people had told us, and passed through N'yakinyama just before I reached it. What had really happened I knew not, and was puzzled to think. To insist on a treaty, demanding an answer, to the Queen, seemed the only chance left; so I wrote to Grant to let me know all about it, and waited the result. He very obligingly came himself, said he left Unyoro after stopping there an age asking for the road without effect, and left by the orders of Kamrasi, thinking obedience the better policy to obtain our ends. Two great objections had been raised against us; one was that we were reported to be cannibals, and the other that our advancing by two roads at once was suspicious, the more especially so as the Waganda were his enemies; had we come from Rŭmanika direct, there would have been no objection to us.

When all was duly considered, it appeared evident to me that the great king of Unyoro, 'the father of all the kings,' was merely a nervous, fidgety creature, half afraid of us because we were attempting his country by the unusual mode of taking two routes at once, but wholly so of the Waganda, who had never ceased plundering his country for years. As it appeared that he would have accepted us had we come by the friendly route of Kisŭéré, a further parley was absolutely necessary, and the more especially so, as now we were all together and in Uganda, which, in consequence, must relieve him from the fear of our harbouring evil designs against him. No one present, however, could be prevailed on to go to him in the capacity of ambassador, as the frontier officer had warned the Wagéni or guests that, if they ever attempted to cross the border again, he was bound in duty, agreeably to the orders of his king, to expel them by force; therefore, should the Wagéni attempt it after this warning, their first appearance would be considered a *casus belli;* and so the matter rested for the day.

To Grant's Camp, 20th: To make the best of a bad bargain, and as N'yakinyama was 'eaten up,' we repaired to Grant's camp to consult with Budja; but Budja was found firm and inflexible against sending men to Unyoro. His pride had been injured by the rebuffs we had sustained. He would wait here three or four days as I proposed, to see what fortune sent us, if I would not be convinced that Kamrasi wished to reject us, and he would communicate with his king in the meanwhile, but nothing more. Here was altogether a staggerer: I would stop for three or four days, but if Kamrasi would not have us by that time, what was to be done? Would it be prudent to try Kisŭéré now Baraka had been refused the Gani route? or would it not be better still for me to sell Kamrasi altogether, by offering Mtésa five hundred loads of ammunition, cloth, and beads, if he would give us a thousand Waganda as a force to pass through the Masai to Zanzibar, this property to be sent back by the escort from the coast? Kamrasi would no doubt catch it if we took this course, but it was expensive.

Thus were we ruminating, when lo, to our delight, as if they had been listening to us, up came Kidgwiga, my old friend, who, at Mtésa's palace, had said Kamrasi would be very glad to see me, and Vittagŭra, Kamrasi's commander-in-chief, to say their king was very anxious to see us, and the Waganda might come or not as they liked. Until now, the deputation said, Kamrasi had doubted Budja's word about our friendly intentions, but since he saw us withdrawing from his country, those doubts were removed. The N'yanswengé, they said – meaning, I thought, Petherick – was still at Gani; no English or others on the Nile ever expressed a wish to enter Unyoro, otherwise they might have done so; and Baraka had left for Karagŭé, carrying off an ivory as a present from Kamrasi.

21st. – I ordered the march to Unyoro; Budja, however, kept brooding over the message sent to the Waganda, to the effect that they might come or not as they liked, and considering us with himself to have all been treated 'like dogs,' begged me to give him my opinion as to what course he had better pursue; for he must, in the first instance, report the whole circumstances to the king, and could not march at once. This was a blight on our prospects, and appeared very vexatious, in the event of Budja waiting for an answer, which, considering Mtésa had ordered his Wakungŭ to accompany us all the way to Gani, might stop our march altogether.

I therefore argued that Kamrasi's treatment of us was easily accounted for: he heard of us coming by two routes from an enemy's country, and was naturally suspicious of us; that had now been changed by our withdrawing, and he invited us to him. Without doubt, his commander-in-chief was never very far away, and followed on our heels. Such precaution was only natural and reasonable on Kamrasi's part, and what had been done need not alarm any one. 'If you do your duty properly, you will take us at once into Unyoro, make your charge over to these men, and return or not as you like; for in doing so you will have fulfilled both Mtésa's and Kamrasi's orders at once.' 'Very good,' says Budja, 'let it be so; for there is great wisdom in your words; but I must first send to my king, for the Waganda villagers have struck two of your men with weapons' (this had happened just before my arrival here), 'and this is a most heinous offence in Uganda, which cannot be overlooked. Had it been done with a common stick, it could have been overlooked; but the use of weapons is an offence, and both parties must go before the king.' This, of course, was objected to on the plea that it was my own affair. I was king of the Wangŭana, and might choose to dispense with the attendance. The matter was compromised, however, on the condition that Budja should march across the border to-morrow, and wait for the return of these men and for further orders on the Unyoro side.

The bait took. Budja lost sight of the necessity there was for his going to Gani to bring back a gun, ammunition, and some medicine – that is to say, brandy – for his king; and sent his men off with mine to tell Mtésa all our adventures – our double repulse, the intention to wait on the Unyoro side for further orders, and the account of some Waganda having wounded my men. I added my excuses for Kamrasi, and laid a complaint against Mtésa's officers for having defrauded us out of ten cows, five goats, six butter, and sixty mbŭgŭ. It was not that we required these things, but I knew that the king had ordered them to be given to us, and I thought it right we should show that his officers, if they professed to obey his orders, had peculated. After these men had started, some friends of the villager who had been apprehended

on the charge of assailing my men, came and offered Budja five cows
to overlook the charge; and Budja, though he could not overlook it
when I pleaded for the man, asked me to recall my men. Discovering
that the culprit was a queen's man, and that the affair would cause bad
blood at court should the king order the man's life to be taken, I tried
to do so, but things had gone too far.

To North Frontier Station, Uganda, 22d: Again the expedition
marched on in the right direction. We reached the last village on the
Uganda frontier, and there spent the night. Here Grant shot a nsunnŭ
buck. The Wangŭana mutinied for ammunition, and would not lift a
load until they got it, saying, 'Unyoro is a dangerous country,' though
they had been there before without any more than they now had in
pouch. The fact was, my men, in consequence of the late issues on
the river, happened to have more than Grant's men, and every man
must have alike. The ringleader, unfortunately for himself, had lately
fired at a dead lion, to astonish the Unyoro, and his chum had fired
a salute, winch was contrary to orders; for ammunition was at a low
ebb, and I had done everything in my power to nurse it. Therefore,
as a warning to the others, the guns of these two were confiscated,
and a caution given that any gun in future let off, either by design or
accident, would be taken.

To South Frontier Station, Unyoro, 23d: To-day I felt very thankful
to get across the much-vexed boundary-line, and enter Unyoro,
guided by Kamrasi's deputation of officers, and so shake off the
apprehensions which had teased us for so many days. This first march
was a picture of all the country to its capital: an interminable forest
of small trees, bush, and tall grass, with scanty villages, low huts,
and dirty-looking people clad in skins; the plantain, sweet potato,
sesamum, and ŭlézi (millet) forming the chief edibles, besides goats
and fowls; whilst the cows, which are reported to be numerous,
being kept, as everywhere else where pasture-lands are good, by the
wandering, unsociable Wahŭma, are seldom seen. No hills, except a
few scattered cones, disturb the level surface of the land, and no pretty
views ever cheer the eye. Uganda is now entirely left behind; we shall
not see its like again; for the further one leaves the equator, and the
rain-attracting influences of the Mountains of the Moon, vegetation
decreases proportionately with the distance.

To Kidgwiga's, 24th: Fortunately the frontier village could not feed so large a party as ours, and therefore we were compelled to move farther on, to our great delight, through the same style of forest acacia, cactus, and tall grass, to Kidgwiga's gardens, where we no sooner arrived than Mtésa's messenger-page, with a party of fifty Waganda, dropped in, in the most unexpected manner, to inquire after 'his royal master's friend, Bana.' The king had heard of the fight upon the river, and thought the Wangŭana must be very good shots. He still trusted we would not forget the gun and ammunition, but, above all, the load of stimulants, for he desired that above all things on earth. This was the fourth message to remind us of these important matters which we had received since leaving his gracious presence, and each time brought by the same page. While the purpose of the boy's coming with so many men was not distinctly known, the whole village and camp were in a state of great agitation, Budja fearing lest the king had some fault to find with his work, and the Wanyoro deeming it a menace of war, whilst I was afraid they might take fright and stop our progress.

But all went well in the end; Massey's log, which I have mentioned as a present I intended for Mtésa, was packed up, and the page departed with it. Some of Rŭmanika's men, who came into Unyoro with Baraka, with four of K'yengo's, were sent to call us by Kamrasi. Through Rŭmanika's men it transpired that he had stood security for our actions, else, with the many evil reports of our being cannibals and suchlike, which had preceded our coming here, we never should have gained admittance to the country. The Wanyoro, who are as squalid-looking as the Wanyamŭézi, and almost as badly dressed, now came about us to hawk ivory ornaments, brass and copper twisted wristlets, tobacco, and salt, which they exchanged for cowries, with which they purchase cows from the Waganda. As in Uganda, all the villagers forsake their huts as soon as they heard the Wagéni (guests) were coming; and no one paid the least attention to the traveller, save the few head-men attached to the escort, or some professional traders.

25th to 28th. – I had no sooner ordered the march than Vittagŭra counter-ordered it, and held a levee to ascertain, as he said, if the Waganda were to go back; for though Kamrasi wished to see us, he did not want the Waganda. It was Kamrasi's orders that Budja should tell this to his 'child the Mkavia,' meaning Mtésa; for when the Waganda came the first time to see him, three of his family died; and when they came the second time, three more died; and as this rate of mortality was quite unusual in his family circle, he could only attribute it to foul magic. The presence of people who brought such results was of course by no means desirable. This neat message elicited a declaration of the necessity of Budja's going to Gani with us, and a response from the commander-in-chief, probably to terrify the Waganda, that although Gani was only nine days' journey distant from Kamrasi's palace, the Gani people were such barbarians, they would call a straight-haired man a magician, and any person who tied his mbŭgŭ in a knot upon his shoulder, or had a full set of teeth as the Waganda have, would be surely killed by them. Finally, we must wait two days, to see if Kamrasi would see us or not. Such was Unyoro diplomacy.

Three days were spent in simply waiting for return messages on both sides, and more might have been lost in the same way, only we amused Vittagŭra and gave him confidence by showing our pictures, looking-glass, scissors, knives, etc., when he promised a march in the morning, leaving a man behind to bring on the Wangŭana sent to Mtésa's, it being the only alternative which would please Budja; for he said there was no security for life in Unyoro, where every Mkungti calls himself the biggest man, and no true hospitality is to be found.

29th, 30th. – The next two days took us through Chagamoyo to Kiratosi, by the aid of the compass; for the route Kamrasi's men took differed from the one which Budja knew, and he declared the Wanyoro were leading us into a trap, and would not be convinced we were going on all right till I pulled out the compass and confirmed the Wanyoro. We were anything but welcomed at Kiratosi, the people asking by what bad-luck we had come there to eat up their crops; but in a little while they flocked to our doors and admired our traps, remarking that they believed each iron box contained a couple of white dwarfs, which we carry on our shoulders, sitting straddle-legs, back to back, and they fly off to eat people whenever they get the order. One of these visitors happened to be the sister of one of my men, named Barŭti, who no sooner recognised her brother, than, without saying a word, she clasped her head with her hands, and ran off, crying, to tell her husband what she had seen. A spy of Kamrasi dropped the report that the Wangŭana were returning from Mtésa's, and hurried on to tell his king.

31st. – Some Waganda hurrying in, confirmed the report of last night, and said the Wangŭana, footsore, had been left at the Uganda frontier, expecting us to return, as Mtésa, at the same time that he approved highly of my having sent men back to inform him of Kamrasi's conduct, begged we would instantly return, even if found within one march of Kamrasi's, for he had much of importance to tell his friend Bana. The message continued to this effect: I need be under no apprehensions about the road to the coast, for he would give me as many men as I liked; and, fearing I might be short of powder, he had sent some with the Wangŭana. Both Wangŭana were by the king given women for their services, and an old tin cartridge-box represented Mtésa's card, it being an article of European manufacture, which, if found in the possession of any Mganda, would be certain death to him. Finally, all the houses and plantains where my men were wounded had been confiscated.

When this message was fully delivered, Budja said we must return without a day's delay. I, on the contrary, called up Kidgwiga. I did not like my men having been kept prisoners in Uganda, and pronounced in public that I would not return. It would be an insult to Kamrasi my doing so, for I was now in his 'house' at his own invitation. I wished Bombay would go with him (Kidgwiga) at once to his king, to say I had hoped, when I sent Budja with Mabrŭki, in the first instance, conveying a friendly present from Mtésa, which was done at my instigation, and I found Kamrasi acknowledged it by a return-present, that there would be no more fighting between them. I said I had left England to visit these countries for the purpose of opening up a trade, and I had no orders to fight my way except with the force of friendship. That Rŭmanika had accepted my views Kamrasi must be fully aware by Baraka's having visited him; and that Mtésa did the same must be also evident, else he would never have ordered his men to accompany me to Gani; and I now fondly trusted that these Waganda would be allowed to go with me, when, by the influence of trade, all animosity would cease, and friendly relations be restored between the two countries.

This speech was hardly pronounced when Kajunjŭ, a fine athletic man, dropped suddenly in, nodded a friendly recognition to Budja, and wished to know what the Waganda meant by taking us back,

for the king had heard of their intention last night; and when told by
Budja his story, and by Kidgwiga mine, he vanished like a shadow.
Budja, now turning to me, said, 'If you won't go back, I shall; for the
orders of Mtésa must always be obeyed, else lives will be lost; and
I shall tell him that you, since leaving his country, and getting your
road, have quite forgotten him.' 'If you give such a message as that,'
I said, 'you will tell a falsehood. Mtésa has no right to order me out
of another man's house, to be an enemy with one whose friendship I
desire. I am not only in honour bound to speak with Kamrasi, but I
am also bound to carry out the orders of my country just as much as
you are yours; moreover, I have invited Petherick to come to Kamrasi's
by a letter from Karagŭé, and it would be ill-becoming in me to desert
him in the hands of an enemy, as he would then certainly find Kamrasi
to be if I went back now.' Budja then tried the coaxing dodge, saying,
'There is much reason in your words, but I am sorry you do not listen
to the king, for he loves you as a brother. Did you not go about like
two brothers – walking, talking, shooting, and even eating together?
It was the remark of all the Waganda, and the king will be so vexed
when he finds you have thrown him over. I did not tell you before, but
the king says, 'How can I answer Rŭmanika if Kamrasi injures Bana?
Had I known Kamrasi was such a savage, I would not have let Bana
go there; and I should now have sent a force to take him away, only
that some accident might arise from it by Kamrasi's taking fright; the
road even to Gani shall be got by force if necessary.' Then, finding me
still persistent, Budja turned again and threatened us with the king's
power, saying, 'If you choose to disobey, we will see whether you ever
get the road to Gani or not; for Kamrasi is at war on all sides with his
brothers, and Mtésa will ally himself with them at any moment that he
wishes, and where will you be then?'

Saying this, Budja walked off, muttering that our being here would
much embarrass Mtésa's actions; whilst my Wangŭana, who have
been attentively listening, like timid hares, made up their minds to
leave me, and tried, through Bombay, to obtain a final interview with
me, saying they knew Mtésa's power, and disobedience to him would
only end in taking away all chance of escape. In reply, I said I would
not listen to them, as I had seen enough of them to know it was no
use speaking with a pack of unreasonable cowards, having tried it so

often before; but I sent a message requesting them, if they did desert me at last, to leave my guns; and, further, added an intimation that, as soon as they reached the coast, they would be put into prison for three years. The scoundrels insolently said 'tŭendé sétu' (let's be off), rushed to the Waganda drums, and beat the march.

1st. – Early in the morning, as Budja drummed the home march, I called him up, gave him a glass rain-gauge as a letter for Mtésa, and instructed him to say I would send a man to Mtésa as soon as I had seen Kamrasi about opening the road; that I trusted he would take all the guns from the deserters and keep them for me, but the men themselves I wished transported to an island on the N'yanza, for I could never allow such scoundrels again to enter my camp. It was the effect of desertions like these that prevented any white men visiting these countries. This said, the Waganda all left us, taking with them twenty-eight Wangŭana, armed with twenty-two carbines. Amongst them was the wretched governess, Manamaka, who had always thought me a wonderful magician, because I possessed, in her belief, an extraordinary power in inclining all the black kings' hearts to me, and induced them to give the roads no one before of my colour had ever attempted to use.

With a following reduced to twenty men, armed with fourteen carbines, I now wished to start for Kamrasi's, but had not even sufficient force to lift the loads. A little while elapsed, and a party of fifty Wanyoro rushed wildly into camp, with their spears uplifted, and looked for the Waganda, but found them gone. The athletic Kajunjŭ, it transpired, had returned to Kamrasi's, told him our story, and received orders to snatch us away from the Waganda by force, for the great Mkamma, or king, was most anxious to see his white visitors; such men had never entered Unyoro before, and neither his father nor his father's fathers had ever been treated with such a visitation; therefore he had sent on these fifty men to fall by surprise on the Waganda, and secure us. But again, in a little while, about 10 A.M., Kajunjŭ, in the same wild manner, at the head of 150 warriors, with the soldier's badge – a piece of mbŭgŭ or plantain-leaf tied round their heads, and a leather sheath on their spearheads, tufted with cow's-tail – rushed in exultingly, having found, to their delight, that there was no one left to fight with, and that they had gained an easy victory. They were certainly a wild set of ragamuffins – as different as possible from the smart, well-dressed, quick-of-speech Waganda as could be, and anything but prepossessing to our eyes. However, they had done their work, and I offered them a cow, wishing to have it shot before them; but the chief men, probably wishing the whole animal to themselves, took it alive, saying the men were all the king's servants, and therefore could not touch a morsel.

Kamrasi expected us to advance next day, when some men would go on ahead to announce our arrival, and bring a letter which was brought with beads by Gani before Baraka's arrival here. It was shown to Baraka in the hope that we would come by the Karagüé route, but not to Mabrŭki, because he came from Uganda. Kidgwiga informed us that Kamrasi never retaliated on Mtésa when he lifted Unyoro cows, though the Waganda keep their cattle on the border – which simply meant he had not the power of doing so. The twenty remaining Wangŭana, conversing over the sudden scheme of the deserters, proposed, on one side, sending for them, as, had they seen the Wanyoro arrive, they would have changed their minds; but the other side said, 'What! those brutes who said we should all die here if we stayed, and yet dared not face the danger with us, should we now give them a helping hand? Never! We told them we would share our fate with Bana, and share it we will, for God rules everything: every man must die when his time comes.'

To Utŭti, 2d: We marched for the first time without music, as the drum is never allowed to be beaten in Unyoro except when the necessities of war demand it, or for a dance. Wanyamŭézi and Wanyoro, in addition to our own twenty men, carried the luggage, though no one carried more than the smallest article he could find. It was a pattern Unyoro march, of only two hours' duration. On arrival at the end, we heard that elephants had been seen close by. Grant and I then prepared our guns, and found a herd of about a hundred feeding on a plain of long grass, dotted here and there by small mounds crowned with shrub. The animals appeared to be all females, much smaller than the Indian breed; yet, though ten were fired at, none were killed, and only one made an attempt to charge. I was with the little twin Manila at the time, when, stealing along under cover of the high grass, I got close to the batch and fired at the largest, which sent her round roaring. The whole of them then, greatly alarmed, packed together and began sniffing the air with their uplifted trunks, till, ascertaining by the smell of the powder that their enemy was in front of them, they rolled up their trunks and came close to the spot where I was lying under a mound. My scent then striking across them, they pulled up short, lifted their heads high, and looked down sideways on us. This was a bad job. I could not get a proper front shot at the boss of any of them, and if I had waited an instant we should both have been picked up or trodden to death; so I let fly at their temples, and instead of killing, sent the whole of them rushing away at a much faster pace than they came. After this I gave up, because I never could separate the ones I had wounded from the rest, and thought it cruel to go on damaging more. Thinking over it afterwards, I came to the conclusion I ought to have put in more powder; for I had, owing to their inferior size to the Indian ones, rather despised them, and fired at them with the same charge and in the same manner as I always did at rhinoceros. Though puzzled at the strange sound of the rifle, the elephants seldom ran far, packed in herd, and began to graze again. Frij, who was always ready at spinning a yam, told us with much gravity that two of my men, Ulédi and Wadi Hamadi, deserters, were possessed of devils (Phépo) at Zanzibar. Ulédi, not wishing to be plagued by his Satanic majesty's angels on the march, sacrificed a cow and fed the poor, according to the great Phépos orders, and had been exempted from it; but Wadi Hamadi, who preferred taking his chance, had been visited several times: once at Usŭi, when he was told the journey would be prosperous, only the devil wanted one man's life, and one man would fall sick; which proved true, for Hassani was murdered, and Grant fell sick in Karagŭé. The second time Wadi Hamadi saw the devil in Karagŭé, and was told one man's life would be required in Uganda, and such also was the case by Kari's murder; and a third time, in Unyoro, he was possessed, when it was said that the journey would be prosperous but protracted.

3d. – Though we stormed every day at being so shamefully neglected and kept in the jungles, we could not get on, nor find out the truth of our position. I asked if Kamrasi was afraid of us, and looking into his magic horn; and was answered, 'No; he is very anxious to see you, or he would not have sent six of his highest officers to look after you, and prevent the unruly peasantry from molesting you.' 'Then by whose orders are we kept here?' 'By Kamrasi's.' 'Why does Kamrasi keep us here?' 'He thinks you are not so near, and men have gone to tell him.' 'How did we come here from the last ground?' 'By Kamrasi's orders; for nothing can be done excepting by his orders.' 'Then he must know we are here?' 'He may not have seen the men we sent to him; for unless he shows in public no one can see him.' The whole affair gave us such an opinion of Kamrasi as induced us to think it would have served him right had we joined Mtésa and given him a thrashing. This, I said, was put in our power by an alliance with his refractory brothers; but Kidgwiga only laughed and said, 'Nonsense! Kamrasi is the chief of all the countries round here – Usoga, Kidi, Chopi, Gani, Uléga, everywhere; he has only to hold up his hand and thousands would come to his assistance.' Kwibéya, the officer of the place, presented us with five fowls on the part of the king, and some baskets of potatoes.

4th. – We halted again, it was said, in order that Kwibéya might give us all the king had desired him to present. I sent Bombay off with a message to Kamrasi explaining everything, and begging for an early interview, as I had much of importance to communicate, and wished, of all things, to see the letter he had from Gani, as it must have come from our dear friends at home. Seven goats, flour, and plantains, were now brought to us; and as Kidgwiga begged for the flour without success, he flew into a fit of high indignation because these things were given and received without his having first been consulted. He was the big man and appointed go-between, and no one could dispute it. This was rather startling news to us, for Vittagŭra said he was commander-in-chief; Kajunjŭ thought himself biggest, so did Kwibéya, and even Dr K'yengo's men justified Budja's speech.

Halt 5th and 6th, change ground, 7th: At last we made a move, but only of two hours' duration, through the usual forest, in which elephants walked about as if it were their park. We hoped at starting to reach the palace, but found we must stop here until the king should send for us. We were informed that doubtless he was looking into his Uganga, or magic horn, to discover what he had to expect from us; and he seemed as yet to have found no ground for being afraid of us. Moreover, it is his custom to keep visitors waiting on him in this way, for is he not the king of kings, the king of Kittara, which includes all the countries surrounding Unyoro?

CHAPTER XIII

Unyoro

To Chagŭzi, on the left bank of the Kafŭ river, 8th: We halted again, but in the evening one of Dr K'yengo's men came to invite us to the palace. He explained that Kamrasi was in a great rage because we only received seven goats instead of thirty, the number he had ordered Kwibéya to give us, besides pombé and plantains without limitation. I complained that Bombay had been shown more respect than myself, obtaining an immediate admittance to the king's presence. To this he gave two ready answers – that every distinction shown my subordinate was a distinction to myself, and that we must not expect court etiquette from savages.

9th. – We set off for the palace. This last march differed but little from the others. Putting Dr K'yengo's men in front, and going on despite all entreaties to stop, we passed the last bit of jungle, sighted the Kidi hills, and, in a sea of swampy grass, at last we stood in front of and overlooked the great king's palace, situated N. lat 1° 37′ 43″, and E. long. 32° 19′ 49″, on a low tongue of land between the Kafŭ and Nile rivers. It was a dumpy, large hut, surrounded by a host of smaller ones, and the worst royal residence we had seen since leaving Uzinza. Here Kajunjŭ, coming from behind, overtook us, and, breathless with running, in the most excited manner abused Dr K'yengo's men for leading us on, and ordered us to stop until he saw the king, and ascertained the place his majesty wished us to reside in. Recollecting Mtésa's words that Kamrasi placed his guests on the N'yanza, I declined going to any place but the palace, which I maintained was my right, and waited for the issue, when Kajunjŭ returned with pombé, and showed us to a small, dirty set of huts beyond the Kafŭ river – the trunk of the Mwérango and N'yanza branches which we crossed in Uganda – and trusted this would do for the present, as better quarters in the palace would be looked for on the morrow. This was a bad beginning, and caused a few of the usual anathemas in which our countrymen give vent to their irritation.

Two loads of flour, neatly packed in long strips of rushpith, were sent for us 'to consume at once,' as more would be given on the morrow. To keep us amused, Kidgwiga informed us that Kamrasi and Mtésa – in fact, all the Wahŭma – came originally from a stock of the same tribe dwelling beyond Kidi. All bury their dead in the same way, under ground; but the kings are toasted first for months till they are like sun-dried meat, when the lower jaw is cut out and preserved, covered with beads. The royal tombs are put under the charge of special officers, who occupy huts erected over them. The umbilical cords are preserved from birth, and, at death, those of men are placed within the door-frame, whilst those of women are buried without – this last act corresponding, according to Bombay, with the custom of the Wahiyow. On the death of any of the great officers of state, the finger-bones and hair are also preserved; or if they have died shaven, as sometimes occurs, a bit of their mbŭgŭ dress will be preserved in place of the hair. Their families guard their tombs.

10th. – I sent Kidgwiga with my compliments to the king, and a request that his majesty would change my residence, which was so filthy that I found it necessary to pitch a tent, and also that he would favour me with an interview after breakfast. The return was a present of twenty cows, ten cocks, two bales of flour, and two pots of pombé, to be equally divided between Grant and myself, as Kamrasi recognised in us two distinct camps, because we approached his country by two different routes – a smart method for expecting two presents from us, which did not succeed, as I thanked for all, Grant being 'my son' on this occasion. The king also sent his excuses, and begged pardon for what happened to us on entering his country, saying it could not have taken place had we come from Rŭmanika direct. His fear of the Waganda gave rise to it, and he trusted we would forget and forgive. To-morrow our residence should be changed, and an interview follow, for he desired being friends with us just as much as we did with him.

At last Bombay came back. He reported that he had not been allowed to leave the palace earlier, though he pleaded hard that I expected his return; and the only excuse he could extract from the king was, that we were coming in charge of many Wakungŭ, and he had found it necessary to retard our approach in consequence of the famine at Chagŭzi. His palace proper was not here, but three marches westward: he had come here and pitched a camp to watch his brothers, who were at war with him. Bombay, doing his best to escape, or to hurry my march, replied that he was very anxious on our account, because the Waganda wished to snatch us away.

It was no doubt this hint that brought the messenger to our relief yesterday; and otherwise we might have been kept in the jungle longer. When told by Bombay of our treatment on the Nile, the king first said he did not think we wished to see him, else we would have come direct from Rŭmanika; but when asked if Baraka's coming with Rŭmanika's officers was not sufficient to satisfy him on this point, he hung down his head, and evaded the question, saying he had been the making of king Mtésa of Uganda; but he had turned out a bad fellow, and now robbed him right and left. The Gani letter, supposed to be from Petherick, was now asked for, and a suggestion made about opening a trade with Gani, but all with the provoking result we had been so well accustomed to. No letter like that referred to had ever been received, so that Frij's interpretation about Grant's letter-dream was right; and if we wished to go to Gani, the king would send men travelling by night, for his brothers at war with him lay upon the road. As to the Uganda question, and my desiring him to make friends with Mtésa, in hopes that the influence of trade would prevent any plundering in future, he merely tossed his head. He often said he did not know what to think about his guests, now he had got them; to which Bombay, in rather successful imitation of what he had heard me say on like occasions, replied, 'If you do not like them after you have seen them, cut their heads off, for they are all in your hands.'

11th. – With great apparent politeness Kamrasi sent in the morning to inquire how we had slept. He had 'heard our cry' – an expression of regal condescension – and begged we would not be alarmed, for next morning he would see us, and after the meeting change our residence, when, should we not approve of wading to his palace, he would bridge all the swamps leading up to it; but for the present he wanted two rounds of ball-cartridge – one to fire before his women, and the other before his officers and a large number of Kidi men who were there on a visit. To please this childish king, Bombay was sent with two other of my men, and no sooner arrived than a cow was placed before them to be shot Bombay, however, thinking easy compliance would only lead to continued demands on our short store of powder, said he had no order to shoot cows, and declined. A strong debate ensued, which Bombay, by his own account, turned to advantage by saying, 'What use is there in shooting cows? we have lots of meat; what we want is flour to eat with it.' To which the great king retorted, 'If you have not got flour, that is not my fault, for I ordered your master to come slowly, and to bring provisions along with him.'

12th. – To back Bombay in what he had said, I gave him two more cartridges to shoot the cow with, and orders as well to keep Kamrasi to his word about the oft-promised interview and change of residence. He gave me the following account on his return: Upwards of a thousand spectators were present when he killed the cow, putting both bullets into her, and all in a voice, as soon as they saw the effect of the shot, shouted in amazement; the Kidi visitors, all terror-stricken, crying out, as they clasped their breasts, 'Oh, great king, do allow us to return to our country, for you have indeed got a new species of man with you, and we are greatly afraid!' – a lot of humbug and affectation to flatter the king, which pleased him greatly. It was not sufficient, however, to make him forget his regal pride; for though Bombay pleaded hard for our going to see him, and for a change of residence, the immovable king, to maintain the imperial state he had assumed as 'king of kings,' only said, 'What difference does it make whether your master sees me to-day or to-morrow? If he wants to communicate about the road to Gani, his property at Karagŭé, or his guns at Uganda, he can do so as well through the medium of my officers as with me direct, and I will send men whenever he wishes to do so. Perhaps you don't know, but I expect men from Gani every day, who took a present of slaves, ivory, and monkey-skins to the foreigners residing there, who, in the first instance, sent me a necklace of beads [showing them] by some men who wore clothes. They said white men were coming from Karagüé, and requested the beads might be shown them should they do so. They left this two moons before Baraka arrived here, and I told them the white men would not come here, as I heard they had gone to Uganda.'

Bombay then, finding the king very communicative, went at him for his inhospitality towards us, his turning us back from his country twice, and now, after inviting us, treating us as Süwarora did. On this he gave, by Bombay's account, the following curious reason for his conduct: 'You don't understand the matter. At the time the white men were living in Uganda, many of the people who had seen them there came and described them as such monsters, they ate up mountains and drank the N'yanza dry; and although they fed on both beef and mutton, they were not satisfied until they got a dish of the 'tender parts' of human beings three times a-day. Now, I was extremely anxious to see men of such wonderful natures. I could have stood their mountain-eating and N'yanza-drinking capacities, but on no consideration would I submit to sacrifice my subjects to their appetites, and for this reason I first sent to turn them back; but afterwards, on hearing from Dr Kyengo's men that, although the white men had travelled all through their country, and brought all the pretty and wonderful things of the world there, they had never heard such monstrous imputations cast upon them, I sent a second time to call them on: these are the facts of the case. Now, with regard to your accusation of my treating them badly, it is all their own fault I ordered them to advance slowly and pick up food by the way, as there is a famine here; but they, instead, hurried on against my wishes. That they want to see and give me presents you have told me repeatedly – so do I them; for I want them to teach me the way to shoot, and when that is accomplished, I will take them to an island near Kidi, where there are some men [his refractory brothers] whom I wish to frighten away with guns; but still there is no hurry, – they can come when I choose to call them, and not before.' Bombay to this said, 'I cannot deliver such a message to Bana; I have told so many falsehoods about your saying you will have an interview to-morrow, I shall only catch a flogging; and forthwith departed.

13th. – More disgusted with Kamrasi than ever, I called Kidgwiga up, and told him I was led to expect from Rŭmanika that I should find his king a good and reasonable man, which I believed, considering it was said by an unprejudiced person. Mtésa, on the contrary, told me Kamrasi treated all his guests with disrespect, sending them to the farther side of the N'yanza. I now found his enemy more truthful than his friend, and wished him to be told so. 'For the future, I should never,' I said, 'mention his name again, but wait until his fear of me had vanished; for he quite forgot his true dignity as a host and king in his surprise and fear, merely because we were in a hurry and desired to see him.' He was reported to-day, by the way, to be drunk.

Change to West End, 14th: As nothing could be done yesterday, in consequence of the king being in his cups, the Wakungŭ conveyed my message to-day, but with the usual effect, till a diplomatic idea struck me, and I sent another messenger to say, if our residence was not changed at once, both Grant and myself had made up our minds to cut off our hair and blacken our faces, so that the king of all kings should have no more cause to fear us. Ignoring his claims to imperial rank, I maintained that his reason for ill-treating us must be fear, – it could be nothing else. This message acted like magic; for he fully believed we would do as we said, and disappoint him altogether of the strange sight of us as pure white men. The reply was, Kamrasi would not have us disfigured in this way for all the world; men were appointed to convey our traps to the west end at once; and Kidgwiga, Vittagŭra, and Kajunjŭ rushed over to give us the news in all haste lest we should execute our threat, and they were glad to find us with our faces unchanged. I now gave one cow to the head of Dr K'yengo's party, and one to the head of Rŭmanika's men, because I saw it was through their instrumentality we gained admittance in the country; and we changed residence to the west end of Chagŭzi, and found there comfortable huts close to the Kafŭ, which ran immediately between us and the palace.

Still our position in Unyoro was not a pleasant one. In a long field of grass, as high as the neck, and half under water, so that no walks could be taken, we had nothing to see but Kamrasi's miserable huts and a few distant conical hills, of which one,

Udongo, we conceive, represents the Padongo of Brun-Bollet, placed by him in 1° south latitude, and 35° east longitude. We were scarcely inside our new dwelling when Kamrasi sent a cheer of two pots pombé, five fowls, and two bunches of plantains, hoping we were now satisfied with his favour; but he damped the whole in a moment again, by asking for a many-bladed knife which his officers had seen in Grant's possession. I took what he sent, from fear of giving offence, but replied that I was surprised the great king should wish to see my property before seeing myself, and although I attached no more value to my property than he did to his, I could not demean myself by sending him trifles in that way. However, should he, after hearing my sentiments, still persist in asking for the knife to be sent by the hands of a black man, I would pack it up with all the things I had brought for him, and send them by a black man, judging that he liked black men more than white.

Dr K'yengo's men then informed us they had been twice sent with an army of Wanyoro to attack the king's brothers, on a river-island north of this about three days' journey, but each time it ended in nothing. You fancy yourself they said, in a magnificent army, but the enemy no sooner turn out than the cowardly Wanyoro fly, and sacrifice their ally as soon as not into the hands of the opponents. They said Kamrasi would now expect us to attack them with our guns. Rionga was the head of the rebels; there were formerly five, but now only two of the brothers remained.

15th. – Kamrasi, after inquiring after our health, and how we had slept, through a large deputation of head men, alluded to the knife question of yesterday, thinking it very strange that after giving me such nice food I should deny him the gratification of simply looking at a knife; he did not intend to keep it if it was not brought for him, but merely to look at and return it. To my reply of yesterday I added, I had been led, before entering Unyoro, to regard Kamrasi as the king of all kings – the greatest king that ever was, and one worthy to be my father; but now, as he expected me to amuse him with toys, he had lowered himself in my estimation to the position of being my child. To this the sages said, 'Bana speaks beautifully, feelingly, and moderately. Of course he is displeased at seeing his property preferred before himself; all the right is on his side: we will now return and see what can be done – though none but white men in their greatness dare send such messages to our king.'

Dr K'yengo's men were now attacked by Kidgwiga for having taken a cow from me yesterday, and told they should not eat it, because both they and myself were the king's guests, and it ill became one to eat that which was given as a dinner for the other. Fortunately, foreseeing this kind of policy, as Kamrasi had been watching our actions, I invariably gave in presents those cows which came with us from Uganda, and therefore defied any one to meddle with them. This elicited the true facts of the case. Dr K'yengo's men had been sent out to our camp to observe if anybody received presents from us, as Kamrasi feared his subjects would have the fleecing of us before his turn came; and those men had reported the two cows given by me as mentioned above. Kamrasi no sooner heard of this than he took the cows and kept them himself. In their justification, Dr K'yengo's men said that had they not been in the country before us, Kamrasi would not have had such guests at all; for when he asked them if the Waganda reports about our cannibalism and other monstrosities were true, their head man denied it all, offered to stand security for our actions, and told the king if he found us cannibals he might make a Mohammedan of him, and sealed the statement with his oath by throwing down his shield and bow and walking over them. To this Kamrasi was said to have replied, 'I will accept your statements, but you must remain with me until they come.'

Kajunjŭ came with orders to say Kamrasi would seize anybody found staring at us. I requested a definite answer would be given as regards Kamrasi's seeing us. Dr K'yengo's men then said they were kept a week waiting before they could obtain an interview, whilst Kajunjŭ excused his king by saying, 'At present the court is full of Kidi, Chopi, Gani, and other visitors, who he does not wish should see you, as some may be enemies in disguise. They are all now taking presents of cows from Kamrasi, and going to their homes, and, as soon as they are disposed of, your turn will come.'

16th. – We kept quiet all day, to see what effect that would have upon the king. Kidgwiga told us that, when he was a lad, Kamrasi sent him with a large party of Wanyoro to visit a king who lived close to a high mountain, two months' journey distant, to the east or south-east of this, and beg for a magic horn, as that king's doctor was peculiarly famed for his skill as a magician. The party carried with them 600 majembé (iron spades), two of which expended daily paid for their board and lodgings on the way. The horn applied for was sent by a special messenger to Kamrasi, who, in return, sent one of his horns; from which date, the two kings, whenever one of them wishes to communicate with the other, sends, on the messenger's neck, the horn that had been given him, which both serves for credentials and security, as no one dare touch a Mbakka with one of these horns upon his neck.

17th. – Tired and out of patience with our prison – a river of crocodiles on one side, and swamps in every other direction, while we could not go out shooting without a specific order from the king – I sent Kidgwiga and Kajunjŭ to inform Kamrasi that we could bear this life no longer. As he did not wish to see white men, our residing here could be of no earthly use. I hoped he would accept our present from Bombay, and give us leave to depart for Gani. The Wakungŭ, who thought, as well as ourselves, that we were in nothing better than a prison, hurried off with the message, and soon returned with a message from their king that he was busily engaged decorating his palace to give us a triumphant reception; for he was anxious to pay us more respect than anybody who had ever visited him before. We should have seen him yesterday, only that it rained; and, as a precaution against our meeting being broken up, a shed was being built. He could not hear of our leaving the country without seeing him.

18th. – At last we were summoned to attend the king's levee; but the suspicious creature wished his officers to inspect the things we had brought for him before we went there. Here was another hitch. I could not submit to such disrespectful suspicions, but if he wished Bombay to convey my present to him, I saw no harm in the proposition. The king waived the point, and we all started, carrying as a present the things enumerated in the note. The Union Jack led the way. At the ferry three shots were fired, when, stepping into two large canoes, we all went across the Kafŭ together, and found, to our surprise, a small hut built for the reception, low down on the opposite bank, where no strange eyes could see us.

Within this, sitting on a low wooden stool placed upon a double matting of skins – cows' below and leopards' above – on an elevated platform of grass, was the great king Kamrasi, looking, enshrouded in his mbŭgŭ dress, for all the world like a pope in state – calm and actionless. One bracelet of fine-twisted brass wire adorned his left wrist, and his hair, half an inch long, was worked up into small peppercorn-like knobs by rubbing the hand circularly over the crown of the head. His eyes were long, face narrow, and nose prominent, after the true fashion of his breed; and though a finely-made man, considerably above six feet high, he was not so large as Rŭmanika. A cow-skin, stretched out and fastened to the roof, acted as a canopy to prevent dust falling, and a curtain of mbŭgŭ concealed the lower parts of the hut, in front of which, on both sides of the king, sat about a dozen head men.

This was all. We entered and took seats on our own iron stools, whilst Bombay placed all the presents upon the ground before the throne. As no greetings were exchanged, and all at first remained as silent as death, I commenced, after asking about his health, by saying I had journeyed six long years (by the African computation of five months in the year) for the pleasure of this meeting, coming by Karagŭé instead of by the Nile, because the 'Wanya Béri' (Bari people at Gondokoro) had defeated the projects of all former attempts made by white men to reach Unyoro. The purpose of my coming was to ascertain whether his majesty would like to trade with our country, exchanging ivory for articles of European manufacture; as, should he do so, merchants would come here in the same way as they went from Zanzibar to Karagŭé. Rŭmanika and Mtésa were both anxious for trade, and I felt sorry he would not listen to my advice and make friends with Mtésa; for unless the influence of trade was brought in to check the Waganda from pillaging the country, nothing would do so.

Kamrasi, in a very quiet, mild manner, instead of answering the question, told us of the absurd stories which he had heard from the Waganda, said he did not believe them, else his rivers, deprived of their fountains, would have run dry; and he thought if we did eat hills and the tender parts of mankind, we should have had enough to satisfy our appetites before we reached Unyoro. Now, however, he was glad to see that, although our hair was straight and our faces white, we still possessed hands and feet like other men.

The present was then opened, and everything in turn placed upon the red blanket. The goggles created some mirth; so did the scissors, as Bombay, to show their use, clipped his beard, and the lucifers were considered a wonder; but the king scarcely moved or uttered any remarks till all was over, when, at the instigation of the courtiers, my chronometer was asked for and shown. This wonderful instrument, said the officers (mistaking it for my compass), was the magic horn by which the white men found their way everywhere. Kamrasi said he must have it, for, besides it, the gun was the only thing new to him. The chronometer, however, I said, was the only one left, and could not possibly be parted with; though, if Kamrasi liked to send men to Gani, a new one could be obtained for him.

19th. – As the presents given yesterday occupied the king's mind too much for other business, I now sent to offer him one-third of the guns left in Uganda, provided he would send some messengers with one of my men to ask Mtésa for them, and also the same proportion of the sixty loads of property left in charge of Rŭmanika at Karagŭé, if he would send the requisite number of porters for its removal. But of all things, I said, I most wished to send a letter to Petherick at Gani, to apprise him of our whereabouts, for he must have been four years waiting our arrival there, and by the same opportunity I would get a watch for the king. He sent us to-day two pots of pombé, one sack of salt, and what might be called a screw of butter, with an assurance that the half of everything which came to his house – and everything was brought from great distances in boats – he would give me; but for the present the only thing he was in need of was some medicine or stimulants. Further, I need be under no apprehension if I did not find men at once to go on the three respective journeys; it should be all done in good time, for he loved me much, and desired to show us so much respect that his name should be celebrated for it in songs of praise until he was bowed down by years, and even after death it should be remembered.

I ascertained then that the salt, which was very white and pure, came from an island on the Little Lŭta Nzigé, about sixty miles west from the Chagŭzi palace, where the lake is said to be forty or fifty miles wide. It is the same piece of water we heard of in Karagŭé as the Little Lŭta Nzigé, beyond Utŭmbi; and the same story of Unyoro being an island circumscribed by it and the Victoria N'yanza connected by the Nile, is related here, showing that both the Karagŭé and Unyoro people, as indeed all negroes and Arabs, have the common defect in their language, of using the same word for a peninsula and an island. The Waijasi – of whom we saw a specimen in the shape of an old woman, with her upper lip edged with a row of small holes, at Karagŭé – occupy a large island on this lake named Gasi, and sometimes come to visit Kamrasi. Ugungŭ, a dependency of Kamrasi's, occupies this side the lake, and on the opposite side is Ulégga; beyond which, in about 2° N. lat and 28° E. long., is the country of Namachi; and further west still about 2°, the Wilyanwantŭ, or cannibals, who, according to the report both here and at Karagŭé, 'bury cows but eat men.' These distant people pay their homage to Kamrasi, though they have six degrees of longitude to travel over. They are, I believe, a portion of the N'yam N'yams – another name for cannibal – whose country Petherick said he entered in 1857-58. Among the other wild legends about this people, it was said that the Wilyanwantŭ, in making brotherhood, exchanged their blood by drinking at one another's veins; and, in lieu of butter with their porridge, they smear it with the fat of fried human flesh.

20th. – I had intended for to-day an expedition to the lake; but Kamrasi, harbouring a wicked design that we should help in an attack on his brothers, said there was plenty of time to think of that; we would only find that all the waters united go to Gani, and he wished us to be his guests for three or four months at least. Fifty Gani men had just arrived to inform him that Rionga had lately sent ten slaves and ten ivory tusks to Petherick's post, to purchase a gun; but the answer was, that a thousand times as much would not purchase a weapon that might be used against us; for our arrival with Kamrasi had been heard of, and nothing would be done to jeopardise our road.

To talk over this matter, the king invited us to meet him. We went as before, minus the flag and firing, and met a similar reception.

The Gani news was talked over, and we proposed sending Bombay with a letter at once. I could get no answer; so, to pass the time, we wished to know from the king's own lips if he had prevented Baraka from going to Gani, as he had carried orders from Rŭmanika as well as from myself to visit Kamrasi, to give him fifty egg-beads, seventy necklaces of mtendé, and seventy necklaces of kŭtŭamnazi beads, and then to pass on to Gani and give its chief fifty egg-beads and forty necklaces of kŭtŭamnazi. Kamrasi replied, 'I did not allow him to go, because I heard you had gone to Uganda' and Dr K'yengo's men happening to be present, added, 'Baraka used up all the beads save forty which he gave to Kamrasi, living upon goats all the way; and when he left, took back a tusk of ivory.'

This little controversy was amusing, but did not suit Kamrasi, who had his eye on a certain valuable possession of mine. He made his approach towards it by degrees, beginning with a truly royal speech thus: 'I am the king of all these countries, even including Uganda and Kidi – though the Kidi people are such savages they obey no man's orders – and you are great men also, sitting on chairs before kings; it therefore ill becomes us to talk of such trifles as beads, especially as I know if you ever return this way I shall get more from you.' 'Begging your majesty's pardon,' I said, 'the mention of beads only fell in the way of our talk like stones in a walk; our motive being to get at the truth of what Baraka did and said here, as his conduct in returning after receiving strict orders from Rŭmanika and ourselves to open the road, is a perfect enigma to us. We could not have entered Unyoro at all excepting through Uganda, and we could not have put foot in Uganda without visiting its king.' Without deigning to answer, Kamrasi, in the metaphorical language of a black man, said, 'It would be unbecoming of me to keep secrets from you, and therefore I will tell you at once; I am sadly afflicted with a disorder which you alone can cure.' 'What is it, your majesty? I can see nothing in your face; it may perhaps require a private inspection.' 'My heart,' he said, 'is troubled, because you will not give me your magic horn – the thing, I mean, in your pocket, which you pulled out one day when Budja and Vittagŭra were discussing the way; and you no sooner looked at it than you said, "That is the way to the palace."'

So! the sly fellow has been angling for the chronometer all this time, and I can get nothing out of him until he has got it – the road to the lake, the road to Gani, everything seemed risked on his getting my watch – a chronometer worth £50, which would be spoilt in his hands in one day. To undeceive him, and tell him it was the compass which I looked at and not the watch, I knew would only end with my losing that instrument as well; so I told him it was not my guide, but a time-keeper, made for the purpose of knowing what time to eat my dinner by. It was the only chronometer I had with me; and I begged he would have patience until Bombay returned from Gani with another, when he should have the option of taking this or the new one. 'No; I must have the one in your pocket; pull it out and show it.' This was done, and I placed it on the ground, saying, 'The instrument is yours, but I must keep it until another one comes.' 'No; I must have it now, and will send it you three times every day to look at.'

The watch went, gold chain and all, without any blessings following it; and the horrid king asked if I could make up another magic horn, for he hoped he had deprived us of the power of travelling, and plumed himself on the notion that the glory of opening the road would devolve upon himself. When I told him that to purchase another would cost five hundred cows, the whole party were more confirmed than ever as to its magical powers; for who in his senses would give five hundred cows for the mere gratification of seeing at what time his dinner should be eaten? Thus ended the second meeting. Kamrasi now said the Gani men would feast on beef to-morrow, and the next day be ready to start with my men for Petherick's camp. He then accompanied us to the boats, spear in hand, and saw us cross the water. Long tail-hairs of the giraffe surrounded his neck, on which little balls and other ornaments of minute beads, after the Uganda fashion, were worked. In the evening four pots of pombé and a pack of flour were brought, together with the chronometer, which was sent to be wound up – damaged of course – the seconds-hand had been dislodged.

21st. – I heard from Kidgwiga that some of those Gani men now ordered to go with Bombay had actually been visiting here when the latter shot his first cow at the palace, but had gone to their homes to give information of us, and had returned again. Eager to get on with my journey, and see European faces again, I besought the king to let us depart, as our work was all finished here, since he had assured us he would like to trade with England. The N'yanswengé – meaning Petherick's party – who have hitherto been afraid to come here, would do so now, when they had seen us pass safely down, and could receive my guns and property left to come from Uganda and Karagüé, which we ourselves could not wait for. Kamrasi, thinking me angry for his having taken the watch so rudely out of my pocket, took fright at the message, sent some of his attendants quickly back to me, requesting me to keep the instrument until another arrived, and begged I would never say I wished to leave his house again.

22d. – Kamrasi sent to say Bombay was not to start to-day, but to-morrow, so we put the screw on again, and said we must go at once; if he would give us guides to Gani, we would return him his twenty cows and seven goats with pleasure. I let him understand we suspected he was keeping us here to fight his brothers, and told him he must at once know we would never lift hand against them. It was contrary to the laws of our land. 'I have got no orders to enter into black men's quarrels, and my mother' (the Queen), 'whom I see every night in my sleep calling me home, would be very angry if she heard of it. Rŭmanika once asked me to fight his brothers Rogéro and M'yongo, but my only reply to all had been the same – I have no orders to fight with, only to make friends of, the great kings of Africa.'

The game seemed now to be won. At once Kamrasi ordered Bombay to prepare for the journey. Five Wanyoro, five Chopi men, and five Gani men, were to escort him. There was no objection to his carrying arms. The moment he returned, which ought to be in little more than a fortnight, we would all go together. An earnest request was at the same time made that I would not bully him in the mean time with any more applications to depart. So Bombay and Mabrŭki, carrying their muskets, and a map and letter for Petherick, departed.

23d and 24th. – Kamrasi, presuming he had gained favour in our eyes, sent, begging to know how we had slept, and said he would like us to inform him what part of his journey Bombay had this morning reached – a fact which he had no doubt must be divinable through the medium of our books. The reply was, that Bombay's luck was so good we had no doubt regarding his success; but now he had gone, and our days here were numbered, we should like to see the palace, his fat wives and children, as well as the Wanyoro's dances, and all the gaiety of the place. We did not think our reception-hut by the river sufficiently dignified, and our residence here was altogether like that of prisoners – seeing no one, knowing no one. In answer to this, Kamrasi sent one pot of pombé and five fowls, begging we would not be alarmed; we should see everything in good time, if we would but have patience, for he considered us very great men, as he was a great man himself, and we had come at his invitation. He must request, in the mean time, that we would send no more messages by his officers, as such messages are never conveyed properly. At present there was a great deal of business in the palace.

We asked for some butter, but could get none, as all the milk in the palace was consumed by the wives and children, drinking all day long, to make themselves immovably fat.

25th. – In the morning, the commander-in-chief wished us to cast a horoscope, and see where Bombay was, and if he were getting on well. That being negatived, he told us to put our hut in order, as Kamrasi was coming to see us. Accordingly we made everything as smart as possible, hanging the room round with maps, horns, and skins of animals, and placed a large box covered with a red blanket, as a throne for the king to sit upon. As he advanced, my men, forming a guard of honour, fired three shots immediately on his setting foot upon our side the river; whilst Frij, with his boatswain's whistle, piped the 'Rogue's March,' to prepare us for his majesty's approach. We saluted him, hat in hand, and, leading the way, showed him in. He was pleased to be complimentary, remarking, what Waséja (fine men) we were, and took his seat. We sat on smaller boxes, to appear humble, whilst his escort of black 'swells' filled the doorway, squatting on the ground, so as to stop the light and interfere with our decorations.

After the first salutations, the king remarked the head of a nsamma buck, and handled it; then noticed my mosquito-curtains hanging over the bed, and begged for them. He was told they could not be given until Bombay returned, as the mosquitoes would eat us up. 'But there were two,' said the escort, 'for we have seen one in the other hut.' That was true; but were there not two white men? However, if the king wanted gauze, here was a smart gauze veil – and the veil vanished at once. The iron camp-bed was next inspected, and admired; then the sextant, which was coveted and begged for, but without success, much to the astonishment of the king, as his attendants had led him to expect he would get anything he asked for. Then the thermometers were wanted and refused; also table-knives, spoons, forks, and even cooking-pots, for we had no others, and could not part with them. The books of birds and animals had next to be seen, and being admired were coveted, the king offering one of the books I first gave him in exchange for one of these. In fact, he wanted to fleece us of everything; so, to shut him up, I said I would not part with one bird for one hundred tusks of ivory; they were all the collections I had made in Africa, and if I parted with them my journey would go for nothing; but if he wanted a few drawings of birds I would do some for him – at present I wished to speak to him. 'Well, what is it? we are all attention.' 'I wish to know positively if you would like English traders to come here regularly, as the Arabs do to trade at Karagŭé? and if so, would you give me a pembé (magic horn) as a warrant, that everybody may know Kamrasi, king of Unyoro, desires it?'

Kamrasi replied, 'I like your proposition very much; you shall have the horn you ask for, either large or small, just as you please; and after you have gone, should we hear any English are at Gani wishing to come here, as my brothers are in the way we will advance with spears whilst they approach with guns, and, between us both, my brothers must fly – for I myself will head the expedition. But now you have had your say I will have mine if you will listen.' 'All right, your majesty; what is it?' 'I am constantly stricken with fever and pains, for which I know no remedy but cautery; my children die young; my family is not large enough to uphold my dignity and station in life; in fact, I am infirm and want stimulants, and I wish you to prescribe for me, which, considering you have found your way to this, where nobody came before, must be easy to you.' Two pills and a draught for the morning were given as a preliminary measure, argument being of no avail; and to our delight the king said it was time to go.

We jumped off our seats to show him the way, hoping our persecutions were over; but still he sat, and sat, until at length, finding we did not take the hint to give him a parting present, he said, 'I never visited any big man's house without taking home some trifle to show my wife and children.' 'Indeed, great king! then you did not come to visit us, but to beg, eh? You shall have nothing, positively nothing; for we will not have it said the king did not come to see us, but to beg.' Kamrasi's face changed colour; he angrily said, 'Irokh togend' (let us rise and go), and forthwith walked straight out of the hut. Frij piped, but no guns fired; and as he asked the reason why, he was told it would be offensive to say we were glad he was going. The king was evidently not pleased, for no pombé came to-day.

CHAPTER XIV

Unyoro – Continued

26th. – We found that the palace was shut up in consequence of the new moon, seen for the first time last evening; and incessant drumming was the order of the day. Still, private interviews might be granted, and I sent to inquire after the state of the king's health. The reply was, that the medicine had not been taken, and the king was very angry because nothing was given him when he took the trouble to call on us. He never called at a big man's house and left it mwiko (empty-handed) before; if there was nothing else to dispose of, could Bana not have given him a bag of beads?

To save us from this kind of incessant annoyance, I now thought it would be our best policy to mount the high horse and bully him. Accordingly, we tied up a bag of the commonest mixed beads, added the king's chronometer, and sent them to Kamrasi with a violent message that we were thoroughly disgusted with all that had happened; the beads were for the poor beggar who came to our house yesterday, not to see us, but to beg; and as we did not desire the acquaintance of beggars, we had made up our minds never to call again, nor receive any more bread or wine from the king.

This appeared to be a hit. Kamrasi, evidently taken aback, said, if he thought he should have offended us by begging, he would not have begged. He was not a poor man, for he had many cows, but he was a beggar, of course, when beads were in the question; and, having unwittingly offended, as he desired our friendship, he trusted his offence would be forgiven. On opening the chronometer, he again wrenched back the seconds-hand, and sent it for repair, together with two pots of pombé as a peace-offering. Frij, who accompanied the deputation, overheard the counsellors tell their king that the Waganda were on their way back to Unyoro to snatch us away; on hearing which the king asked his men if they would ever permit it; and, handling his spear as if for battle, said at the same time he would lose his own head before they should touch his guests. Then, turning to Frij, he said, 'What would you do if they came? – go back with them?' To which Frij said, 'No, never, when Gani is so near; they might cut our heads off, but that is all they could do.' The watch being by this time repaired, it gave me the opportunity of sending Kidgwiga back to the palace to say we trusted Kamrasi would allow Budja to come here, if only with one woman to carry his pombé, else Mtésa would take offence, form an alliance with Rionga, and surround the place with warriors, for it was not becoming in great kings to treat civil messengers like dogs.

The reply to this was, that Kamrasi was very much pleased with my fatherly wisdom and advice, and would act up to it, allowing Budja only to approach with one woman; we need, however, be under no apprehensions, for Kamrasi's power was infinite; the Gani road should be opened even at the spear's point; he had been beating the big drum in honour of us the whole day; he would not allow any beggars to come and see us, for he wanted us all to himself, and for this reason had ordered a fence to be built all round our house; but he had got no present from Grant yet, though all he wanted was his mosquito-curtains, whilst he wished my picture-books to show his women, and be returned. We sent a picture of Mtésa as a gift, the two books to look at, and an acknowledgment that the mosquito-curtains were his, only he must have patience until Bombay arrived; but his proposition about the fence we rejected with scorn. The king had been raising an army to fight Rionga – the true reason, we suspect, for the beating of the drum.

27th and 28th. – There was drumming and music all day and night, and the army was being increased to a thousand men, but we poor prisoners could see nothing of it. Frij was therefore sent to inspect the armament and bring us all the news. Some of N'yamyonjo's men, seeing mine armed with carbines, became very inquisitive about them, and asked if they were the instruments which shot their men on the Nile – one in the arm, who died; the other on the top of the shoulder, who was recovering. The drums were kept in private rooms, to which a select few only were admitted. Kamrasi conducts all business himself, awarding punishments and seeing them carried out. The most severe instrument of chastisement is a knob-stick, sharpened at the back, like that used in Uganda, for breaking a man's neck before he is thrown into the N'yanza; but this severity is seldom resorted to, Kámrasi being of a mild disposition compared with Mtésa, whom he invariably alludes to when ordering men to be flogged, telling them that were they in Uganda, their heads would suffer instead of their backs. In the day's work at the palace, army collecting, ten officers were bound because they failed to bring a sufficient number of fighting men, but were afterwards released on their promising to bring more.

Dr K'yengo's men, who had been sent three times into action against the refractory brothers, asked leave to return to Karagŭé; but the king, who did not fear for their lives when his work was to be done, would not give them leave, lest accident should befall them on the way. We found no prejudice against eating butter amongst these Wahŭma, for they not only sold us some, but mixed it with porridge and ate it themselves.

29th. – The king has appointed a special officer to keep our table supplied with sweet potatoes, and sent us a pot of pombé, with his excuses for not seeing us, as business was so pressing, and would continue to be so until the army marched. Budja and Kasoro were again reported to be near with a force of fifty Waganda, prepared to snatch us away; and the king, fearing the consequences, had sent to inform Budja, that if he dared attempt to approach, he would slip us off in boats to Gani, and then fight it out with the Waganda; for his guests, since they had been handed over to him, had been treated with every possible respect.

To keep Kamrasi to his promise, as we particularly wished to hear the Uganda news, Frij was sent to inform him on my behalf that Mtésa only wished to make friends with all the great kings surrounding his country before his coronation took place, when his brothers would be burnt, and he would cease to take advice from his mother. To treat his messengers disrespectfully could do no good, and might provoke a war, when we should see my deserters joined with the Waganda really coming in force against us; whereas, if we saw Budja, we could satisfy him, and Mtésa too, and obviate any such calamity. The reply was, that Kamrasi would arrange for our having a meeting with Budja alone if we wished it; he did not fear my deserters siding with king Mtésa, but he detested the Waganda, and could not bear to see them in his country.

30th. – At breakfast-time we heard that my old friend Kasoro had come to our camp without permission, to the surprise of everybody, attended by all his boys, leaving Budja and his children, on account of sickness, at the camp assigned to the Waganda, five miles off. Kasoro wished to speak to us, and we invited him into the hut; but the interview could not be permitted until Kamrasi's wishes on the subject had been ascertained. In a little while the Kamraviona, having seen Kamrasi, said we might converse with one another whilst his officers were present listening, and sent a cow as a present for the Waganda. Kasoro with his children now came before us in their usual merry manner, and, after saluting, told us how the deserters, on reaching Uganda, begged for leave to proceed to Karagŭé; but Mtésa, who would only allow two of them to approach him, abused them, saying, 'Did I not command you to take Bana to Gani at all risks? If there was no road by land, you were to go by water; or, if that failed, to go under-ground, or in the air above; and if he died, you were to die with him: what, then, do you mean by deserting him and flying here? You shall not move a yard from this until I receive a messenger from him to hear what he has got to say on the matter.'

Mtésa would not take their arms, even at the desire of Budja, on my behalf; for as no messenger on my behalf came to him, he would not believe what Budja said, and feared to touch any of our property. The chief item of court news was, that Mtésa had shot a buffalo which was attacking him behind his palace, and made his Wakungŭ carry the animal bodily, whilst life was in it, into his court. The ammunition I wrote for to Rŭmanika had been brought by Maŭla.

As Kasoro still remained silent with regard to Mtésa's message, I told him we shot two of N'yamyonjo's men on our retreat up the Nile, and that Kamrasi turned us back because some miscreant Waganda had forged lies and told him we were terrible monsters, who ate hills and human flesh, and drank up all the water of the lake. He laughed, but still was silent; so I said, 'What message have you brought from Mtésa?' To which, in a timid, modest kind of manner, he said, 'Bana knows – what more need I say? Has he forgotten Mtésa, who loves him so?' I said,

'No, indeed, I have not forgotten Mtésa; and, moreover, as I expected you back again, I have sent Bombay to bring the stimulants and all the things I promised Mtésa from Gani; in two or three days, he will return.' 'No,' said Kasoro, 'that is not it; we must go to Gani with you; for Mtésa says he loves you so much he will never allow you to part from his hand until his servants have seen you safely at your homes.'

I replied, 'If Mtésa wishes you to see my vessels and all the wonders they contain, as far as I am concerned you may do so, and I shall be only too happy to show you a little English hospitality; but the road is in Kamrasi's hands, and his wishes must now be heard.' The commander-in-chief, now content with all he had heard, went to Kamrasi to receive his orders, whilst I gave Kasoro a feast of porridge and salt, with pombé to wash it down, and a cow to take home with him; for the poor creatures said they were all starving, as the Wanyoro would not allow them to take a single plantain from the field until Kamrasi's permission had been given.

Kamrasi's reply now arrived; it was to the following effect: 'Tell my children, the Waganda, they were never turned out of Unyoro by my orders: if they wish to go to Gani, they can do so; but, first of all, they must return to Mtésa, and ask him to deliver up all of Bana's men.' I answered, 'No; if any one of those scoundrels who has deserted me ever dares show his face to me again, I will shoot him like a dog. Moreover, I want Mtésa to take their guns from them, and, without taking life, to transport them all to an island on the N'yanza, where they can spend their days in growing plantains; for it is such men who prevent our travelling in the country and visiting kings.' Kasoro on this said, 'Mtésa will do so in a minute if you send a servant to him, but he won't if we only say you wish it.'

The commander-in-chief then added, as to Kasoro's wish to accompany me, 'If Mtésa will send another time one of his people whose life he wishes sacrificed on the journey, or tells us, Here is a man whom I wish you to send to Gani at all hazards, and without responsibility for his life on our part, we will be very glad to send him; but as we are at war with the Gani people continually, there will be no security for a Mganda's life there.' To this I added, 'Now, Kasoro, you see how it is; Kamrasi does not wish you to go to Gani, so if you take my advice you will return to Mtésa. Give this tin cartridge-box, which first came from him, back to him again, to show him you have seen me, and say, This is Bana's letter; he wishes you to transport the deserters and seize their guns. The guns, of course, I shall want again at some other time, when I will send one of my English children to visit him; for now Kamrasi has opened his country to us, and given us leave to come and purchase ivory, I never shall be very far away.' I gave them three pills for Budja, blistered two of the pages, and started the whole merrily off, Kasoro asking me to send Mtésa some pretty things from England such as he never saw.

1st.- Kamrasi sent his commander-in-chief to inquire after my health, and to say Budja had left in fear and trembling lest Mtésa should cut all their heads off for failing in the mission; but he had sent Kidgwiga's brother with a pot of pombé to escort the Waganda beyond his frontier, and cheer them on the way; for the tin cartridge-box, he thought, would save their lives by satisfying Mtésa they had seen me. The commander-in-chief then told me Kamrasi did not wish them to accompany me through Kidi, for the Kidi people don't like the Waganda, and, discovering their nationality by the fulness of their teeth, would bring trouble on us whilst trying to kill them. I said I thanked Kamrasi for his having treated the Waganda with such marked respect, in allowing them to see me, and sending them back with an escort; but I thought it would have been better if he had spoken the truth plainly out, for then I could have told them I feared to have them in company with me. In return for my civilities, the king then sent one of his Chopi officers to see me, who went four stages with Bombay, and he also sent some rich beads which he wished me to look at. They were nicely kept in a neat though very large casing of rush pith, and were those sent as a letter from Gani, to inform him that we were expected to come *viâ* Karagŭé. After this, to keep us in good-humour, Kamrasi sent to inform us that some Gani men, twenty-five in number, had just arrived, and had given him a lion-skin, several tippet monkey-skins, and some giraffe hair, as well as a stick of copper or brass wire. Bombay was met by them on the confines of Gani.

2d. – The king sent me a pot of pombé to-day, inquiring after my health, and saying he would like to take the medicine I gave him if I would send Frij over to administer it, but he would be ashamed to swallow pills before me. Hitherto he had not been able to take the medicine from press of business in collecting an army to fight his brothers; but as his troops would all leave for war to-day, he expected to have leisure.

In plying the Kamraviona to *try* if we could get rid of the annoying restraints which made our residence here a sort of imprisonment, I discovered that the whole affair was not one of blunder or accident, but that we actually were prisoners thus by design. It appeared that Kamrasi's brothers, when they heard we were coming into Unyoro, murmured, and said to the king, 'Why are you bringing such guests amongst us, who will practise all kinds of diabolical sorcery, and bring evil on us?' To which Kamrasi replied, 'I have invited them to come, and they shall come; and if they bring evil with them, let that all fall on my shoulders, for you shall not see them.' He then built a palaver-house on the banks of the Kafŭ to receive us in privately; and when we were to go to Gani, it was his intention to slip us off privately down the Kafŭ. The brothers were so thoroughly frightened, that when Kamrasi opened his chronometer before them to show them the works in motion, they turned their heads away. The large block-tin box I gave Kamrasi, as part of his hongo, was, I heard, called Mzungŭ, or the white man, by him.

In the evening the beads recently brought from Gani were sent for my inspection, with an intimation that Kamrasi highly approved of them, and would like me to give him a few like them. Some of Kamrasi's spies, whom he had sent to the refractory allies of Rionga his brother, returned bringing a spear and some grass from the thatch of the hut of a Chopi chief. The removal of the grass was a piece of state policy. It was stolen by Kamrasi's orders, in order that he might spread a charm on the Chopi people, and gain such an influence over them that their spears could not prevail against the Wanyoro; but it was thought we might possess some still superior magic powder, as we had come from such a long distance, and Kamrasi would prefer to have ours. These Chopi people were leagued with the brothers, and thus kept the highroad to Gani, though the other half of Chopi remained loyal; and though Kamrasi continually sent armies against the refractory half which aided his brothers, they never retaliated by attacking this place.

3d. – Kamrasi's political department was active again to-day. Some Gani officials arrived to inform him that there were two white men in the vessel spoken of as at Gani; a second vessel was coming in there, and several others were on their way. A carnelian was shown me which the Gani people gave to Kamrasi many years ago. Kamrasi expressed a wish that I would exchange magic powders with him. He had a very large variety, and would load a horn for me with all those I desired most. He wanted also medicines for longevity and perpetual strength. Those I had given him had, he said, deprived him of strength, and he felt much reduced by their effects. He would like me to go with him and attack the island his three brothers, Rionga, Wahitŭ, and Pohŭka, are in possession of. When I said I never fought with black men, he wished to know if I would not shoot them if they attacked me. My reply was, alluding to our fight in the river, 'How did N'yamyonjo s men fare?' I found that Kamrasi had thirty brothers and as many sisters.

4th. – I gave Kamrasi a bottle of quinine, which we call 'strong back,' and asked him in return for a horn containing all the powders necessary to give me the gift of tongues, so that I should be able to converse with any black men whom I might meet with. We heard that Kamrasi has called all his Gani guests to play before him, and a double shot from his Blissett rifle announced to our ears that he in turn was amusing them. This was the first time the gun had been discharged since he received it, and, fearing to fire it himself, he called one of my men to do it for him.

5th. – At 9 A.M., the time for measuring the fall of rain for the last twenty-four hours, we found the rain-gauge and bottle had been removed, so we sent Kidgwiga to inform the king we wished his magicians to come at once and institute a search for it. Kidgwiga immediately returned with the necessary adept, an old man, nearly blind, dressed in strips of old leather fastened to the waist, and carrying in one hand a cow's horn primed with magic powder, carefully covered on the mouth with leather, from which dangled an iron bell. The old creature jingled the bell, entered our hut, squatted on his hams, looked first at one, then at the other – inquired what the missing things were like, grunted, moved his skinny arm round his head, as if desirous of catching air from all four sides of the hut, then dashed the accumulated air on the head of his horn, smelt it to see if all was going right, jingled the bell again close to his ear, and grunted his satisfaction; the missing articles must be found.

To carry out the incantation more effectually, however, all my men were sent for to sit in the open before the hut, when the old doctor rose, shaking the horn and tinkling the bell close to his ear. He then, confronting one of the men, dashed the horn forward as if intending to strike him on the face, then, smelt the head, then dashed at another, and so on, till he became satisfied that my men were not the thieves. He then walked into Grant's hut, inspected that, and finally went to the place where the bottle had been kept. There he walked about the grass with his arm up, and jingling the bell to his ear, first on one side, then on the other, till the track of a hyena gave him the clue, and in two or three more steps he found it. A hyena had carried it into the grass and dropped it. Bravo, for the infallible horn! and well done the king for his honesty in sending it! So I gave the king the bottle and gauge, which delighted him amazingly; and the old doctor, who begged for pombé, got a goat for his trouble. My men now, recollecting the powder robbery at Uganda, said king Mtésa would not send his horn when I asked for it, because he was the culprit himself.

7th. – In the morning the Kamraviona called, on the kings behalf, to inquire after my health, and also to make some important communications. First he was to request a supply of bullets, that the king might fire a salute when Bombay returned from Gani; next, to ask for stimulative medicine, now that he had consumed all I gave him, and gone through the preliminary course; further, to request I would spread a charm over all his subjects, so that their hearts might be inclined towards him, and they would come without calling and bow down at his feet; finally, he wished me to exchange my blood with him, that we might be brother's till death. I sent the bullets, advised him to wait a day or two for the medicine, and said there was only one charm by which he could gain the influence he required over his subjects – this was, knowledge and the power of the pen. Should he desire some of my children (meaning missionaries) to come here and instruct his, the thing would be done; but not in one year, nor even ten, for it takes many years to educate children.

As to exchanging my blood with a black man's, it was a thing quite beyond my comprehension; though Rǔmanika, I must confess, had asked me to do the same thing. The way the English make lasting friendships is done either by the expressions of their hearts, or by the exchange of some trifles, as keepsakes; and now, as I had given Kamrasi some specimens of English manufacture, he might give me a horn, or anything else he chose, which I could show to my friends, so as to keep him in recollection all my life.

The Kamraviona, before leaving, said, for our information, that a robbery had occurred in the palace last night; for this morning, when Kamrasi went to inspect his Mzungǔ (the block-tin box), which he had forgotten to lock, he found all his beads had been stolen. After sniffing round among the various wives, he smelt the biggest one to be the culprit, and turned the beads out of her possession. Deputies came in the evening with a pot of pombé and small screw of butter, to tell me some Gani people had just arrived, bringing information that the vessel at Gani had left to go down the river; but when intelligence reached the vessel of the approach of my men they turned and came back again. Bombay was well feasted on the road by Kamrasi's people, receiving eight cows from one and two cows from another.

8th and 9th. – We had a summons to attend at the Kafǔ palace with the medicine-chest, a few select persons only to be present. It rained so much on the 8th as to stop the visit, but we went next day. After arriving there, and going through the usual salutations, Kamrasi asked us from what stock of people we came, explaining his meaning by saying, 'As we, Rǔmanika, Mtésa, and the rest of us (enumerating the kings), are Wawitǔ (or princes), Uwitǔ (or the country of princes) being to the east.' This interesting announcement made me quite forget to answer his question, and induced me to say, 'Omwita, indeed, was the ancient name for Mombas, if you came from that place: I know all about your race for two thousand years or more. Omwita, you mean, was the last country you resided in before you came here, but originally you came from Abyssinia, the sultan of which, our great friend, is Sahéla Sélassie.'

He pronounced this name laughing, and said, 'Formerly our stock was half-white and half-black, with one side of our heads covered with straight hair, and the other side frizzly: you certainly do know everything.' The subject then turned upon medicine, and, after inspecting the chest, and inquiring into all its contents, it ended by his begging for the half of everything. The mosquito-curtains were again asked for, and refused until I should leave this. As Kamrasi was anxious I should take two of his children to England to be instructed, I agreed to do so, but said I thought it would be better if he invited missionaries to come here and educate all his family. His cattle were much troubled with sickness, dying in great numbers – could I cure them? As he again began to persecute us with begging, wanting knives and forks, etc., I advised his using ivory as money, and purchasing what he wanted from Gani. This brought out the interesting fact, the truth of which we had never reached before, that when Petherick's servant brought him one necklace of beads, and asked after us, he gave in return fourteen ivories, thirteen women, and seven mbŭgŭ cloths. One of his men accompanied the visitors back to the boats, and saw Petherick, who took the ivory and rejected the women.

10th. – At 2 P.M. we were called by Kamrasi to visit him at the Kafŭ palace again, and requested to bring a lot of medicines tied up in various coloured cloths, so that he might know what to select for different ailments. We repaired there as before, putting the medicines into the sextant-stand box, and found him lying at full length on the platform of his throne, with a glass-bead necklace of various colours, and a charm tied on his left arm. Nobody was allowed to be present at our interview. The medicines, four varieties, were weighed out into ten doses each, and their uses and effects explained. He begged for four bottles to put them in, till he was laughed out of it by our saying he required forty bottles; for if the powders were mixed, how could he separate them again? And to keep his mind from the begging tack, which he was getting alarmingly near, I said, 'Now I have given you these things because you would insist on having them. I must also tell you they are dangerous in your hands, in consequence of your being ignorant of their properties. If you take my advice you won't meddle with them until the two children you wish educated have learnt the use of them in England; and if I have to take boys from this, I hope they will be of your family.' He said, 'You speak like a father to us, and we very much approve. Here is a pot of pombé; I did not give you one yesterday.'

12th. – The Kamraviona was sent to inquire after our health, and to ascertain from me all I knew respecting the origin of Kamrasi's tribe, the distribution of countries, and the seat of the government. I sent the king a diagram, painted in various colours, with full explanations of everything, and asked permission to send two more of my men in search of Bombay, who had now been absent twenty days. The reply was, that if Bombay did not return within four days, Kamrasi would send other men after him on the fifth day; and, in the mean time, he sent one pot of pombé as a token of his kind regard.

13th. – The Kamraviona was sent to inquire after our health, to ask for medicine for himself, and to inquire more into the origin of his race. I, on the other hand, wishing to make myself as disagreeable as possible, in order that Kamrasi might get tired of us, sent Frij to ask for fresh butter, eggs, tobacco, coffee, and fowls, every day, saying, I will pay their price when I reach Gani, for we were suffering from want of proper food. Kamrasi was surprised at this clamour for food, and inquired what we ate at home that we were so different from everybody else.

We heard to-day a strange story, involving the tragic fate of Budja. On coming here, he had been bewitched by Kamrasi's frontier officer, who put the charm into a pot of pombé. From the moment Budja drank it he was seized with sickness, and remained so until he reached the first station in Uganda, when he died. The facts of the bewitchment had been found out by means of the perpetrator's wives, who, from the moment the pombé was drunk, took to precipitate flight, well knowing what effects would follow, and dreading the chastisement Mtésa would bring upon their household. We heard, too, that the deserters had returned to the place they deserted from, with thirty Waganda, and a present of some cows for me.

15th. – Getting more impatient, and desirous to move on at any sacrifice, I proposed giving up all claims to my muskets, as well as the present of cows from Mtésa, if Kamrasi would give us boats to Gani at once; but the reply was simply, Why be in such a hurry?

16th. – The Kamraviona was sent to us with a load of coffee, which Kamrasi had purchased with cowries, and to inquire how we had slept. Very badly, was the reply, because we knew Bombay would have been back long ago if Kamrasi was not concealing him somewhere, and we did not know what he was doing with deserters and Waganda. Kamrasi then wanted us to paint his mbŭgŭ cloths in different patterns and colours; but we sent him instead six packages of red-ink powder, and got abused for sauciness. He then wanted black ink, else how could he put on the red with taste; but we had none to give him. Next, he asked leave for my men to shoot cows before his Kidi visitors, which they did to his satisfaction, instructing him at the same time to fire powder with his own rifle; when, triumphant with his success, he protested he would never use anything but guns again, and threw away his spear as useless. Bombay, we learned, had reached Gani, and ought to return in eight days.

17th and 18th. – A large party of Chopi people arrived, by Kamrasi's orders, to tell the reason which induced them to apply for guns to the white men at Gani, as it appeared evident they must have wished to fight their king. The Kidi visitors got broken heads for helping themselves from the Wanyoro's fields, and when they cried out against such treatment, were told they should rob the king, if they wished to rob at all.

20th. – Having asked Kamrasi to return my pictures, he sent the book of birds, but not of animals; and said he could not see us until a new hut was built, because the old one was flooded by the Kafŭ, which had been rising several days. We must not, he said, talk about Bombay any more, because everybody said he was detained by the N'yanswengé (Petherick's party), and would return here with the new moon. I would not accept the lie, saying, How can my 'children' at Gani detain my messengers, when they have received strict orders from me by letter to send an answer quickly? It was all Kamrasi's doing, for he had either hidden Bombay, or ordered his officers to take him slowly, as he did us, stopping four days at each stage.

Frij again told me he was present when Said Said, the Sultan of Zanzibar, sent an army to assist the Wagŭnya at Amŭ, on the coast, against the incursions of the Masai. These Amŭ people have the same Wahŭma features as Kamrasi, whom they also resemble both in general physical appearance, and in many of them having circular marks, as if made by cautery, on the forehead and temples. These marks I took not to be tatooing or decorative, but as a cure for disease – cautery being a favourite remedy with both races.

The battle lasted only two days, though the Masai brought a thousand spears against the Arabs' cannon. But this was not the only battle Said Said had to fight on those grounds; for some years previously he had to subdue the Waziwa, who live on very marshy land, into respect for his sovereignty, when the battle lasted years, in consequence of the bad nature of the ground, and the trick the Waziwa had of staking the ground with spikes. The Wasŭahili, or coast-people, by his description, are the bastards or mixed breeds who live on the east coast of Africa, extending from the Somali country to Zanzibar. Their language is Kisŭahili; but there is no land Usŭahili, though people talk of going to the Sŭahili in the same vague sense as they do of going to the Mashenzi, or amongst the savages. The common story amongst the Wasŭahili at Zanzibar, in regard to the government of that island, was, that the Wakhadim, or aborigines of Zanzibar, did not like the oppressions of the Portuguese, and therefore allied themselves to the Arabs of Muscat – even compromising their natural birthright of freedom in government, provided the Arabs, by their superior power, would secure to them perpetual equity, peace, and justice. The senior chief, Sheikh Mŭhadim, was the mediator on their side, and without his sanction no radical changes compromising the welfare of the land could take place; the system of arbitration being, that the governing Arab on the one side, and the deputy of the Wakhadim on the other, should hold conference with a screen placed between them, to obviate all attempts at favour, corruption, or bribery.

The former report of the approach of all of my men, with as many Waganda and cows for me, turned out partly false, inasmuch as only one of my men was with 102 Waganda, whilst the whole of the deserters were left behind in Uganda with cows; and Kamrasi hearing this, ordered all to go back again until the whole of my men should arrive.

22d. – I sent Frij to Kamrasi to find out what he was doing with the Waganda and my deserters, as I wished to speak with their two head representatives. I also wanted some men to seek for and fetch Bombay, as I said I believed him to be tied by the leg behind one of the visible hills in Kidi. The reply was, 102 Waganda, with one of my men only, had been stationed at the village my men deserted from since the date (13th) we heard of them last. They had no cows for me, but each of the Waganda bore a log of firewood, which Mtésa had ordered them to carry until they either returned with me or brought back a box of gunpowder, in default of which they were to be all burnt in a heap with the logs they carried. Kamrasi, still acting on his passive policy, would not admit them here, but wished them to return with a message, to the effect that Mtésa had no right to hold me as his guest now I had once gone into another's hands. We were all three kings to do with our subjects as we liked, and for this reason the deserters ought to be sent on here; but if I wished to speak to the Waganda, he would call their officer. There was no fear, he said, about Bombay; he was on his way; but the men who were escorting him were spinning out the time, stopping at every place, and feasting every day. Tomorrow, he added, some more Gani people would arrive here, when we should know more about it. I still advised Kamrasi to give the road to Mtésa, provided he gave up plundering the Wanyoro of women and cattle; but if my counsel was listened to, I could get no acknowledgment that it was so.

23d and 24th. – I sent to inquire what news there was of Bombay's coming, and what measures Kamrasi had taken to call the Waganda's chief officer and my deserters here; as also to beg he would send us specimens of all the various tribes that visit him, in order that we might draw them. He sent four loads of dried fish, with a request for my book of birds again, as it contains a portrait of king Mtésa, and proposed seeing us at the newly-constructed Kafŭ palace to-morrow, when all requests would be attended to. In the meanwhile, we were told that Bombay had been seen on his way returning from Gani; and the Waganda had all run away frightened, because they were told the Kidi and Chopi visitors, who had been calling on Kamrasi lately, were merely the nucleus of an army forming to drive them away, and to subdue Uganda. Mtésa was undergoing the coronation formalities, and for this reason had sent the deserters to Kari's hill, giving them cows and a garden to live on, as no visitors can remain near the court whilst the solemnities of the coronation were going on. The thirty-odd brothers will be burnt to death, saving two or three, of which one will be sent into this country – as was the case with one of the late king Sunna's brothers, who is still in Unyoro – and the others will remain in the court with Mtésa as playfellows until the king dies, when, like Sunna's two brothers still living in Uganda, one at N'yama Goma and one at Ngambézi, they will be pensioned off. After the coronation is concluded, it is expected Mtésa will go into Kittara, on the west of Uganda, to fight first, and then, turning east, will fight with the Wasoga; but we think, if he fights anywhere, it will be with Kamrasi.

25th and 26th. – I sent Frij to the palace to inquire after Bombay, and got the usual reply: 'Why is Bana in such a hurry? He is always for doing things quickly. Tell my "brother" to keep his mind at rest; Bombay is now on the boundary of Gani coming here, and will in due course arrive.' Both Rŭmanika's men and those belonging to Dr K'yengo asked Kamrasi's leave to return to their homes, but were refused, because the road was unsafe. 'Had they not,' it was said, 'heard of Budja's telling Mtésa that K'yengo's children prevented the white men from returning to Uganda? and since then Mtésa had killed his frontier officer for being chicken-hearted, afraid to carry out his orders, and had appointed another in his stead, giving him strict orders to make prisoners of all foreigners who might pass that way; and, further, when some twenty Wanyoro were going to Karagŭé, they were hunted down by Mtésa's orders, and three of their number killed; for he was determined to cut off all intercourse between this country and Karagŭé. They must therefore wait till the road is safe.'

Hearing this, Dr Kyengo's men, who happened to be as well off here as anywhere, accepted the advice; but Rŭmanika's men said, 'We are starving; we have been here too long already doing nothing, and must go, let what will happen to us.' Kamrasi said, 'What will be the use of your going empty-handed? I cannot send cows and slaves to Rŭmanika when the road is so unsafe; you must wait a bit.' But they still urged as before, and so forced the king reluctantly to acquiesce, but only on the condition that two of their head men should remain behind until some more of Rŭmanika's men came to fetch them away – in fact, as we had been accredited to him by Rŭmanika, he wanted to keep some of that king's people as a security until we were out of his hands.

27th. – I sent Frij to the palace to ask once more for leave to visit the Lŭta Nzigé river-lake to the westward, and to request Kamrasi would send men to fetch my property from Karagŭé. He sent four loads of small fish and one pot of pombé, to say he would see me on the morrow, when every arrangement would be made. Late at night orders came announcing that I might write my despatches, as sixty men were ready to start for Karagŭé.

28th. – I sent one of my men with despatches to Kamrasi, who detained him half the day, and then ordered him to call tomorrow. This being the fifteenth or twentieth time Kamrasi had disappointed me, after promising an interview, that we might have a proper understanding about everything, and when no begging on his part was to interrupt our conversation, I sent him a threatening message, to see what effect that would have. The purport of it was, that I was afraid to send men to Karagŭé, now I had seen his disposition to make prisoners of all who visit him. Here had I been kept six weeks waiting for Bombay's return from Gani, where I only permitted him to go because I was told the journey to and fro would only occupy from eight to ten days at most. Then Rŭmanika's men, who came here with Baraka, though daily crying to get away, were still imprisoned here, without any hope before them. If I sent Msalima, he would be kept ten years on the road. If I went to the lake Lŭta Nzigé, God only knows when he would let me come back; and now, for once and for all, I wished to sacrifice all my property, and leave the countries of black kings; for what Kamrasi had done, Mtésa had done likewise, detaining the two men I detached on a friendly mission, which made me fear to send any more and inquire after my guns, lest he should seize them likewise. I would stay no longer among such people.

Kamrasi, in answer, begged I would not be afraid; there was no occasion for alarm; Bombay would be here shortly. I had promised to wait patiently for his return, and as soon as he did return, I would be sent off without one day's delay, for I was not his slave, that he should use violence upon me. Rŭmanika's men, too, would be allowed to go, only that the road was unsafe, and he feared Rŭmanika would abuse him if any harm befell them.

29th. – To-day I met Kamrasi at his new reception-palace on this side the Kafŭ. I begged for my picture-books, which were only lent him at his request for a few days; and then began a badgering verbal conflict: he would not return them until I drew others like them; he would not allow me to go to the Little Lŭta Nzigé, west of this, until

Bombay returned, when he would send me with an army of spears to lead the way, and my men with their guns behind to protect the rear. This was for the purpose of making us his tools in his conflict with his brothers. I complained that he had, without consulting me, ordered away the men who had been sent, either to fetch me back to Uganda, or else get powder from me, although they had orders to carry out their king's desire, under the threat of being burnt with the fire logs they carried; and all this Kamrasi had professed to do merely out of respect for my dignity, as I was no slave, that Mtésa should order me about. I argued, founding on each particular in succession, that his conduct throughout was most unjustifiable, and anything but friendly. He then produced an officer, who was to escort my man Msalima to Karagué, giving him orders to collect the sixty men required on the way; five of Rŭmanika's men could go with him, but five must stop, until other Karagué men came to say the road was safe, when he would, send by them the present he had prepared for Rŭmanika.

Then, turning to us, he said, 'Why have you not brought the medicine-chest and the saw? We wish to see everything you have got, though we do not wish to rob you.' When these things came for inspection, he coveted the saw, and discovered there were more varieties of medicine in the chest than had been given him. This he was told was not the case, because the papers given him contained mixed medicines – a little being taken from every bottle. 'But there are no pills; why won't you give us pills? We have men, women, and children who require pills as well as you do.' We were much annoyed by this dogged begging; and as he said, 'Well, if you won't give me anything, I will go,' we at once rose, hat in hand; when, regretting the hastiness of his speech, he begged us to be seated again, and renewed his demands. We told him the road to Gani was the only condition on which we would part with any more medicine; we had asked leave to go a hundred times, and that was all we now desired. At last he rose and walked off in a huff; but, repenting before he reached home, he sent us a pot of pombé, when, in return, I finished the farce by sending him a box of pills.

30th. – I gave Msalima a letter in the Kisŭahili or coast language to convey to Rŭmanika, ordering all my property to be sent here, his account of the things as they left him to be given to Msalima to convey to the coast, while I sent him one pound of gunpowder as a sort of agency fee. Msalima also took a map of all the countries we had passed, with lunar observations, and a letter to Rigby, by which he, Baraka, and Ulédi would be able to draw their pay on arrival.

31st. – I sent Frij with a letter to the king, containing an acknowledgment that, on the arrival of the rear property from Karagŭé, he would be entitled to the half of everything, reserving the other half for any person I might in future send to take them from him. He accepted the letter, and put it into his mzungŭ – the tin box I had given him. He said he would take every care of the kit from the time it arrived, and would not touch his share of it until my deputy arrived. An inhabitant of Chopi reported that he heard Bombay's gun fire the evening before he left home, and was rewarded with the present of a cow.

1st. – I purchased a small kitten, *Felis serval,* from an Unyoro man, who requested me to give it back to him to eat if it was likely to die, for it is considered very good food in Unyoro.

Bombay at last arrived with Mabrŭki in high glee, dressed in cotton jumpers and drawers, presents given them by Petherick's outpost. Petherick himself was not there. The journey to and fro was performed in fourteen days' actual travelling, the rest of the time being frittered away by the guides. The jemadar of the guard said he commanded two hundred Turks, and had orders to wait for me, without any limit as to time, until I should arrive, when Petherick's name would be pointed out to me cut on a tree; but as no one in camp could read my letter, they were doubtful whether we were the party they were looking out for.

They were all armed with elephant-guns, and had killed sixteen elephants. Petherick had gone down the river eight days' journey, but was expected to return shortly. Kamrasi would not see Bombay immediately on his return, but sent him some pombé, and desired an interview the following day.

2d. – I sent Bombay with a farewell present to Kamrasi, consisting of one tent, one mosquito-curtain, one roll of bindera or red cotton cloth, one digester pot, one saw, six copper wires, one box of beads, containing six varieties of the best sort, and a request to leave his country. Much pleased with the things, Kamrasi ordered the tent to be pitched before all his court, pointed out to them what clever people the white people are, making iron pots instead of earthen ones. Covetous and never satisfied, however, instead of returning thanks, he said he was sure I must have more beads than those I sent him; and, instead of granting the leave asked for, said he would think about it, and send the Kamraviona in the evening with his answer. This, when it came, was anything but satisfactory; for we were required to stop here until the king should have prepared the people on the road for our coming, so that they might not be surprised, or try to molest us on the way. Kamrasi, however, returned the books of birds and animals, requesting a picture of the king of Uganda to be drawn for him, and gave us one pot of pombé.

3d. – I sent the picture required, and an angry message to Kamrasi for breaking his word, as he promised us we should go without a day's delay; and go we must, for I could neither eat nor sleep from thinking of my home. His only reply to this was, Bana is always in a preposterous hurry. He answered, that for our gratification he had directed a dwarf called Kimenya to be sent to us, and the Kamraviona should follow after. Kimenya, a little old man, less than a yard high, called on us with a walking-stick higher than himself, made his salaam, and sat down very composedly. He then rose and danced, singing without invitation, and following it up with queer antics. Lastly, he performed the tambŭra, or charging-march, in imitation of Wakungŭ, repeating the same words they use, and ending by a demand for simbi, or cowrie-shells, modestly saying, 'I am a beggar, and want simbi; if you have not 500 to spare, you must at any rate give me 400.'

He then narrated his fortune in life. Born in Chopi, he was sent for by Kamrasi, who first gave him two women, who died; then another, who ran away; and, finally, a distorted dwarf like himself, whom he rejected, because he thought the propagation of his pigmy breed would not be advantageous to society. Bombay then marched him back to the palace, with 500 simbi strung in necklaces round his neck. When these two had gone, the Kamraviona arrived with two spears, one load of flour, and a pot of pombé, which he requested me to accept, adding that the spears were given as it was observed I had accepted some from the king of Uganda; a shield was still in reserve for me, and spears would be sent for Grant. Then with regard to my going, Kamrasi must beg us to have patience until he had sent messengers into Kidi, requesting the natives there not to molest me on the way, for they had threatened they would do so, and, if they persisted, he would send us with a force by another route *viâ* Ugungŭ – another attempt to draw us off to fight against his brothers.

I stormed at this announcement as a breach of faith; said I had given the king my only tent, my only digester, my only saw, my only wire, my only mosquito-curtains, and my last of everything, because he had assured me I should have to pay no more chiefs, and he would give me the road at once. If he did not intend now to fulfil his promise, I begged he would take back his spears, for I would only accept them as a farewell present. The Kamraviona finding me rather warm, with the usual pertinacious duplicity of a negro, then said, 'Well, let that subject drop, and consider the present Kamrasi promised you when you gave him the Uganga' (meaning the watch); 'Kamrasi's horn is not ready yet.' This second prevarication completely set my dander up. If I did not believe in his dangers of the way before, it quite settled my opinion of the worth of his words now. I therefore tendered him what might be called the ultimatum to this effect. There was no sincerity in such haggling; I would not submit to being told lies by kings or anybody else. He must take back the spears, or give us the road to-morrow; and unless the Kamraviona would tell him this and bring me an answer at once, the spears should not remain in my hut during the night. Evidently in alarm, the Kamraviona, with Kidgwiga and Frij in company to bear him witness, returned to the palace, telling Kamrasi that he saw we were in thorough earnest. He extracted a promise that Kamrasi would have a farewell meeting with us either to-morrow or the next day, when we should have a large escort to Petherick's boats, and the men would be able to bring back anything that he wanted; but he could not let us go without a parting interview, such as we had at Uganda with Mtésa.

The deputation, delighted with their success and the manner in which it was effected, hurried back to me at once, and said they were so frightened themselves that they would have skulked away to their homes and not come near me if they could not have

arranged matters to my satisfaction. Kamrasi would not believe
I had threatened to turn out his spears until Frij testified to their
statements; and he then said, 'Let Bana keep the spears and drink
the pombé, for I would not wish him to be a prisoner against his
will.' Bombay, after taking back the dwarf, met one of N'yamasoré's
officers, just arrived from Uganda on some important business, and
upbraided Mtésa for not having carried out my instructions. The
officer in turn tried to defend Mtésa's conduct by saying he had given
the deserters seventy cows and four women, as well as orders to join
us quickly; but they had been delayed on the road, because wherever
they went they plundered, and no one liked their company. Had we
returned to Uganda, Mtésa would have given us the road through
Masai, which, in their opinion, is nearer for us than this one.

This officer had been wishing to see us as much as we had been
to see him; but Kamrasi would not allow him to get access to us,
from fear, it was said, lest the Waganda should know where we
were hidden, and enable Mtésa to send an army to come and snatch
us away. As the officer said he would deliver any message I might
wish to send to Uganda, I folded a visiting-card as a letter to the
queen-dowager, intimating that I wished the two men whom I
sent back to Mtésa to be forwarded on to Karagüé; but desired that
the remainder, who deserted their master in difficulty, should be
placed on an island of the N'yanza to live in exile until some other
Englishmen should come to release them; that their arms should be
taken from them and kept in the palace. I said further, that should
Mtésa act up to my desires, I would then know he was my friend,
and other white men would not fear to enter Uganda; but if he acted
otherwise, they would fear lest he should imprison them, or seize
their property or their men. If these deserters escaped punishment,
no white men would ever dare trust their lives with such men again.
The officer said he should be afraid to deliver such a message to
Mtésa direct; but he certainly would tell the queen every word of it,
which would be even more efficacious.

4th. – I bullied Kamrasi by telling him we must go with this moon,
for the benefit of its light whilst crossing the Kidi wilderness; as if
we did not reach the vessels in time for seasonable departure down
the Nile, we should have to wait another year for their return from

Khartŭm. 'What!' said Kamrasi, 'does Bana forget my promised appointment that I would either see him to-day or to-morrow? I cannot do so to-day, and therefore to-morrow we will certainly meet and bid good-bye.' The Gani men, who came with Bombay, said they would escort us to their country, although, as a rule, they never cross the Kidi wilderness above once in two years, from fear of the hunting natives, who make game of everybody and everything they see; in other words, they seize strangers, plunder them, and sell them as slaves. To cross that tract, the dry season is the best, when all the grass is burnt down, or from the middle of December to the end of March. I gave them a cow, and they at once killed it, and, sitting down, commenced eating her flesh raw, out of choice.

5th. – The Kamraviona came to inform us that the king was ready for the great interview, where we could both speak what we had at heart, for as yet he had only heard what our servants had to say; and there was a supplement to the message, of the usual kind, that he would like a present of a pencil. The pencil was sent in the first place, because we did not like talking about trifles when we visited great kings.

The interview followed. It was opened on our side by our saying we had enjoyed his hospitality a great number of days, and wished to go to our homes; should he have any message to send to the great Queen of England, we should be happy to convey it. A long yarn then emanated from the throne. He defended his over-cautiousness when admitting us into Unyoro. It was caused at first by wicked men who did not wish us to visit him; he subsequently saw through their representations, and now was very pleased with us as he found us. Of course he could not tie us down to stopping here against our wish, but, for safety's sake, he would like us to stop a little longer, until he could send messengers ahead, requesting the wild men in Kidi not to molest us. That state trick failing to frighten and stop us, he tried another, by saying, when we departed, he hoped we would leave two men with guns behind, to occupy our present camp, and so delude the people into the belief that merely a party of their followers, and not the white men themselves, had left his house, for the purpose of spreading terror in the minds of the people we might meet, who, not knowing the number of men behind, would naturally conclude there was a large reserve force ready to release us in case of necessity.

This foxy speech was too transparent to require one moment's reflection. In a country where men were property, the fate of one or two left behind was obvious; and had we doubted that his object was to get possession of them, his next words would have sufficiently revealed it. He said, 'As you gave men to Mtésa, why would you refuse them to me?' but was checkmated on being told, 'Should any of those men who deserted us in this country ever reach their homes, they will all be hung for breaking their allegiance or oath.' 'Well,' says the king, 'I have acceded to everything you have to say; and the day after to-morrow, when I shall have had time to collect men to go with you, and selected the two princes you have promised to educate, we will meet again and say good-bye; but you must give me a gun and some more medicine, as well as the powder and ball you promised after reaching the vessels.' This was all acquiesced in, and we wished to take his portrait, but he would not have it done on any consideration. The Kamraviona and Kidgwiga followed us home, and told Bombay the king did not wish us to leave till next moon, and then he would like us to fight his brothers on the way. This message, sent in such an underhand manner after the meeting, Bombay refused to deliver, telling them he should be afraid to do so.

6th. – The Kamraviona was sent to us with four loads of fish and a request for ammunition, notwithstanding everything asked for yesterday had been refused until we reached the vessels. 'Confound Kamrasi!' was the reply; 'does he think we came here to trick kings that he doubts our words? We came to open the road; and, as sure as we wish it, we will send him everything that has been promised. Why should he doubt our word more than anybody else? We are not accustomed to be treated in this manner, and must beg he won't insult us any more. Then about fighting his brothers, we have already given answer that we never fight with black men; and should the king persist in it, we will never take another thing from his hands. The boys shall not go to England, neither will any other white men come this way.' The Kamraviona made the following answer: 'But there are two more things the king wishes to know about: he has asked the question before, but forgotten the answers. Is there any medicine for women or children which will prevent the offspring from dying shortly after birth? – for it is a common infirmity in this country with some women, that all their children die before they are able to walk, whilst others never lose a child. The other matter of inquiry was, What medicine will attach all subjects to their king? – for Kamrasi wants some of that most particularly.' I answered, 'Knowledge of good government, attended with wisdom and justice, is all the medicine we know of; and this his boys can best learn in England, and instruct him in when they return.'

7th. – We went to meet Kamrasi at his Kafŭ palace to bid good-bye. After all the huckstering and begging with which he had tormented us, the state he chose to assume on this occasion was very ludicrous. He sat with an air of the most solemn dignity, upon his throne of skins, regarding us like mere slaves, and asking what things we intended to send to him. On being told we did not like being repeatedly reminded of our promises, he came down a little from his dignity, saying, 'And what answer have you about the business on the island?' – meaning the request to fight his brothers. That, of course, could not be listened to, as it was against the principles of our country. Grant's rings were then espied, and begged for, but without success. We told him it was highly improper to beg for everything he saw, and if he persisted in it, no one would ever dare to come near him again.

Then, to change the subject, we begged K'yengo's men might be allowed to go as far as Gani with us; but no reply was given, until the question was put again, with a request that the reasons might be told us for his not wishing it, as we saw great benefit would be derived to Unyoro, as the Wanyamŭézi, instead of trading merely with Karagŭé and Zanzibar, would bring their ivory through this country and barter it, thus converting Unyoro into a great commercial country; when Kamrasi said, 'We don't want any more ivory in Unyoro; for the tusks are already as numerous as grass.' Kidgwiga was then appointed to receive all the things we were to send back from Gani; our departure was fixed for the 9th; and the king walked away as coldly as he came, whilst we felt as jolly as birds released from a cage.

Floating islands of grass were seen going down the Kafŭ, reminding us of the stories told at Kazé by Mŭsa Mzŭri, of the violent manner in which, at certain seasons, the N'yanza was said to rise and rush with such velocity that islands were uprooted and carried away. In the evening a pot of pombé was brought, when the man in charge, half-drunk, amused us with frantic charges, as if he were fighting with his spear; and after settling the supposed enemy, he delighted in trampling him under foot, spearing him repeatedly through and through, then wiping the blade of the spear in the grass, and finally polishing it on his tufty head, when, with a grunt of satisfaction, he shouldered arms and walked away a hero.

8th. – As the king seemed entirely to disregard our comfort on the journey, we made a request for cows, butter, and coffee, in answer to which we only got ten cows, the other things not being procurable without delay. Twenty-four men were appointed to escort us and bring back our presents from Gani, which were to be – six carbines, with a magazine of ammunition, a large brass or iron water-pot, a hair-brush, lucifers, a dinner-knife, and any other things procurable that had never been seen in Unyoro.

Two orphan boys, seized by the king as slaves, were brought for education in England; but as they were both of the common negro breed, with nothing attractive about them, and such as no one could love but their mothers, we rejected them, fearing lest no English boys would care to play with them, and told Kamrasi that his offspring only could play with our children, and unless I got some princes of that interesting breed, no one would ever undertake to teach children brought from his country. The king was very much disappointed at this announcement; said they were his adopted children, and the only ones he could part with, for his own boys were mere balls of fat, and too small to leave home.

CHAPTER XV

The March to Madi

To North Chagŭzi, 9th: After giving Kamrasi a sketching-stool, we dropped down the Kafŭ two miles in a canoe, in order that the common people might not see us; for the exclusive king would not allow any eyes but his own to be indulged with the extraordinary sight of white men in Unyoro! The palace side of the river, however, as we paddled away, was thronged with anxious spectators, amongst whom the most conspicuous was the king's favourite nurse. Dr K'yengo's men were very anxious to accompany us, even telling the king, if he would allow the road to be opened to their countrymen, all would hongo, or pay customs-duty, to him; but the close, narrow-minded king could not be persuaded. Bombay here told us Kamrasi at the last moment wished to give me some women and ivory; and when told we never accepted anything of that sort, wished to give them to my head servants; but this being contrary to standing orders also, he said he would smuggle them down to the boats for Bombay in such a manner that I should not find it out.

To Kitwara, 10th: We were now expected to march again, but being anxious myself to see more of the river, before starting, I obtained leave to go by boat as far as the river was navigable, sending our cattle by land. To this concession was accompanied a request for a few more gun-caps, and liberty was given us to seize any pombé which might be found coming on the river in boats, for the supplies to the palace all come in this manner. We then took boat again, an immense canoe, and, after going a short distance, emerged from the Kafŭ, and found ourselves on what at first appeared a long lake, averaging from two hundred at first to one thousand yards broad, before the day's work was out; but this was the Nile again, navigable in this way from Urondogani.

Both sides were fringed with the huge papyrus rush. The left one was low and swampy, whilst the right one – in which the Kidi people and Wanyoro occasionally hunt – rose from the water in a gently sloping bank, covered with trees and beautiful convolvuli, which hung in festoons. Floating islands, composed of rush, grass, and ferns, were continually in motion, working their way slowly down the stream, and proving to us that the Nile was in full flood. On one occasion we saw hippopotami, which our men said came to the surface because we had domestic fowls on board, supposing them to have an antipathy to that bird. Boats there were, which the sailors gave chase to; but, as they had no liquor, they were allowed to go their way, and the sailors, instead, set to lifting baskets and taking fish from the snares which fishermen, who live in small huts amongst the rushes, had laid for themselves.

After arrival, as we found the boatmen wished to make off, instead of carrying out their king's orders to take us to the waterfall, we seized all the paddles, and kept their tongues quiet by giving them a cow to eat. The overland route, by which Kidgwiga and the cattle went, was not so interesting, by all accounts, as the river one; for they walked the whole way through marshy ground, and crossed one drain in boats, where some savages struggled to plunder our men of their goats.

To Koki, 11th: With a great deal of difficulty, and after hours of delay, we managed to get under way with two boats besides the original one; and, after an hour and a half's paddling in the laziest manner possible, the men seized two pots of pombé and pulled in to Koki, guided by a king's messenger, who said this was one of the places appointed by order to pick up recruits for the force which was to take us to Gani. We found, however, nothing but loss and disappointment – one calf stolen, and five goats nearly so. Fortunately, the thief who attempted to run off with the goats was taken by my men in the act, tied with his hands painfully tight behind his back, and left, with his face painted white, till midnight, when his comrades stole into Bombay's hut and released him. After all these annoyances, the chief officer of the place offered us a present of a goat, but was sent to the right-about in scorn. How could he be countenanced as a friend when the men under him steal from us?

To Gŭéni, S., 12th: The big boat gave us the slip, floating away and leaving its paddles behind. To supply its place, we took six small boats, turning my men into sailors, and going as we liked. The river still continued beautiful; but after paddling three hours we found it bend considerably, and narrow to two hundred yards, the average depth being from two to three fathoms. At the fourth hour, imagining our cattle to be far behind, we pulled in, and walked up a well-cultivated hill to Yaragonjo's, the governor of these parts. The guide, however, on first sighting his thorn-fenced cluster of huts, regarding it apparently with the awe and deference due to a palace, shrank from advancing, and merely pointed, till he was forced on, and in the next minute we found ourselves confronted with the heads of the establishment. The father of the house, surprised at our unexpected manner of entrance – imagining, probably, we were the king's sorcerers, in consequence of our hats, sent to fight 'the brothers' – without saying a word, quietly beckoned us to follow him out of the gate by the same way as we came. Preferring, however, to have a little talk where we were, we remained.

The eldest son, a fine young man considerably above six feet high, with large gashes on his body received in war during late skirmishes with the refractory brothers, now came in, did the honours, and, on hearing of the importance of his visitors, directed us to some huts a little distance off, where we could rest for the night, for there was no accommodation for such a large party in the palace. The red hill we were now on, with plantain-gardens, fine huts neatly kept, and dense grasses covering the country, reminded us of our residence in Uganda. The people seemed of a decidedly sporting order, for they kept hippopotamus-harpoons, attached to strong ropes with trimmers of pith wood, in their huts; and, outside, trophies of their toil in the shape of a pile of heads, consisting of those of buffalo and hippopotami. The women, anything but pretty, wore their mbŭgŭ cut into two flounces, fastened with a drawing-string round the waist; and, in place of stockings, they bound strings of small iron beads, kept bright and shining, carefully up the leg from the ankle to the bottom of the calf.

To Gŭéni, N., 13th: Kidgwiga with our cattle arrived in the morning. A bundle of cartridges, stolen from one of the men's pouches, which we knew could only have been done by some comrade, was discovered by stopping the rations of flesh. The guilty person, to save detection, threw it on the road, and allowed some of the natives to pick it up. Strange as it may appear, the only motive for this petty theft was the hope of being able to sell the cartridges for a trifle at Gani. Yaragonjo brought us a present of a goat and plantains. He was sorry he sent us back yesterday from his house; and invited us to change ground to another village close by, where he would make arrangements for our receiving other boats, as the ones we had in possession must go back. Presuming this to be a very fair proposition, and thinking we would only have to walk across an elbow of land where the river bends considerably, we gave him a return-present of beads, and did as we were bid; but, after moving, it was obvious we had been sold. We had lost our former boats, and no others were near us; therefore, feeling angry with Yaragonjo, I walked back to his palace, taking the presented goat with me, as I knew that would touch the savage in the most tender part; then flaring up with the officer for treating the king's orders with contempt, as well as his guests, by sending us into the jungles like a pack of thieves, whose riddance from his presence was obviously his only intent, I gave him his goat again, and said I would have nothing more to say to him, for I should look to the king for redress.

This frightened him to such an extent that he immediately produced another and finer goat, which he begged me to accept, promising to convey all my traps to the next governor's, where there would be no doubt about our getting boats. He did not intend to deceive us, but committed an error in not informing us he had no boats of his own; and, to show his earnestness, accompanied us to the camp. Here I found the missing calf taken at Koki, and a large deputation of natives awaiting our arrival. They told me that the Koki governor had taken such fright in consequence of my anger when I refused his proffered goat, that he had traced the calf back to Kitwara, and now wished to take Kidgwiga a prisoner to Kamrasi's for having seized five cows of his, and a woman from another governor. As yet I had not heard of this piece of rough justice; and, on inquiry, found out that he had been compelled to do as he had done, because those officers, on finding we had gone ahead in boats, would not produce the complement of men required of them by the king's orders for escorting us to Gani; but now they sent the men, the woman and cows could not be returned, as they had been sent overland by the ordinary route to the ferry on the Nile.

Of course we would not listen to this reference for justice with Kamrasi, as the woman and cows were still all alive; commended Kidgwiga for carrying out his orders so well, and told the officers they had merited their punishment – as how could the affairs of government be carried on, when subordinate officers refused immediate compliance? The sub-mkungŭ of Northern Gŭéni, Kasoro, now proffered a goat and plantains, and everything was settled for the day.

To Kijumbŭra, 14th: With a full complement of porters, travelling six miles through cultivation and jungle, we reached the headquarters of governor Kaérŭ, where all the porters threw down their loads and bolted, though we were still two miles from the post. We inquired for the boats at once, but were told they were some distance off, and we must wait here for the night. Four pots of pombé were sent us, and Kaérŭ thought we would be satisfied and conform. We suspected, however, that there was some trick at the bottom of all; so, refusing the liquor, we said, with proper emphasis, 'Unless we are forwarded to the boats at once, and get them on the following morning, we cannot think of receiving presents from any one.' This served our purpose, for a fresh set of porters was found like magic, and traps, pombé, and all together, were forwarded to the journey's end – a snug batch of huts imbedded in large plantain cultivation surrounded by jungle, and obviously near the river, as numerous huge harpoons, intended for striking hippopotami, were suspended from the roof. Kaérŭ here presented us with a goat, and promised the boats in the morning.

To Koki in Chopi, 16th: After walking two miles to the boats, we entered the district of Chopi, subject to Unyoro, and went down the river, keeping the Kikungŭrŭ cone in view. On arrival at camp, Viarwanjo, the officer of the district, a very smart fellow, arrived with a large escort of spearmen, presented pombé, ordered fowls to be seized for us, and promised one boat in the morning, for he had no more disposable, and even that one he felt anxious about lest the men on ahead should seize it.

To Parangoni, 17th: I gave Viarwanjo some beads, and dropped down the river in his only wretched little canoe – he with Grant and the traps, going overland. I caught a fever, and so spent the night.

Halt, 18th: Here I halted to please Magamba, the governor, who is a relation of the king. He called in great state, presented a cow and pombé, was much pleased with the picture-books, and wished to feast his eyes on all the wonders in the hut. He was very communicative, also, as far as his limited knowledge permitted. He said the people are only a sub-tribe of the Madi; and the reason why the right bank of the river is preferred to the left for travelling is, that Rionga, who lives down the river, is always on the look-out for Kamrasi's allies, with a view to kill them. Magamba also, on being questioned, told us about Urŭri, a province of Unyoro, under the jurisdiction of Kiméziri, a noted governor, who covers his children with bead ornaments, and throws them into the N'yanza, to prove their identity as his own true offspring; for should they sink, it stands to reason some other person must be their father; but should they float, then he recovers them. One of Kamrasi's cousins, Kaoroti, with his chief officer, called on us, presenting five fowls as an honorarium. He had little to say, but begged for medicine, and when given some in a liquid state, said his sub would like some also; then Kidgwiga's wife, who was left behind, must have some; and as pills were given for her, the two men must have dry medicine too, to take home with them.

Severe drain as this was on the medicine-chest, Magamba and his wife must have both wet and dry; and even others put in a claim, but were told they were too healthy to require physicking. Many Kidi men, dressed as in the woodcut, crossed the river to visit Kamrasi; they could not, however, pass us without satisfying their curiosity with a look. Usually these men despise clothes, and never deign to put any covering on except out of respect, when visiting Kamrasi. Their 'sou'-wester'-shaped wigs are made of other men's hair, as the negro hair will not grow long enough. A message came from Ukéro, the governor-general of Chopi, to request we would not go down the river in boats to-morrow, lest the Chopi ferry-men at the falls should take fright at our strange appearance, paddle precipitately across the river, hide their boats, and be seen no more.

To Wiré, over the Karŭma Falls, 19th: We started, leaving all the traps and men to follow, and made this place in a stride, as a whisper warned me that Kamrasi's officers, who are as thick as thieves about here, had made up their minds to keep us each one day at his abode, and show us 'hospitality.' Such was the case, for they all tried their powers of persuasion, which failing, they took the alternative of making my men all drunk, and sending to camp sundry pots of pombé. The ground on the line of march was highly cultivated, and intersected by a deep ravine of running water, whose sundry branches made the surface very irregular. The sand-paper tree, whose leaves resemble a cat's tongue in roughness, and which is used in Uganda for polishing their clubs and spear-handles, was conspicuous; but at the end of the journey only was there anything of much interest to be seen. There suddenly, in a deep ravine one hundred yards below us, the formerly placid river, up which vessels of moderate size might steam two or three abreast, was now changed into a turbulent torrent. Beyond lay the land of Kidi, a forest of mimosa trees, rising gently away from the water in soft clouds of green. This, the governor of the place, Kija, described as a sporting-field, where elephants, hippopotami, and buffalo are hunted by the occupants of both sides of the river. The elephant is killed with a new kind of spear, with a double-edged blade a yard long, and a handle which, weighted in any way most easy, is pear-shaped.

With these instruments in their hands, some men climb into trees and wait for the herd to pass, whilst others drive them under. The hippopotami, however, are not hunted, but snared with lŭnda, the common tripping-trap with spike-drop, which is placed in the runs of this animal, described by every South African traveller, and generally known as far as the Hametic language is spread. The Karŭma Falls, if such they may be called, are a mere sluice or rush of water between high syenitic stones, falling in a long slope down a ten-feet drop. There are others of minor importance, and one within ear-sound, down the river, said to be very grand.

The name given to the Karŭma Falls arose from the absurd belief that Karŭma, the agent or familiar of a certain great spirit, placed the stones that break the waters in the river, and, for so doing, was applauded by his master, who, to reward his services by an appropriate distinction, allowed the stones to be called Karŭma. Near this is a tree which contains a spirit whose attributes for gratifying the powers and pleasures of either men or women who summon its influence in the form appropriate to each, appear to be almost identical with that of Mahadeo's Ligna in India.

21st and 22d. – The governor, who would not let us go until we saw him, called on the 22d with a large retinue, attended by a harpist, and bringing a present of one cow, two loads flour, and three pots of pombé. He expected a chair to sit upon, and got a box, as at home he has a throne only a little inferior to Kamrasi's. He was very generous to Bombay on his former journey to Gani; and then said he thought the white men were all flocking this way to retake their lost country; for tradition recorded that the Wahŭma were once half-black and half-white, with half the hair straight and the other half curly; and how was this to be accounted for, unless the country formerly belonged to white men with straight hair, but was subsequently taken by black men? We relieved his apprehensions by telling him his ancestors were formerly all white, with straight hair, and lived in a country beyond the salt sea, till they crossed that sea, took possession of Abyssinia, and are now generally known by the name of Hubshies and Gallas; but neither of these names was known to him.

On the east, beyond Kidi, he only knew of one clan of Wahŭma, a people who subsist entirely on meat and milk. The sportsmen of this country, like the Wanyamŭézi, plant a convolvulus of extraordinary size by the side of their huts, and pile the jaw-bones and horns of their spoils before, as a means of bringing good-luck. This same flower, held in the hand when a man is searching for anything that he has lost, will certainly bring him to the missing treasure. In the evening, Kidgwiga, at the head of his brave army, made one of their theatrical charges on 'Bana' with spear and shield, swearing they would never desert him on the march, but would die to a man if it were necessary; and if they deserted him, then might they be deprived of their heads, or of other personal possessions not much less valuable.

To 1st Camp in Kidi, 23d: Just as we were ready for crossing the river, a line of Kidi men was descried filing through the jungle on the opposite side, making their way for a new-moon visit to Rionga, who occasionally leads them in battle against Ukéro. The last time they fought, two men only were killed on Kamrasi's side, whilst nine fell on Rionga's. There was little done besides crossing, for the last cow was brought across at sunset – the ferrying-toll for the whole being one cow, besides a present of beads to the head officer. Kidgwiga's party sacrificed two kids, one on either side the river, flaying them with one long cut each down their breasts and bellies. These animals were then, spread-eagle fashion, laid on their backs upon grass and twigs, to be stepped over by the travellers, that their journey might be prosperous; and the spot selected for the ordeal was chosen in deference to the Mzimŭ, or spirit – a sort of wizard or ecclesiastical patriarch, whose functions were devoted to the falls.

To 2nd Camp, 24th, to 3d Camp, 25th: After a soaking night, we were kept waiting till noon for the forty porters ordered by Kamrasi, to carry our property to the vessels wherever they might be. Only twenty-five men arrived, notwithstanding the wife and one slave belonging to a local officer, who would not supply the men required of him, were seized and confiscated by Ukéro, of Wiré. We now mustered twenty Wangŭana, twenty-five country porters, and thirty-one of Kidgwiga's 'children' – making a total, with ourselves, of seventy-eight souls. By a late arrival a message came from Kamrasi. Its import was, that we must defer the march, as it was reported the refractory brother Rionga harboured designs of molesting us on the way, and therefore the king conceived it prudent to clear the road by first fighting him. Without heeding this cunning advice, we made a short march across swamps, and through thick jungle and long grasses, which proved anything but pleasant – wet and labouring hard all the way.

To 4th Camp, 26th: After toiling five miles through the same terrible grasses, and crossing swamp after swamp, we were at last rewarded by a striking view. The jungles had thinned; we found ourselves unexpectedly standing on the edge of a plateau, on the west of which, for distance interminable, lay apparently a low flat country of grass, yellowed by the sun, with a few trees or shrubs only thinly scattered over the surface; while, from fifteen to twenty miles in the rear, bearing south by west, stood conspicuously the hill of Kistiga, said to be situated in Chopi, not far from the refractory brothers. But this view was only for the moment; again we dived into the grasses and forced our way along. Presently elephants were seen, also buffalo; and the guide, to make the journey propitious, plucked a twig, denuded it of its leaves and branches, waved it like a wand up the line of march, muttered some unintelligible words to himself, broke it in twain, and threw the separated bits on either side of the path.

To 5th Camp, 27th: Immediately after starting, the guide ran up on an ant-hill and pointed out to us all the glories of the country round. In our rear we could see back upon Wiré and the hill of Kisŭga; to the west were the same low plains of grass; east and by south, the jungles of Kidi; and to the northward, over downs of grass, the tops of some hills, which marked the neighbouring village of Koki, which we were making for. Its appearance in the distance warned us that we were closing on the habitations of men, and we were told that Bombay had drunk pombé there. Then plunging through grass again over our heads, and crossing constant swamps, we arrived at a stream which drains all these lands to westward, and rested a while that the men might bathe, and also that they might set fire to the grass as a telegraph to the settlement of Koki, to apprise the people of our advance, and be ready with their pombé ere our arrival. Shortly after, towards the close of the day's work, as a solitary buffalo was seen grazing by a brook, I put a bullet through him, and allowed the savages the pleasure of despatching him in their own wild fashion with spears.

It was a sight quite worthy of a little delay. No sooner was it observed that the huge beast could not retire, than, with springing bounds, the men, all spear in hand, as if advancing on an enemy, went top speed at him, over rise and fall alike, till, as they neared the maddened bull, he instinctively advanced to meet his assailants with the best charge his exhausted body could muster up. Wind, however, failed him soon; he knew his disadvantage, and tried to hide by plunging in the water, – the worst policy he could have pursued, for the men from the bank above him soon covered him with bristling spears, and gained their victory. Now, what was to be done with this huge carcass? No one could be induced to leave it. A cow was offered as a bribe on reaching camp; but no, the buffalo was bigger than a cow, and must be quartered on the spot; so, to gain our object, we went ahead and left the rear men to follow, thus saving a cow in rations, for we required to slaughter one every day.

To 6th Camp, 28th: By dint of hard perseverance we accomplished ten miles over the same downs of tall grass with occasional swamps. We saw a herd of hartebeest, and reached at night a place within easy run of Koki in Gani.

To Koki in Gani, 29th: The weather had now become fine. At length we reached the habitations of men – a collection of conical huts on the ridge of a small chain of granitic hills lying north-west. As we approached the southern extremity of this chain, knots of naked men, perched like monkeys on the granite blocks, were anxiously watching our arrival. The guides, following the usages of the country, instead of allowing us to mount the hill and look out for accommodation at once, desired us to halt, and sent on a messenger to inform Chongi, the governor-general, that we were visitors from Kamrasi, who desired he would take care of us and forward us to our brothers. This Mercury brought forth a hearty welcome; for Chongi had been appointed governor by Kamrasi of this district, which appears to have been the extreme northern limit of the originally vast kingdom of Kittara. All the *élite* of the place, covered with warpaints, and dressed, so far as their nakedness was covered at all, like clowns in a fair, charged down the hill full tilt with their spears, and, after performing their customary evolutions, mingled with our men, and invited us up the hill, where we no sooner arrived than Chongi, a very old man, attended by his familiar, advanced to receive us – one holding a white hen, the other a small gourd of pombé and a little twig.

Chongi gave us all a friendly harangue by way of greeting; and taking the fowl by one leg, swayed it to and fro close to the ground in front of his assembled visitors. After this ceremony had been also repeated by the familiar, Chongi then took the gourd and twig, and sprinkled the contents all over us; retired to the Uganga, or magic house – a very diminutive hut – sprinkled pombé over it; and, finally, spreading a cow-skin under a tree, bade us sit, and gave us a jorum of pombé, making many apologies that he could not show us more hospitality, as famine had reduced his stores. What politeness in the midst of such barbarism!!! Nowhere had we seen such naked creatures, whose sole dress consisted of bead, iron, or brass ornaments, with some feathers or cowrie-beads on the head. Even the women contented themselves with a few fibres hung like tails before and behind. Some of our men who had seen the Watŭta in Utambara, declared these savages to resemble them in every particular, save one small specialty in their costume, alluded to in the description of the Zŭlŭ Kafirs' dress. The hair of the men was dressed in the same fantastic fashion, and the women placed half-gourds over the baby as it rode on its mother's back. They also, like the Kidi people, whom they much fear, carry diminutive stools to sit upon wherever they go.

Their habitat extends from this to the Asha river, whilst the Madi occupy all the country west of this meridian to the Nile, which is far beyond sight. The villages are composed of little conical huts of grass, on a framework of bamboo raised above low mud walls. There are no sultans here of any consequence, each village appointing its own chief. The granitic hills, like those of Unyamŭézi, are extremely pretty, and clad with trees, contrasting strangely with the grassy downs of indefinite extent around, which give the place, when compared with the people, the appearance of a paradise within the infernal regions. From the site of Koki we saw the hills behind which, according to Bombay, Petherick was situated with his vessels; and we also saw a nearer hill, behind which his advanced post of elephant-hunters were waiting our arrival.

30th. – We halted, at the earnest solicitation of Chongi, as well as of the Chopi porters, who said they required a day to lay in grain, as the Wichwézi, or mendicant sorcerers – for so they thought fit to designate Petherick's elephant-hunters – had eaten up the country all about them, and those who went before with Bombay to visit their camp could get no food.

1st. – We halted again at the request of all parties, and much to the delight of old Chongi, who supplied us with abundant pombé, promised a cow, that we should not be put to any extra expense by stopping, and said that without fail he would furnish us with guides who knew a short cut across country, by which we might reach the Wichwézi camp in one march, instead of going by the circuitous route which Bombay formerly took. The cow, however, never came, as the old man did not intend to give his own, and his officers refused to obey his orders in giving one of theirs.

To Mŭdŭa, 2d: We left Koki with difficulty, in consequence of the Chopi porters refusing to carry any loads, leaving the burden of lifting them on the country people, as they said, 'We have endured all the trouble and hardships of bringing these visitors through the wilderness; and now, as they have visited you, it is your place to help them on.' The consequence was, we had to engage fresh porters at every village, each in turn saying he had done all the work which with justice fell to his lot, till at last we arrived at the borders of a jungle, where the men last engaged, feeling tired of their work, pleaded ignorance of the direct road, and turned off to the longer one, where villages and men were in abundance, thus upsetting all our plans, and doubling the actual distance.

To pass the night half-way was now imperative, as we had been the whole day travelling without making good much ground. From the Gani people we had, without any visible change, mingled with the Madi people, who dress in the same naked fashion as their neighbours, and use bows and arrows. Their villages were all surrounded with bomas (fences), and the country in its general aspect resembled that of Northern Unyamŭézi. At one place, the good-natured simple people, as soon as we reached their village, spread a skin, deposited a stool upon it, and placed in front two pots of pombé. At the village where we put up, however, the women and children of the head man at first all ran away, and the head man himself was very shy of us, thinking we were some unearthly creatures. He became more reconciled to us, however, when he perceived we fed like rational beings; and, calling his family in by midnight, presented us with pombé, and made many apologies for having allowed us to dine without a drop of his beer, for he was very glad to see us.

CHAPTER XVI

Madi

To Faloro, 3d: After receiving more pombé from the chief, and, strange to say, hot water to wash with – for he did not know how else he could show hospitality better – we started again in the same straggling manner as yesterday. In two hours we reached the palace of Piéjoko, a chief of some pretensions, and were summoned to stop and drink pombé. In my haste to meet Petherick's expedition, I would listen to nothing, but pushed rapidly on, despite all entreaties to stop, both from the chief and from my porters, who, I saw clearly, wished to do me out of another day.

Half my men, however, did stop there, but with the other half Grant and I went on; and, as the sun was setting, we came in sight of what we thought was Petherick's outpost, N. lat. 3° 10' 33'',and E. long. 31°50' 45''. My men, as happy as we were ourselves, now begged I would allow them to fire their guns, and prepare the Turks for our reception. Crack, bang, went their carbines, and in another instant crack, bang, was heard from the northerners' camp, when, like a swarm of bees, every height and other conspicuous place was covered with men. Our hearts leapt with an excitement of joy only known to those who have escaped from long-continued banishment among barbarians, once more to meet with civilised people, and join old friends. Every minute increased this excitement. We saw three large red flags heading a military procession, which marched out of the camp with drums and fifes playing. I halted and allowed them to draw near. When they did so, a very black man, named Mahamed, in full Egyptian regimentals, with a curved sword, ordered his regiment to halt, and threw himself into my arms, endeavouring to hug and kiss me. Rather staggered at this unexpected manifestation of affection, which was like a conjunction of the two hemispheres, I gave him a squeeze in return for his hug, but raised my head above the reach of his lips, and asked who was his master? 'Petrik,' was the reply. 'And where is Petherick now?' 'Oh, he is coming.' 'How is it you have not got English colours, then?' 'The colours are Debono's.' 'Who is Debono?' 'The same as Petrik; but come along into my camp, and let us talk it out there; saying which, Mahamed ordered his regiment (a ragamuffin mixture of Nubians, Egyptians, and slaves of all sorts, about two hundred in number) to right-about, and we were guided by him, whilst his men kept up an incessant drumming and fifing, presenting arms, and firing, until we reached his huts, situated in a village, kept exactly in the same order as that of the natives. Mahamed then gave us two beds to sit upon, and ordered his wives to advance on their knees and give us coffee, whilst other men brought pombé, and prepared us a dinner of bread and honey and mutton.

A large shed was cleared for Grant and myself, and all my men were ordered to disperse, and chum in ones and twos with Mahamed's men; for Mahamed said, now we had come there, his work was finished. 'If that is the case,' I said, 'tell us your orders; there must be some letters.' He said, 'No, I have no letters or written orders; though I have directions to take you to Gondokoro as soon as you come. I am Debono's Vakil, and am glad you are come, for we are all tired of waiting here for you. Our business has been to collect ivory whilst waiting for you.' I said, 'How is it Petherick has not come here to meet me? is he married?' 'Yes, he is married; and both he and his wife ride fore-and-aft on one animal at Khartŭm.' 'Well, then, where is the tree you told Bombay you would point out to us with Petherick's name on it?' 'Oh, that is on the way to Gondokoro. It was not Petherick who wrote, but some one else, who told me to look out for your coming this way. We don't know his name, but he said if we pointed it out to you, you would know at once.'

4th. – After spending the night as Mahamed's guest, I strolled round the place to see what it was like, and found the Turks were all married to the women of the country, whom they had dressed in clothes and beads. Their children were many, with a prospect of more. Temporary marriages, however, were more common than others – as, in addition to their slaves, they hired the daughters of the villagers, who remained with them whilst they were trading here, but went back to their parents when they marched to Gondokoro.

They had also many hundreds of cattle, which it was said they had plundered from the natives, and now used for food, or to exchange for ivory, or other purposes. The scenery and situation were perfect for health, and beauty. The settlement lay at the foot of small, well-wooded granitic hills, even prettier than the out-crops of Unyamŭézi, and was intersected by clear streams.

At noon, all the rear troops arrived with Bombay and Piéjoko in person. This good creature had treated Bombay very handsomely on his former journey. He said he felt greatly disappointed at my pushing past him yesterday, as he wished to give me a cow, but still hoped I would go over and make friends with him. I gave him some beads, and off he walked. Old Chongi's 'children,' who had escorted us all the way from Kamrasi's, then took some beads and cast-off clothes for themselves and their father, and left us in good-humour.

This reduced the expedition establishment to my men and Kidgwiga's. With these, now, as there was no letter from Petherick, I ordered a march for the next morning, but at once met with opposition. Mahamed told me that there were no vessels at Gondokoro; we must wait two months, by which time he expected they would arrive there, and some one would come to meet him with beads. I said in answer, that Petherick had promised to have boats there all the year round, so I would not wait. 'Then,' said Mahamed, 'we cannot go with you, for there is a famine at this season at Gondokoro.' I said, 'Never mind; do you give me an interpreter, and I will go as I am.' 'No,' said Mahamed, 'that will not do, as the Bari people are so savage, you could not get through them with so small a force; besides which, just now there is a stream which cannot be crossed for a month or more.'

Unable to stand Mahamed's shifting devices with equanimity any longer, I accused him of trying to trick me in the same way as all the common savage chiefs had done wherever I went, because they wished me to stop for their own satisfaction, quite disregarding my wishes and interests; so I said I would not stop there any longer; I would raft over the river, and find my way through the Bari, as I had through the rest of the African savages. We talked and talked, but could make nothing of it. I maintained that if he was commissioned to help me, he at least could not refuse to give me a guide and interpreter; when, if I failed in the direct route, I would try another, but go I must, as I could not hold out any longer, being short of beads and cows. I had just enough, but none to spare. He told me not to think of such a thing, as he would give me all that was needful, both for myself and my men; but if I would have patience, he would collect all his officers, and the next morning would see what their opinions were on the subject.

5th. – I found that every one of Mahamed's men was against our going to Gondokoro. They told me, in fact, with one voice, that it was quite impossible; but they said, if I liked they would furnish me guides to escort me on ten marches to a depôt at the further end of the Madi country, and if I chose to wait there until they could collect all their ivory tusks together and join us, we would be a united party too formidable to be resisted by the Bari people. This offer of immediate guides I of course accepted at once, as to keep on the move was my only desire at that time; for my men were all drunk, and Kidgwiga's were deserting. Once more on the way, I did not despair of reaching Gondokoro by myself. In the best good-humour now, I showed Mahamed our picture-books; and as he said he always drilled his two hundred men every Friday, I said I would, if he liked, command them myself. This being agreed to, all the men turned out in their best, and, to my surprise, they not only knew the Turkish words of command, but manoeuvred with some show of good training; though, as might have been expected with men of this ragamuffin stamp, all the privates gave orders as well as their captains.

When the review was over, I complimented Mahamed on the efficiency of his corps, and, retiring to my hut, as I thought I had him now in a good-humour, again discussed our plans for going ahead the next day. Scarcely able to look me in the face, the humbugging scoundrel said he could not think of allowing me to go on without him, for if any accident happened he would be blamed for it. At the same time, he could not move for a few days, as he expected a party of men to arrive about the next new moon with ivory. My hurry he thought very uncalled for; for, as I had spent so many days with Kamrasi, why could I not be content to do so with him?

I was provoked beyond measure with this, as it upset all my plans. Kidgwiga's men were deserting, and I feared I should not be able to keep my promise to Kamrasi of sending him another white visitor, who would perhaps do what I had left undone, when I did not follow up the connection of the Little Lŭta Nzigé with the Nile. We battled away again, and then Mahamed said there was not one man in his camp who would go with me until their crops were cut and taken in; for whilst residing here they grew grain for their support. We battled again, and Mahamed at last, out of patience himself, said, 'Just look here, what a fix I am in,' showing me a hut full of ivory. 'Who,' he said, 'is to carry all this until the natives have got in their crops?' This, I said, so far as I was concerned, was all nonsense. I merely had asked him for a guide and interpreter, for go I must. In a huff he then absconded; and my men – those of them who were not too drunk – came and said to me, 'For Godsake let us stop here. Mahamed says the road is too dangerous for us to go alone; he has promised to carry all our loads for us if we stop; and all Kamrasi's men are running away, because they are afraid to go on.'

6th. – Next morning I called Kidgwiga, and begged him to procure two men as guides and interpreters. He said he could not find any. I then went at Mahamed again, who first said he would give me the two men I wanted, then went off, and sent word to say he would not be visible for three days. This was too much for my patience, so I ordered all my things to be tied up in marching order, and gave out that I should leave and find out the way myself the following morning. Like an evil spirit stirred up, my preparations for going no sooner were heard of than Mahamed appeared again, and after a long and sharp contest in words, he promised us guides if I would consent to write him a note, testifying that my going was against his expressed desire.

This was done; but the next morning (7th), after our things were put out for the march, all Kidgwiga's men bolted, and no guides would take service with us. It was now obvious that, even supposing I succeeded in taking Kidgwiga to Gondokoro, he would not have a sufficient escort to come back with, unless, indeed, it happened that Englishmen might be there who might wish to carry out my investigations by penetrating to the Little Lŭta Nzigé, and to pay a visit to Kamrasi. I therefore called Kidgwiga, and after explaining these circumstances, advised him to go back to Kamrasi. He was loth to leave, he said, until his commission was fully performed; but as I thought it advisable, he would consent. I then gave him a double gun and ammunition, as well as some very rich beads which I obtained from Mahamed's stores, to take back to Kamrasi, with orders to say that, as soon as I reached Gondokoro or Khartŭm, I would send another white man to him – not by the way I had come through Kidi, but by the left bank of the Nile: to which Kidgwiga replied, 'That will do famously, for Kamrasi will change his residence soon, and come on the Nile this side of Rionga's palace, in order that he may cut in between his brother and the Turks' guns.'

After this, I gave a lot of rich beads to Kidgwiga for himself, and a lot also for the senior officers at the Chopi and Kamrasi's palaces, and sent the whole set off as happy as birds. When these men were gone, I tried to get up an elephant-shooting excursion due west of this, with a view to see where the Nile was, for I would not believe it was very far off, although no one as yet, since I left Chopi, either would or could tell me where the stream had gone to.

8th. – Mahamed professed to be delighted I had made up my mind to such a scheme. He called the heads of the villages to give me all the information I sought for, and went with me to the top of a high rock, from which we could see the hills I first viewed at Chopi, sweeping round from south by east to north, which demarked the line of the Astia river. The Nile at that moment was, I believed, not very far off; yet, do or say what I would, everybody said it was fifteen marches off, and could not be visited under a month. It would be necessary for me to take thirty-six of Mahamed's men, besides all my own, to go there, which, he said, I was welcome to, but I should have to pay them for their services. This was a damper at once.

I knew in my mind all these reports were false, but, rather than be out of the way when the time came for marching, I agreed to wait patiently, write the history of the Wahŭma, and make collections, till Mahamed was ready, trusting that I might find some one at Gondokoro who would finish what I had left undone; or else, after arriving there, I might go up the Nile in boats and see for myself. The same evening I was attracted by the sound of drums to a neighbouring village, where, by the moonlight, I found the natives were dancing. A more indecent or savage spectacle I never witnessed. The whole place was alive with naked humanity in a state of constant motion. Drawing near, I found that a number of drums were beaten by men in the centre. Next to them was a deep ring of women, half of whom carried their babies; and outside these again was a still deeper circle of men, some blowing horns, but most holding their spears erect. To the sound of the music both these rings of the opposite sexes kept jumping and sidling round and round the drummers, making the most grotesque and obscene motions to one another.

9th to 14th. – Nothing of material consequence happened until the 14th, when eighty of Rionga's men brought in two slaves and thirty tusks of ivory, as a present to Mahamed. Of course, I knew this was a bribe to induce Mahamed to fight with Rionga against Kamrasi; but, counting that no affair of mine, I tried to induce these men to give me some geographical information of the countries they had just left. Not one of them would come near me, for they knew I was friends with Kamrasi; and Mahamed's men, when they saw mine attempting to converse with them, abused them for 'prying into other men's concerns.' 'These men,' they said, 'are our friends, and not yours; if we choose to give them presents of cloth and beads, and they give us a return in ivory, what is that to you?' Mysterious Mahamed next came to me, and begged for a blanket, as he said he was going off for a few days to a depôt where he had some ivory; and he also wanted to borrow a musket, as one of his had been burnt.

My suspicions, and even apprehensions, were now greatly excited. I began to think he had prevailed on me to stop here, that I might hold the place whilst he went to fight Kamrasi with Rionga's men; so I begged him to listen to my advice, and not attempt to cross the Nile, 'else,' I said, 'all his guns would be taken from him, and his passage back cut off.' At once he saw the drift of my thought, and said he was not going towards the Nile, but, on the contrary, he was going with Rionga's men in the opposite direction, to a place called Paira. 'If that is the case,' I said, 'why do you want a gun?' 'Because there are some other matters to settle. I shall not be long away, and my men will take care of you whilst I am gone.' I gave him the blanket after this, but was too suspicious of his object to lend him a gun.

15th to 20th. – I saw Mahamed march his regiment out of the place, drums and fifes playing, colours flying, a hundred guns firing, officers riding, – some of them on donkeys, and others – yes, actually – on cows! while a host of the natives, Rionga's men included, carrying spears and bows and arrows, looked little like a peaceful caravan of merchants, but very much resembled a band of marauders. After this I heard they were not going to Rionga himself, but were going to show Rionga's men the way that they made friends with old Chongi of Koki. In reality, Chongi had invited Mahamed to fight against an enemy of his, in whose territories immense stores of ivory were said to be buried, and the people had an endless number of cattle – for they lived by plunder, and had lifted most of old Chongi's; and this was the service on which the expedition had set off.

21st to 31st. – I had constantly wondered, ever since I first came here, and saw the brutal manner in which the Turks treated the natives, that these Madi people could submit to their 'Egyptian taskmasters,' and therefore was not surprised now to find them pull down their huts and march off with the materials to a distant site. Every day this sort of migration continued, just as you see in the picture; and nothing more important occurred until Christmas-day, when an armadillo was caught, and I heard from Mahamed's head wife that the Turks had plundered and burnt down three villages, and in all probability they would return shortly laden with ivory. This was a true anticipation; for, on the 31st, Mahamed came in with his triumphant army laden with ivory, and driving in five slave-girls and thirty head of cattle.

1st to 3d. – I now wished to go on with the journey, as I could get no true information out of these suspicious blackguards who called themselves Turks; but Mahamed postponed it until the 5th, by which time he said he would be able to collect all the men he wanted to carry his ivory. Rionga's men then departed, and Mahamed showed some signs of getting ready by ordering one dozen cows to be killed, the flesh of which was to be divided amongst those villagers who would carry his ivory, and the skins to be cut into thongs for binding the smaller tusks of ivory together in suitable loads.

4th and 5th. – Another specimen of Turkish barbarity came under my notice, in the head man of a village bringing a large tusk of ivory to Mahamed, to ransom his daughter with; for she had been seized as a slave on his last expedition, in common with others who could not run away fast enough to save themselves from the Turks. Fortunately for both, it was thought necessary for the Turks to keep on good terms with the father as an influential man; and therefore, on receiving the tusk, Mahamed gave back the girl, and added a cow to seal their friendship.

6th to 10th. – I saw this land-pirate Mahamed take a blackmail like a negro chief. Some men who had fled from their village when Mahamed's plundering party passed by them the other day, surprised that he did not stop to sack their homes, now brought ten large tusks of ivory to him to express the gratitude they said they felt for his not having molested them. Mahamed, on finding how easy it was to get taxes in this fashion, instead of thanking them, assumed the air of the great potentate, whose clemency was abused, and told the poor creatures that, though they had done well in seeking his friendship, they had not sufficiently considered his dignity, else they would have brought double that number of tusks, for it was impossible he could be satisfied at so low a price. 'What,' said these poor creatures, 'can we do then? for this is all that we have got.' 'Oh,' says Mahamed, 'if it is all you have got now in store, I will take these few for the present; but when I return from Gondokoro, I expect you will bring me just as many more. Good-bye, and look out for yourselves.'

To Panyoro, 11th: Tired beyond all measure with Mahamed's procrastination, as I could not get him to start, I now started myself, much to his disgust, and went ahead again, leaving word that I would wait for him at the next place, provided he did not delay more than one day. The march led us over long rolling downs of grass, where we saw a good many antelopes feeding; and after going ten miles, we came, among other villages, to one named Panyoro, in which we found it convenient to put up. At first all the villagers, thinking us Turks bolted away with their cattle and what stores they could carry; but, after finding out who we were, they returned again, and gave us a good reception, helping us to rig up a shed with grass, and bringing a cow and some milk for our dinner.

12th. – To-day I went out shooting, but though I saw and fired at a rhinoceros, as well as many varieties of antelopes, I did not succeed in killing one head. All my men were surprised as well as myself; and the villagers who were escorting me in the hope of getting flesh, were so annoyed at their disappointment, they offered to cut my fore-finger with a spear and spit on it for good-luck. Joining in their talk, I told them the powder must be crooked; but, on inspecting my rifle closer, I found that the sights had been knocked on one side a little, and this created a general laugh at all in turn. Going home from the shooting, I found all the villagers bolting again with their cattle and stores, and, on looking towards Faloro, saw a party of Turks coming.

As well as I could I reassured the villagers, and brought them back again, when they said to me, 'Oh, what have you done? We were so happy yesterday when we found out who you were, but now we see you have brought those men, all our hearts have sunk again; for they beat us, they make us carry their loads, and they rob us in such a manner, we know not what to do.' I told them I would protect them if they would keep quiet; and, when the Turks came, I told them what I had said to the head man. They were the vanguard of Mahamed's party, and said they had orders to march on as far as Apuddo with me, where we must all stop for Mahamed, who, as well as he could, was collecting men. There was a certain tree near Apuddo which was marked by an Englishman two years ago, and this, Mahamed thought, would keep us amused.

To Paira, 13th: The next march brought us to Paira, a collection of villages within sight of the Nile. It was truly ridiculous; here had we been at Faloro so long, and yet could not make out what had become of the Nile. In appearance it was a noble stream, flowing on a flat bed from west to east, and immediately beyond it were the Jbl (hills) Kŭkŭ, rising up to a height of 2000 feet above the river. Still we could not make out all, until the following day, when we made a march parallel to the Nile, and arrived at Jaifi.

To Jaifi, 14th: This was a collection of huts close to a deep nullah which drains the central portions of Eastern Madi. At this place the Turks killed a crocodile and ate him on the spot, much to the amusement of my men, who immediately shook their heads laughingly, and said, 'Ewa, Allah! are these men, then, Mussulmans? Savages in our country don't much like a crocodile.'

To Apuddo, 15th: After crossing two nullahs, we reached Apuddo, and at once I went to see the tree said to have been cut by an Englishman some time before. There, sure enough, was a mark, something like the letters M.I., on its bark, but not distinct enough to be ascertained, because the bark had healed up. In describing the individual who had done this, the Turks said he was exactly like myself, for he had a long beard, and a voice even much resembling mine. He came thus far with Mahamed from Goudokoro two years ago, and then returned, because he was alarmed at the accounts the people gave of the countries to the southward, and he did not like the prospect of having to remain a whole rainy season with Mahamed at Faloro. He knew we were endeavouring to come this way, and directed Mahamed to point out his name if we did so.

We took up our quarters in the village as usual, but the Turks remained outside, and carried off all the tops of the villagers' huts to make a camp for themselves. I rebuked them for doing so, but was mildly told they had no huts of their own. They carried no pots either for cooking their dinners, and therefore took from the villagers all that they wanted. It was a fixed custom now, they told us, and there was no use in our trying to struggle against it. If the natives were wise, they would make enough to sell; but as they would not, they must put up with their lot; for the 'government' cannot be baulked of its ivory. Truly there seemed to be nothing but misery here; food was so scarce the villagers sought for wild berries and fruits; whilst the Turks helped themselves out of their half-filled bins – a small reserve store to last up to the far-distant harvest. Then, to make matters worse, all the village chiefs were at war with one another.

Halt, 16th and 17th: At night a party of warriors walked round our village, but feared to attack it because we were inside. Next morning the villagers turned out and killed two of the enemy; but the rest, whilst retreating, sang out that they would not attempt to fight until 'the guns' were gone – after that, the villagers had better look out for themselves. I now proposed going on if the Apina, or chief of the village, would give me a guide; but he feared to do so lest I should come to grief, and Mahamed would then be down upon him. Struggling was useless, for I had no beads to pay my way with, and my cows were now all finished; so I took the matter quietly, and went out foraging with the rifle.

24th to 30th. – Bŭkhet, Mahamed's factotum, arrived with the greater part of the Turk's property. He then confirmed a report we had heard before, that, some few days previously, Mahamed had ordered Bŭkhet to go ahead and join us, which he attempted to do; but, on arrival at Panyoro, his party had a row with the villagers, and lost their property. Bŭkhet then returned to Mahamed and reported his defeat and losses; upon hearing which, Mahamed at once said to him, 'What do you mean by returning to me empty-handed? go back at once and recover your things, else how can I make my report at Gondokoro?' With these peremptory orders Bŭkhet went back to Panyoro, and commenced to attack it. The contest did not last long; for, after three of Bŭkhet's men had been wounded, he set fire to the villages, killed fifteen of the natives, and, besides recovering his own lost property, took one hundred cows.

31st. – To-day Mahamed came in, and commenced to arrange for the march onwards. This, however, was no easy matter, for the Turks alone required six hundred porters – half that number to carry their ivory, and the other half to carry their beds and bedding; whilst from fifty to sixty men was the most a village had to spare, and all the village chiefs were at enmity with one another. The plan adopted by Mahamed was, to summon the heads of all the villages to come to him, failing which, he would seize all their belongings. Then, having once got them together, he ordered them all to furnish him with so many porters a-head, saying he demanded it of them, for the 'great government's property' could not be left on the ground. Their separate interests must now be sacrificed, and their feuds suspended; and if he heard, on his return again, that one village had taken advantage of the other's weakness caused by their employment in his service, he would then not spare his bullets, – so they might look out for themselves.

Some of the Turks, having found ninety-nine eggs in a crocodile's nest, had a grand feast. They gave us two of the eggs, which we ate, but did not like, for they had a highly musky flavour.

1st. – On the 1st of February we went ahead again, with Bukhet and the first half of Mahamed's establishment, as a sufficient number of men could not be collected at once to move all together. In a little while we struck on the Nile, where it was running like a fine Highland stream between the gneiss and mica-schist hills of Kŭkŭ, and followed it down to near where the Asha river joined it. For a while we sat here watching the water, which was greatly discoloured, and floating down rushes. The river was not as full as it was when we crossed it at the Karŭma Falls, yet, according to Dr Khoblecher's account, it ought to have been flooding just at this time: if so, we had beaten the stream. Here we left it again as it arched round by the west, and forded the Asha river, a stiff rocky stream, deep enough to reach the breast when waded, but not very broad. It did not appear to me as if connected with the Victoria N'yanza, as the waters were falling, and not much discoloured; whereas, judging from the Nile's condition, it ought to have been rising. No vessel ever could have gone up it, and it bore no comparison with the Nile itself. The exaggerated account of its volume, however, given by the expeditionists who were sent up the Nile by Mehemet Ali, did not surprise us, since they had mistaken its position; for we were now 3° 42' north, and therefore had passed their 'farthest point' by twenty miles.

In two hours more we reached a settlement called Madi, and found it deserted. Every man and woman had run off into the jungles from fright, and would not come back again. We wished ourselves at the end of the journey; thought anything better than this kind of existence – living entirely at the expense of others; even the fleecings in Usŭi felt less dispiriting; but it could not be helped, for it must always exist as long as these Turks are allowed to ride rough-shod over the people. The Turks, however, had their losses also; for on the way four Bari men and one Bari slave-girl slipped off with a hundred of their plundered cattle, and neither they nor the cattle could be found again. Mijalwa was here convicted of having stolen the cloth of a Turk whilst living in his hut when he was away at the Paira plundering, and got fifty lashes to teach him better behaviour for the future.

Halt, 3d to 5th: A party of fifty men came from Labŭré, a station on ahead of this, to take service as porters, knowing that at this season the Turks always come with a large herd of plundered cattle, which they call government property, and give in payment to the men who carry their tusks of ivory across the Bari country.

Barwŭdi, 6th; and Labŭré, 7th and 8th: We now marched over a rolling ground, covered in some places with bush-jungle, in others with villages, where there were fine trees, resembling oaks in their outward appearance; and stopping one night at the settlement of Barwŭdi, arrived at Labŭré, where we had to halt a day for Mahamed to collect some ivory from a depôt he had formed near by. We heard there was another ivory party collecting tusks at Obbo, a settlement in the country of Panŭquara, twenty miles east of this.

To Mŭgi, 9th. Halt, 10th and 11th: Next we crossed a nullah draining into the Nile, and, travelling over more rolling ground, flanked on the right by a range of small hills, put up at the Madi frontier station, Mŭgi, where we had to halt two days to collect a full complement of porters to traverse the Bari country, the people of which are denounced as barbarians by the Turks, because they will not submit to be bullied into carrying their tusks for them. Here we felt an earthquake. The people would not take beads, preferring, they said, to make necklaces and belts out of ostrich-eggs, which they cut into the size of small shirt-buttons, and then drill a hole through their centre to string them together. A passenger told us that three white men had just arrived in vessels at Gondokoro; and the Bari people, hearing of our advance, instead of trying to kill us with spears, had determined to poison all the water in their country. Mahamed now disposed of half of his herd of cows, giving them to the chiefs of the villages in return for porters. These, he said, were all that belonged to the government; for the half of all captures of cows, as well as all slaves, all goats, and sheep, were allowed to the men as part of their pay.

To Wurŭngi, 12th. To Marsan, 13th: When all was settled we marched, one thousand strong, to Wurŭngi; and next day, by a double march, arrived at Marsan, in the Bari country. I wished still to put up in the native villages, but Mahamed so terrified all my men, by saying these Bari would kill us in the night if we did not all sleep together in one large camp, that we were obliged to submit. The country, still flanked on the right by hills, was undulating and very prettily wooded. Villages were numerous, but as we passed them the inhabitants all fled from us, save a few men, who, bolder than the rest, would stand and look on at us as we marched along. Both night and morning the Turks beat their drums; and whenever they stopped to eat they sacked the villages.

To Doro, 14th: Pushing on by degrees, stopping at noon to eat, we came again in sight of the Nile, and put up at a station called Doro, within a short distance of the well-known hill Rijeb, where Nile voyagers delight in cutting their names. The country continued the same, but the grass was conspicuously becoming shorter and finer every day – so much so, that my men all declared it was a sign of our near approach to England. After we had settled down for the night, and the Turks had finished plundering the nearest villages, we heard two guns fired, and immediately afterwards the whole place was alive with Bari people. Their drums were beaten as a sign that they would attack us, and the war-drums of the villages around responded by beating also. The Turks grew somewhat alarmed at this, and as darkness began to set in, sent out patrols in addition to their nightly watches. The savages next tried to steal in on us, but were soon frightened off by the patrols cocking their guns. Then, seeing themselves defeated in that tactic, they collected in hundreds in front of us, set fire to the grass, and marched up and down, brandishing ignited grass in their hands, howling like demons, and swearing they would annihilate us in the morning.

To Gondokoro, 15th: We slept the night out, nevertheless, and next morning walked in to Gondokoro, N. lat. 4° 54' 5", and E. long. 31° 46' 9", where Mahamed, after firing a salute, took us in to see a Circassian merchant, named Kŭrshid Agha. Our first inquiry was, of course, for Petherick. A mysterious silence ensued; we were informed that Mr Debono was *the* man we had to thank for the assistance we had received in coming from Madi; and then in hot haste, after warm exchanges of greeting with Mahamed's friend, who was Debono's agent here, we took leave, to hunt up Petherick. Walking down the bank of the river – where a line of vessels was moored, and on the right hand a few sheds, one-half broken down, with a brick-built house representing the late Austrian Church Mission establishment – we saw hurrying on towards us the form of an Englishman, who, for one moment, we believed was the Simon Pure; but the next moment my old friend Baker, famed for his sports in Ceylon, seized me by the hand. A little boy of his establishment had reported our arrival, and he in an instant came out to welcome us. What joy this was I can hardly tell. We could not talk fast enough, so overwhelmed were we both to meet again. Of course we were his guests in a moment, and learned everything that could be told. I now first heard of the death of H.R.H. the Prince-Consort, which made me reflect on the inspiring words he made use of, in compliment to myself, when I was introduced to him by Sir Roderick Murchison a short while before leaving England. Then there was the terrible war in America, and other events of less startling nature, which came on us all by surprise, as years had now passed since we had received news from the civilised world.

Baker then said he had come up with three vessels – one dyabir and two nuggers – fully equipped with armed men, camels, horses, donkeys, beads, brass wire, and everything necessary for a long journey, expressly to look after us, hoping, as he jokingly said, to find us on the equator in some terrible fix, that he might have the pleasure of helping us out of it. He had heard of Mahamed's party, and was actually waiting for him to come in, that he might have had the use of his return-men to start with comfortably. Three Dutch ladies, also, with a view to assist us in the same way as Baker (God bless them), had come here in a steamer, but were driven back to Khartŭm by sickness. Nobody had even dreamt for a moment it was possible we could come through. An Italian, named Miani, had gone farther up the Nile than any one else; and he, it now transpired, was the man who had cut his name on the tree by Apuddo. But what had become of Petherick? He was actually trading at N'yambara, seventy miles due west of this, though he had, since I left him in England, raised a subscription of £1000, from those of my friends to whom this Journal is most respectfully dedicated as the smallest return a grateful heart can give for their attempt to succour me, when knowing the fate of the expedition was in great jeopardy.

Instead of coming up the Nile at once, as Petherick might have done – so I was assured – he waited, whilst a vessel was building, until the season had too far advanced to enable him to sail up the river. In short, he lost the north winds at 7° north, and went overland to his trading depôt at N'yambara. Previously, however, he had sent some boats up to this, under a Vakil, who had his orders to cross to his trading depôt at N'yambara, and to work from his trading station due south, ostensibly with a view to look after me, though contrary to my advice before leaving him in England, in opposition to his own proposed views of assisting me when he applied for help to succour me, and against the strongly-expressed opinions of every European in the same trade as himself; for all alike said they knew he would have gone to Faloro, and pushed south from that place, had his trade on the west of the Nile not attracted him there.

Baker now offered me his boats to go down to Khartŭm, and asked me if there was anything left undone which it might be of importance for him to go on and complete, by survey or otherwise; for, although he should like to go down the river with us, he did not wish to return home without having done something to recompense him for the trouble and expense he had incurred in getting up his large expedition. Of course I told him how disappointed I had been in not getting a sight of the Little Lŭta Nzigé. I described how we had seen the Nile bending west where we crossed in Chopi, and then, after walking down the chord of an arc described by the river, had found it again in Madi coming from the west, whence to the south, and as far at least as Koshi, it was said to be navigable, probably continuing to be so right into the Little Lŭta Nzigé. Should this be the case, then, by building boats in Madi above the cataracts, a vast region might be thrown open to the improving influences of navigation. Further, I told Baker of my contract with Kamrasi, and of the property I had left behind, with a view to stimulate any enterprising man who might be found at this place to go there, make good my promise, and, if found needful, claim my share of the things, for the better prosecution of his own travels there. This Baker at once undertook, though he said he did not want my property; and I drew out suggestions for him how to proceed. He then made friends with Mahamed, who promised to help him on to Faloro, and I gave Mahamed and his men three carbines as an honorarium.

I should now have gone down the Nile at once if the moon had been in 'distance' for fixing the longitude; but as it was not, I had to remain until the 26th, living with Baker. Kŭrshid Agha became very great friends with us, and, at once making a present of a turkey, a case of wine, and cigars, said he was only sorry for his own sake that we had found a fellow-countryman, else he would have had the envied honour of claiming us as his guests, and had the pleasure of transporting us in his vessels down to Khartŭm.

On the 18th, Kŭrshid Agha was summoned by the constant fire of musketry, a mile or two down the river, and went off in his vessels to the relief. A party of his had come across from the N'yambara country with ivory, and on the banks of the Nile, a few miles north of this, were engaged fighting with the natives. He arrived just in time to settle the difficulty, and next day came back again, having shot some of the enemy and captured their cows. Petherick, we heard, was in a difficulty of the same kind, upon which I proposed to go down with Baker and Grant to succour him; but he arrived in time, in company with his wife and Dr James Murie, to save us the trouble, and told me he had brought a number of men with him, carrying ivory, for the purpose *now* of looking after me on the east bank of the Nile, by following its course up to the south, though he had given up all hope of seeing me, as a report had reached him of the desertion of my porters at Ugogo. He then offered me his dyabir, as well as anything else that I wanted that lay within his power to give. Suffice it to say, I had, through Baker's generosity, at that very moment enough and to spare; but at his urgent request I took a few more yards of cloth for my men, and some cooking fat; and, though I offered to pay for it, he declined to accept any return at my hands.

Though I naturally felt much annoyed at Petherick – for I had hurried away from Uganda, and separated from Grant at Kari, solely to keep faith with him – I did not wish to break friendship, but dined and conversed with him, when it transpired that his Vakil, or agent, who went south from the N'yambara station, came amongst the N'yam Nyam, and heard from them that a large river, four days' journey more to the southward, was flowing from east to west, beyond which lived a tribe of 'women,' who, when they wanted to marry, mingled with them in the stream and returned and then, again, beyond this tribe of women there lived another tribe of women and dogs. Now, this may all seem a very strange story to those who do not know the negro's and Arab's modes of expression; but to me it at once came very natural, and, according to my view, could be interpreted thus: The river, running from east to west, according to the native mode of expressing direction, could be nothing but the Little Lŭta Nzigé running the opposite way, according to fact and our mode of expression. The first tribe of women were doubtless the Wanyoro – called women by the naked tribes on this side because they wear bark coverings – an effeminate appendage, in the naked man's estimation; and the second tribe must have been in allusion to the dog-keeping Waganda, who also would be considered women, as they wear bark clothes.

In my turn, I told Petherick he had missed a good thing by not going up the river to look for me; for, had he done so, he would not only have had the best ivory-grounds to work upon, but, by building a vessel in Madi above the cataracts, he would have had, in my belief, some hundred miles of navigable water to transport his merchandise. In short, his succouring petition was most admirably framed, had he stuck to it, for the welfare of both of us. We now received our first letters from home, and in one from Sir Roderick Murchison I found the Royal Geographical Society had awarded me their 'founder's medal' for the discovery of the Victoria N'yanza in 1858.

Conclusion

MY journey down to Alexandria was not without adventure, and carried me through scenes which, in other circumstances, it might have been worth while to describe. Thinking, however, that I have already sufficiently trespassed on the patience of the reader, I am unwilling to overload my volume with any matter that does not directly relate to the solution of the great problem which I went to solve. Having now, then, after a period of twenty-eight months, come upon the tracks of European travellers, and met them face to face, I close my Journal, to conclude with a few explanations, for the purpose of comparing the various branches of the Nile with its affluents, so as to show their respective values.

The first affluent, the Bahr el Ghazal, took us by surprise; for instead of finding a huge lake, as described in our maps, at an elbow of the Nile, we found only a small piece of water resembling a duck-pond buried in a sea of rushes. The old Nile swept through it with majestic grace, and carried us next to the Geraffe branch of the Sobat river, the second affluent, which we found flowing into the Nile with a graceful semicircular sweep and good stiff current, apparently deep, but not more than fifty yards broad.

Next in order came the main stream of the Sobat, flowing into the Nile in the same graceful way as the Geraffe, which in breadth it surpassed, but in velocity of current was inferior. The Nile by these additions was greatly increased; still it did not assume that noble appearance which astonished us so much, *immediately after the rainy season,* when we were navigating it in canoes in Unyoro.

I here took my last lunar observations, and made its mouth N. lat. 9° 20' 48", E. long. 31° 24' 0". The Sobat has a third mouth farther down the Nile, which unfortunately was passed without my knowing it; but as it is so well known to be unimportant, the loss was not great.

Next to be treated of is the famous Blue Nile, which we found a miserable river, even when compared with the Geraffe branch of the Sobat. It is very broad at the mouth, it is true, but so shallow that our vessel with difficulty was able to come up it. It had all the appearance of a mountain stream, subject to great periodical fluctuations. I was never more disappointed than with this river; if the White river was cut off from it, its waters would all be absorbed before they could reach Lower Egypt.

The Atbara river, which is the last affluent, was more like the Blue river than any of the other affluents, being decidedly a mountain stream, which floods in the rains, but runs nearly dry in the dry season.

I had now seen quite enough to satisfy myself that the White river which issues from the N'yanza at the Ripon Falls, is the true or parent Nile; for in every instance of its branching, it earned the palm with it in the distinctest manner, viewed, as all the streams were by me, in the dry season, which is the best time for estimating their relative perennial values.

Since returning to England, Dr Murie, who was with me at Gondokoro, has also come home; and he, judging from my account of the way in which we got ahead of the flooding of the Nile between the Karŭma Falls and Gondokoro, is of opinion that the Little Lŭta Nzigé must be a great backwater to the Nile, which the waters of the Nile must have been occupied in filling during my residence in Madi; and then about the same time that I set out from Madi, the Little Lŭta Nzigé having been surcharged with water, the surplus began its march northwards just about the time when we started in the same direction. For myself, I believe in this opinion, as he no sooner asked me how I could account for the phenomenon I have already mentioned of the river appearing to decrease in bulk as we descended it, than I instinctively advanced his own theory. Moreover, the same hypothesis will answer for the sluggish flooding of the Nile down to Egypt.

I hope the reader who has followed my narrative thus far will be interested in knowing how 'my faithful children,' for whose services I had no further occasion, and whom I had taken so far from their own country, were disposed of. At Cairo, where we put up in Shepherd's Hotel, I had the whole of them photographed, and indulged them at the public concerts, tableaux vivants, etc. By invitation, we called on the Viceroy at his Rhoda Island palace, and were much gratified with the reception; for, after hearing all our stories with marked intelligence, he most graciously offered to assist me in any other undertaking which would assist to open up and develop the interior of Africa.

I next appointed Bombay captain of the 'faithfuls,' and gave him three photographs of all the eighteen men and three more of the four women, to give one of each to our Consuls at Suez, Aden, and Zanzibar, by which they might be recognised. I also gave them increased wages, equal to three years' pay each, by orders on Zanzibar, which was one in addition to their time of service; an order for a grand 'freeman's garden,' to be purchased for them at Zanzibar; and an order that each one should receive ten dollars dowry-money as soon as he could find a wife.

With these letters in their hands, I made arrangements with our Consul, Mr Drummond Hay, to frank them through Suez, Aden, and the Seychelles to Zanzibar.

Since then, I have heard that Captain Bombay and his party missed the Seychelles, and went on to the Mauritius, where Captain Anson, Inspector-General of Police, kindly took charge of them, and made great lions of them. A subscription was raised to give them a purse of money; they were treated with tickets to the 'circus,' and sent back to the Seychelles, whence they were transported by steamer to Zanzibar, and taken in charge by our lately-appointed Consul, Colonel Playfair, who appears to have taken much interest in them. Further, they all volunteered to go with me again, should I attempt to cross Africa from east to west, through the fertile zone.